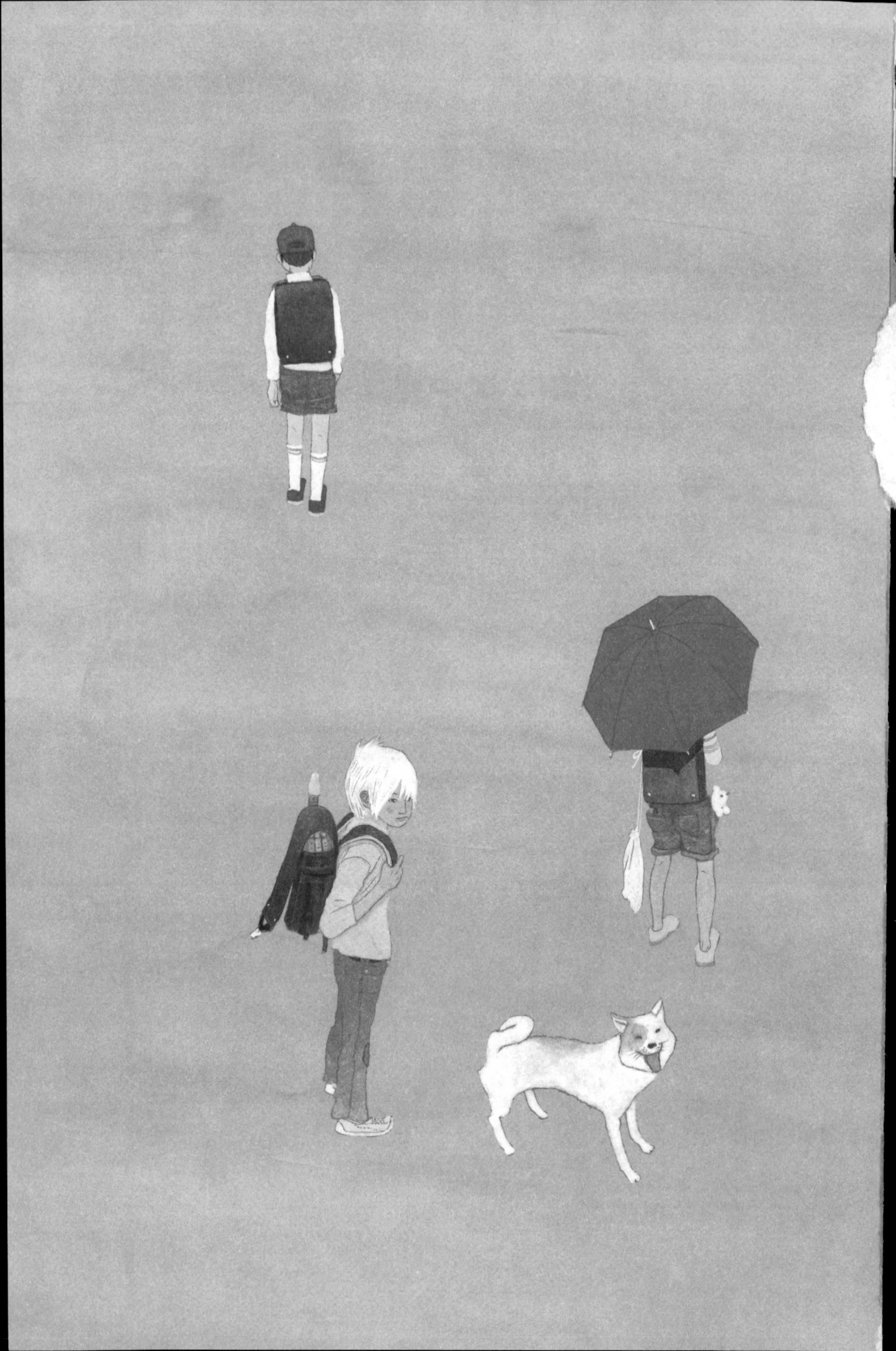

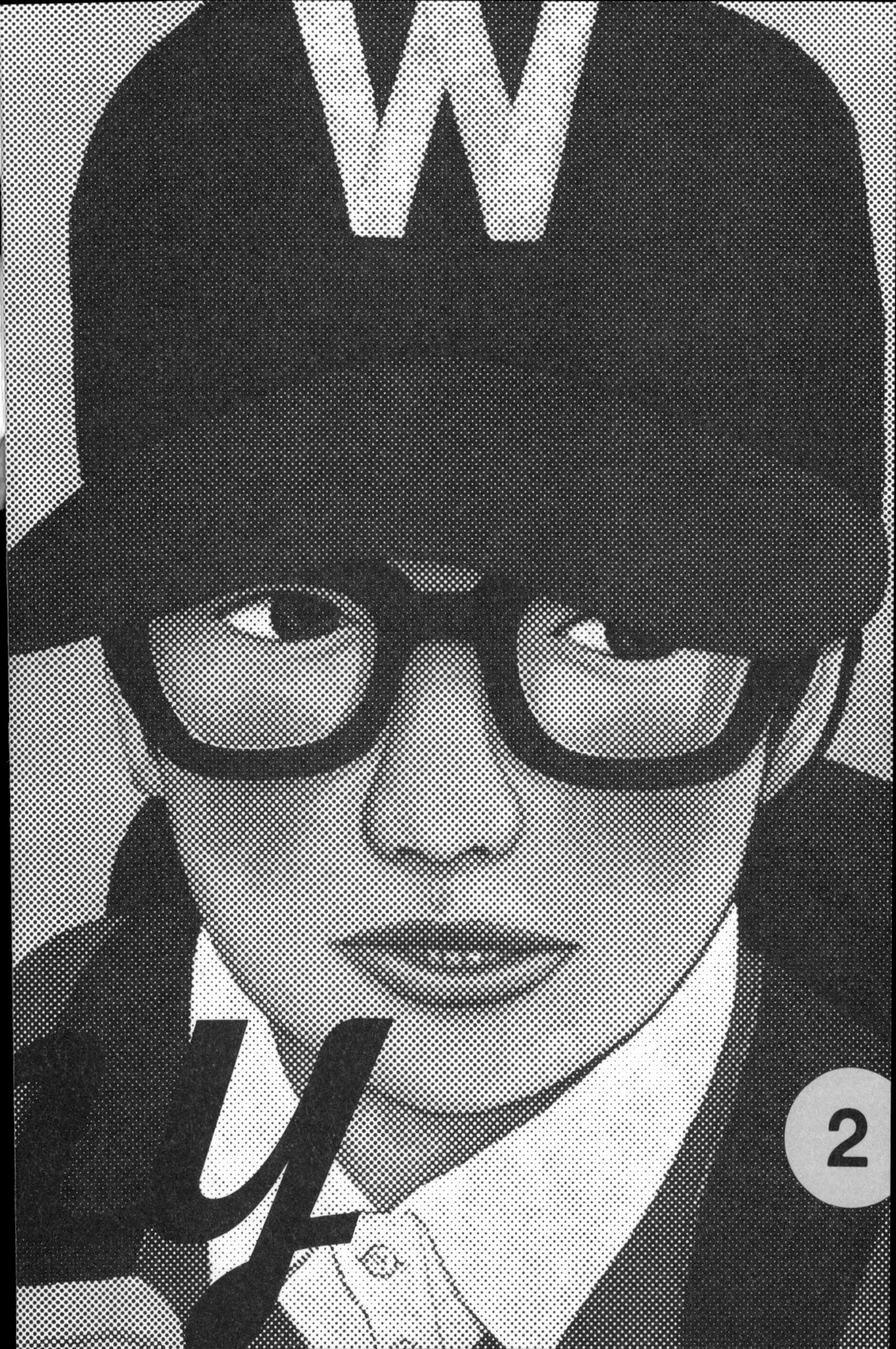
W
y
2

TAIYO MATSUMOTO

Sunn

Y
SUN
v. 2

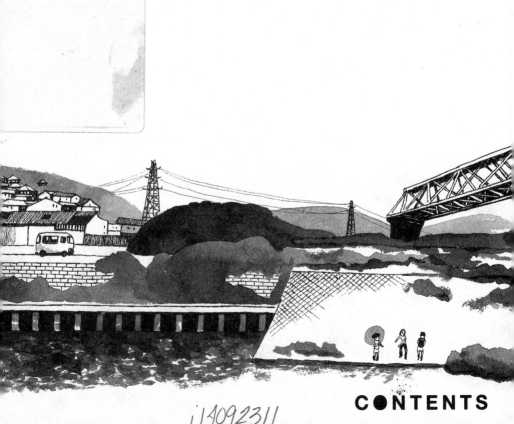

C◯NTENTS

i14092311

TAIYO MATSUMOTO

Sunn

SUN v.2

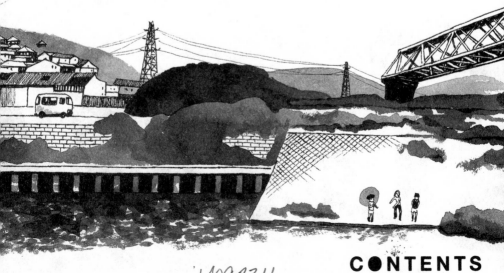

C●NTENTS

i14092311

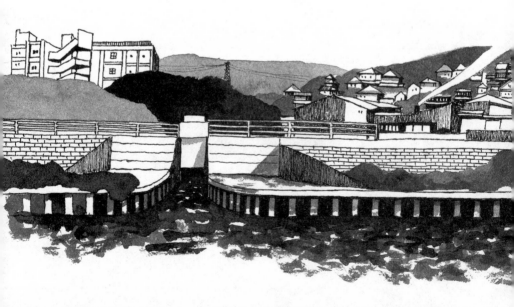

Sunny

2

CHAPTER 7

"When
I get married
I wanna wear
a dress in a
chapel."

"What's a
chapel?"

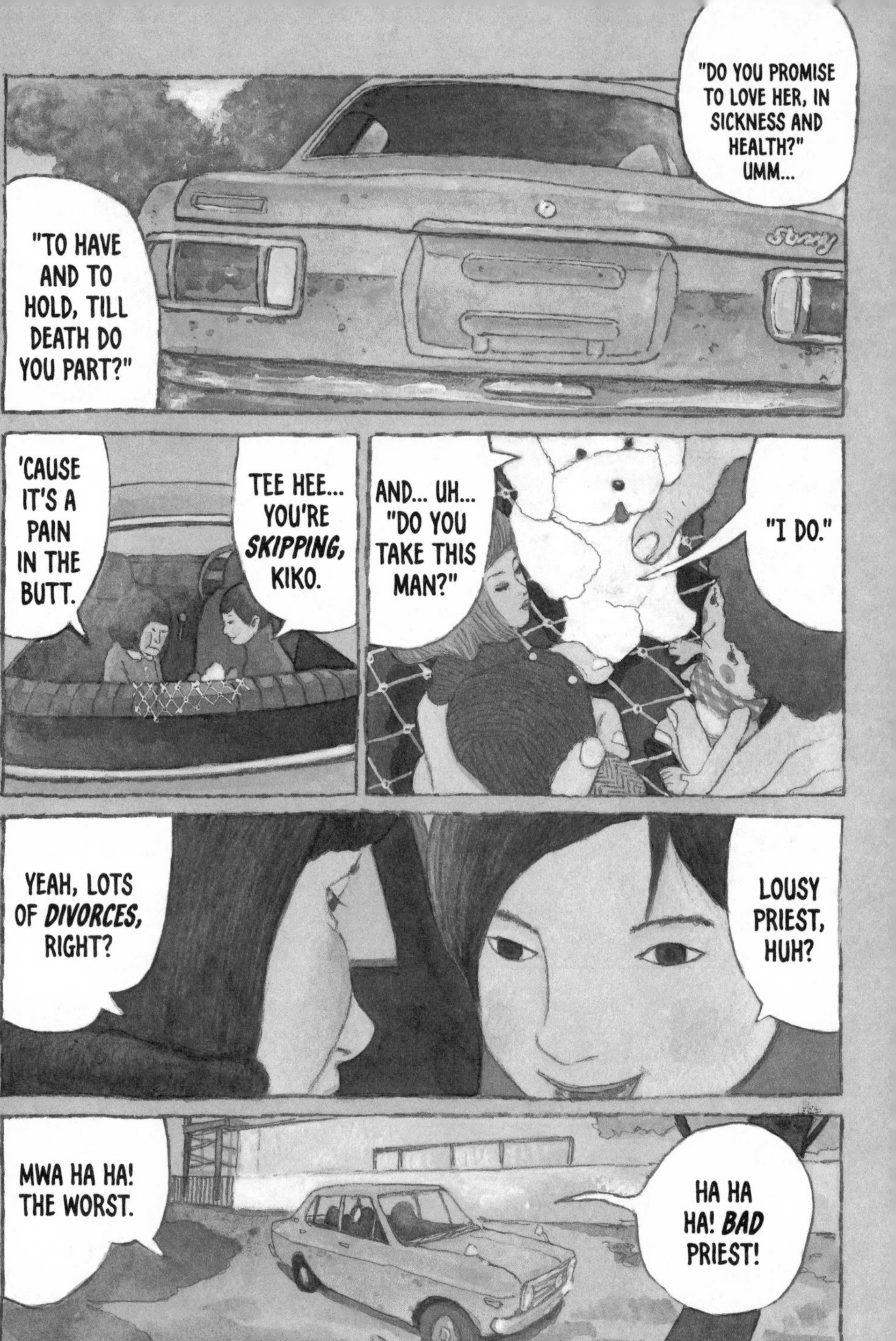
"DO YOU PROMISE TO LOVE HER, IN SICKNESS AND HEALTH?" UMM...
"TO HAVE AND TO HOLD, TILL DEATH DO YOU PART?"
"I DO."
AND... UH... "DO YOU TAKE THIS MAN?"
TEE HEE... YOU'RE *SKIPPING,* KIKO.
'CAUSE IT'S A PAIN IN THE BUTT.
LOUSY PRIEST, HUH?
YEAH, LOTS OF *DIVORCES,* RIGHT?
HA HA HA! *BAD* PRIEST!
MWA HA HA! THE WORST.

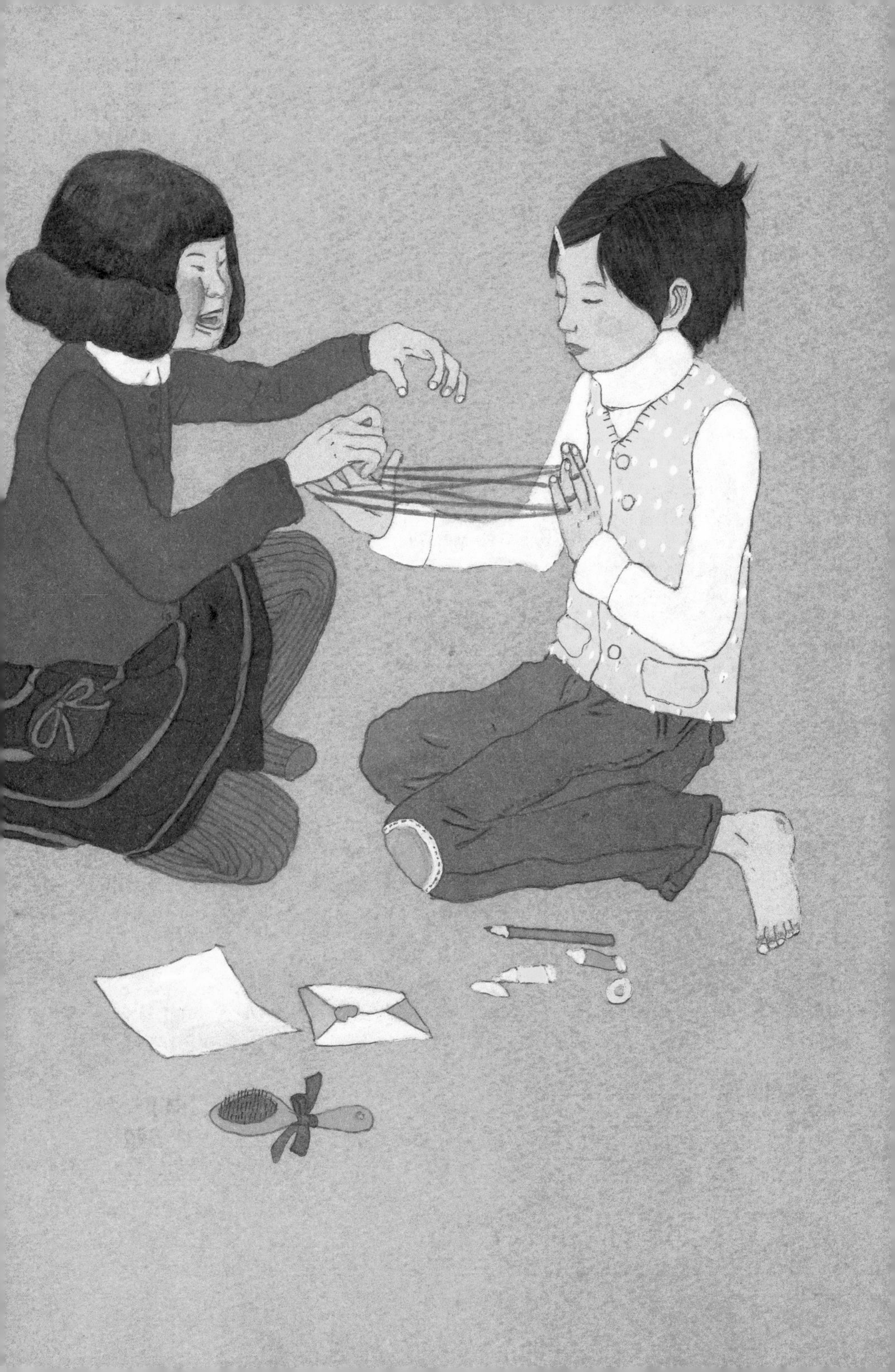

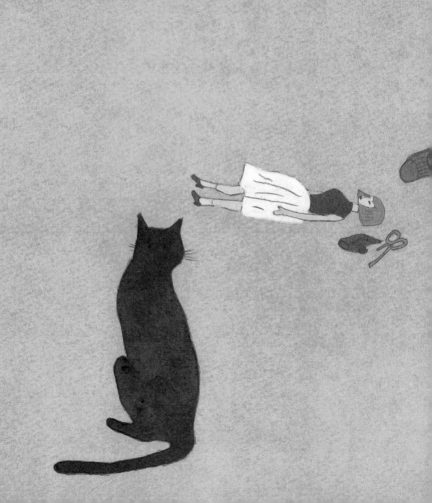

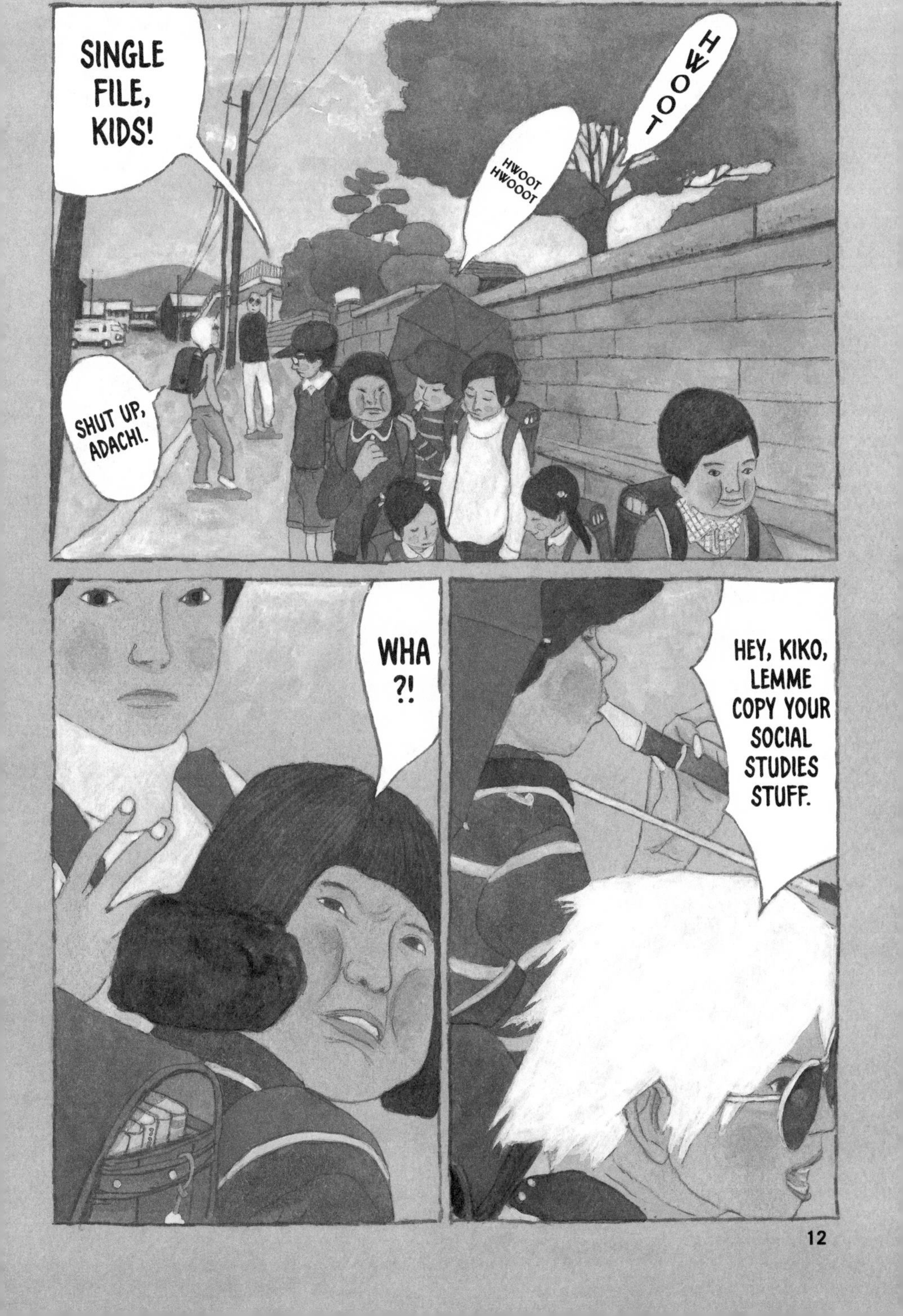
HWOOT
HWOOT HWOOOT
SINGLE FILE, KIDS!
SHUT UP, ADACHI.
HEY, KIKO, LEMME COPY YOUR SOCIAL STUDIES STUFF.
WHA ?!

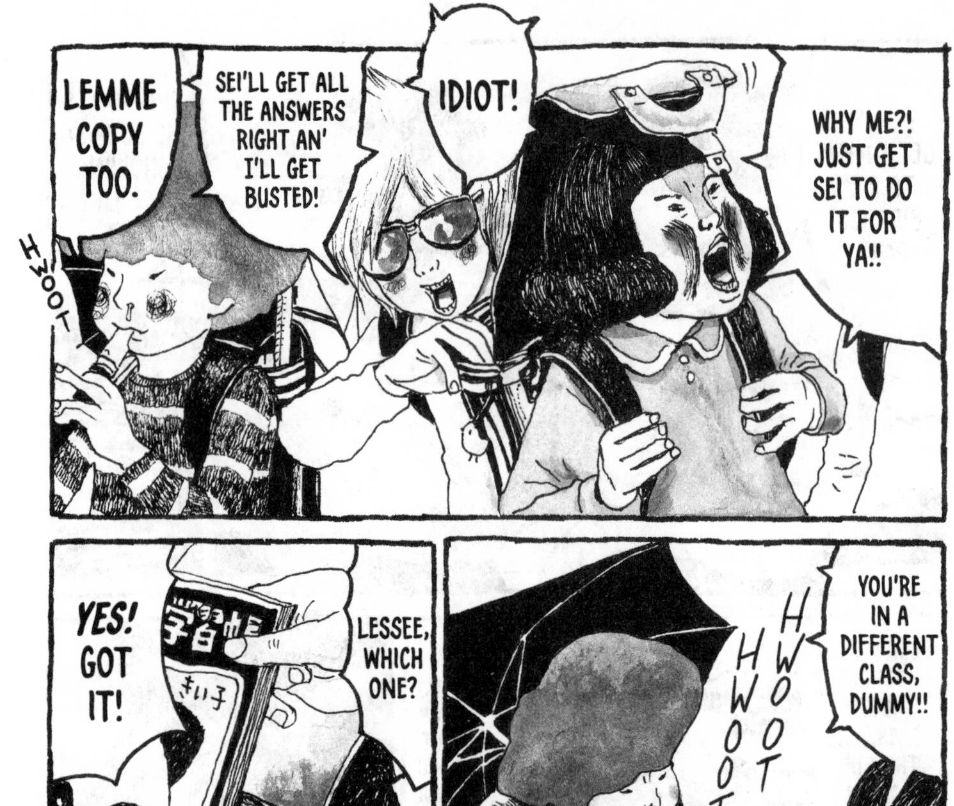
WHY ME?! JUST GET SEI TO DO IT FOR YA!!
IDIOT!
SEI'LL GET ALL THE ANSWERS RIGHT AN' I'LL GET BUSTED!
LEMME COPY TOO.
HWOOT
YOU'RE IN A DIFFERENT CLASS, DUMMY!!
HWOOT
HWOOT
LESSEE, WHICH ONE?
YES! GOT IT!
きい子

**Study guide: Kiko*

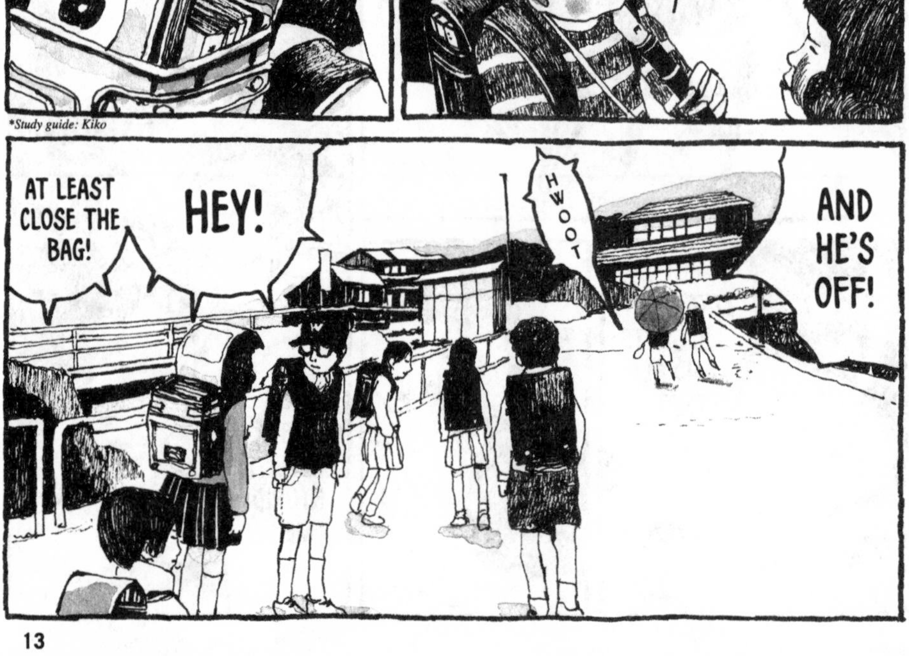
AND HE'S OFF!
HWOOT
HEY!
AT LEAST CLOSE THE BAG!

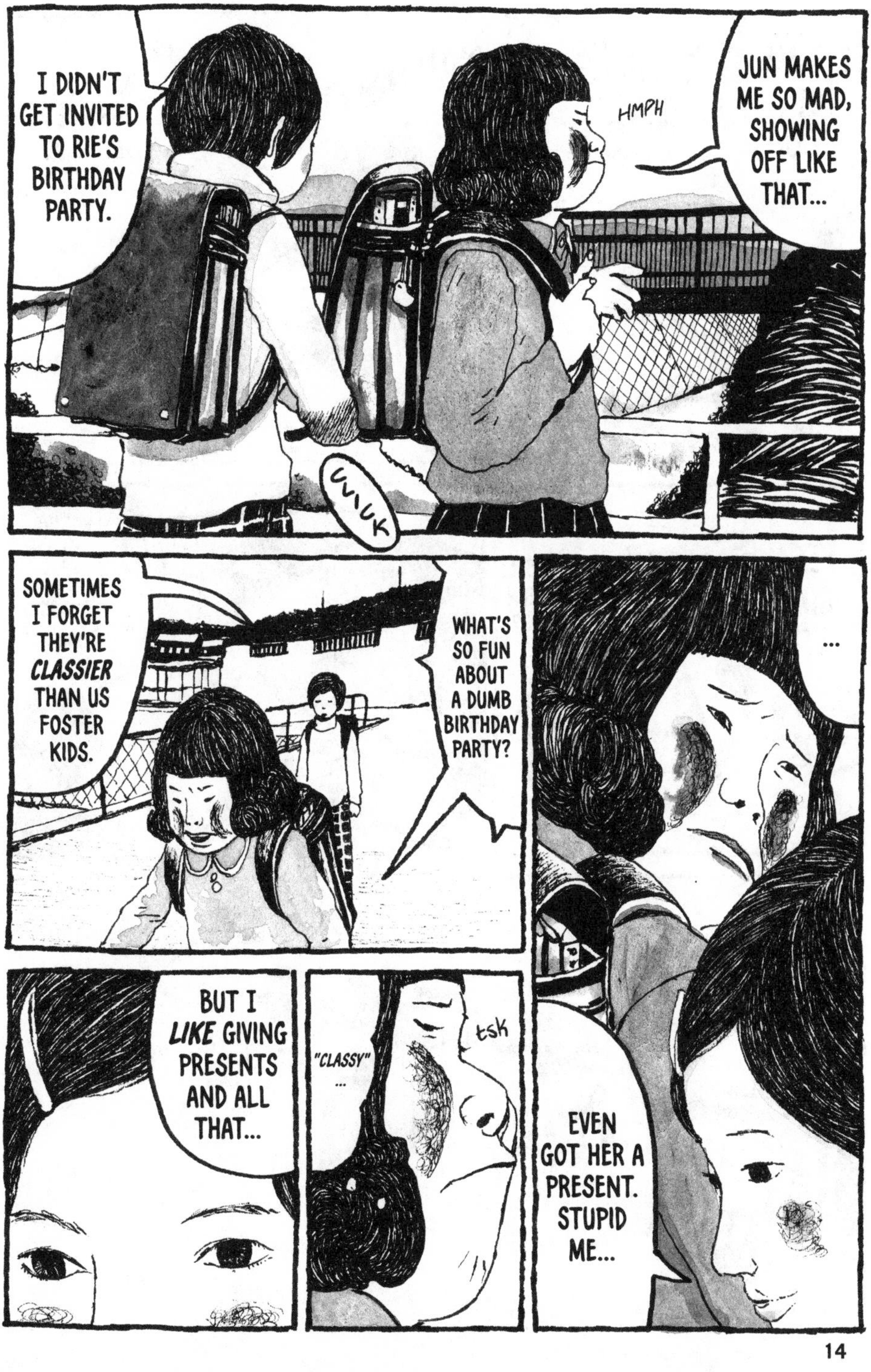
JUN MAKES ME SO MAD, SHOWING OFF LIKE THAT...
HMPH
I DIDN'T GET INVITED TO RIE'S BIRTHDAY PARTY.
...
EVEN GOT HER A PRESENT. STUPID ME...
WHAT'S SO FUN ABOUT A DUMB BIRTHDAY PARTY?
SOMETIMES I FORGET THEY'RE *CLASSIER* THAN US FOSTER KIDS.
tsk
"CLASSY" ...
BUT I *LIKE* GIVING PRESENTS AND ALL THAT...

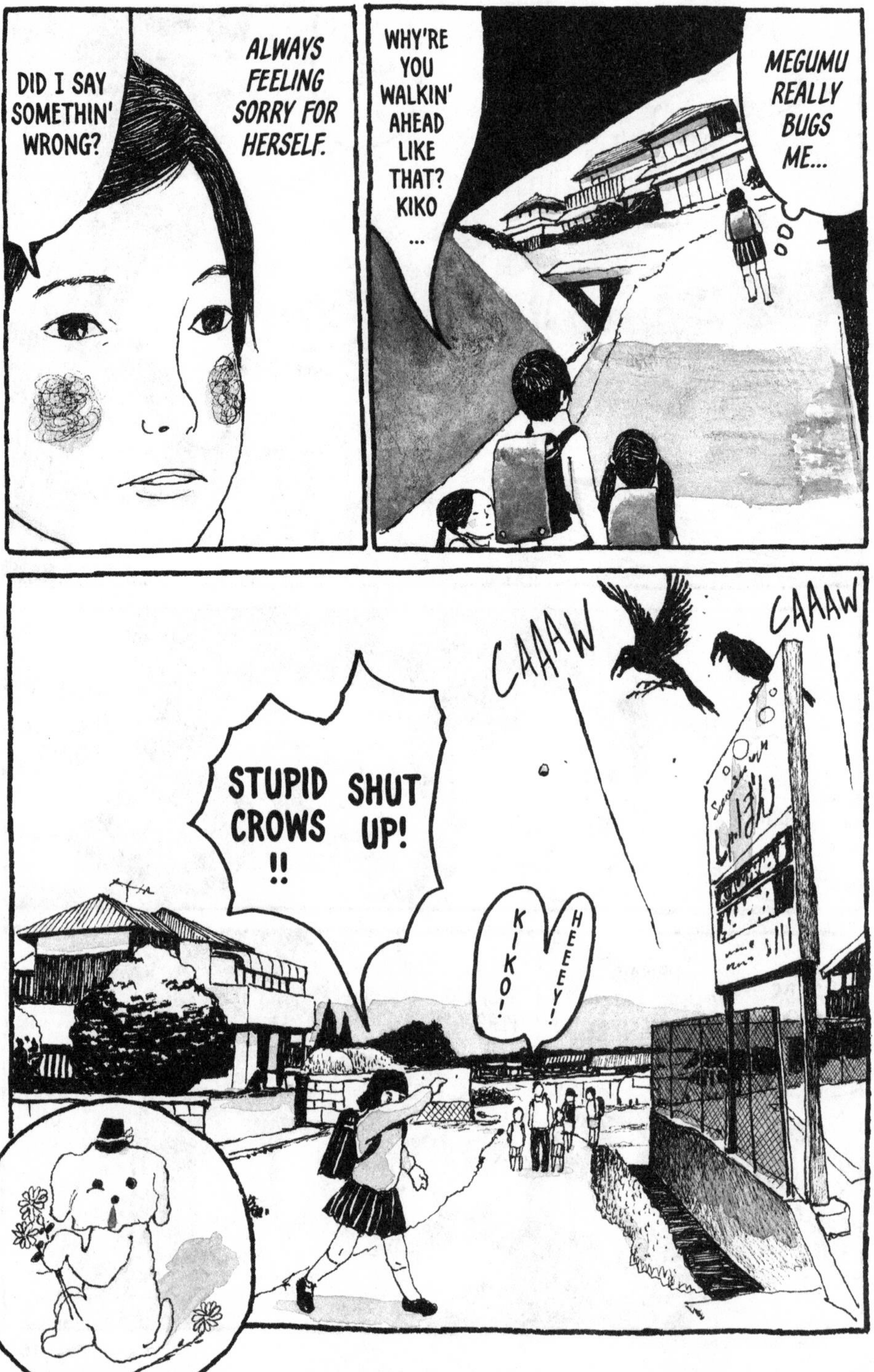
MEGUMU REALLY BUGS ME...
WHY'RE YOU WALKIN' AHEAD LIKE THAT? KIKO ...
ALWAYS FEELING SORRY FOR HERSELF.
DID I SAY SOMETHIN' WRONG?
CAAAW
CAAAW
SHUT UP! STUPID CROWS !!
HEEEEY! KIKO!

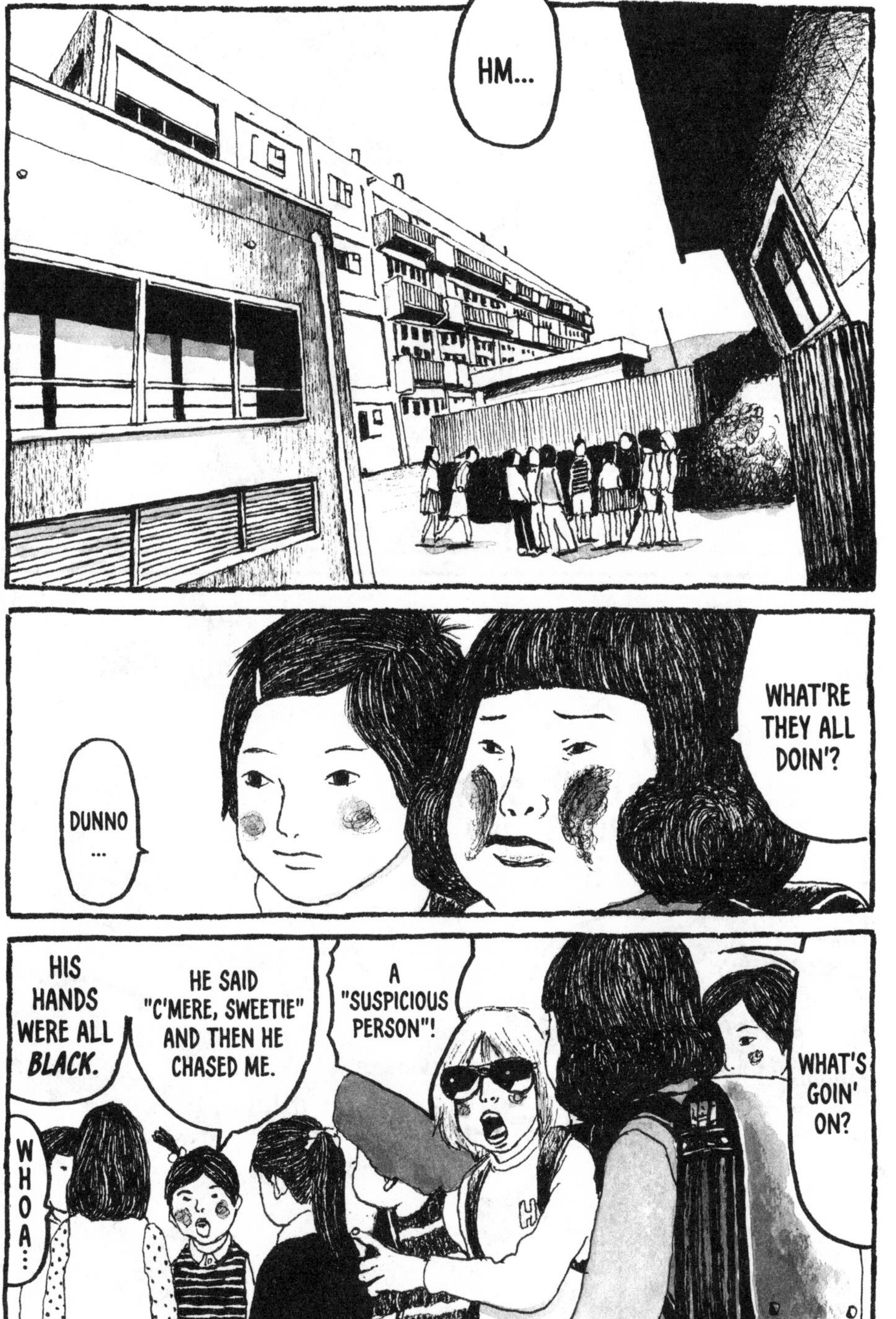
HM...
WHAT'RE THEY ALL DOIN'?
DUNNO ...
WHAT'S GOIN' ON?
A "SUSPICIOUS PERSON"!
HE SAID "C'MERE, SWEETIE" AND THEN HE CHASED ME.
HIS HANDS WERE ALL *BLACK*.
WHOA...

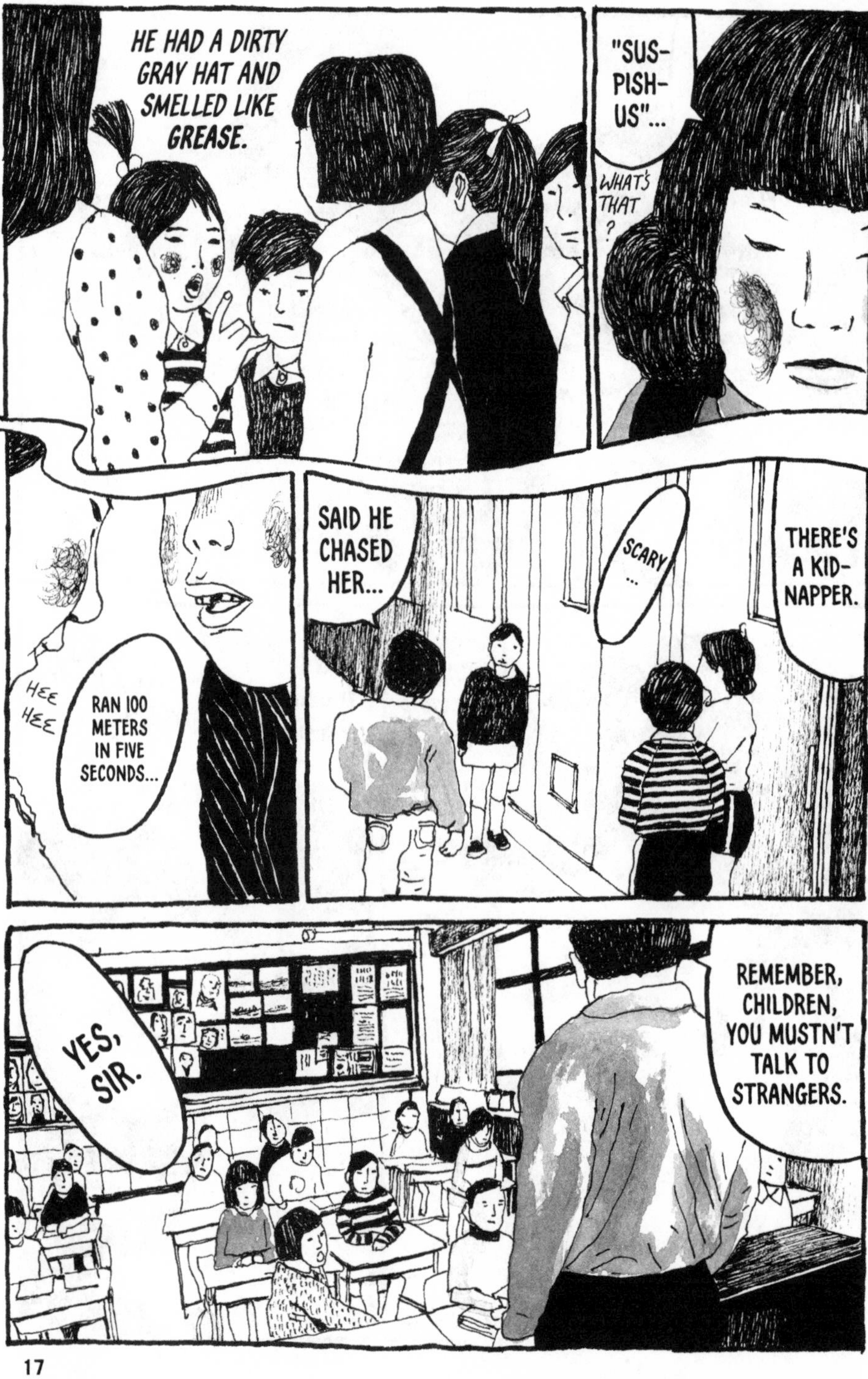
"SUS-PISH-US"...
WHAT'S THAT ?
HE HAD A DIRTY GRAY HAT AND SMELLED LIKE GREASE.
THERE'S A KID-NAPPER.
SCARY...
SAID HE CHASED HER...
RAN 100 METERS IN FIVE SECONDS...
HEE HEE
REMEMBER, CHILDREN, YOU MUSTN'T TALK TO STRANGERS.
YES, SIR.

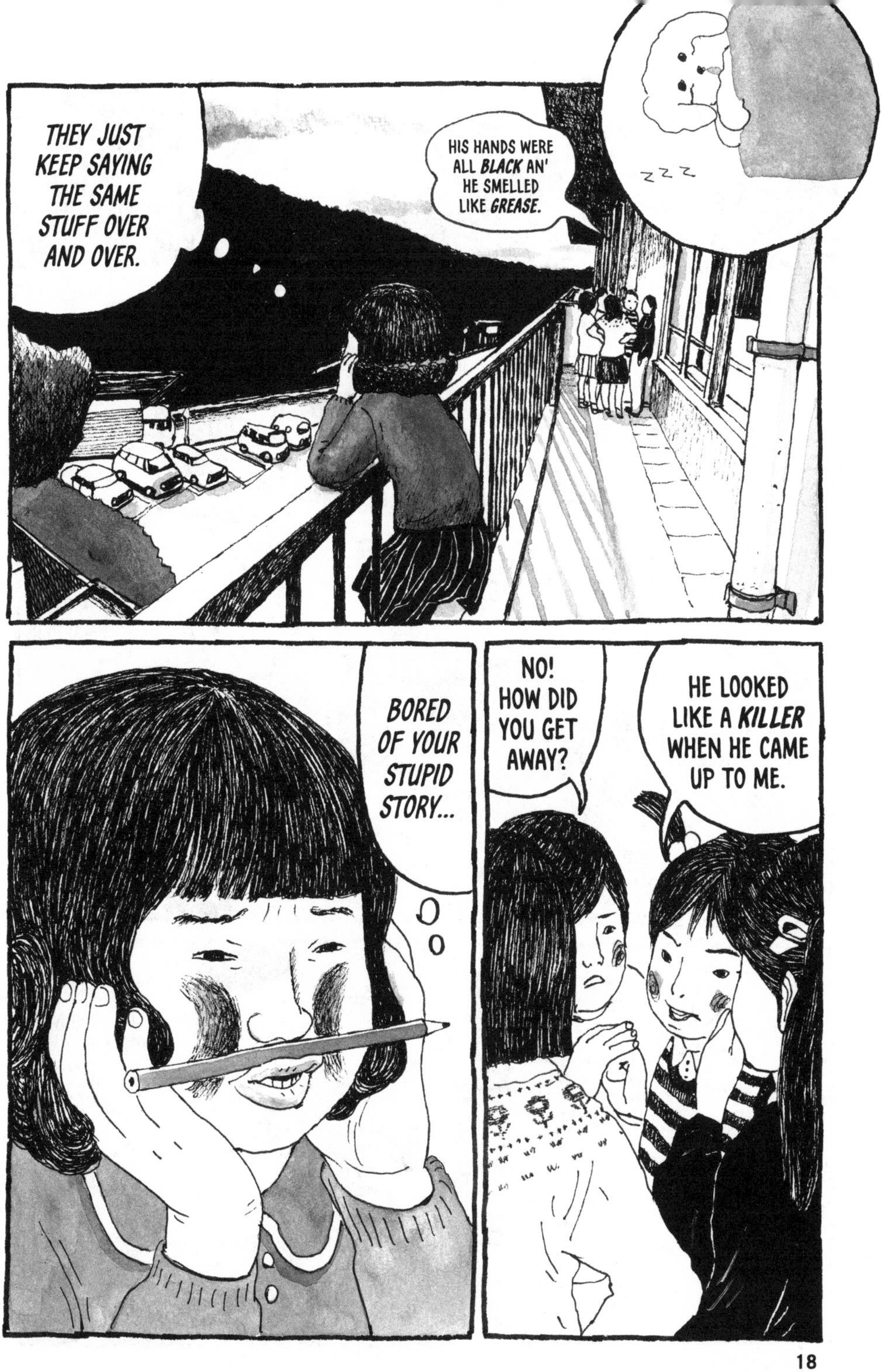
ZZZ
HIS HANDS WERE ALL *BLACK* AN' HE SMELLED LIKE *GREASE*.
THEY JUST KEEP SAYING THE SAME STUFF OVER AND OVER.
HE LOOKED LIKE A *KILLER* WHEN HE CAME UP TO ME.
NO! HOW DID YOU GET AWAY?
BORED OF YOUR STUPID STORY...

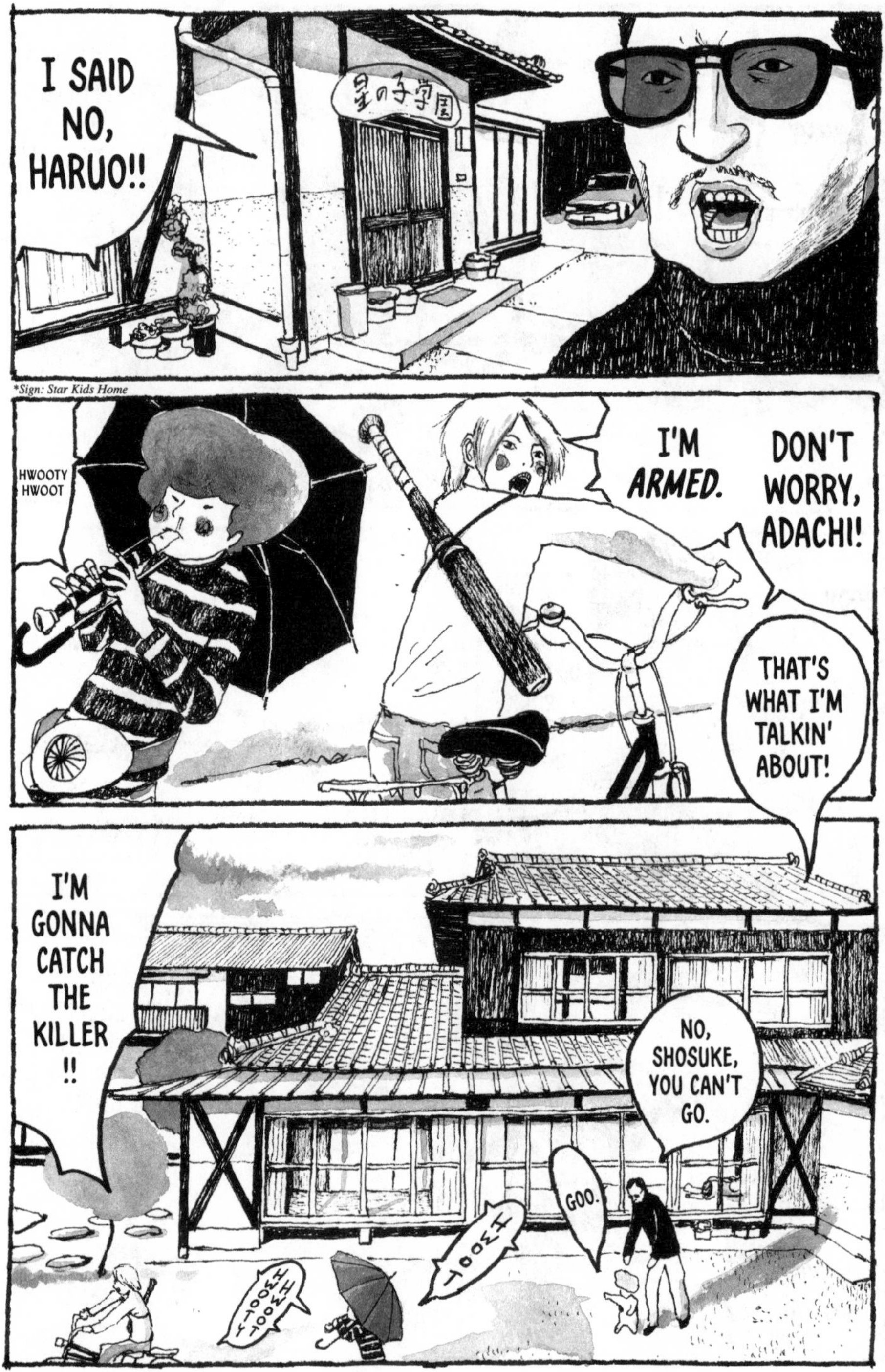
星の子学園
I SAID NO, HARUO!!
DON'T WORRY, ADACHI!
I'M ARMED.
THAT'S WHAT I'M TALKIN' ABOUT!
HWOOTY HWOOT
NO, SHOSUKE, YOU CAN'T GO.
GOO.
HWOOT
HWOOTY HWOOT
I'M GONNA CATCH THE KILLER!!

*Sign: Star Kids Home

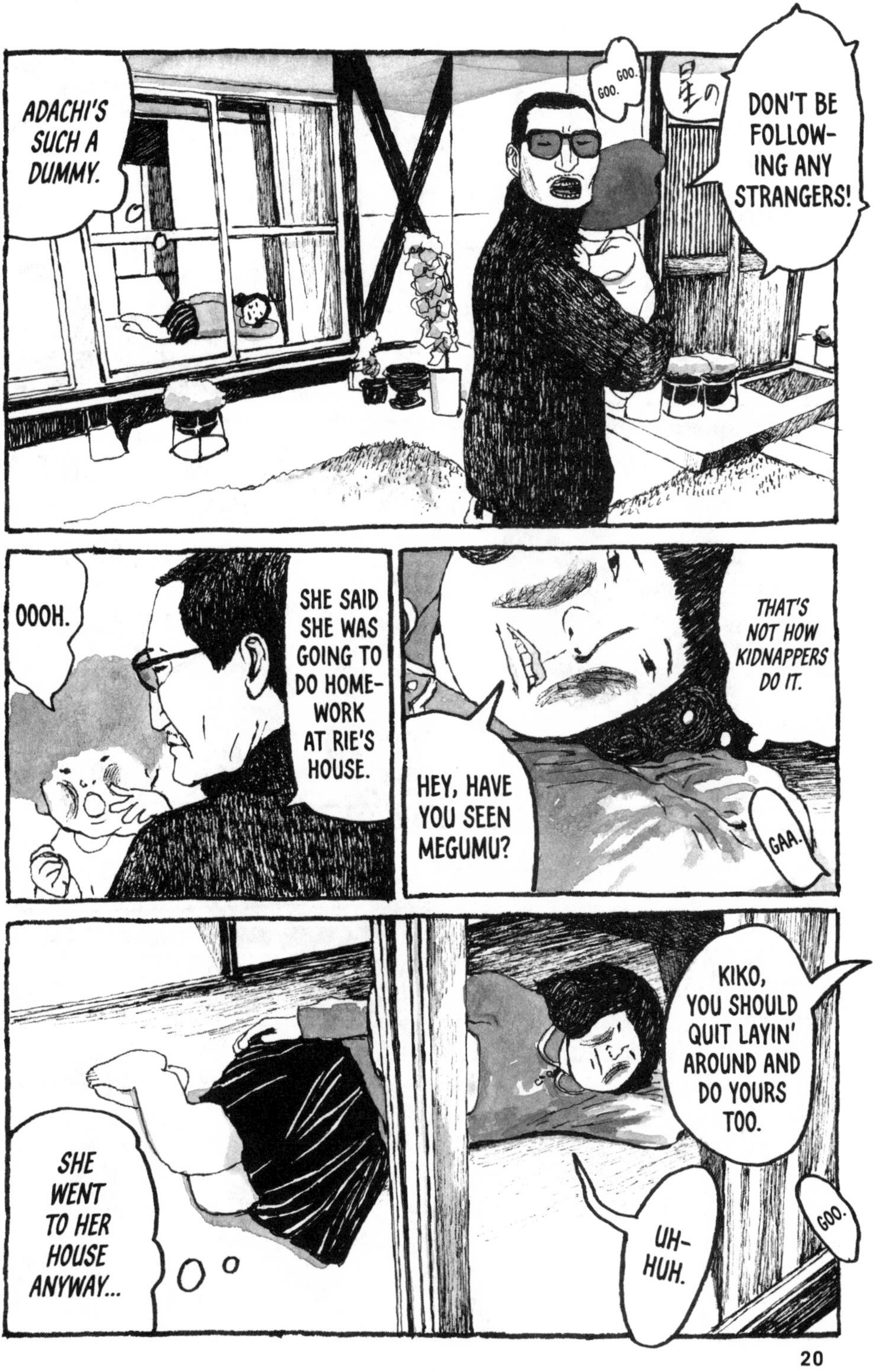

DON'T BE FOLLOWING ANY STRANGERS!
GOO. GOO. GOO.
星の
ADACHI'S SUCH A DUMMY.
THAT'S NOT HOW KIDNAPPERS DO IT.
HEY, HAVE YOU SEEN MEGUMU?
GAA.
SHE SAID SHE WAS GOING TO DO HOMEWORK AT RIE'S HOUSE.
OOOH.
KIKO, YOU SHOULD QUIT LAYIN' AROUND AND DO YOURS TOO.
GOO.
UH-HUH.
SHE WENT TO HER HOUSE ANYWAY...

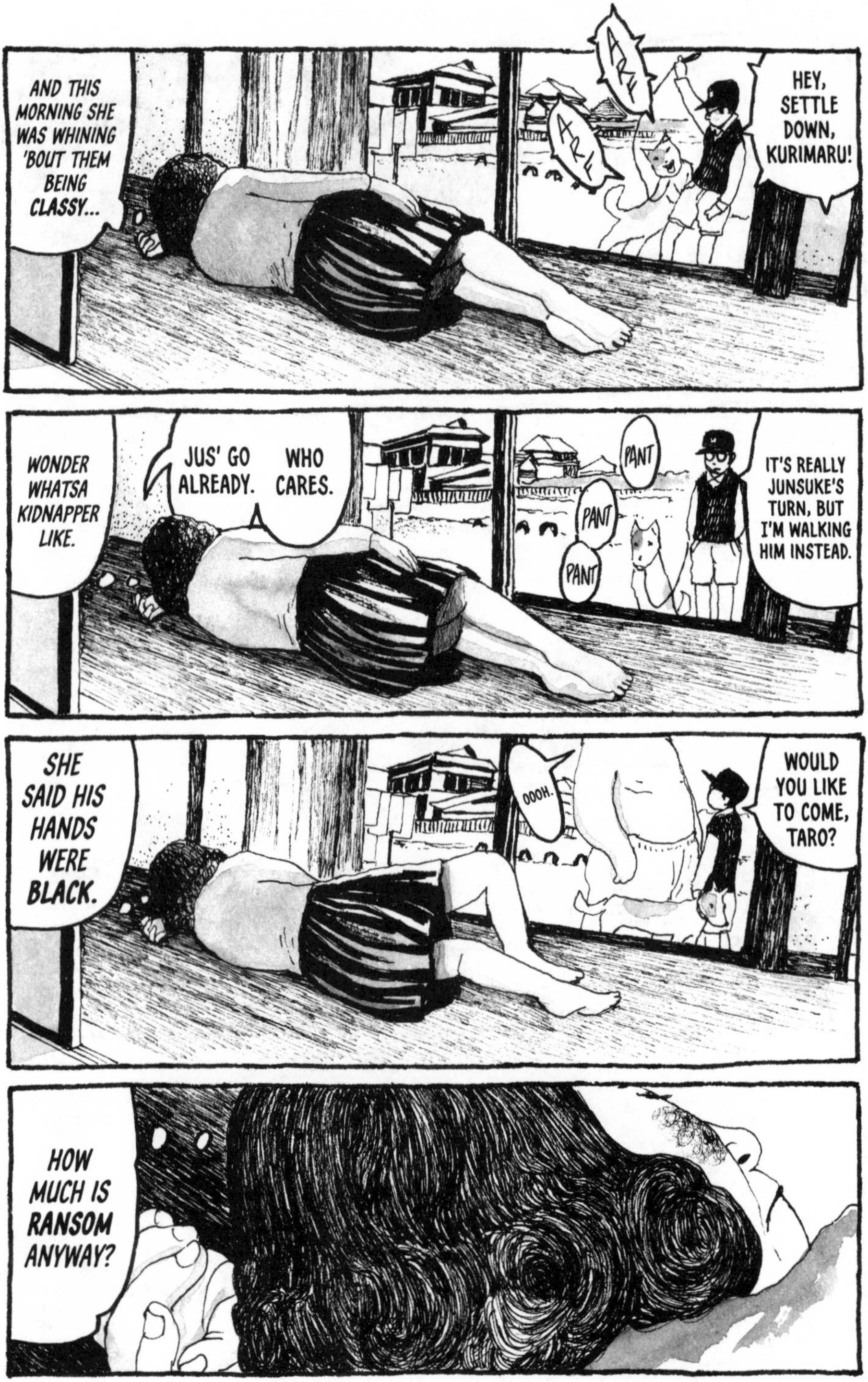
HEY, SETTLE DOWN, KURIMARU!
ARF
ARF
AND THIS MORNING SHE WAS WHINING 'BOUT THEM BEING CLASSY...
IT'S REALLY JUNSUKE'S TURN, BUT I'M WALKING HIM INSTEAD.
PANT
PANT
PANT
WHO CARES.
JUS' GO ALREADY.
WONDER WHATSA KIDNAPPER LIKE.
WOULD YOU LIKE TO COME, TARO?
OOOH.
SHE SAID HIS HANDS WERE BLACK.
HOW MUCH IS RANSOM ANYWAY?

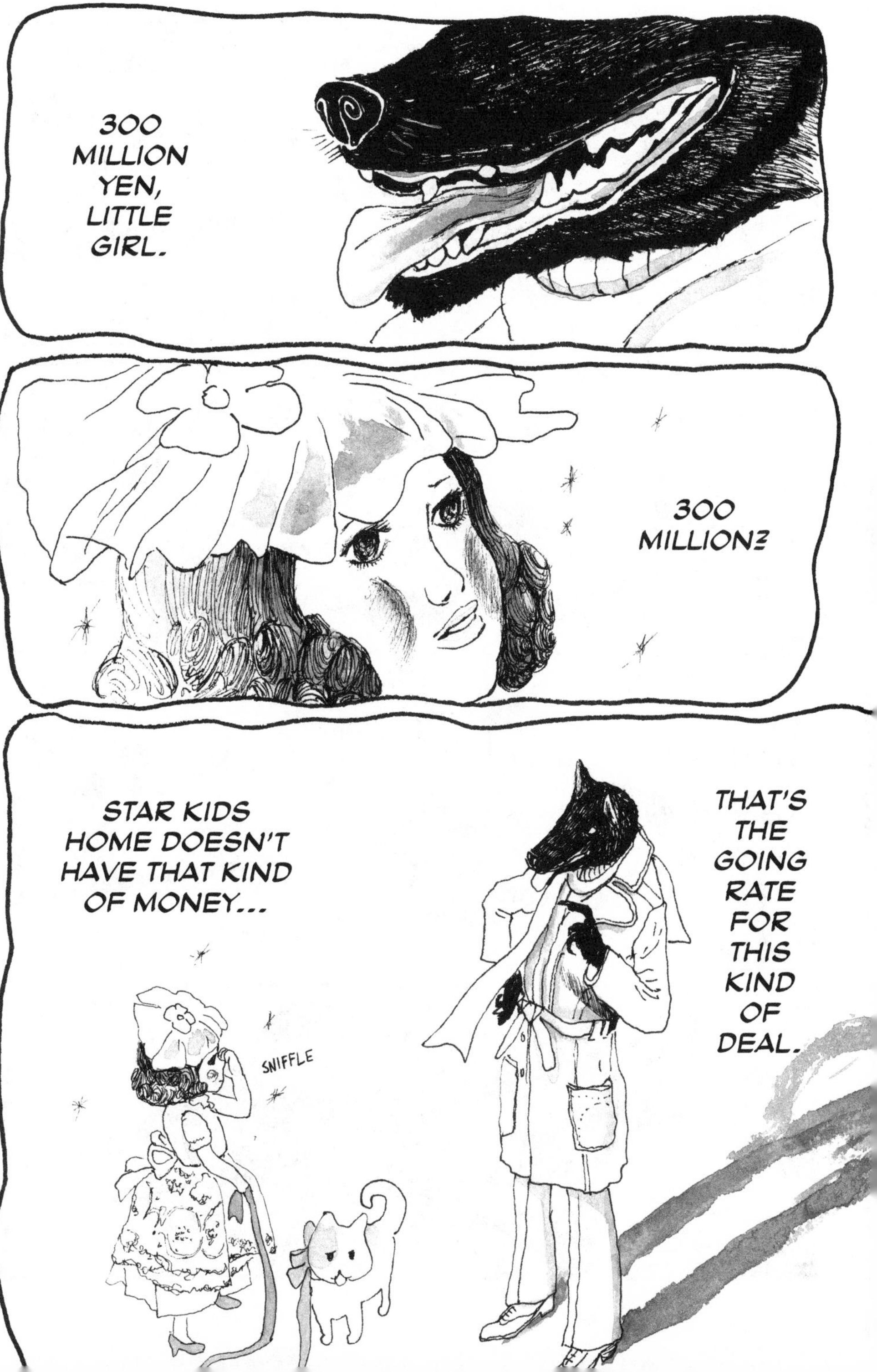
300 MILLION YEN, LITTLE GIRL.
300 MILLION?
THAT'S THE GOING RATE FOR THIS KIND OF DEAL.
STAR KIDS HOME DOESN'T HAVE THAT KIND OF MONEY...
SNIFFLE

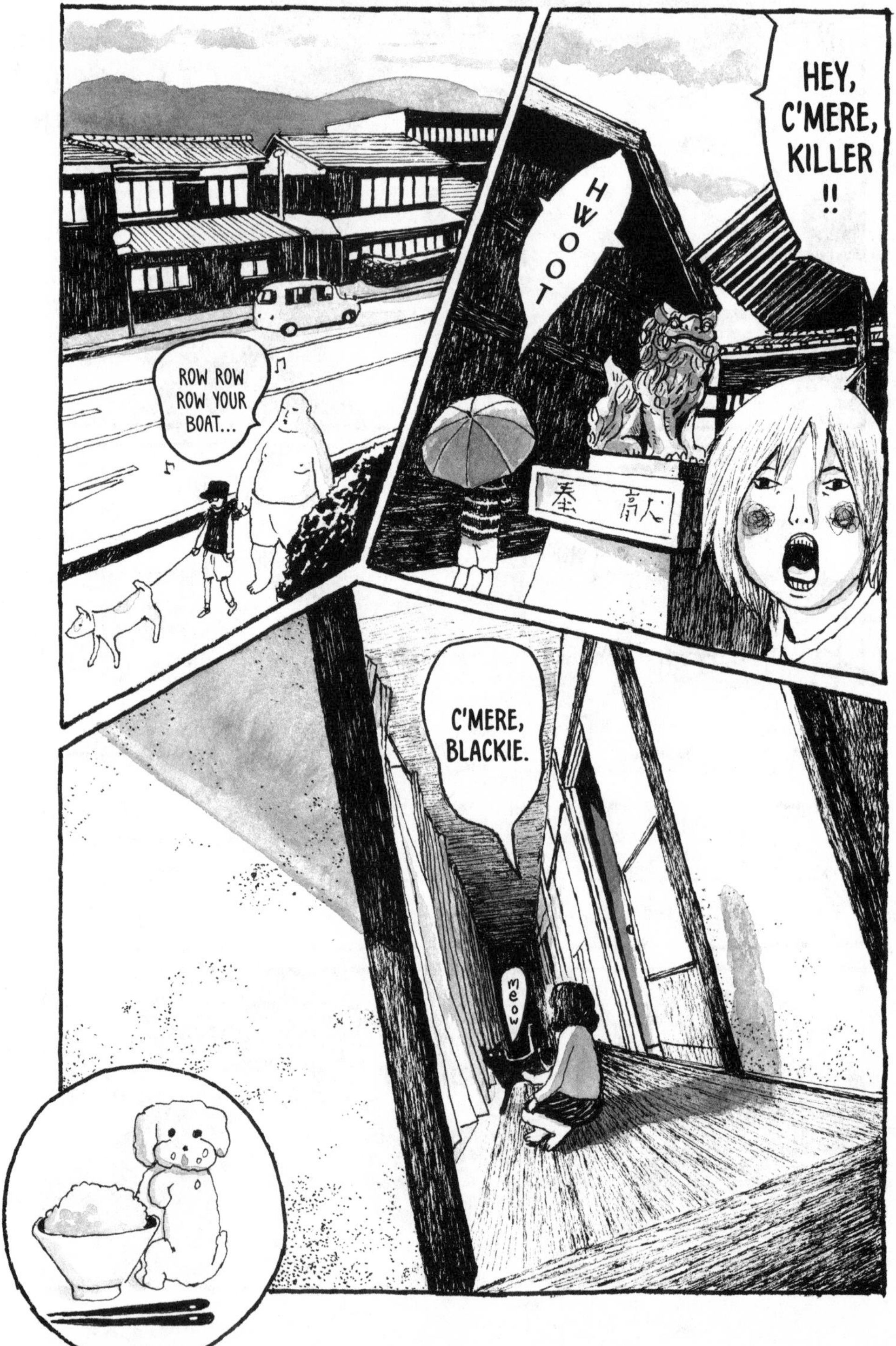
HEY, C'MERE, KILLER !!
HWOOT
ROW ROW ROW YOUR BOAT...
C'MERE, BLACKIE.
meow

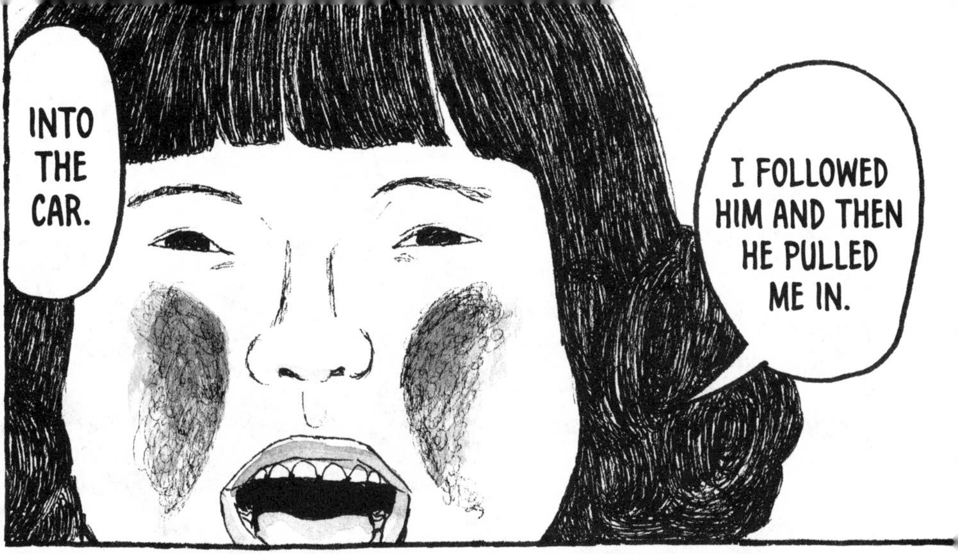
I FOLLOWED HIM AND THEN HE PULLED ME IN.
INTO THE CAR.
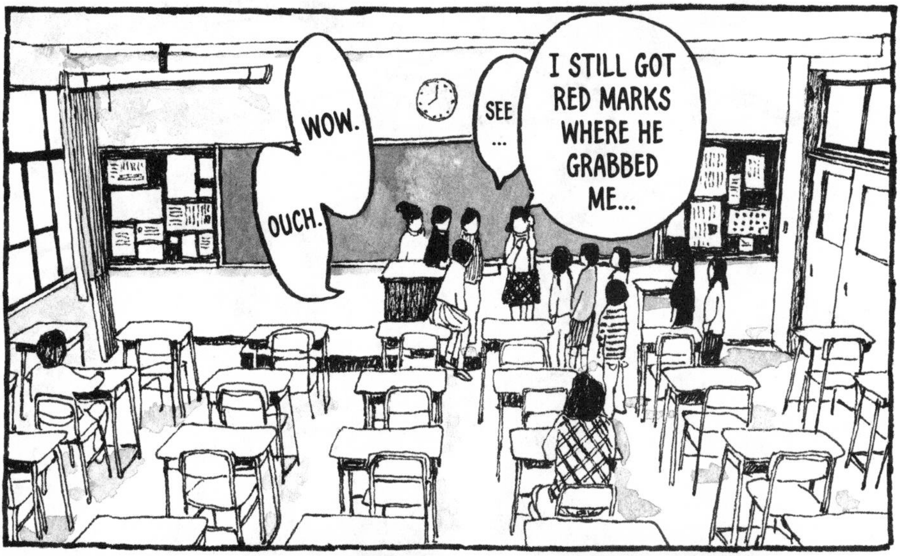
I STILL GOT RED MARKS WHERE HE GRABBED ME...
SEE ...
WOW.
OUCH.
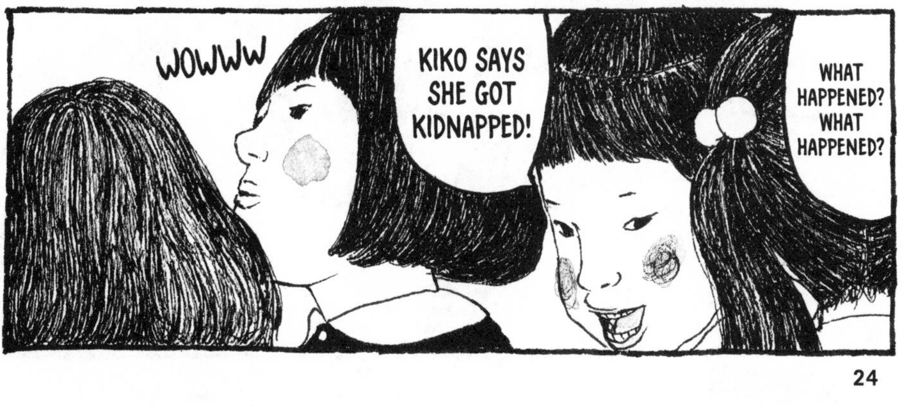
WHAT HAPPENED? WHAT HAPPENED?
KIKO SAYS SHE GOT KIDNAPPED!
WOWWW

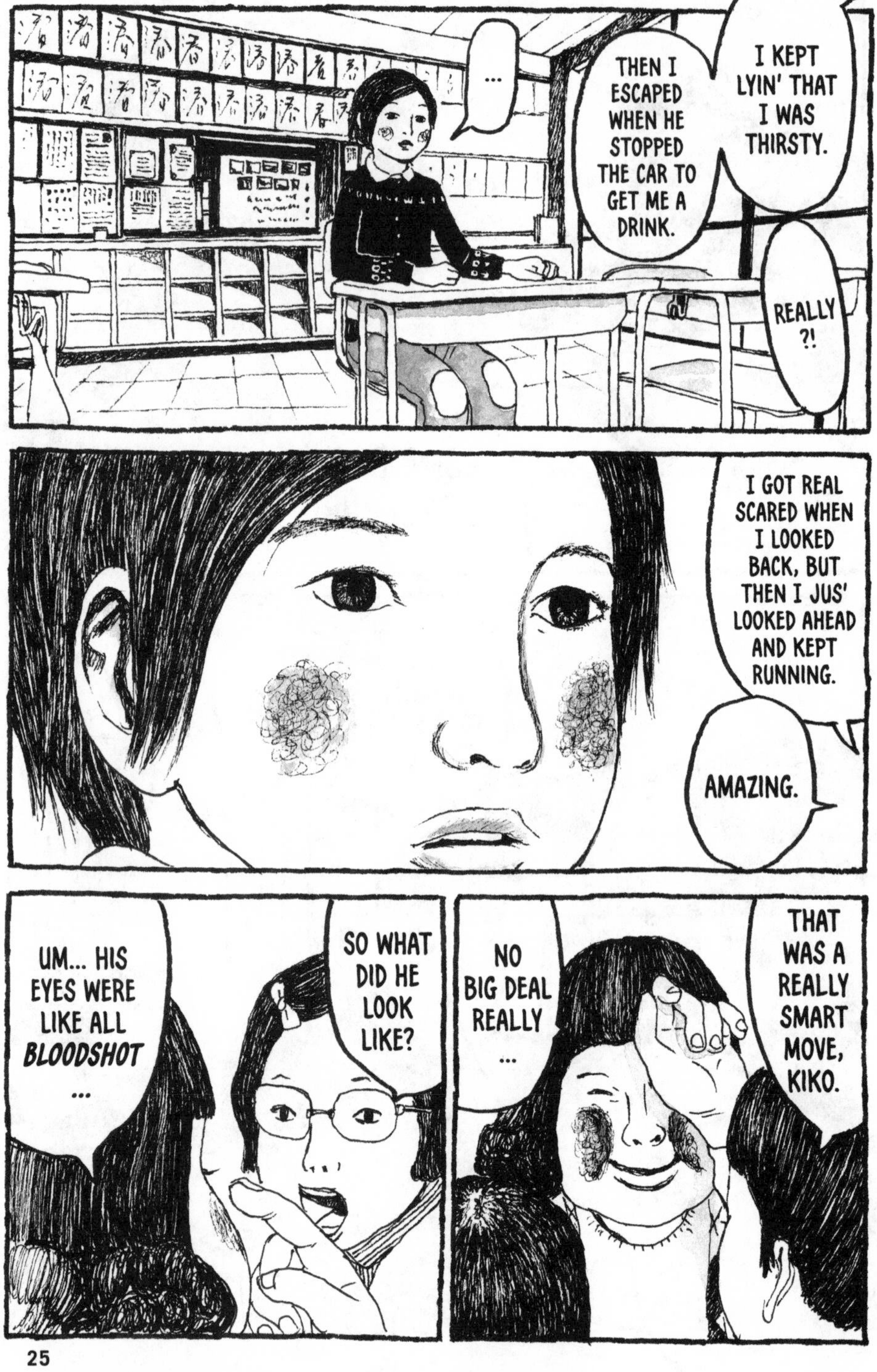
I KEPT LYIN' THAT I WAS THIRSTY.
THEN I ESCAPED WHEN HE STOPPED THE CAR TO GET ME A DRINK.
REALLY?!
...
I GOT REAL SCARED WHEN I LOOKED BACK, BUT THEN I JUS' LOOKED AHEAD AND KEPT RUNNING.
AMAZING.
THAT WAS A REALLY SMART MOVE, KIKO.
NO BIG DEAL REALLY ...
SO WHAT DID HE LOOK LIKE?
UM... HIS EYES WERE LIKE ALL *BLOODSHOT* ...

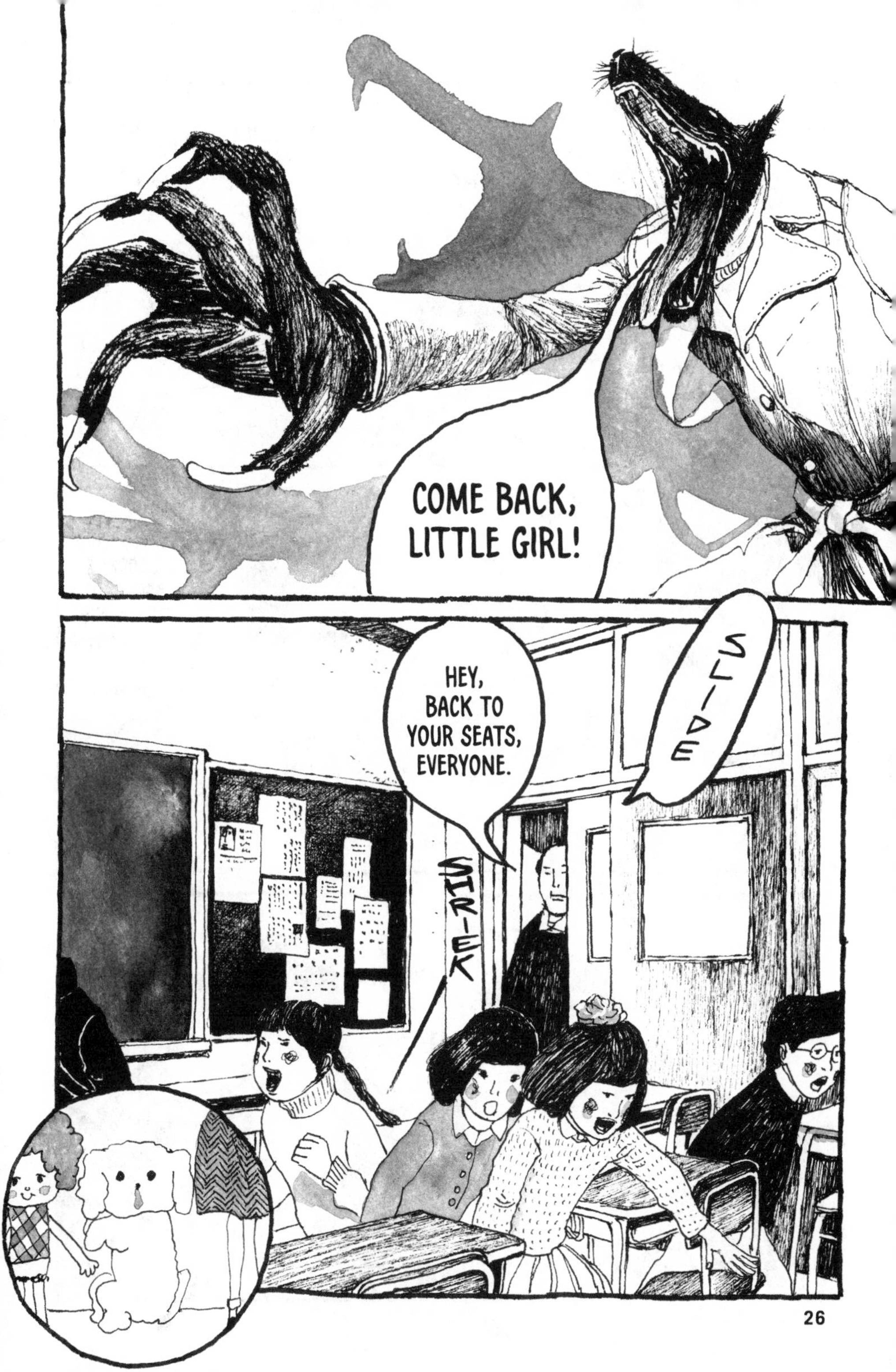
COME BACK, LITTLE GIRL!
SLIDE
HEY, BACK TO YOUR SEATS, EVERYONE.
SHRIEK

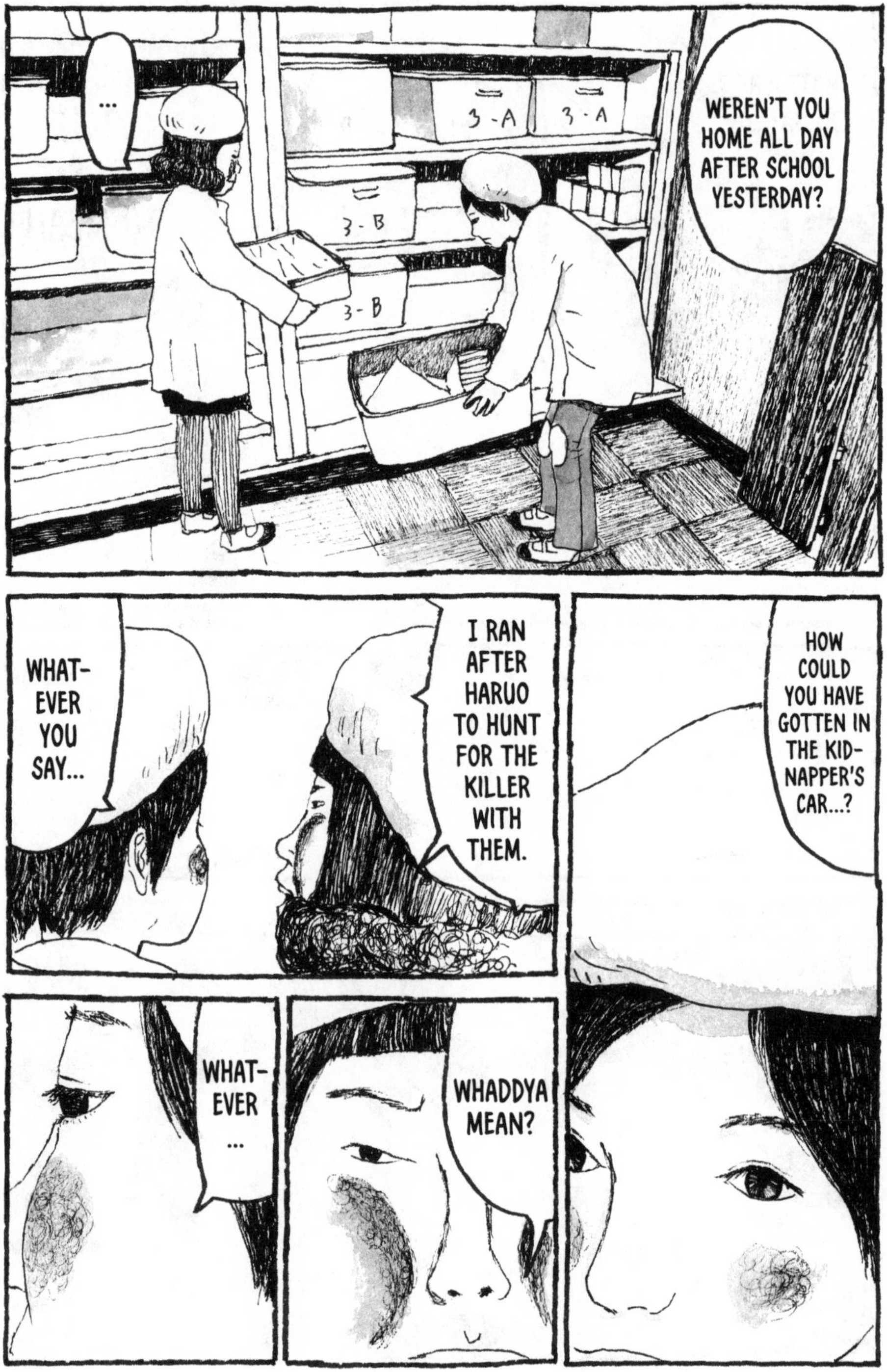
WEREN'T YOU HOME ALL DAY AFTER SCHOOL YESTERDAY?
...
3-A
3-A
3-B
3-B
HOW COULD YOU HAVE GOTTEN IN THE KID-NAPPER'S CAR...?
I RAN AFTER HARUO TO HUNT FOR THE KILLER WITH THEM.
WHAT-EVER YOU SAY...
WHADDYA MEAN?
WHAT-EVER ...

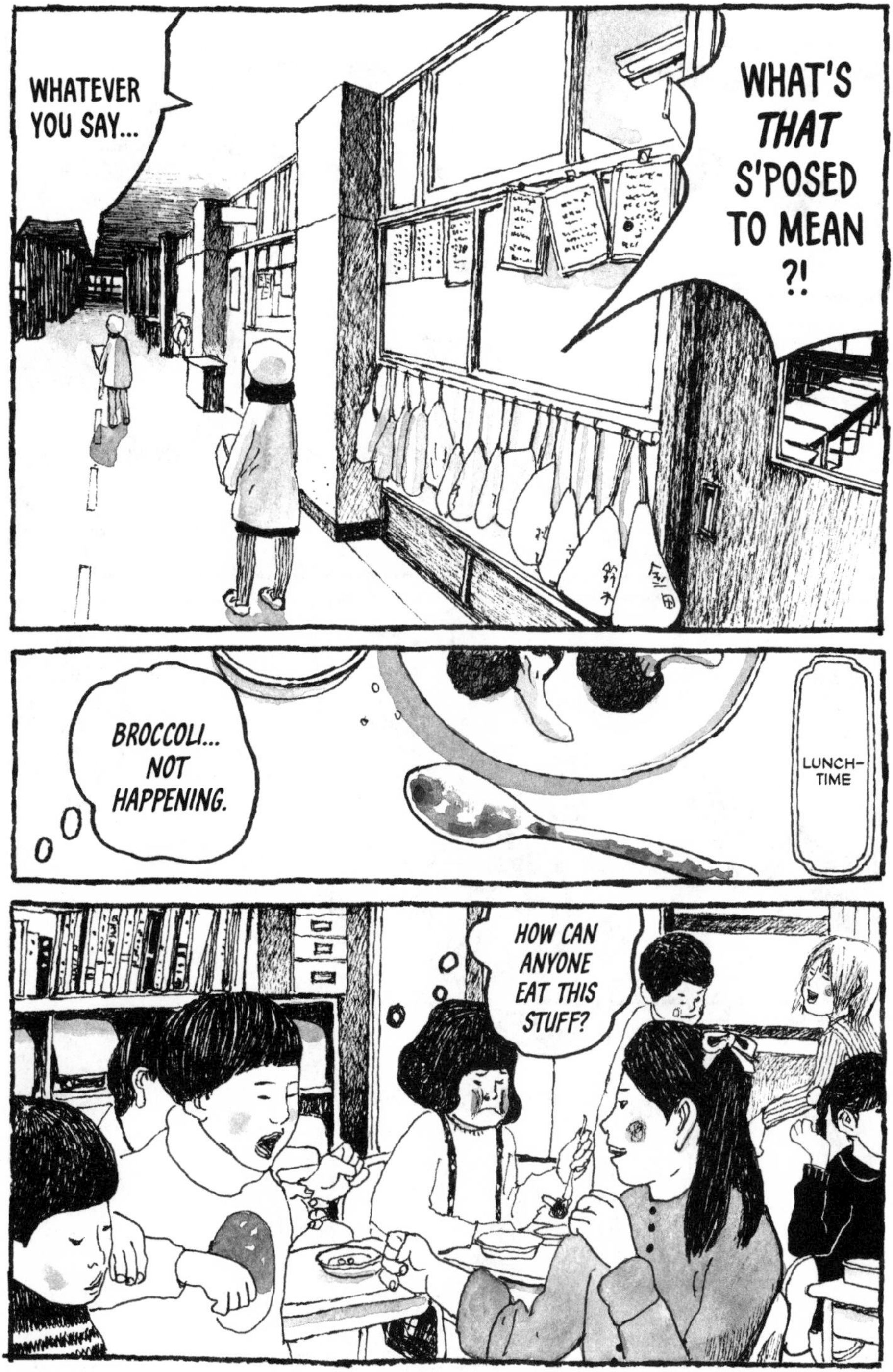
WHAT'S THAT S'POSED TO MEAN ?!
WHATEVER YOU SAY...
LUNCH-TIME
BROCCOLI... NOT HAPPENING.
HOW CAN ANYONE EAT THIS STUFF?

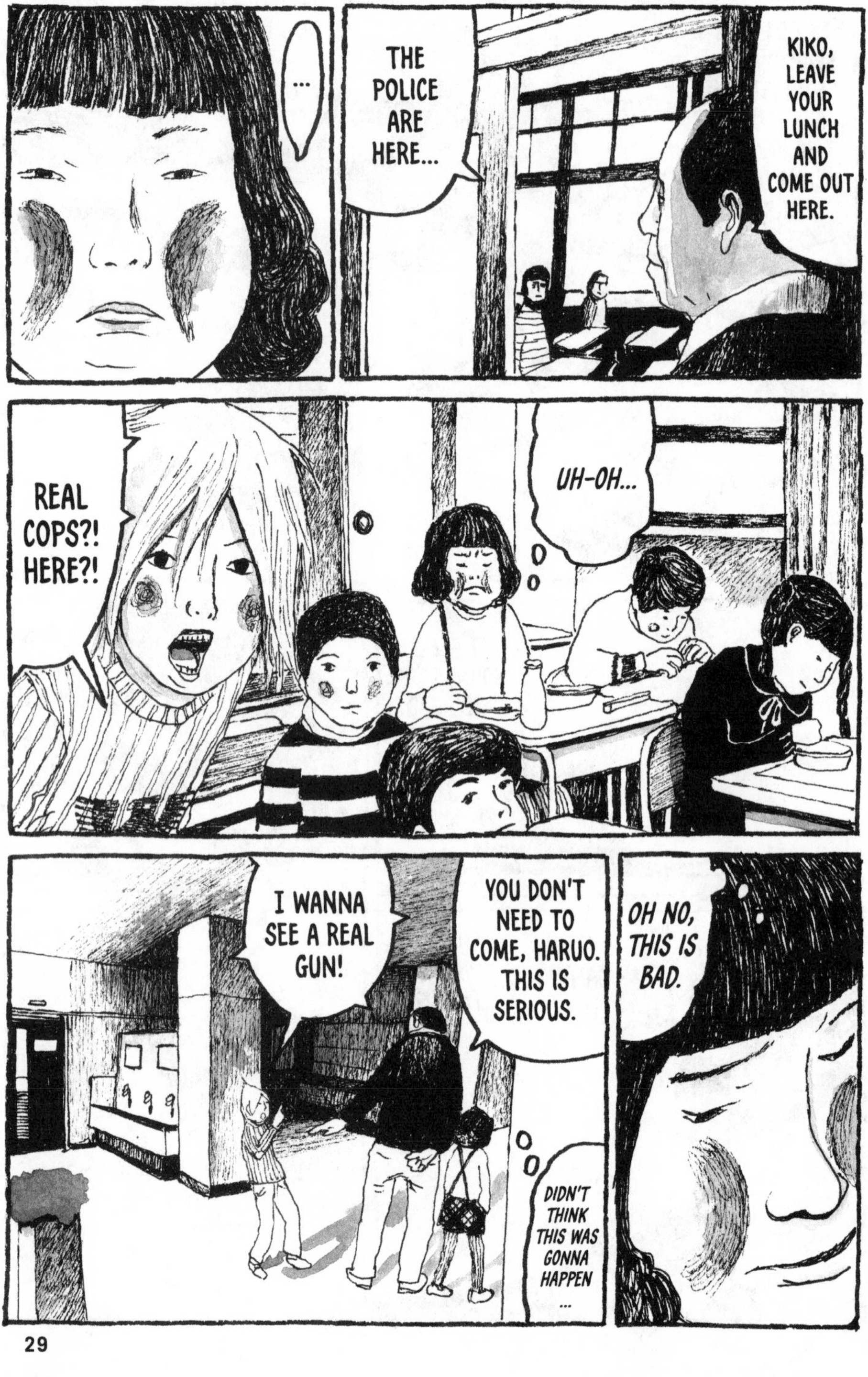
KIKO, LEAVE YOUR LUNCH AND COME OUT HERE.
THE POLICE ARE HERE...
...
UH-OH...
REAL COPS?! HERE?!
OH NO, THIS IS BAD.
YOU DON'T NEED TO COME, HARUO. THIS IS SERIOUS.
I WANNA SEE A REAL GUN!
DIDN'T THINK THIS WAS GONNA HAPPEN ...

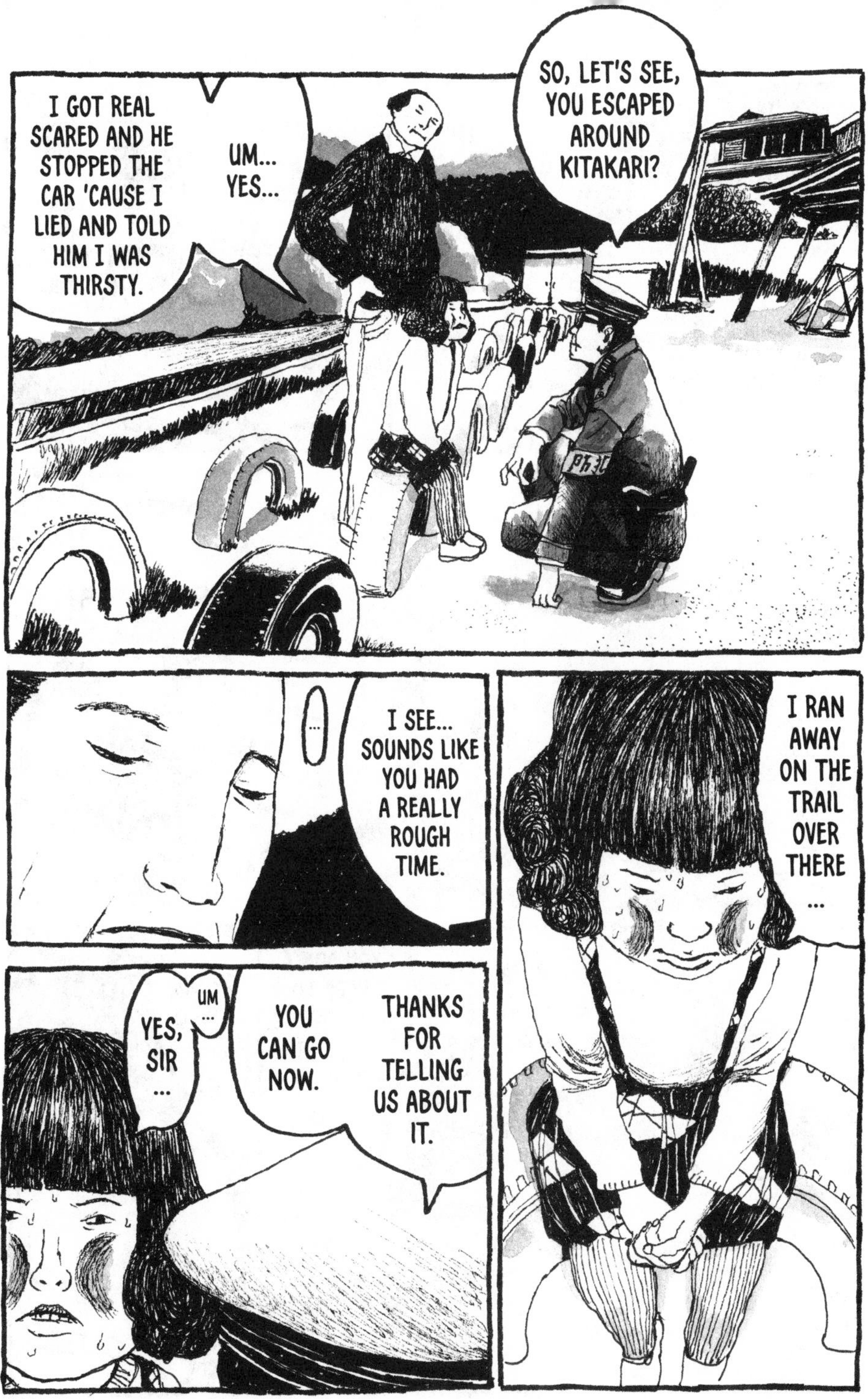
SO, LET'S SEE, YOU ESCAPED AROUND KITAKARI?
UM... YES...
I GOT REAL SCARED AND HE STOPPED THE CAR 'CAUSE I LIED AND TOLD HIM I WAS THIRSTY.
I RAN AWAY ON THE TRAIL OVER THERE ...
I SEE... SOUNDS LIKE YOU HAD A REALLY ROUGH TIME.
...
THANKS FOR TELLING US ABOUT IT.
YOU CAN GO NOW.
UM ...
YES, SIR ...

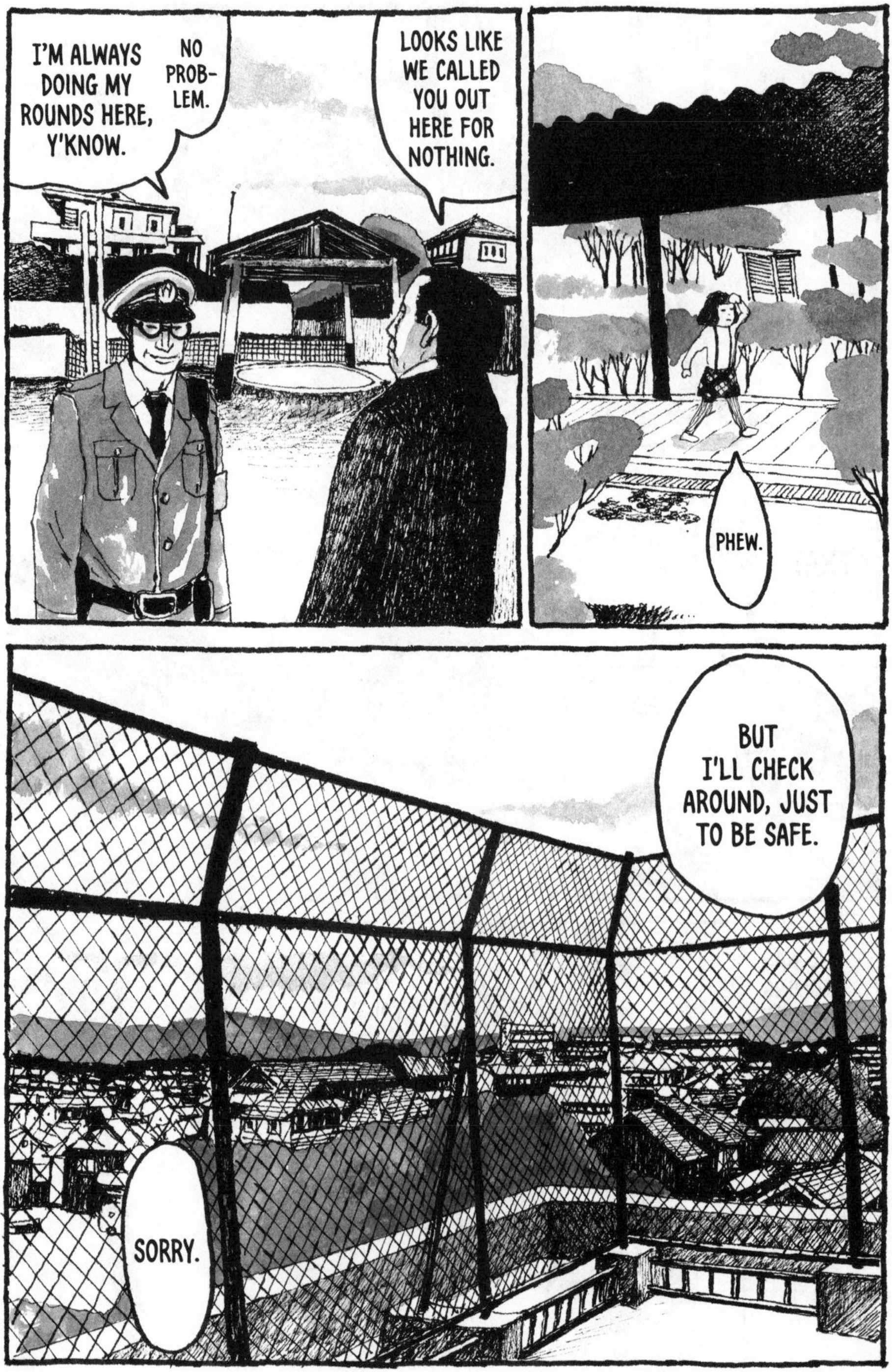
PHEW.
LOOKS LIKE WE CALLED YOU OUT HERE FOR NOTHING.
NO PROB-LEM.
I'M ALWAYS DOING MY ROUNDS HERE, Y'KNOW.
BUT I'LL CHECK AROUND, JUST TO BE SAFE.
SORRY.

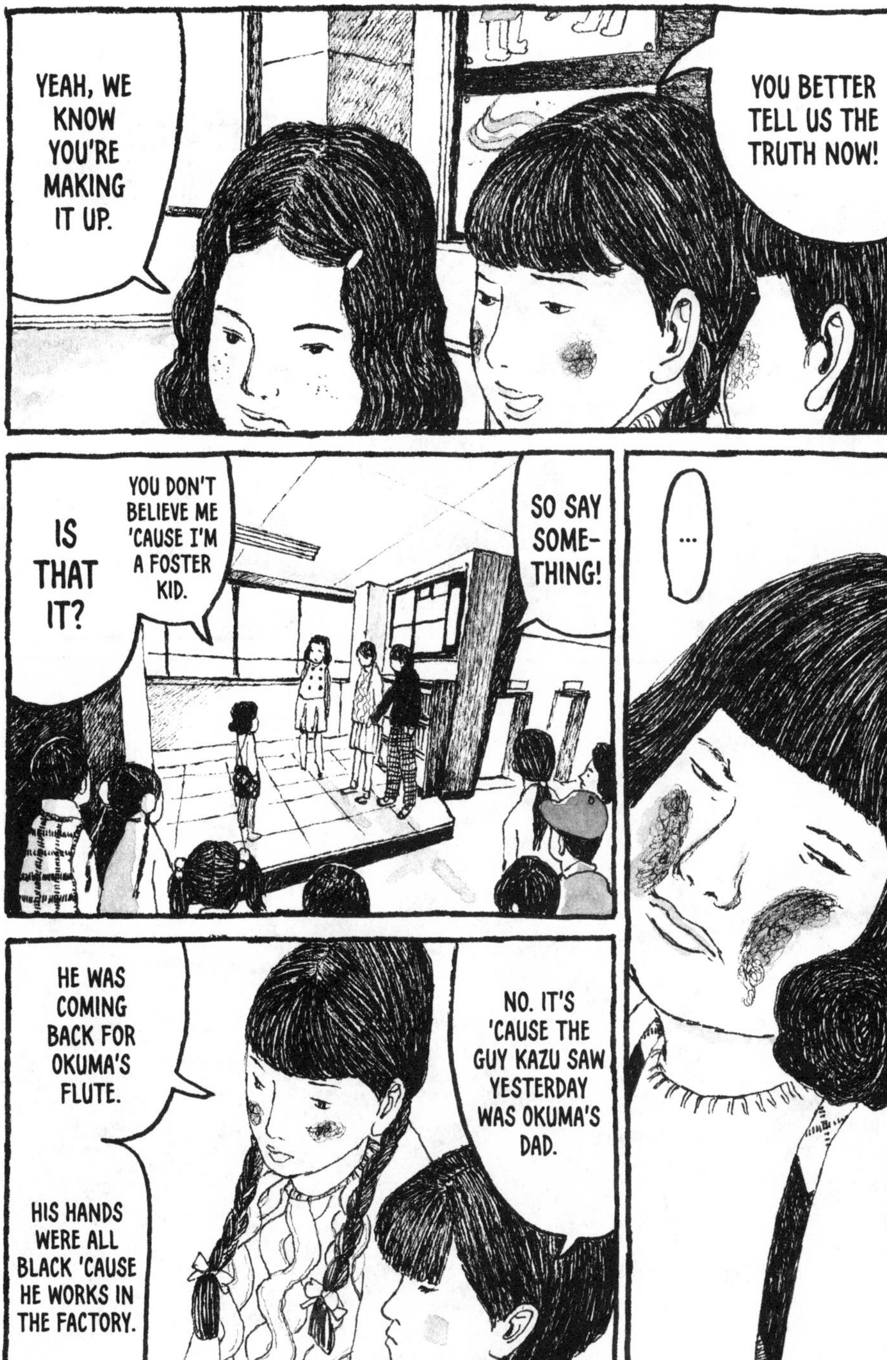
YOU BETTER TELL US THE TRUTH NOW!
YEAH, WE KNOW YOU'RE MAKING IT UP.
...
SO SAY SOME-THING!
YOU DON'T BELIEVE ME 'CAUSE I'M A FOSTER KID.
IS THAT IT?
NO. IT'S 'CAUSE THE GUY KAZU SAW YESTERDAY WAS OKUMA'S DAD.
HE WAS COMING BACK FOR OKUMA'S FLUTE.
HIS HANDS WERE ALL BLACK 'CAUSE HE WORKS IN THE FACTORY.

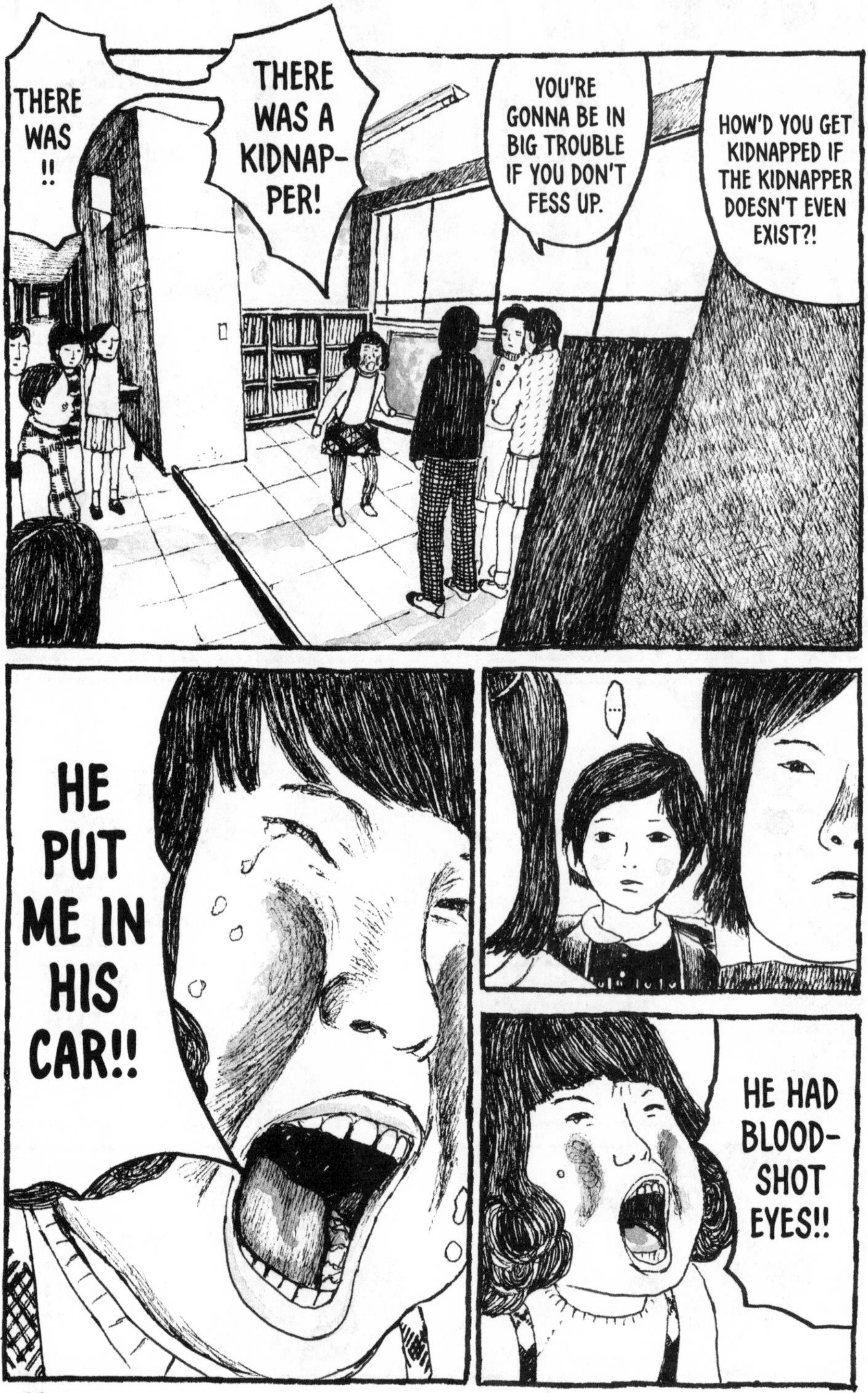
HOW'D YOU GET KIDNAPPED IF THE KIDNAPPER DOESN'T EVEN EXIST?!
YOU'RE GONNA BE IN BIG TROUBLE IF YOU DON'T FESS UP.
THERE WAS A KIDNAP-PER!
THERE WAS !!
...
HE HAD BLOOD-SHOT EYES!!
HE PUT ME IN HIS CAR!!

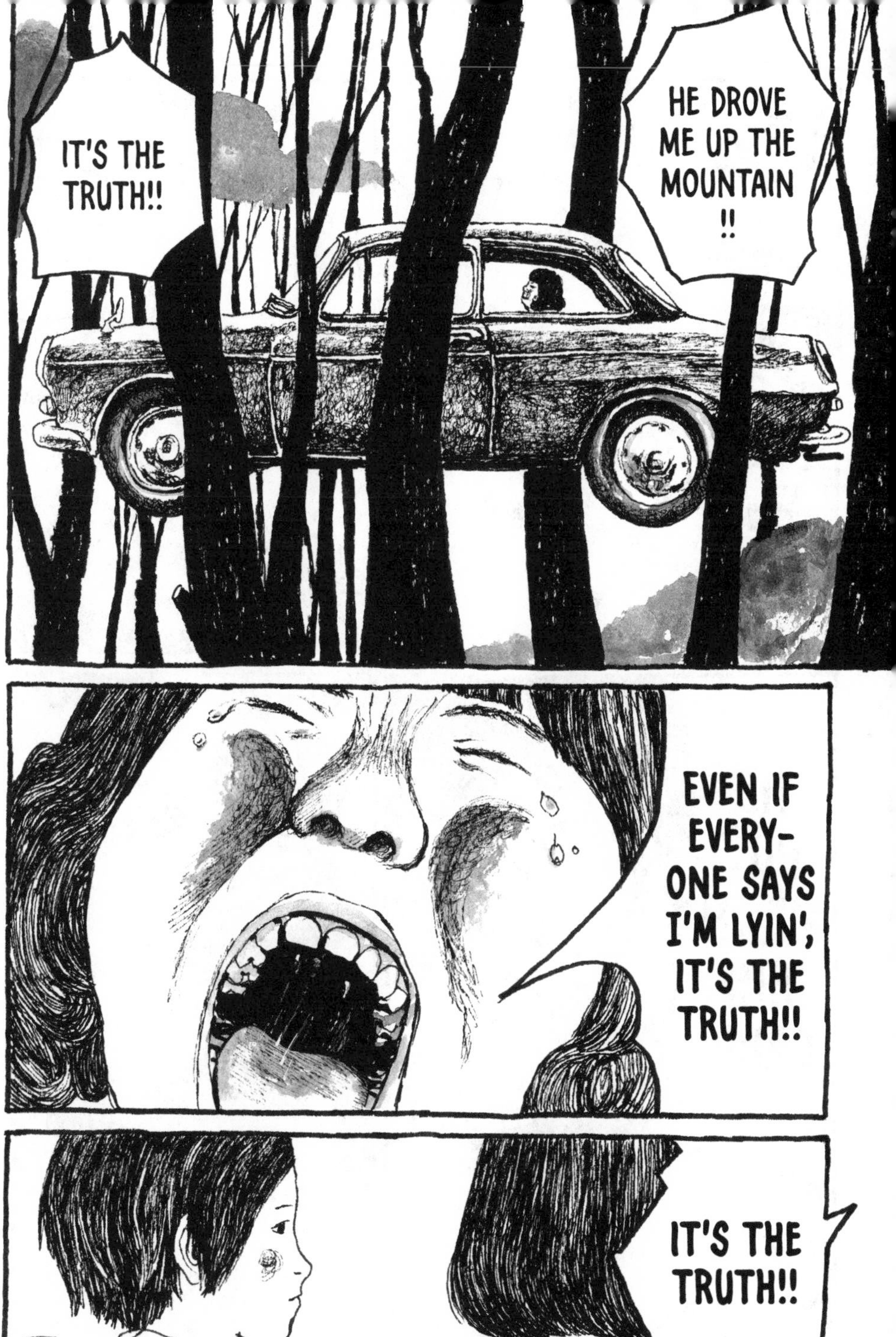
HE DROVE ME UP THE MOUNTAIN !!
IT'S THE TRUTH!!
EVEN IF EVERY-ONE SAYS I'M LYIN', IT'S THE TRUTH!!
IT'S THE TRUTH!!

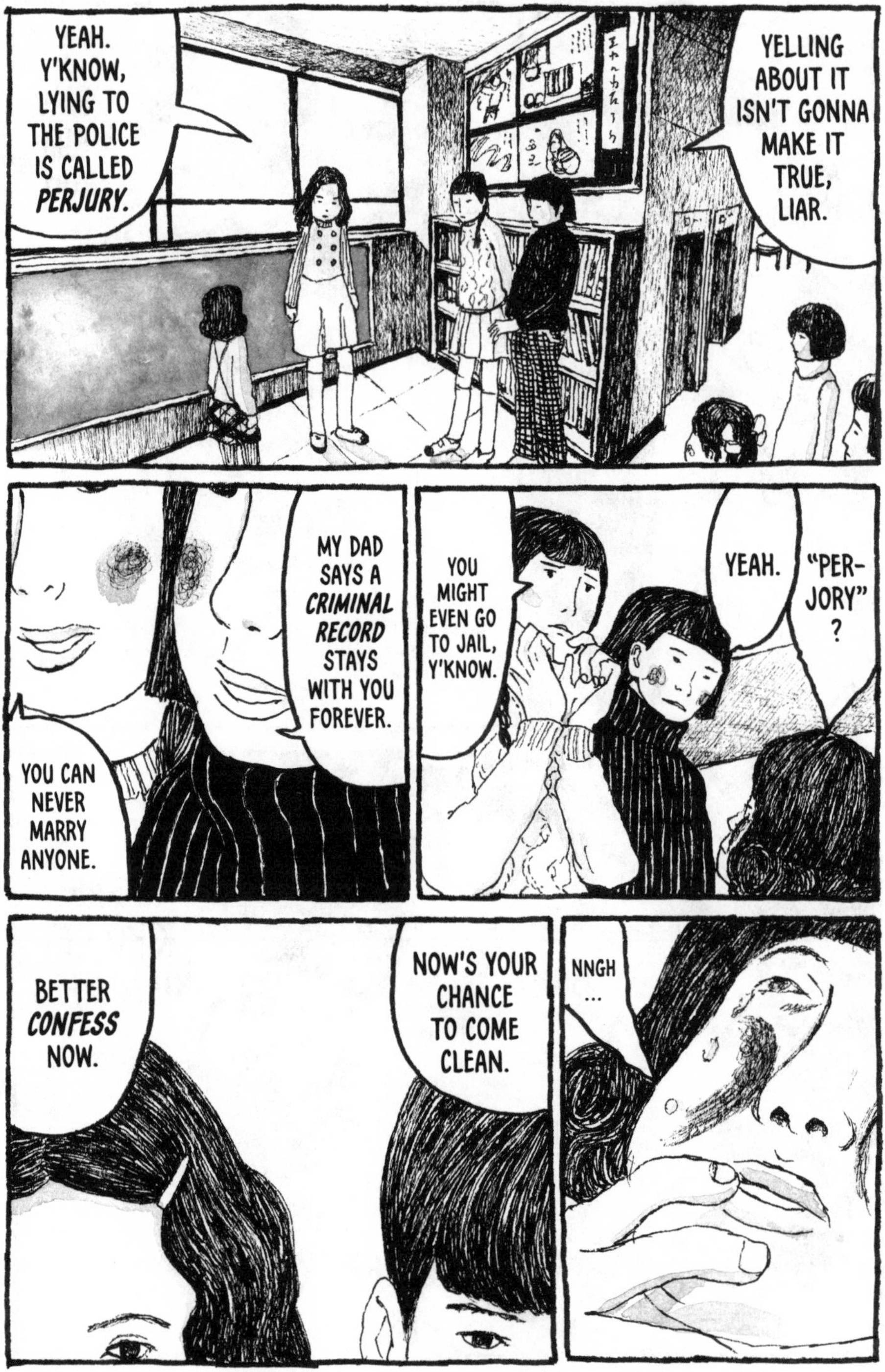
YELLING ABOUT IT ISN'T GONNA MAKE IT TRUE, LIAR.
YEAH. Y'KNOW, LYING TO THE POLICE IS CALLED *PERJURY.*
“PER-JORY”?
YEAH.
YOU MIGHT EVEN GO TO JAIL, Y'KNOW.
MY DAD SAYS A *CRIMINAL RECORD* STAYS WITH YOU FOREVER.
YOU CAN NEVER MARRY ANYONE.
NNGH ...
NOW'S YOUR CHANCE TO COME CLEAN.
BETTER *CONFESS* NOW.

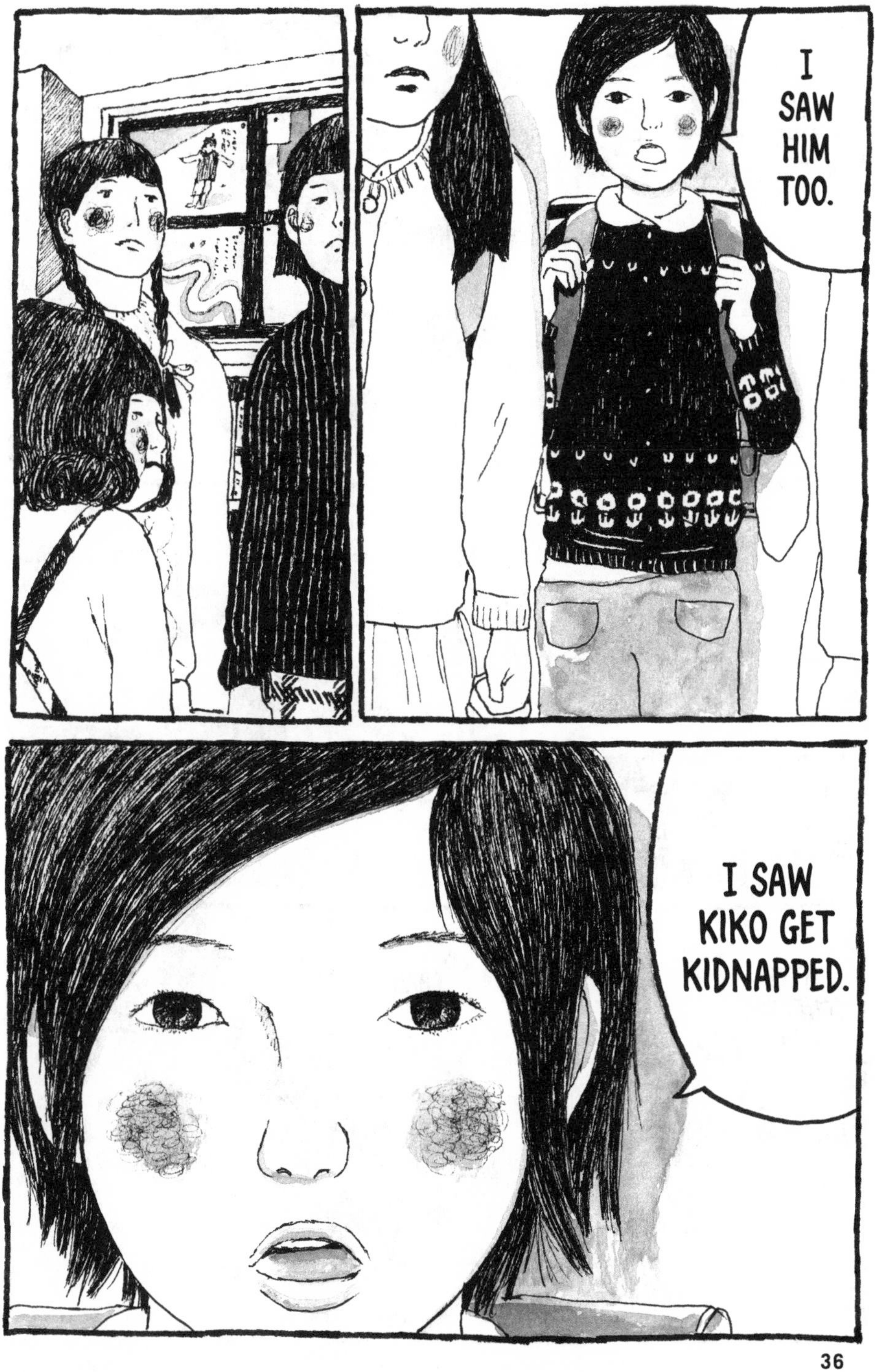
I SAW HIM TOO.
I SAW KIKO GET KIDNAPPED.

I TRIED TO STOP HIM, BUT HE PUT HER IN THE CAR AND TOOK HER AWAY.

CAW
CAW

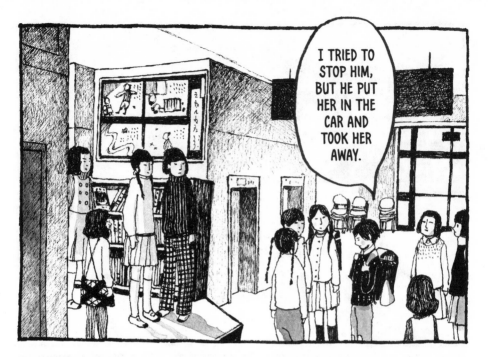

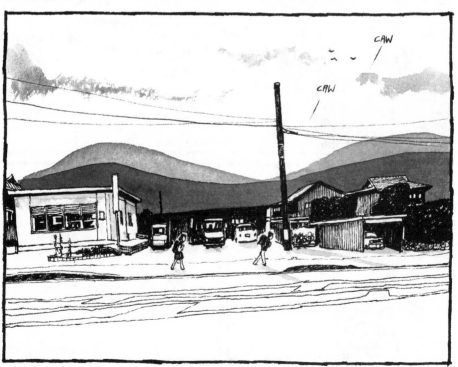

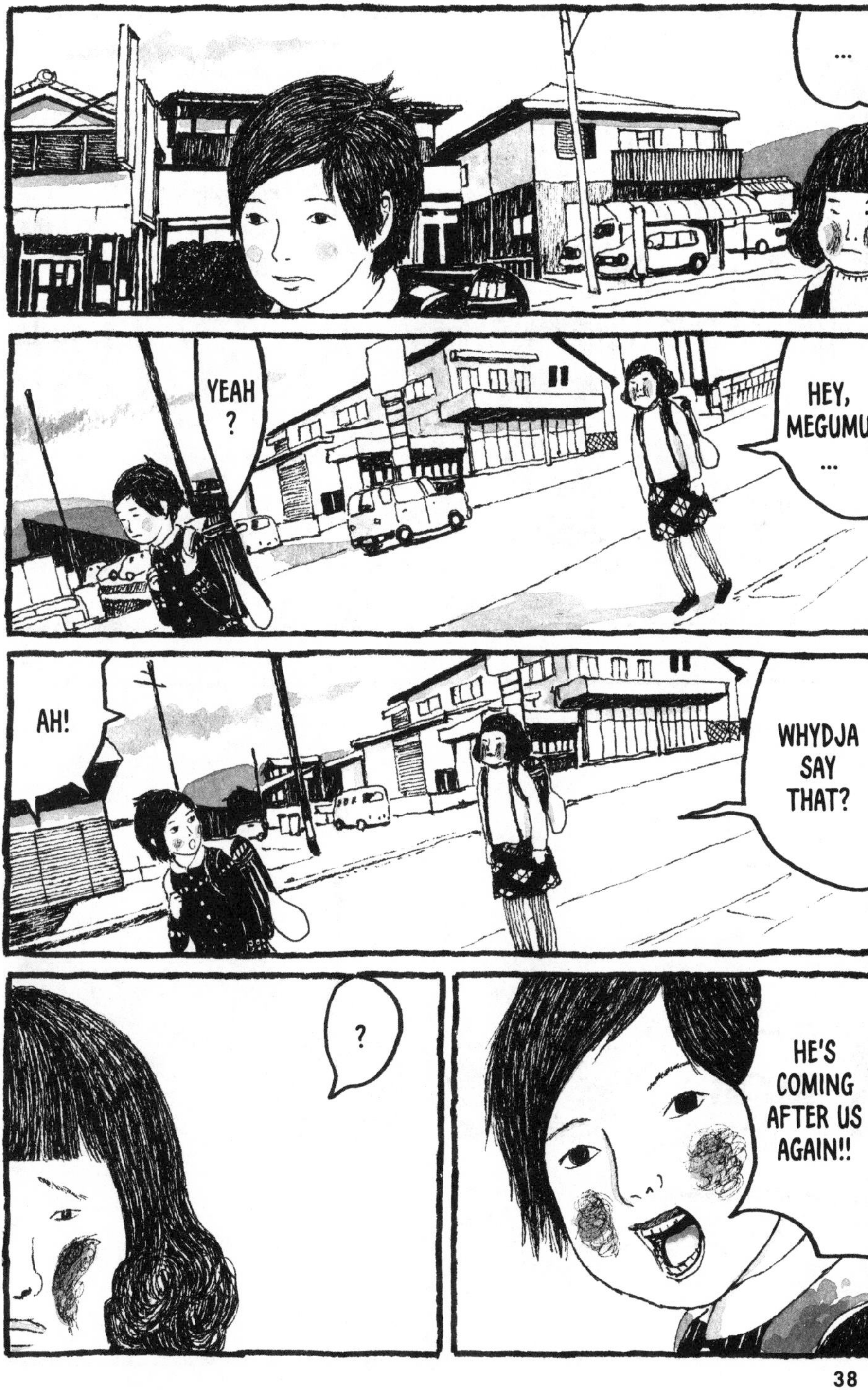
...
HEY, MEGUMU ...
YEAH ?
WHYDJA SAY THAT?
AH!
HE'S COMING AFTER US AGAIN!!
?

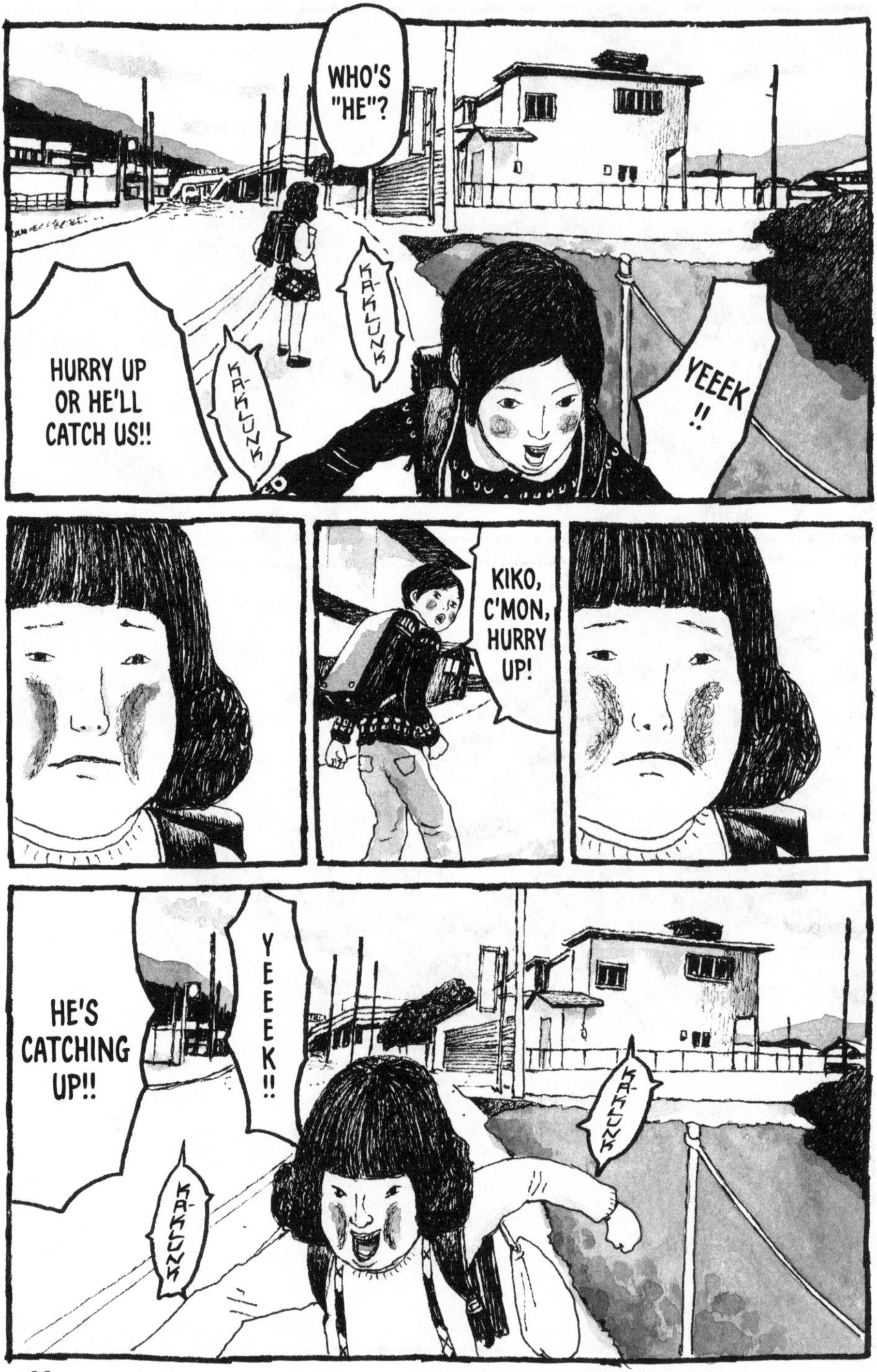
WHO'S "HE"?
YEEEK!!
KA-KLUNK
HURRY UP OR HE'LL CATCH US!!
KA-KLUNK
KIKO, C'MON, HURRY UP!
KA-KLUNK
YEEEK!!
HE'S CATCHING UP!!
KA-KLUNK

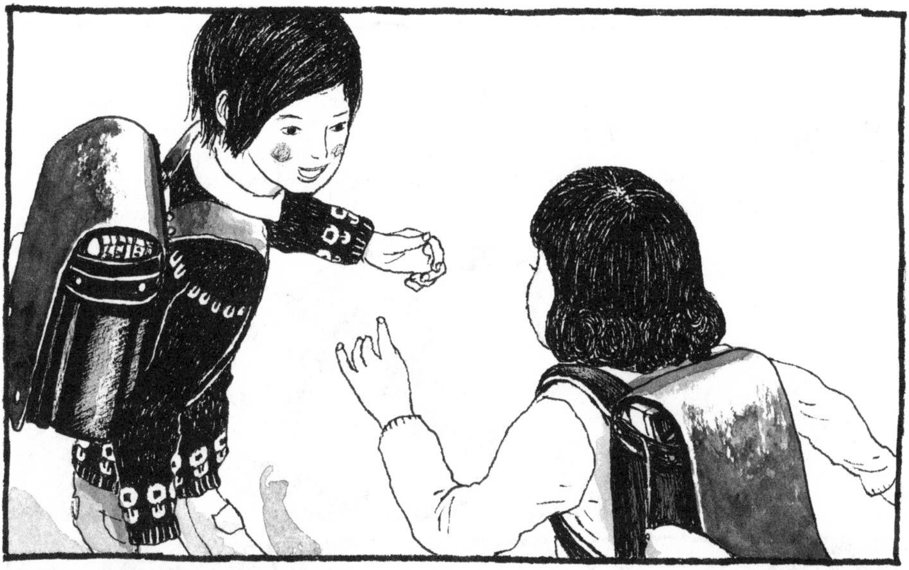
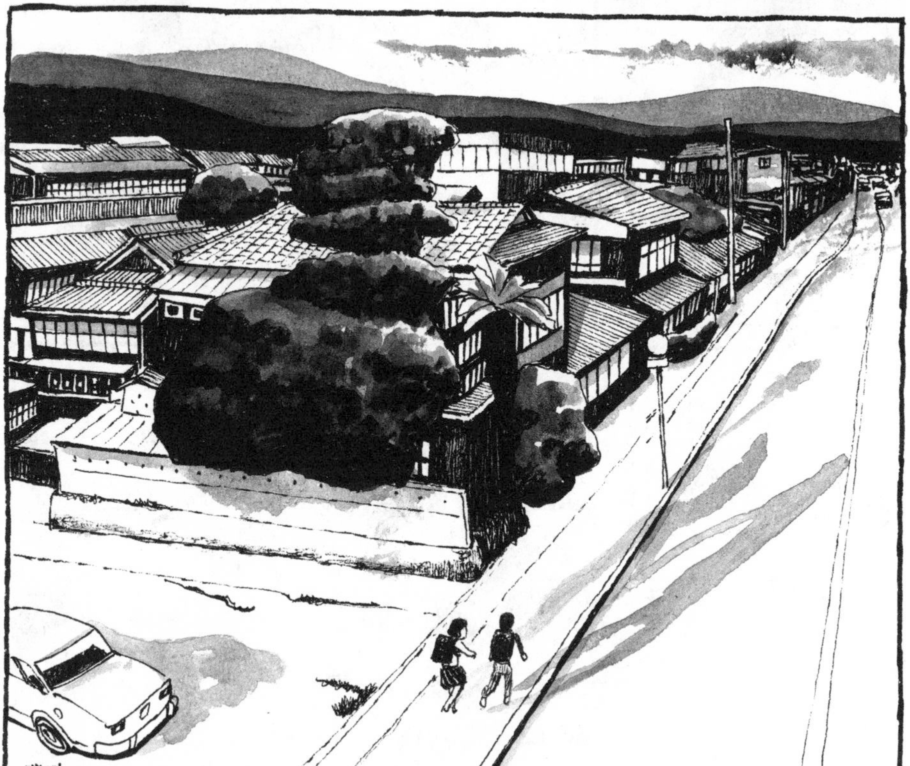

CHAPTER 8

"What's a guppy a baby of?"

"A guppy is a baby guppy."

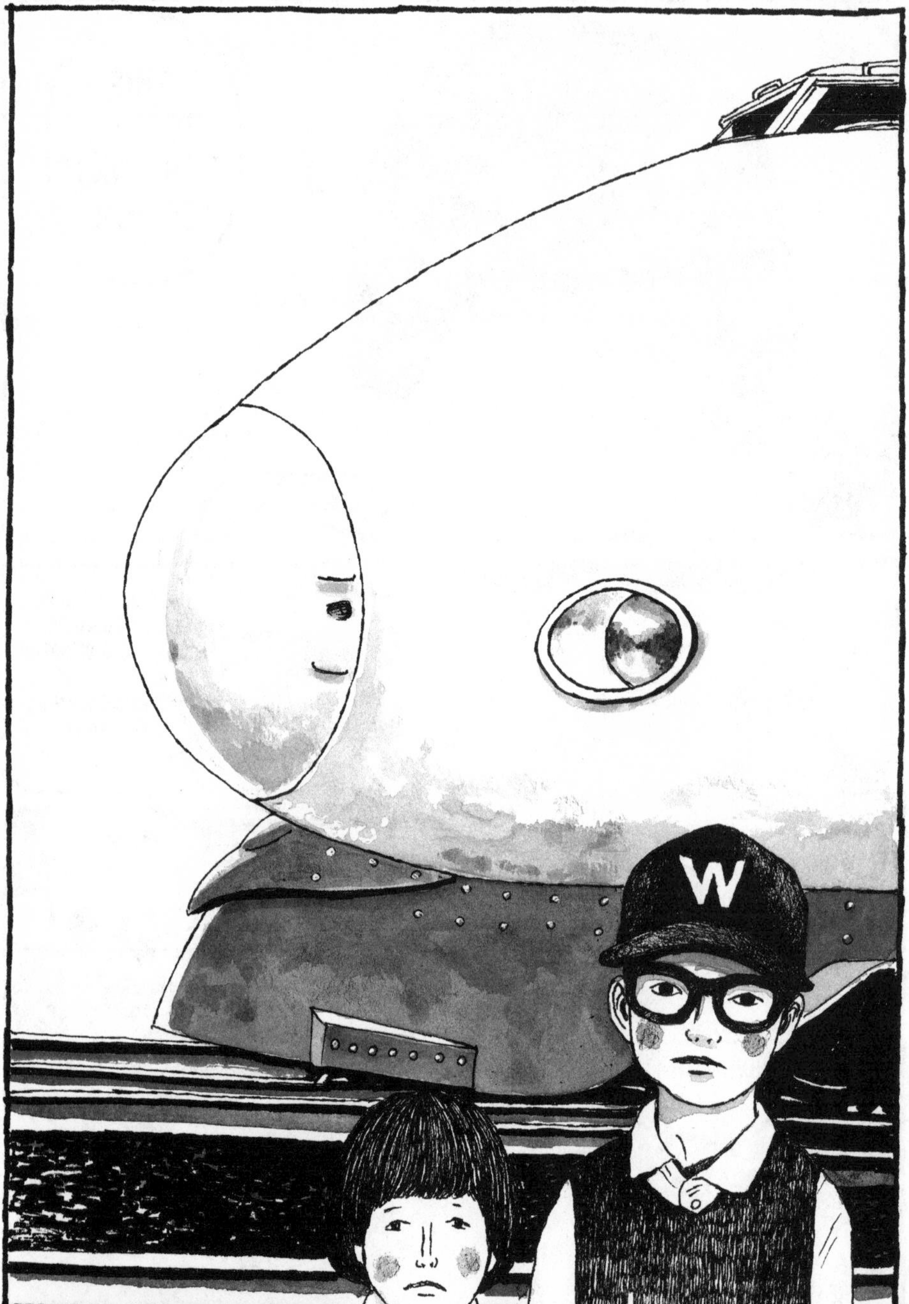
W

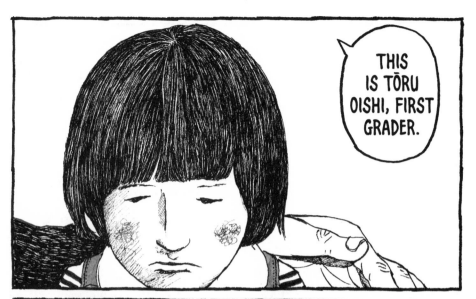

THIS IS TŌRU OISHI, FIRST GRADER.
HE'S MOVING HERE FROM ODAWARA BECAUSE OF A SITUATION AT HOME, AND HE'LL BE STAYING WITH US FOR A WHILE.
ANOTHER BOY?
SIT UP, JUN-SUKE.
WHERE'S ODAWARA?
ODA-WAWA!
SOME-WHERE 'ROUND TOKYO?

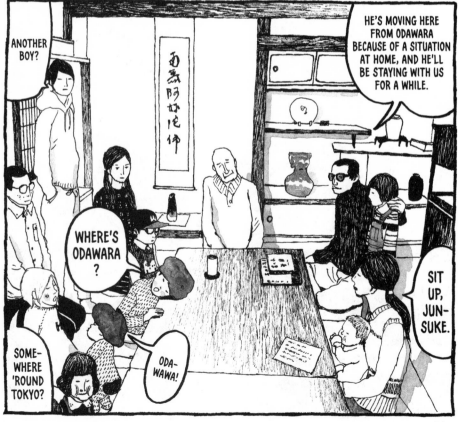

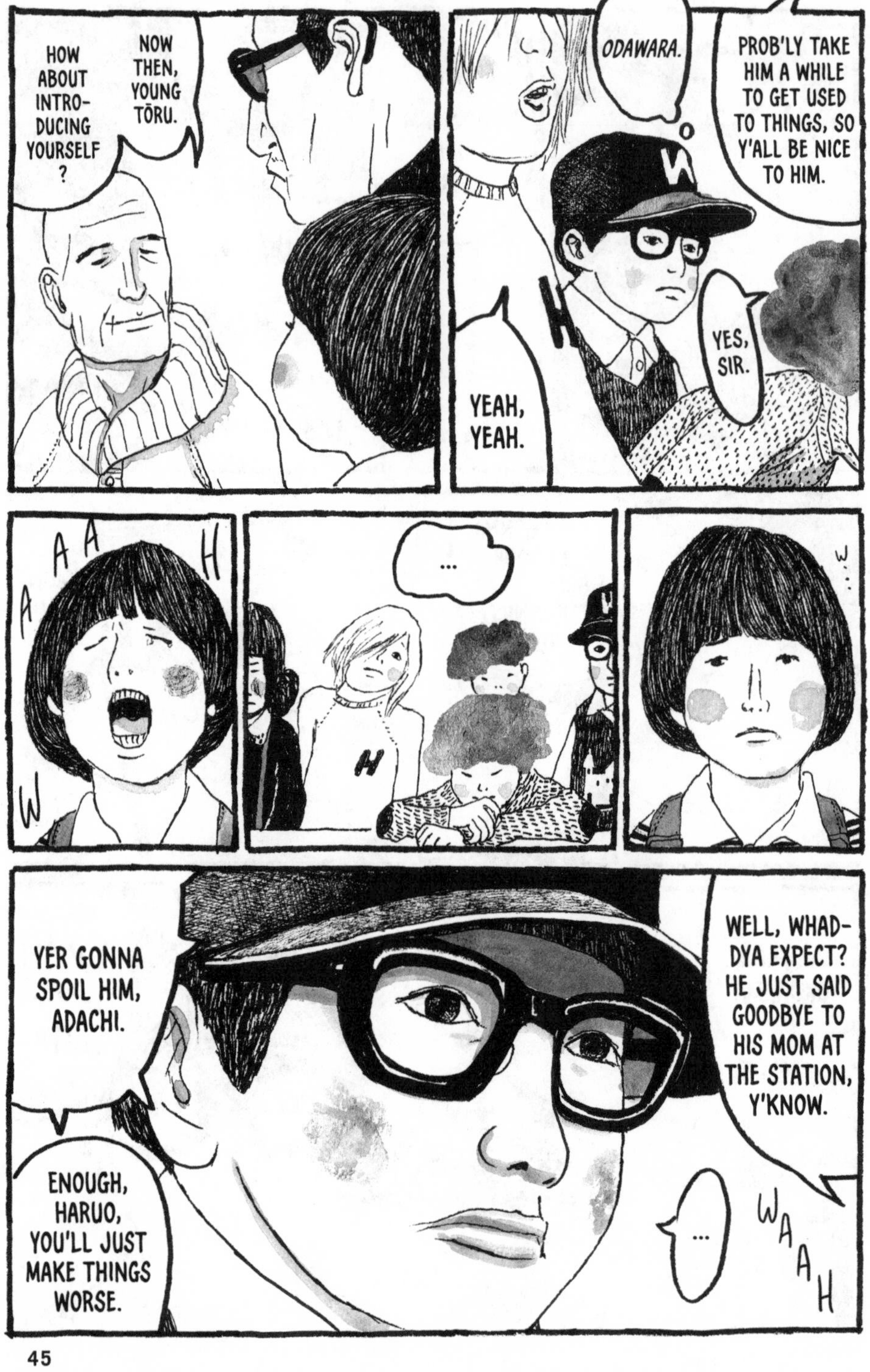
PROB'LY TAKE HIM A WHILE TO GET USED TO THINGS, SO Y'ALL BE NICE TO HIM.
ODAWARA.
YES, SIR.
YEAH, YEAH.
NOW THEN, YOUNG TŌRU.
HOW ABOUT INTRO-DUCING YOURSELF?
W...
...
WAAAH
WELL, WHAD-DYA EXPECT? HE JUST SAID GOODBYE TO HIS MOM AT THE STATION, Y'KNOW.
YER GONNA SPOIL HIM, ADACHI.
WAAAH
...
ENOUGH, HARUO, YOU'LL JUST MAKE THINGS WORSE.

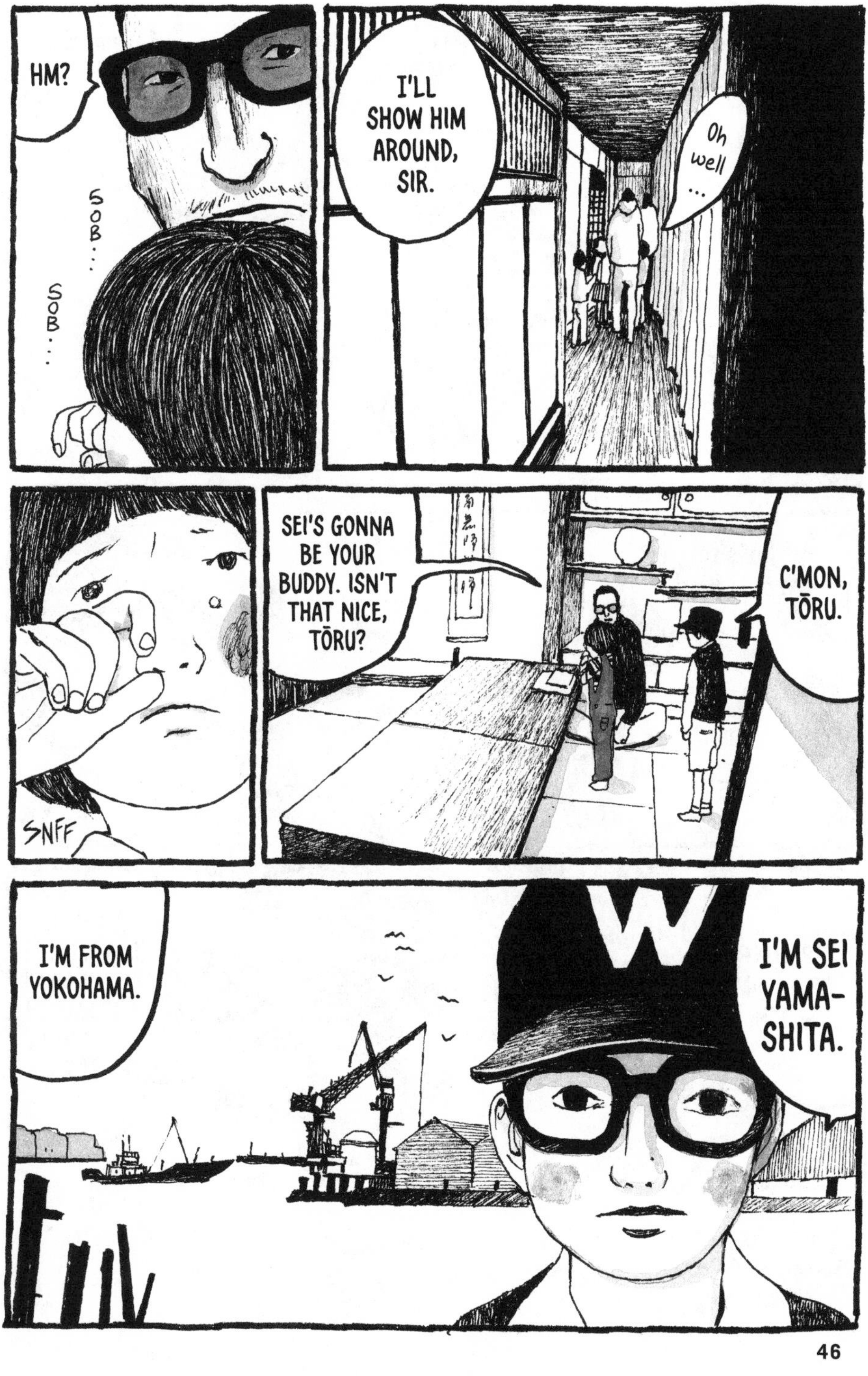
Oh well ...
I'LL SHOW HIM AROUND, SIR.
HM?
SOB...
SOB...
C'MON, TŌRU.
SEI'S GONNA BE YOUR BUDDY. ISN'T THAT NICE, TŌRU?
SNFF
I'M SEI YAMA-SHITA.
I'M FROM YOKOHAMA.

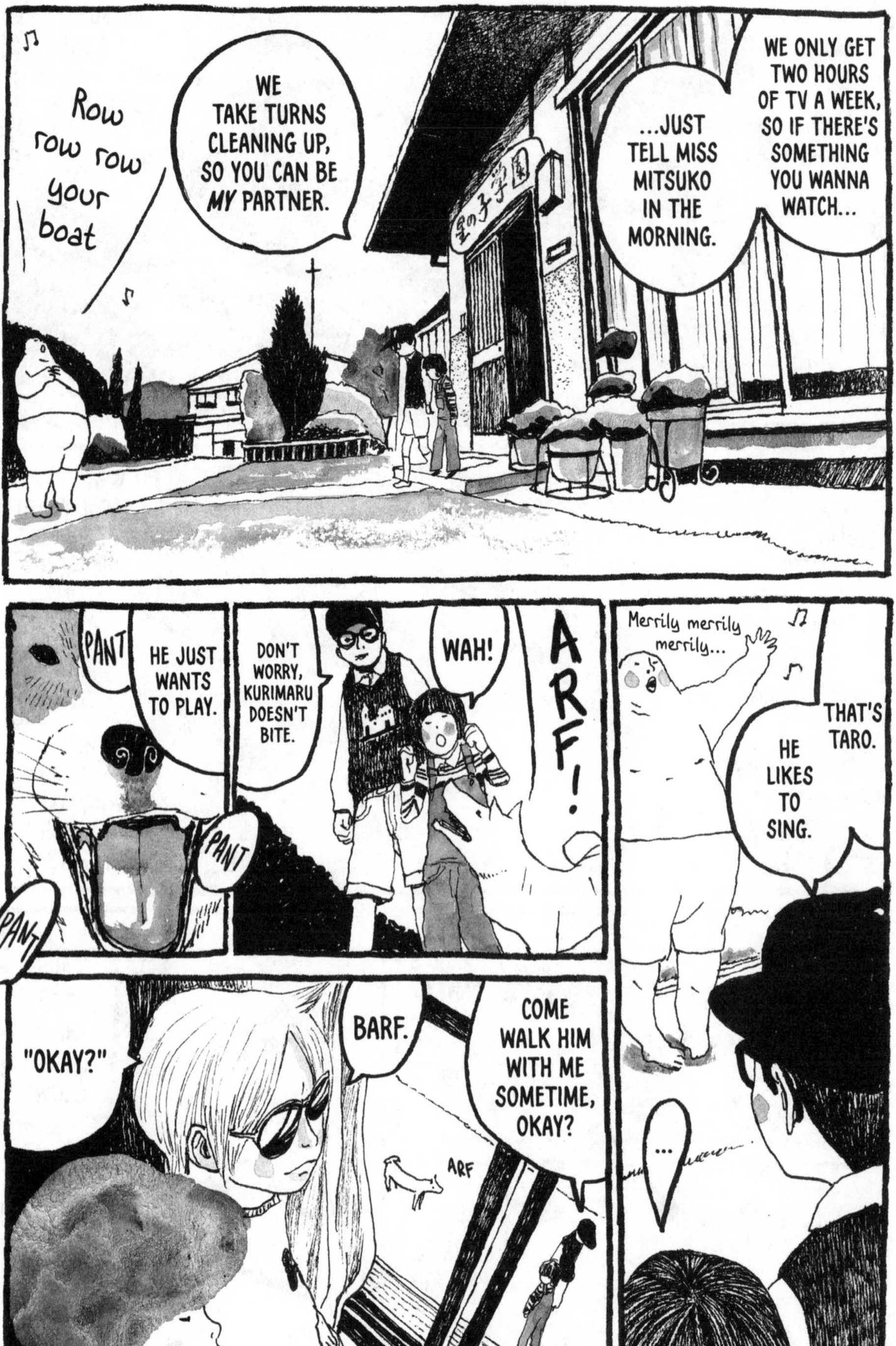
WE ONLY GET TWO HOURS OF TV A WEEK, SO IF THERE'S SOMETHING YOU WANNA WATCH...
...JUST TELL MISS MITSUKO IN THE MORNING.
星の子学園
WE TAKE TURNS CLEANING UP, SO YOU CAN BE *MY* PARTNER.
Row row row row your boat
Merrily merrily merrily...
THAT'S TARO.
HE LIKES TO SING.
...
ARF!
WAH!
DON'T WORRY, KURIMARU DOESN'T BITE.
HE JUST WANTS TO PLAY.
PANT
PANT
PANT
COME WALK HIM WITH ME SOMETIME, OKAY?
BARF.
ARF
"OKAY?"

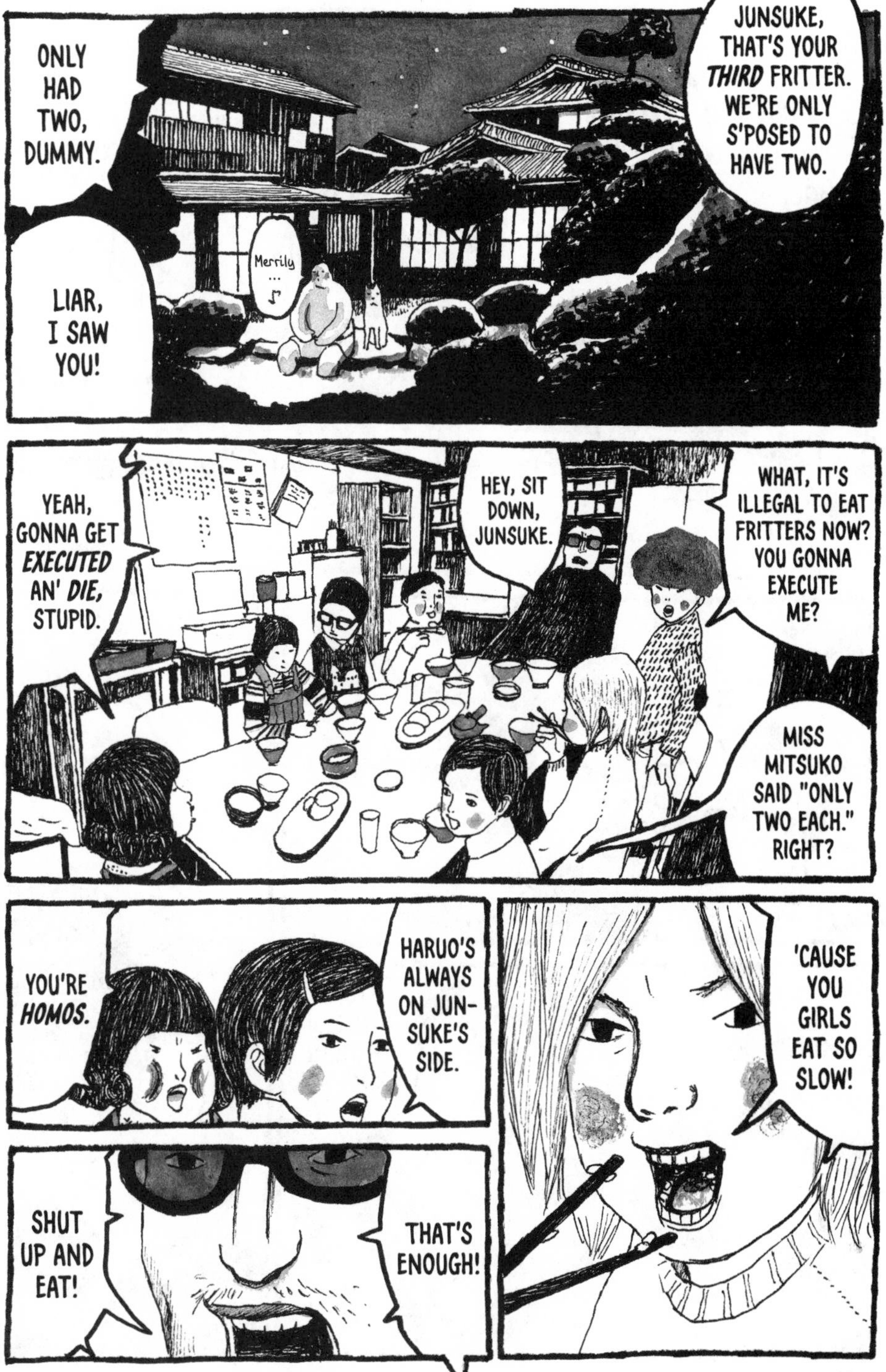
JUNSUKE, THAT'S YOUR *THIRD* FRITTER. WE'RE ONLY S'POSED TO HAVE TWO.
ONLY HAD TWO, DUMMY.
Merrily ... ♪
LIAR, I SAW YOU!
WHAT, IT'S ILLEGAL TO EAT FRITTERS NOW? YOU GONNA EXECUTE ME?
HEY, SIT DOWN, JUNSUKE.
YEAH, GONNA GET *EXECUTED* AN' *DIE,* STUPID.
MISS MITSUKO SAID "ONLY TWO EACH." RIGHT?
'CAUSE YOU GIRLS EAT SO SLOW!
HARUO'S ALWAYS ON JUN-SUKE'S SIDE.
YOU'RE *HOMOS.*
THAT'S ENOUGH!
SHUT UP AND EAT!

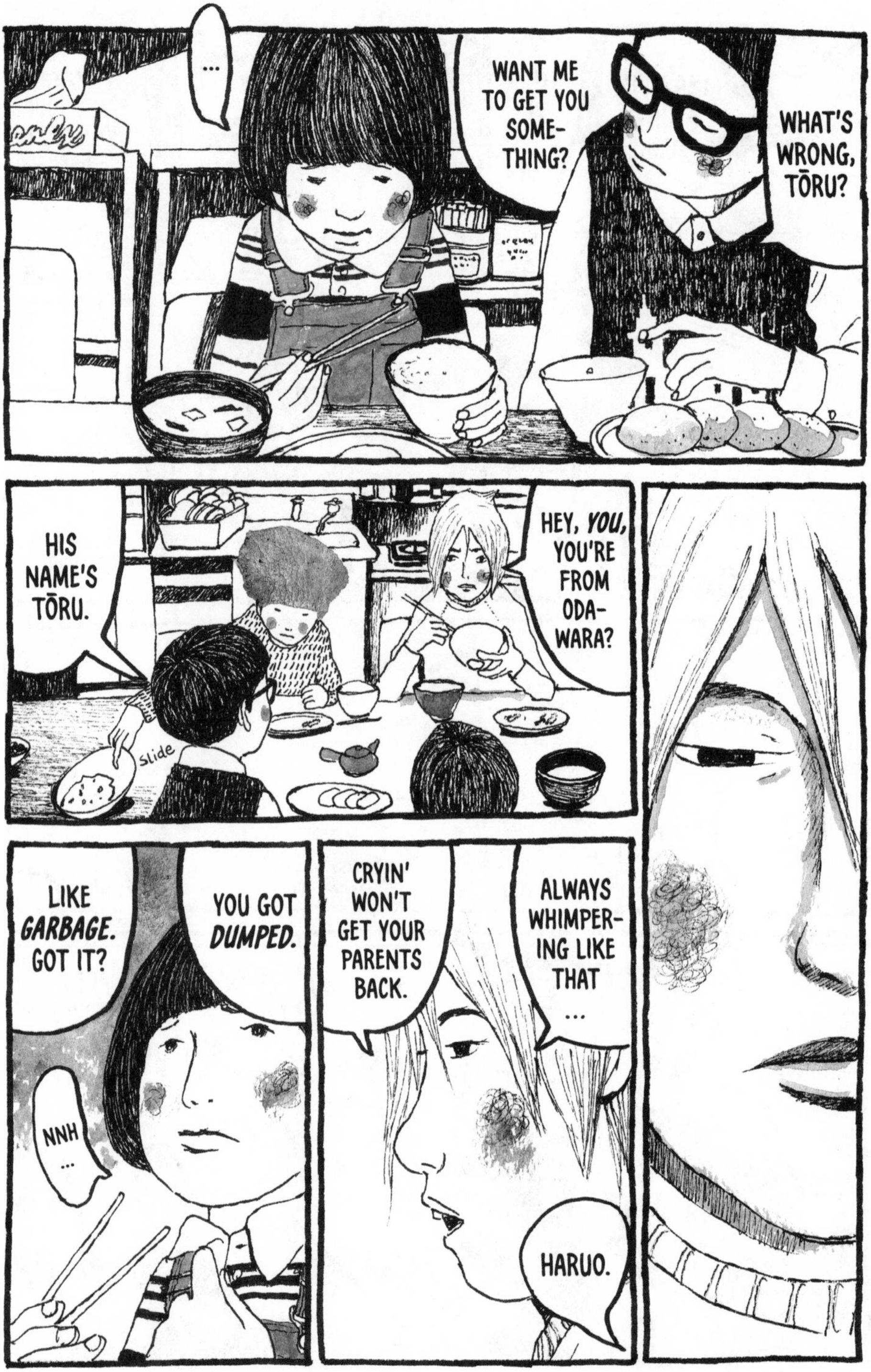
WHAT'S WRONG, TŌRU?
WANT ME TO GET YOU SOME-THING?
...
HEY, *YOU*, YOU'RE FROM ODA-WARA?
HIS NAME'S TŌRU.
slide
ALWAYS WHIMPER-ING LIKE THAT ...
CRYIN' WON'T GET YOUR PARENTS BACK.
HARUO.
YOU GOT *DUMPED*.
LIKE *GARBAGE*. GOT IT?
NNH ...

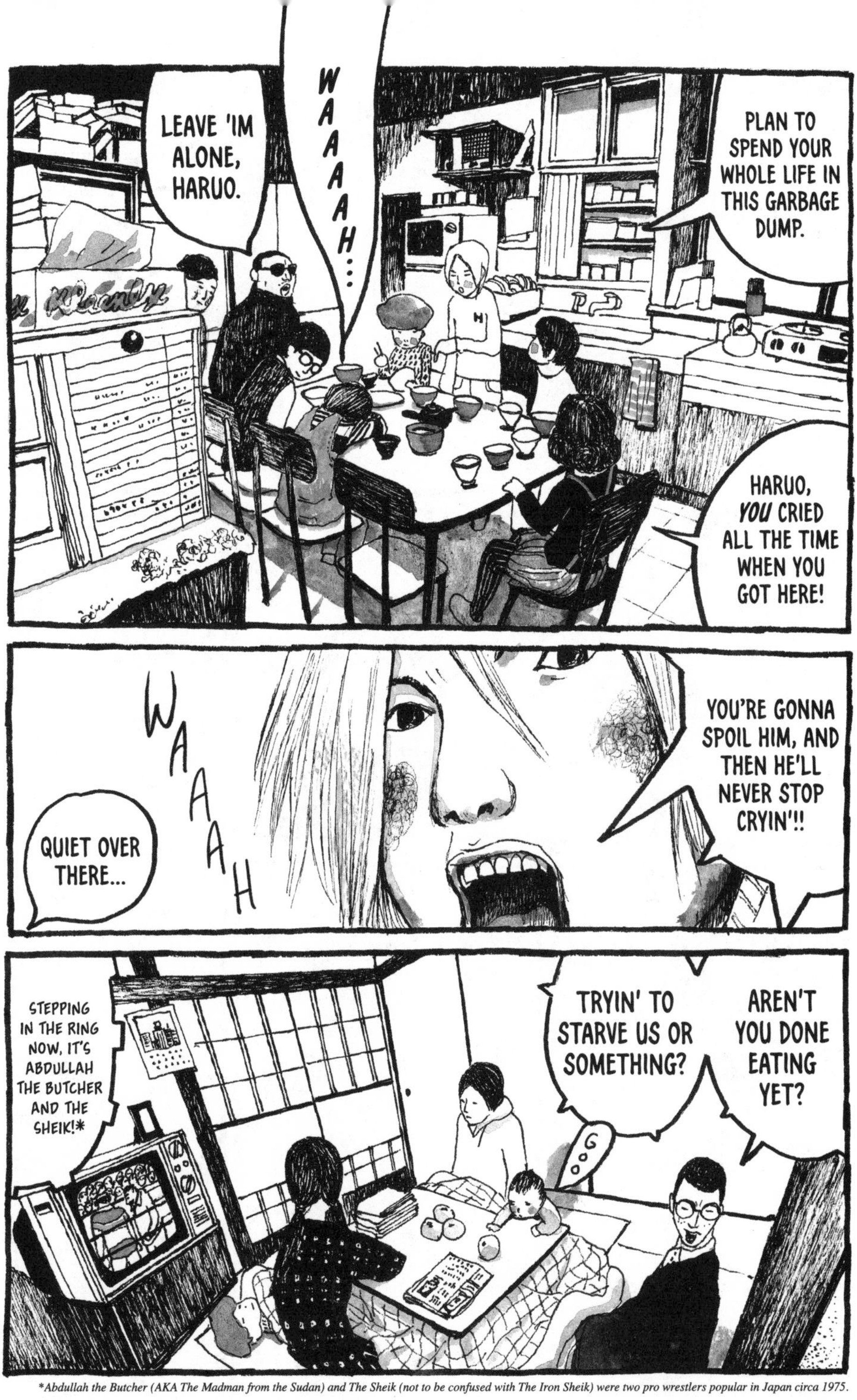
PLAN TO SPEND YOUR WHOLE LIFE IN THIS GARBAGE DUMP.
WAAAAAH...
LEAVE 'IM ALONE, HARUO.
HARUO, *YOU* CRIED ALL THE TIME WHEN YOU GOT HERE!
YOU'RE GONNA SPOIL HIM, AND THEN HE'LL NEVER STOP CRYIN'!!
WAAAAH
QUIET OVER THERE...
AREN'T YOU DONE EATING YET?
TRYIN' TO STARVE US OR SOMETHING?
GOO
STEPPING IN THE RING NOW, IT'S ABDULLAH THE BUTCHER AND THE SHEIK!*

**Abdullah the Butcher (AKA The Madman from the Sudan) and The Sheik (not to be confused with The Iron Sheik) were two pro wrestlers popular in Japan circa 1975.*

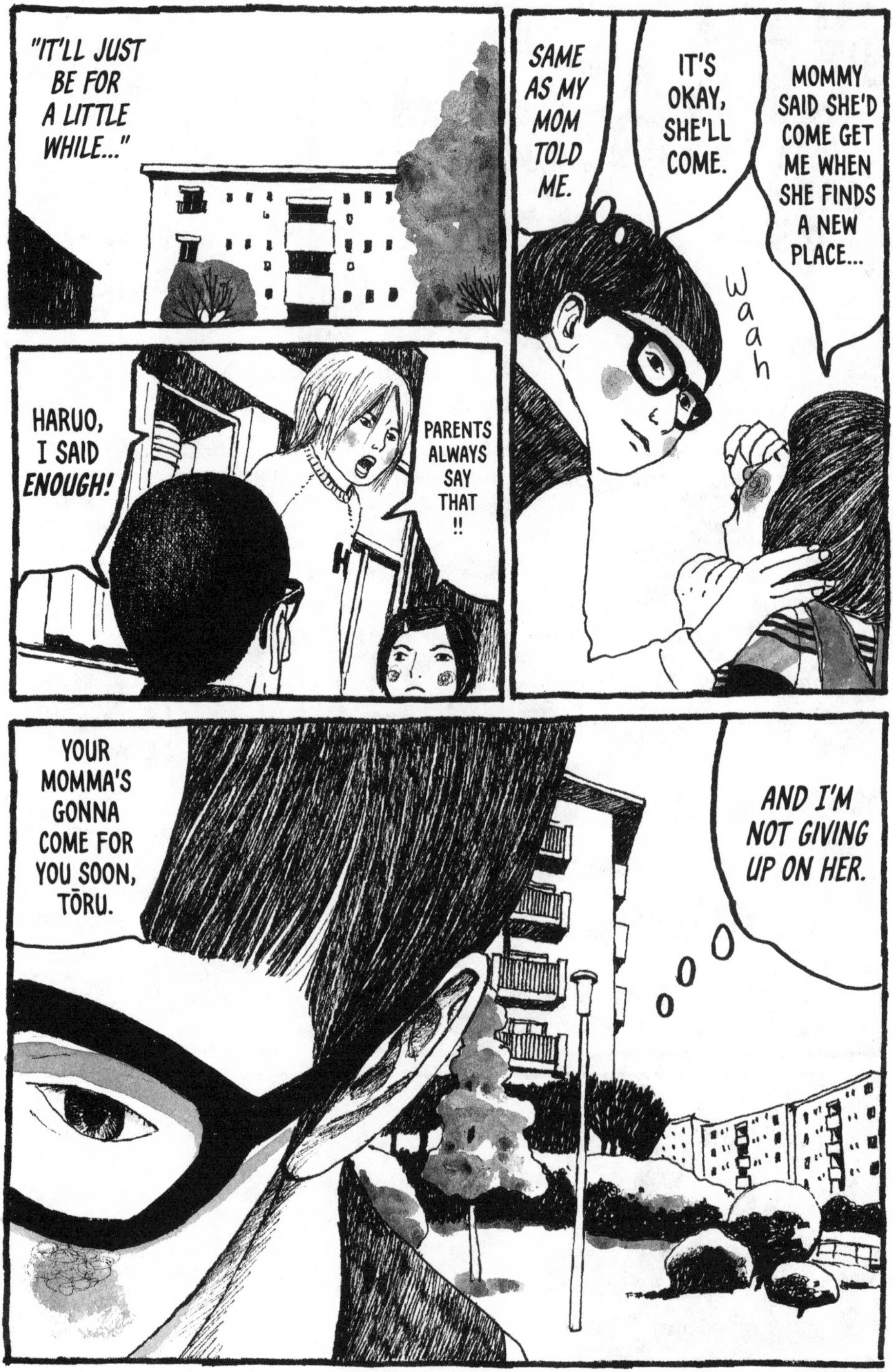
MOMMY SAID SHE'D COME GET ME WHEN SHE FINDS A NEW PLACE...
Waah
IT'S OKAY, SHE'LL COME.
SAME AS MY MOM TOLD ME.
"IT'LL JUST BE FOR A LITTLE WHILE..."
PARENTS ALWAYS SAY THAT !!
HARUO, I SAID *ENOUGH!*
AND I'M NOT GIVING UP ON HER.
YOUR MOMMA'S GONNA COME FOR YOU SOON, TŌRU.

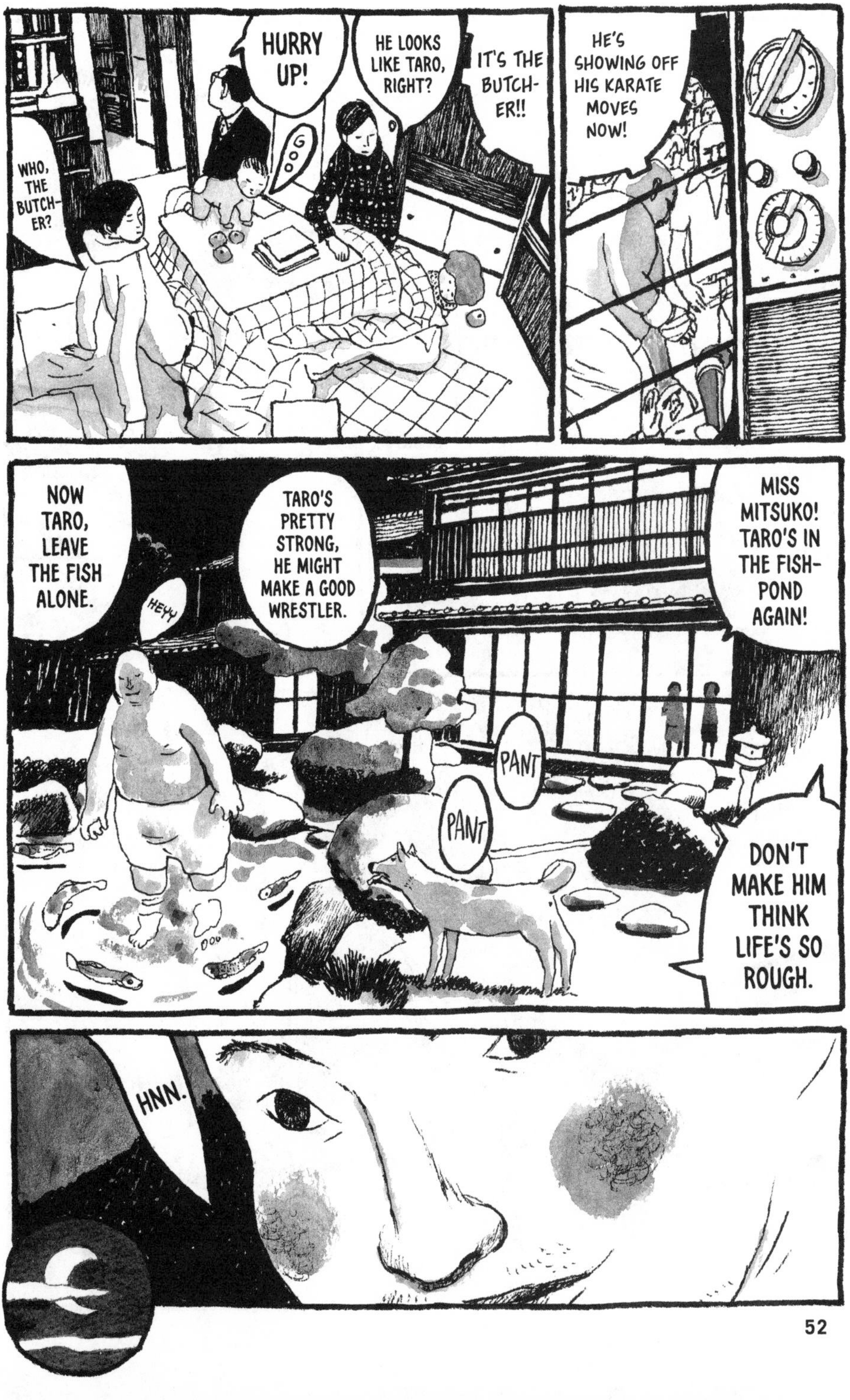
HE'S SHOWING OFF HIS KARATE MOVES NOW!
IT'S THE BUTCHER!!
HE LOOKS LIKE TARO, RIGHT?
HURRY UP!
GOO
WHO, THE BUTCHER?
MISS MITSUKO! TARO'S IN THE FISH-POND AGAIN!
TARO'S PRETTY STRONG, HE MIGHT MAKE A GOOD WRESTLER.
NOW TARO, LEAVE THE FISH ALONE.
HEYY
PANT
PANT
DON'T MAKE HIM THINK LIFE'S SO ROUGH.
HNN.

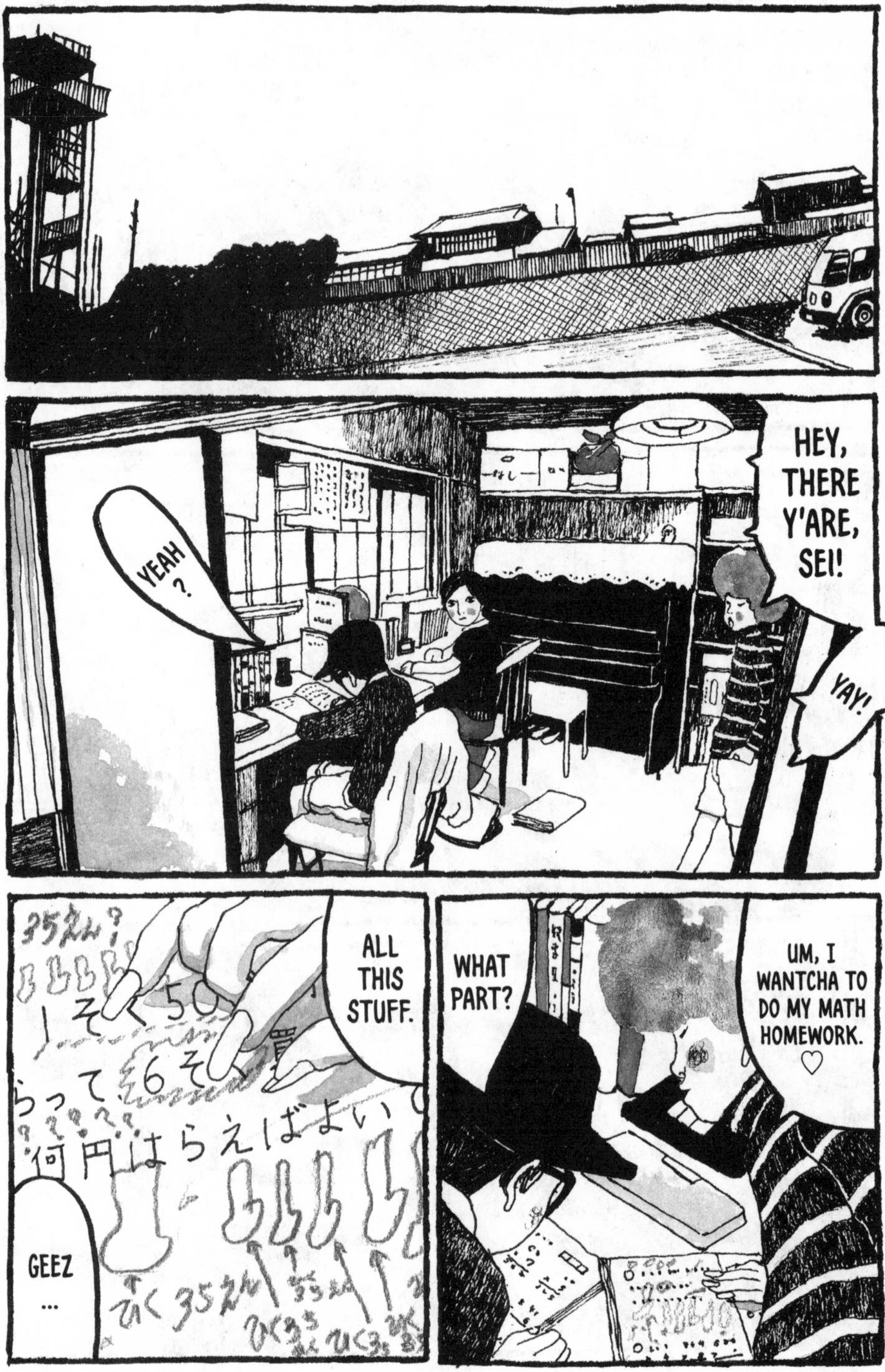

HEY, THERE Y'ARE, SEI!
YEAH ?
YAY!
UM, I WANTCHA TO DO MY MATH HOMEWORK. ♡
WHAT PART?
ALL THIS STUFF.
35えん?
1そく50
らって6そ
何円はらえばよい
ひく35えん
GEEZ ...

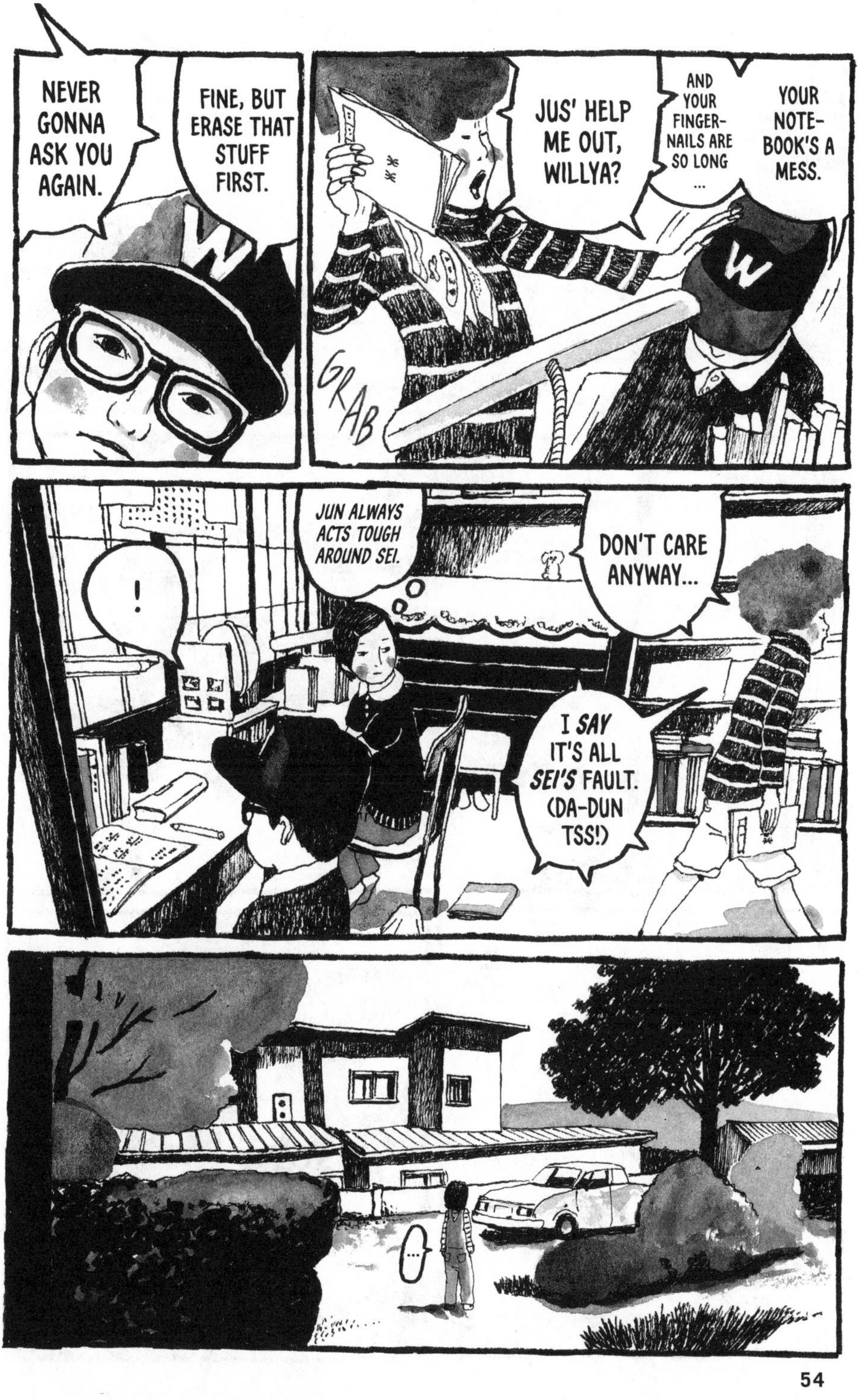
YOUR NOTE-BOOK'S A MESS.
AND YOUR FINGER-NAILS ARE SO LONG ...
JUS' HELP ME OUT, WILLYA?
GRAB
FINE, BUT ERASE THAT STUFF FIRST.
NEVER GONNA ASK YOU AGAIN.
DON'T CARE ANYWAY...
JUN ALWAYS ACTS TOUGH AROUND SEI.
I *SAY* IT'S ALL *SEI'S* FAULT. (DA-DUN TSS!)
!
...

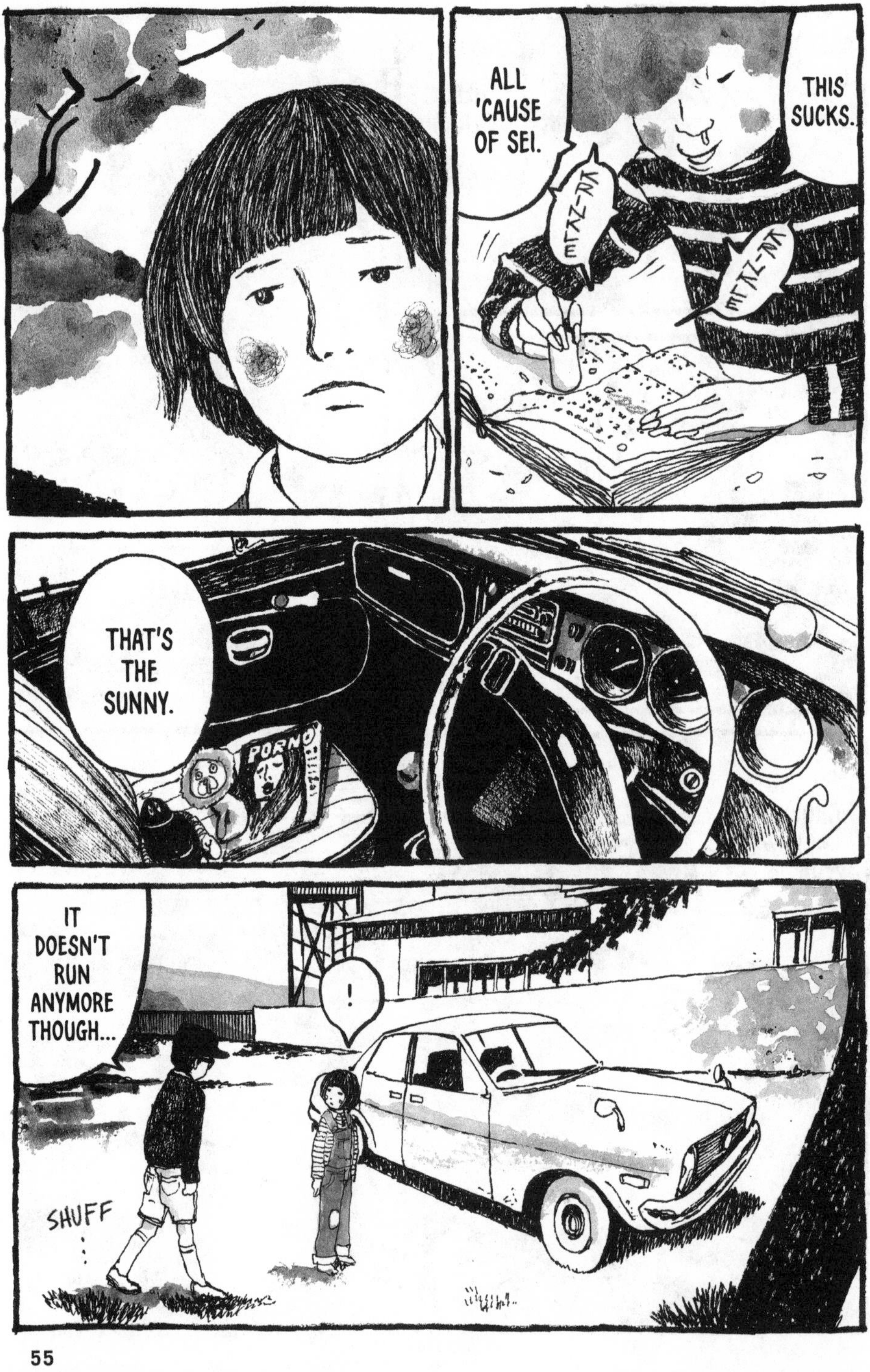
THIS SUCKS.
ALL 'CAUSE OF SEI.
KRINKLE
KRINKLE
THAT'S THE SUNNY.
PORNO
IT DOESN'T RUN ANYMORE THOUGH...
!
SHUFF
...

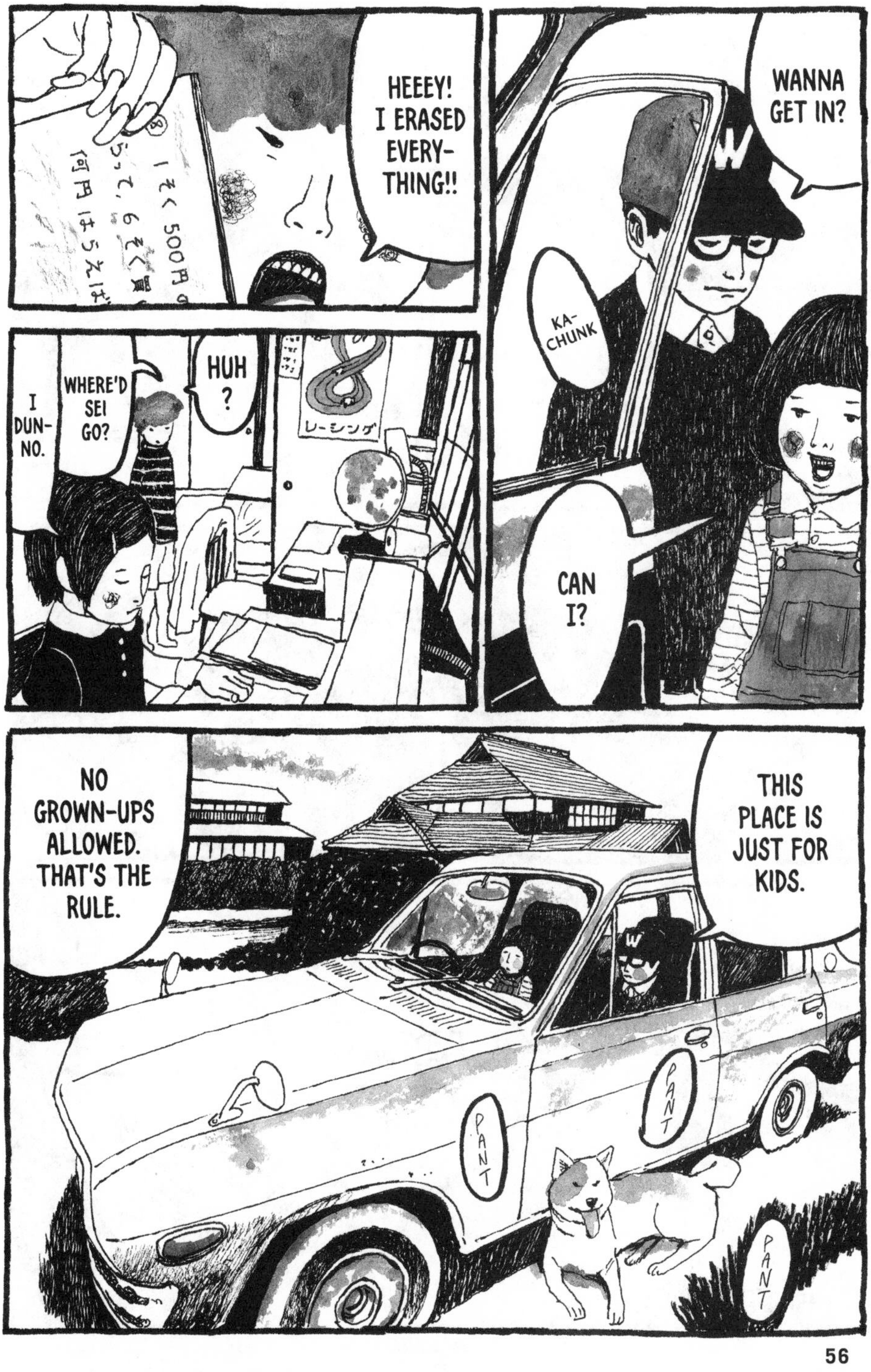
WANNA GET IN?
KA-CHUNK
CAN I?
HEEEY! I ERASED EVERY-THING!!
8
1そく500円の
らって,6そく買
何円はらえば
HUH?
レーシング
WHERE'D SEI GO?
I DUN-NO.
THIS PLACE IS JUST FOR KIDS.
NO GROWN-UPS ALLOWED. THAT'S THE RULE.
PANT
PANT
PANT

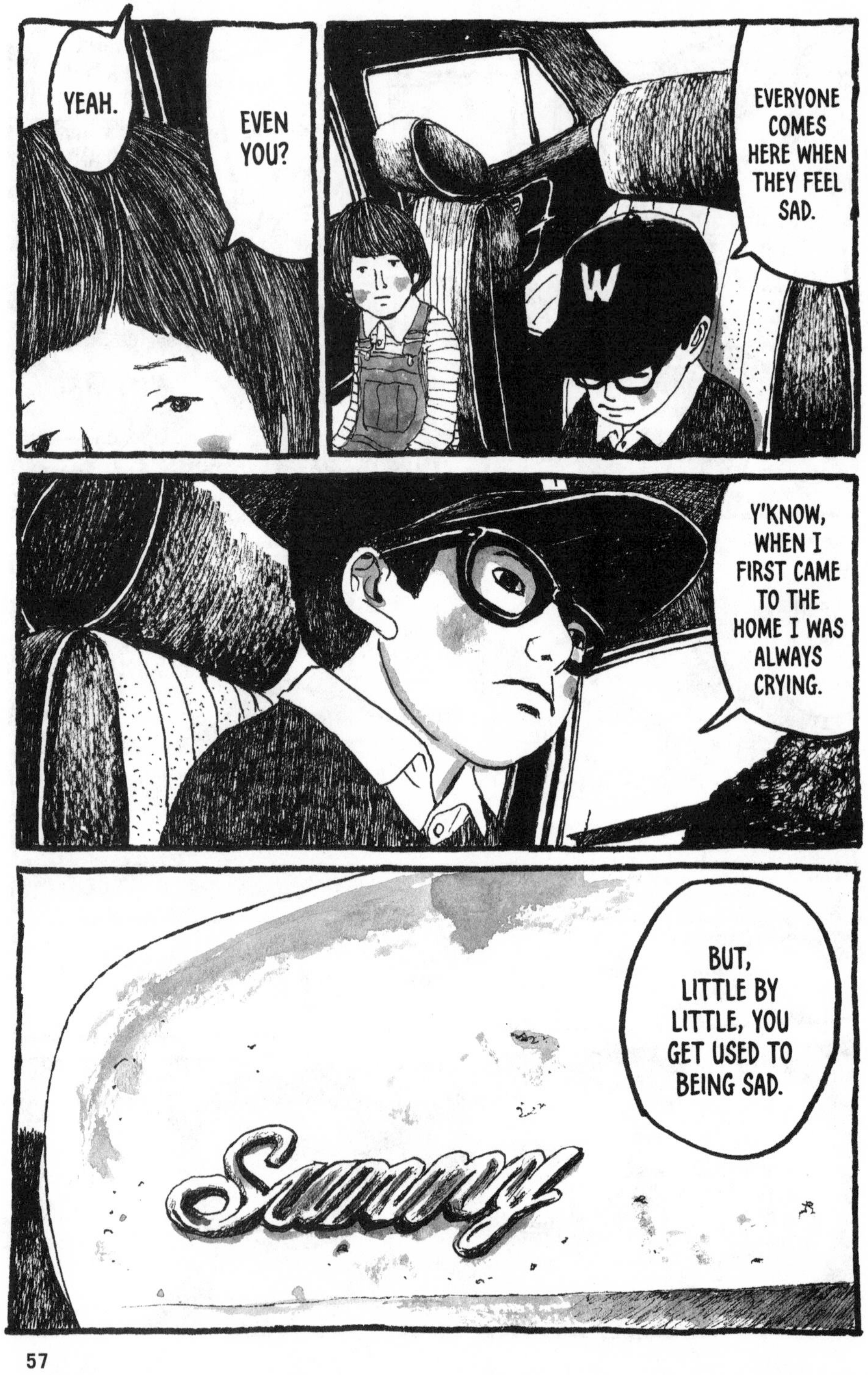
EVERYONE COMES HERE WHEN THEY FEEL SAD.
EVEN YOU?
YEAH.
Y'KNOW, WHEN I FIRST CAME TO THE HOME I WAS ALWAYS CRYING.
BUT, LITTLE BY LITTLE, YOU GET USED TO BEING SAD.
Sunny

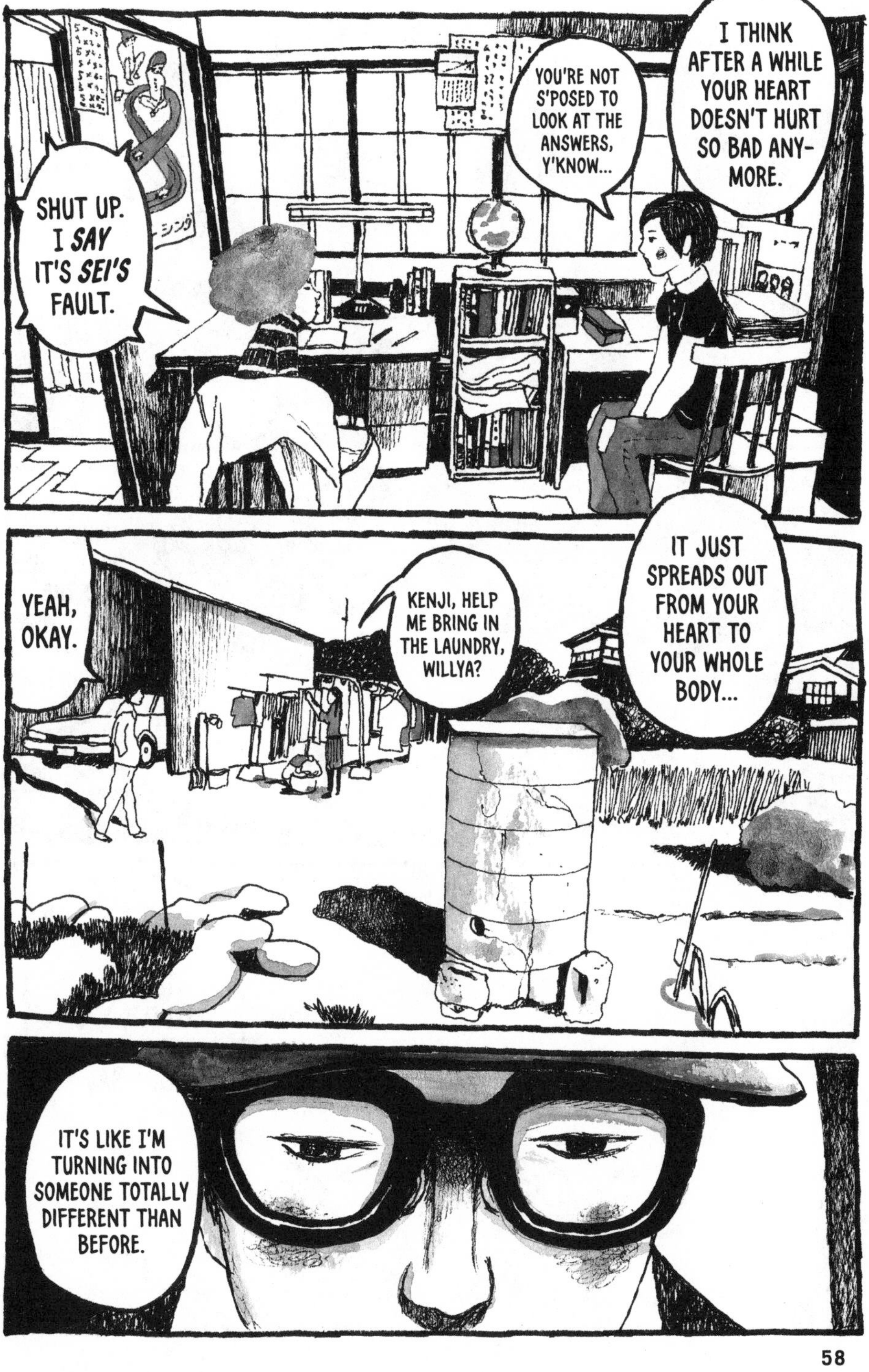

I THINK AFTER A WHILE YOUR HEART DOESN'T HURT SO BAD ANY-MORE.
YOU'RE NOT S'POSED TO LOOK AT THE ANSWERS, Y'KNOW...
SHUT UP. I *SAY* IT'S *SEI'S* FAULT.
IT JUST SPREADS OUT FROM YOUR HEART TO YOUR WHOLE BODY...
KENJI, HELP ME BRING IN THE LAUNDRY, WILLYA?
YEAH, OKAY.
IT'S LIKE I'M TURNING INTO SOMEONE TOTALLY DIFFERENT THAN BEFORE.

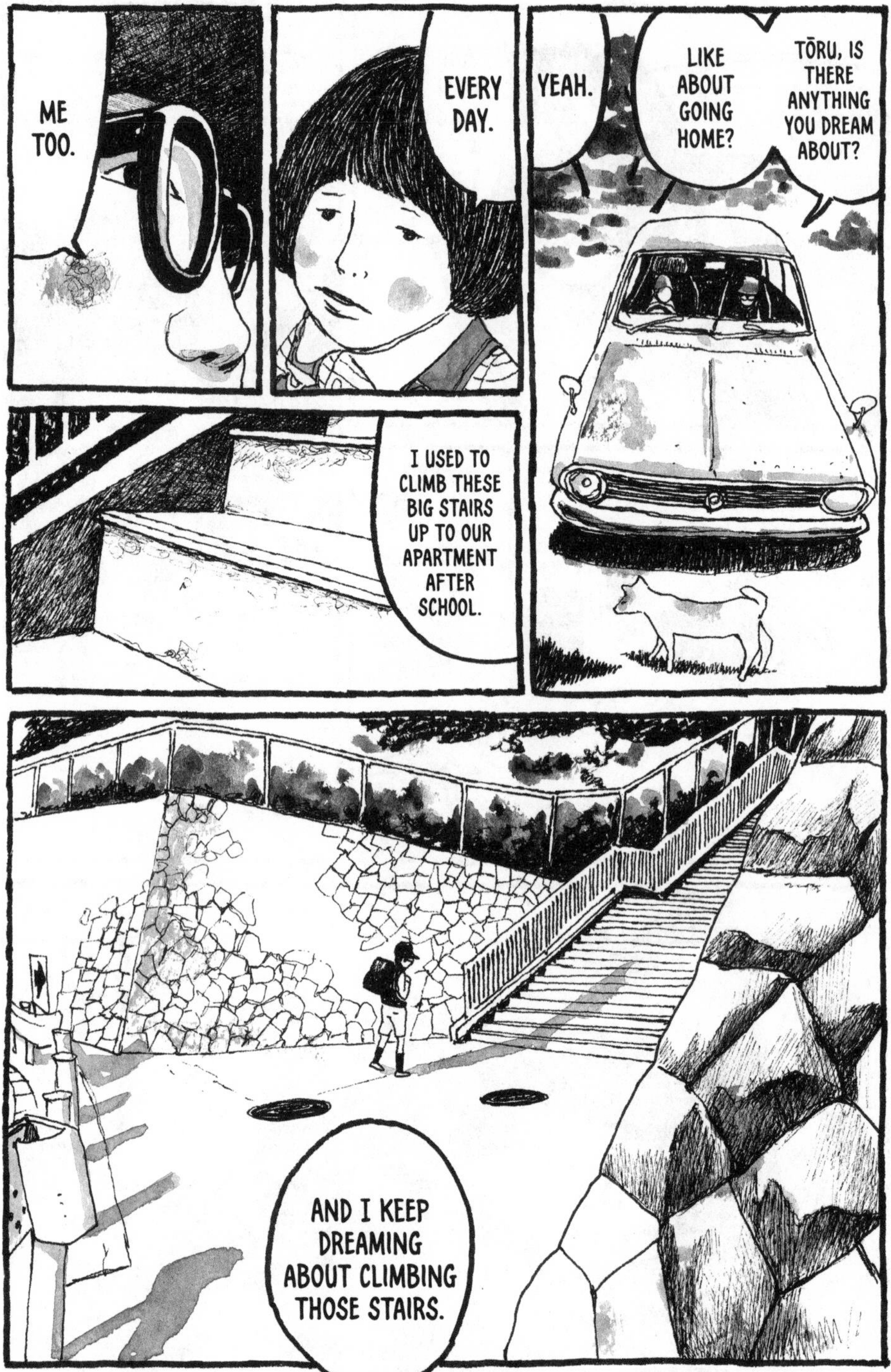
TŌRU, IS THERE ANYTHING YOU DREAM ABOUT?
LIKE ABOUT GOING HOME?
YEAH.
EVERY DAY.
ME TOO.
I USED TO CLIMB THESE BIG STAIRS UP TO OUR APARTMENT AFTER SCHOOL.
AND I KEEP DREAMING ABOUT CLIMBING THOSE STAIRS.

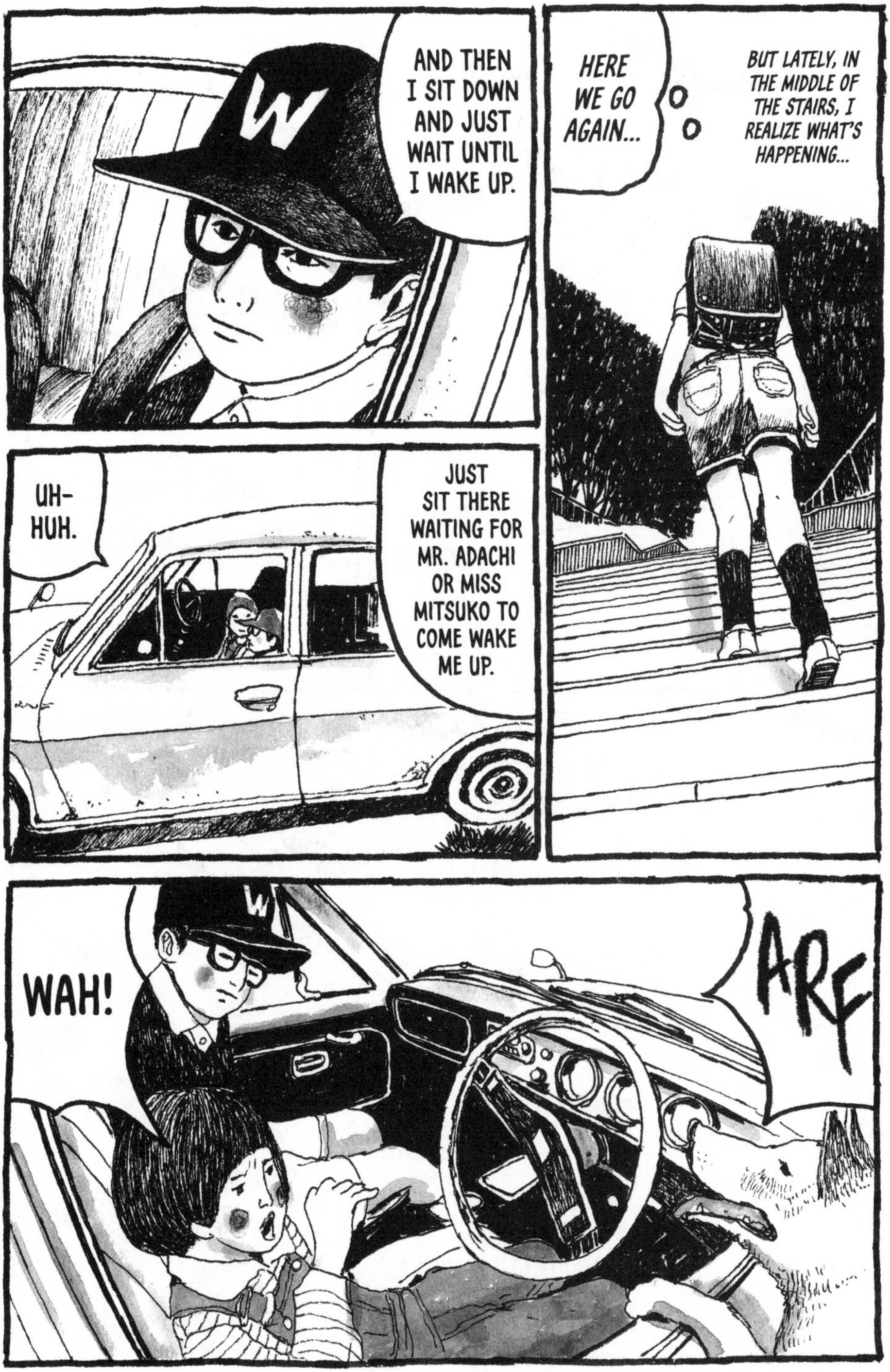
BUT LATELY, IN THE MIDDLE OF THE STAIRS, I REALIZE WHAT'S HAPPENING...
HERE WE GO AGAIN...
AND THEN I SIT DOWN AND JUST WAIT UNTIL I WAKE UP.
JUST SIT THERE WAITING FOR MR. ADACHI OR MISS MITSUKO TO COME WAKE ME UP.
UH-HUH.
ARF
WAH!

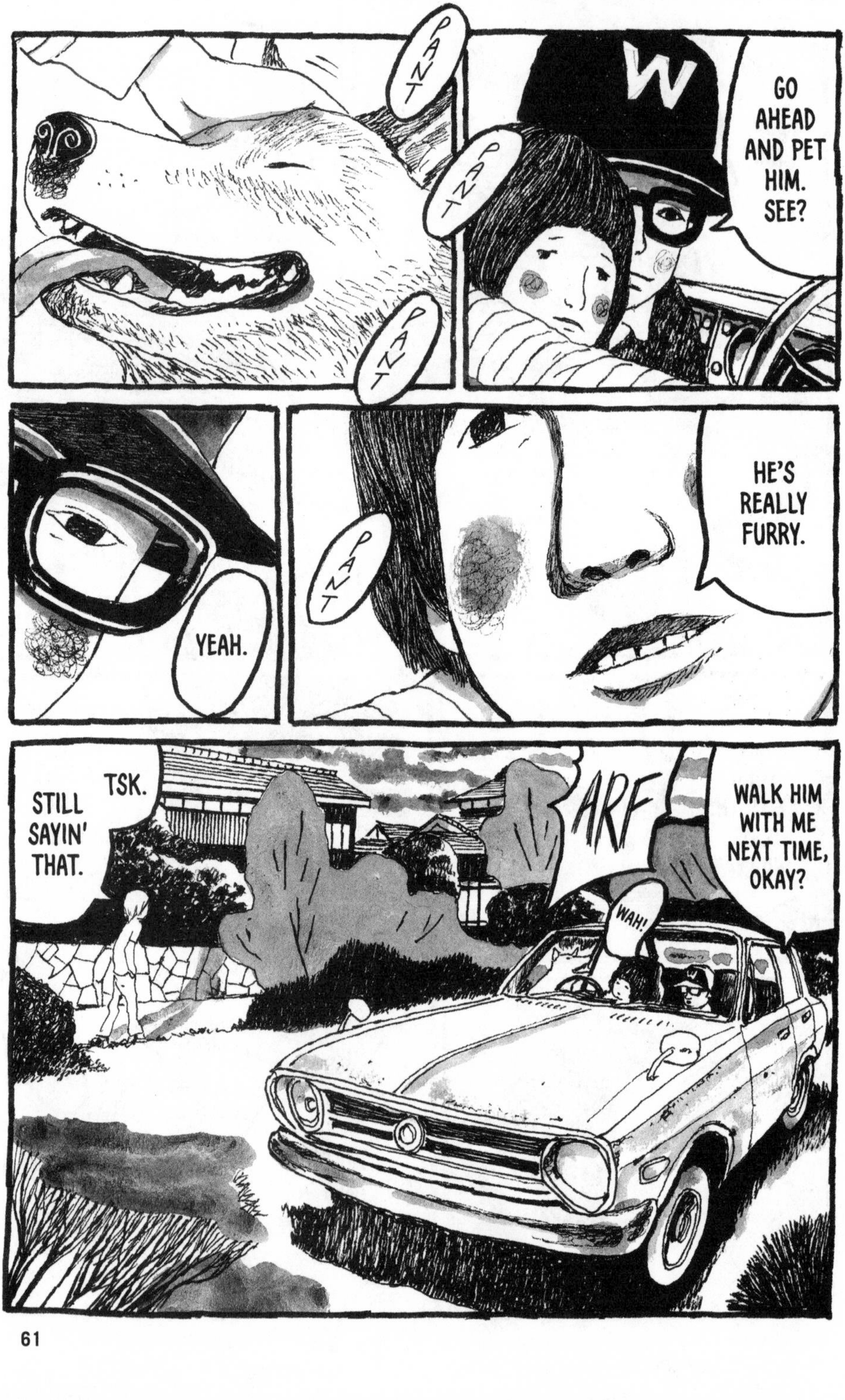
GO AHEAD AND PET HIM. SEE?
PANT
PANT
PANT
HE'S REALLY FURRY.
PANT
YEAH.
WALK HIM WITH ME NEXT TIME, OKAY?
ARF
WAH!
TSK.
STILL SAYIN' THAT.

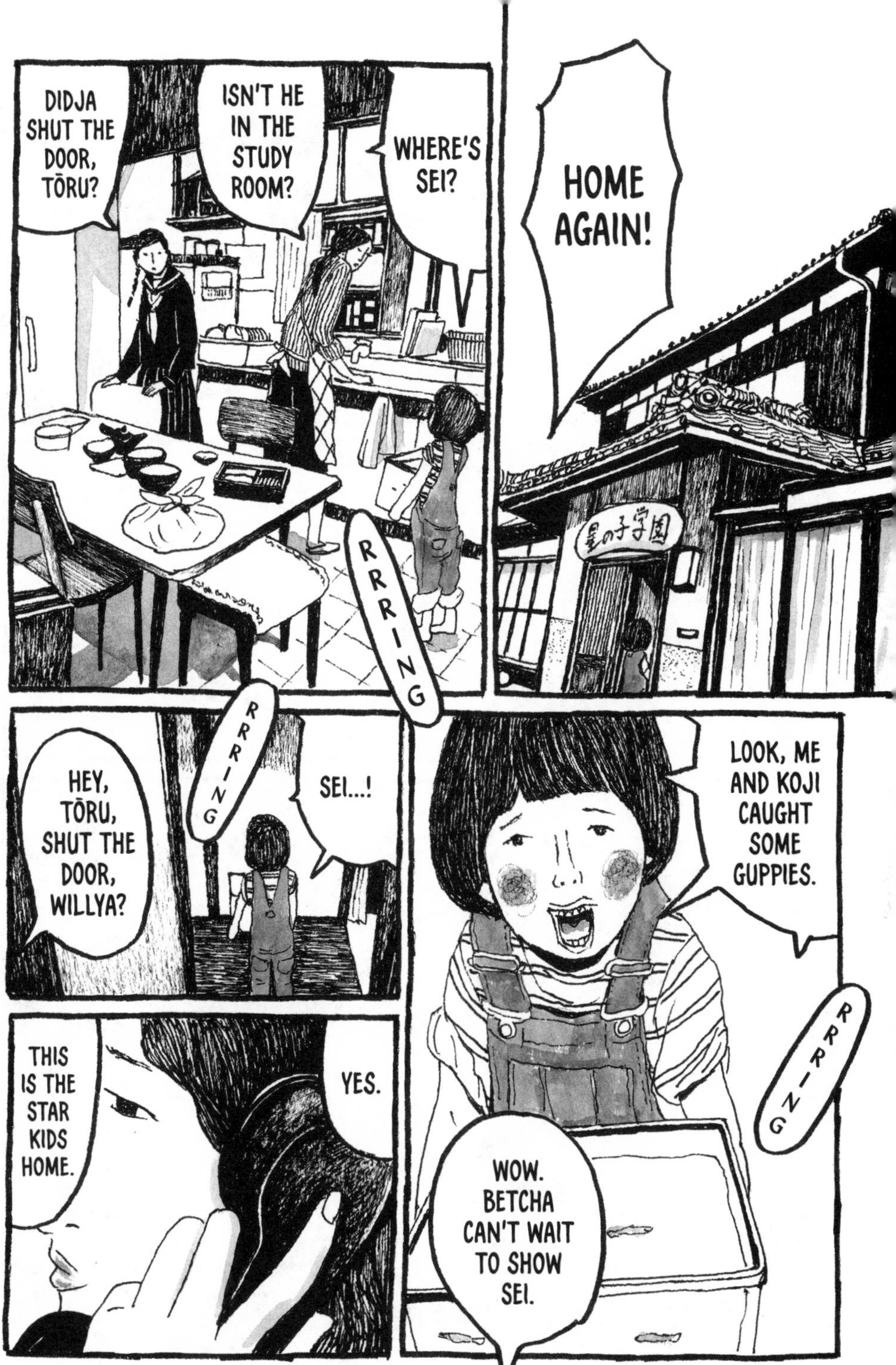
HOME AGAIN!
星の子学園
WHERE'S SEI?
ISN'T HE IN THE STUDY ROOM?
DIDJA SHUT THE DOOR, TŌRU?
RRRING
LOOK, ME AND KOJI CAUGHT SOME GUPPIES.
RRRING
WOW. BETCHA CAN'T WAIT TO SHOW SEI.
SEI...!
RRRING
HEY, TŌRU, SHUT THE DOOR, WILLYA?
YES.
THIS IS THE STAR KIDS HOME.

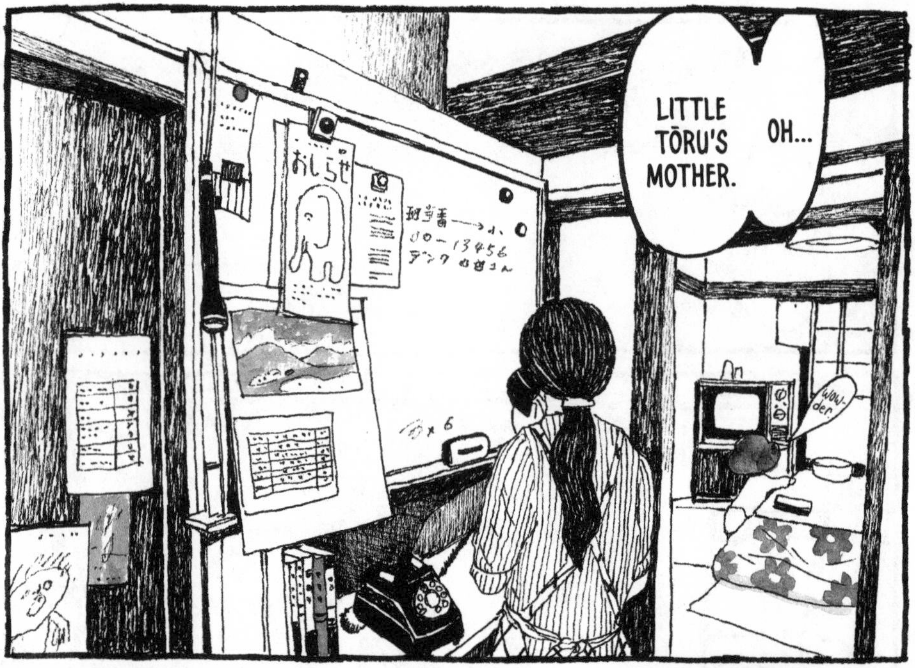
OH...
LITTLE TŌRU'S MOTHER.
おしらせ
wow-der.

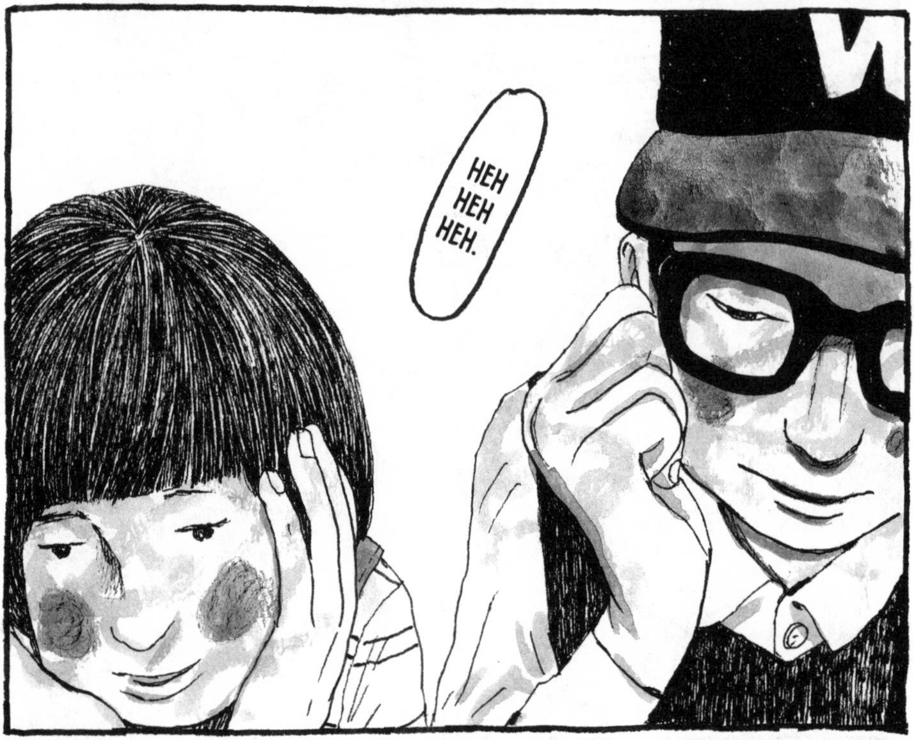
HEH HEH HEH.

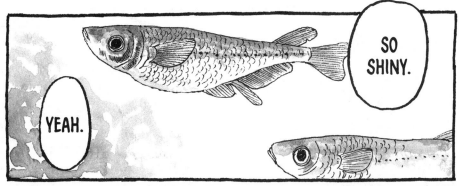

SO SHINY.
YEAH.
THEY'RE ALL SPARKLY.
べんきょう
TŌ-RUU!
YOUR MOMMY'S ON THE PHONE!
meow

*Letters on wall: S-T-U-D-Y

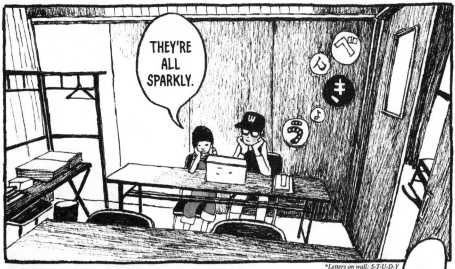

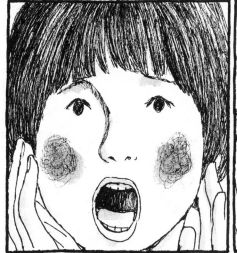

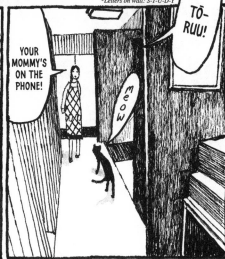

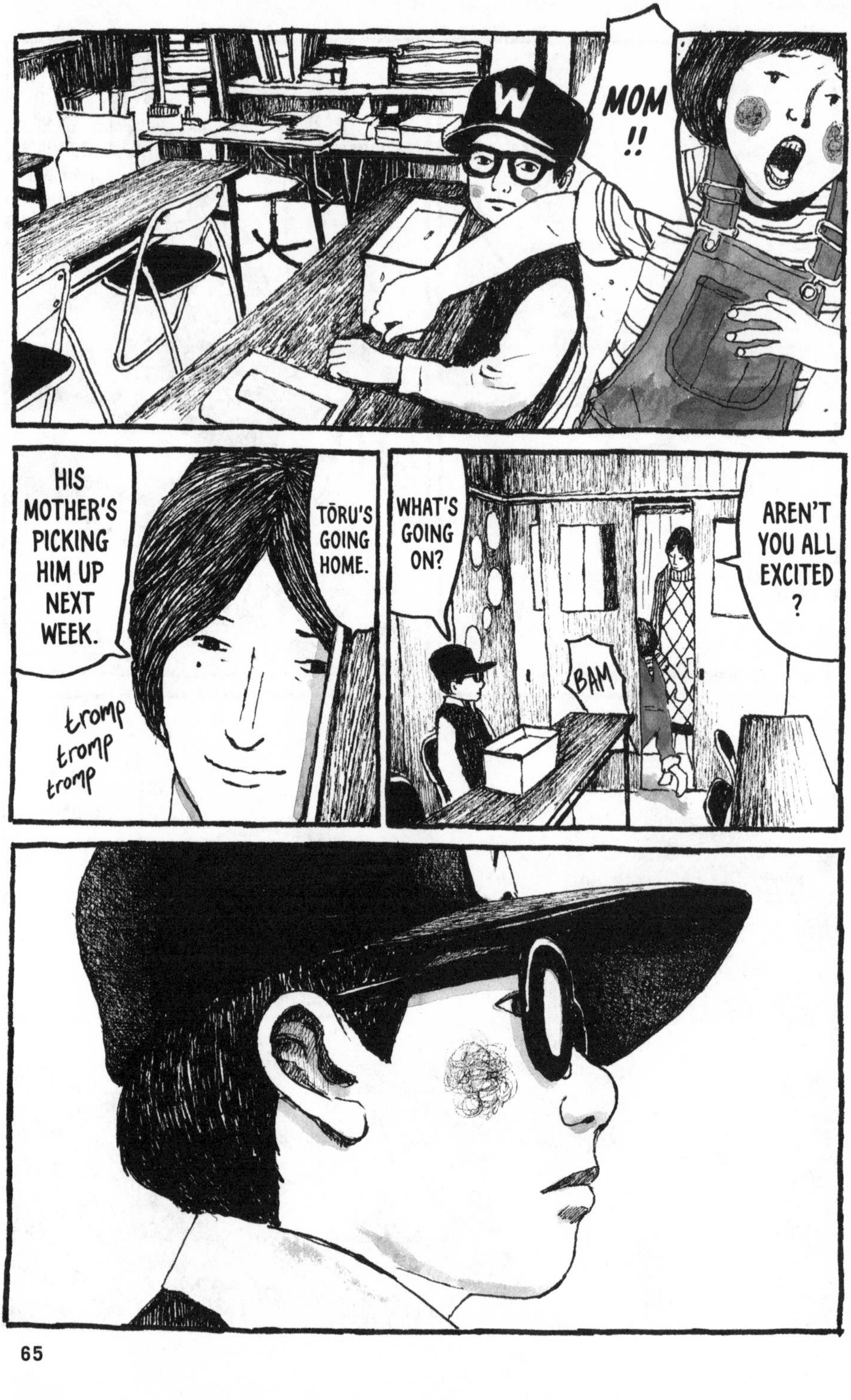
MOM !!
AREN'T YOU ALL EXCITED ?
WHAT'S GOING ON?
BAM
TŌRU'S GOING HOME.
HIS MOTHER'S PICKING HIM UP NEXT WEEK.
tromp tromp tromp

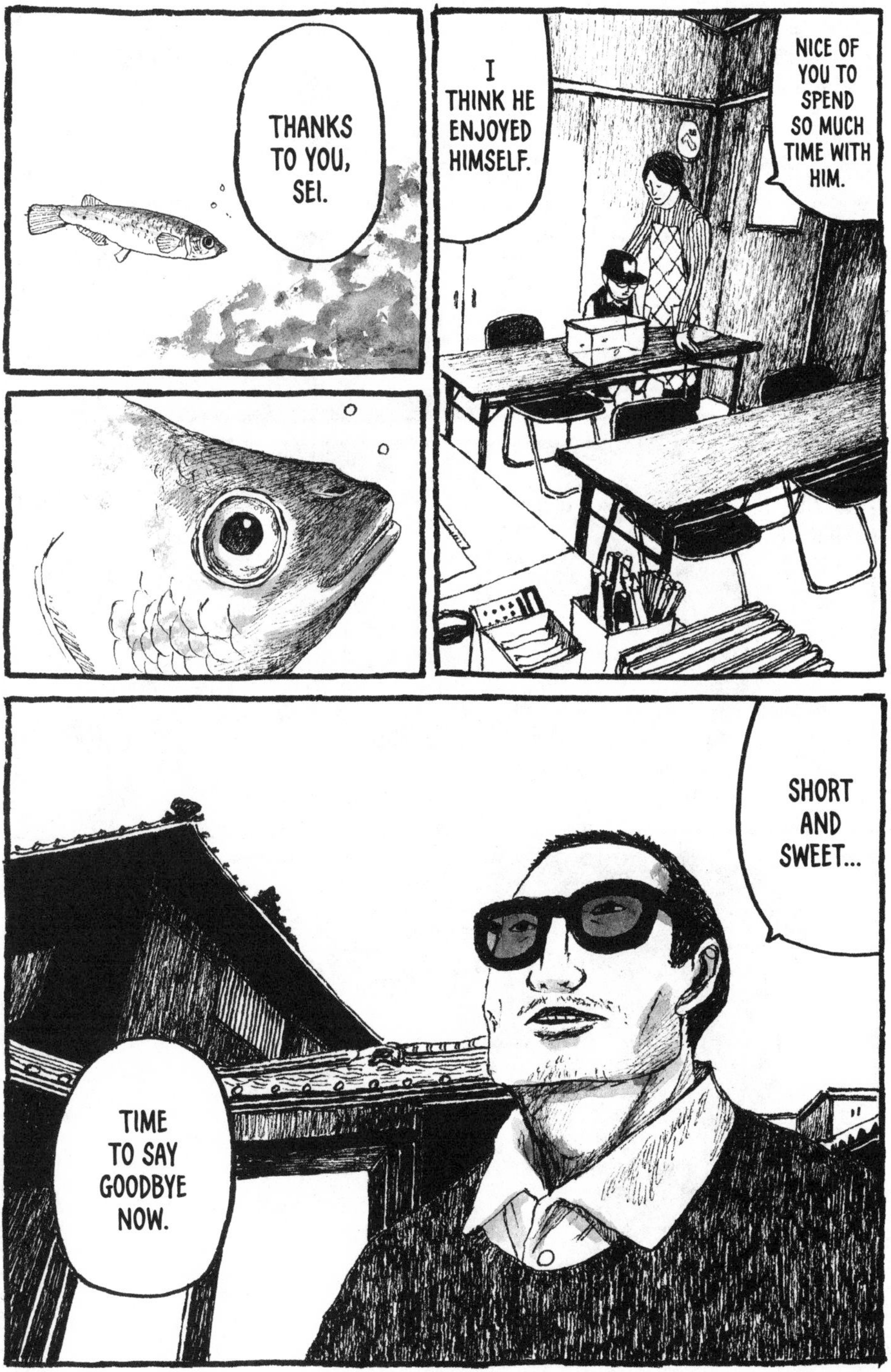
NICE OF YOU TO SPEND SO MUCH TIME WITH HIM.
I THINK HE ENJOYED HIMSELF.
THANKS TO YOU, SEI.
SHORT AND SWEET...
TIME TO SAY GOODBYE NOW.

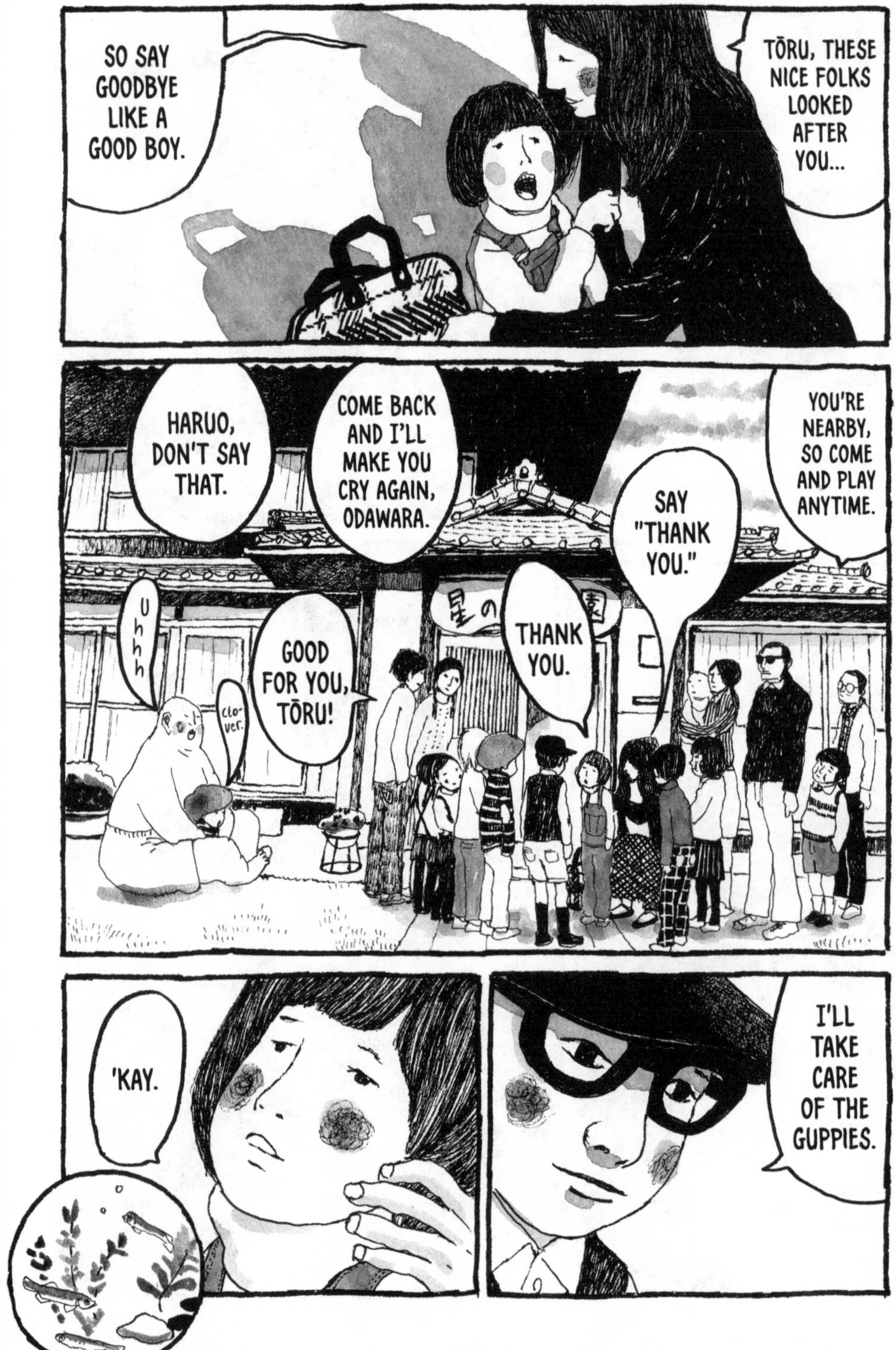
TŌRU, THESE NICE FOLKS LOOKED AFTER YOU...
SO SAY GOODBYE LIKE A GOOD BOY.
YOU'RE NEARBY, SO COME AND PLAY ANYTIME.
SAY "THANK YOU."
THANK YOU.
COME BACK AND I'LL MAKE YOU CRY AGAIN, ODAWARA.
HARUO, DON'T SAY THAT.
星の
園
GOOD FOR YOU, TŌRU!
clo-ver.
Uhhh
I'LL TAKE CARE OF THE GUPPIES.
'KAY.

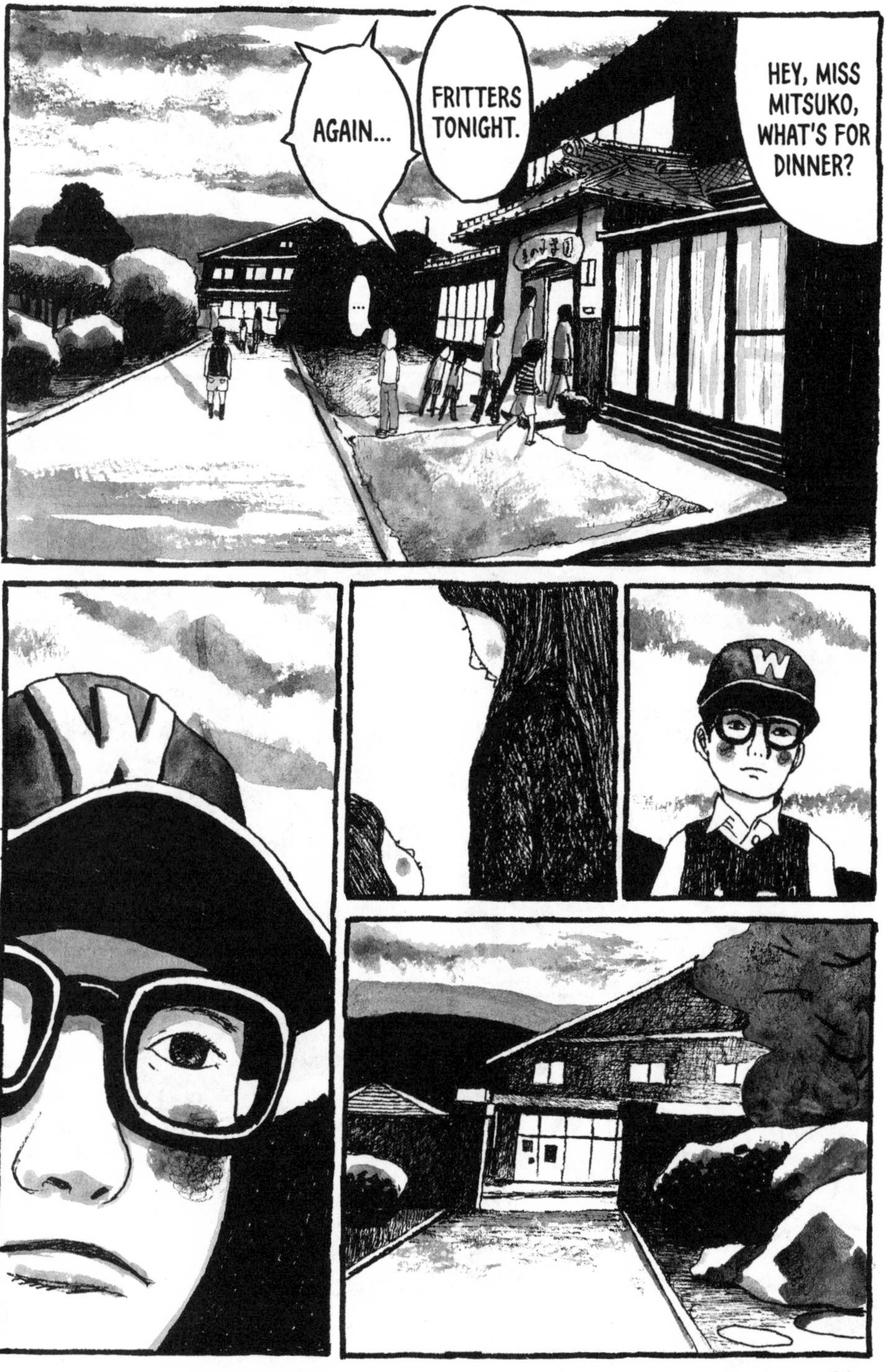
HEY, MISS MITSUKO, WHAT'S FOR DINNER?
FRITTERS TONIGHT.
AGAIN...
...

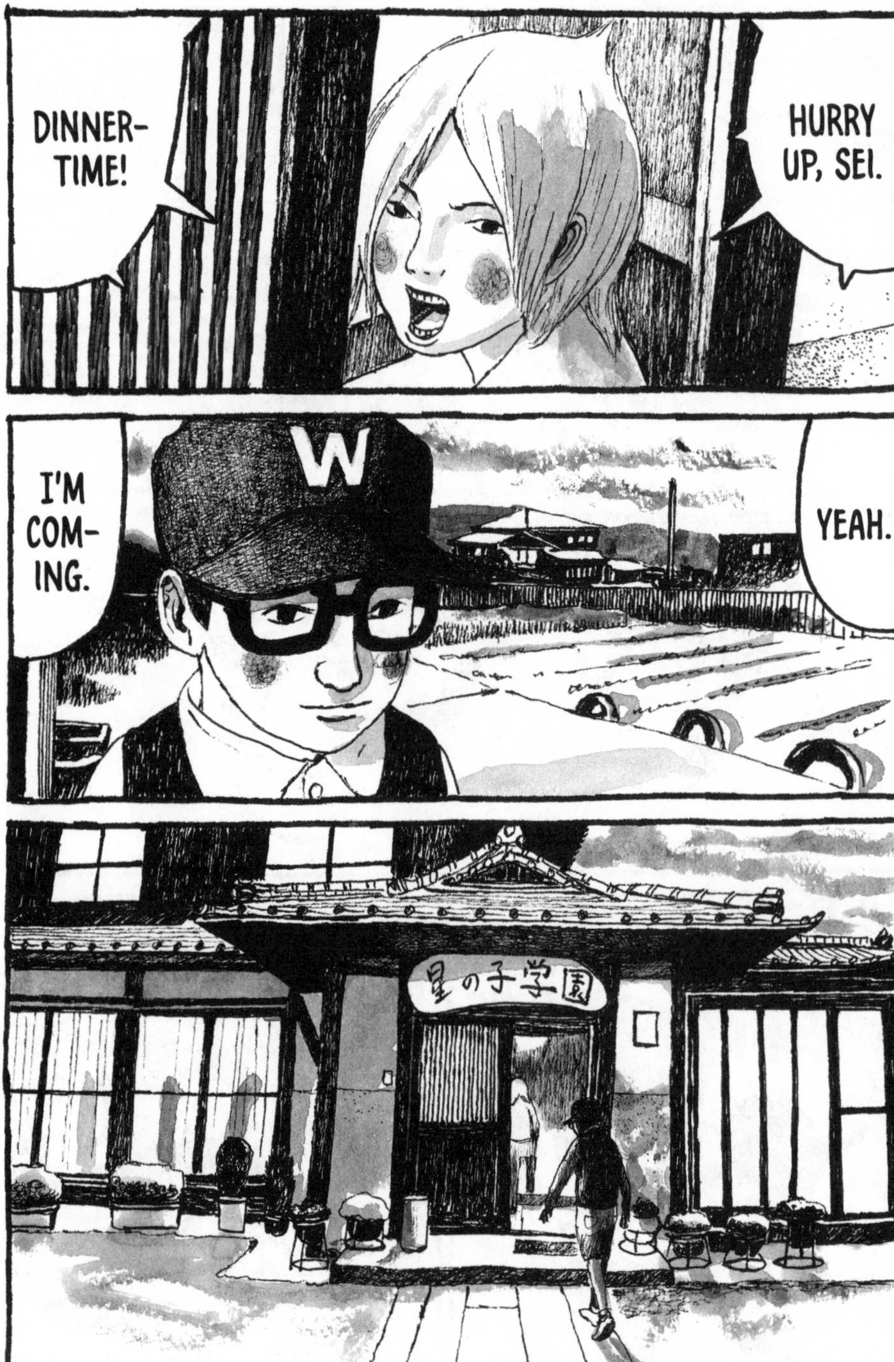
HURRY UP, SEI.
DINNER-TIME!
YEAH.
I'M COM-ING.
星の子学園

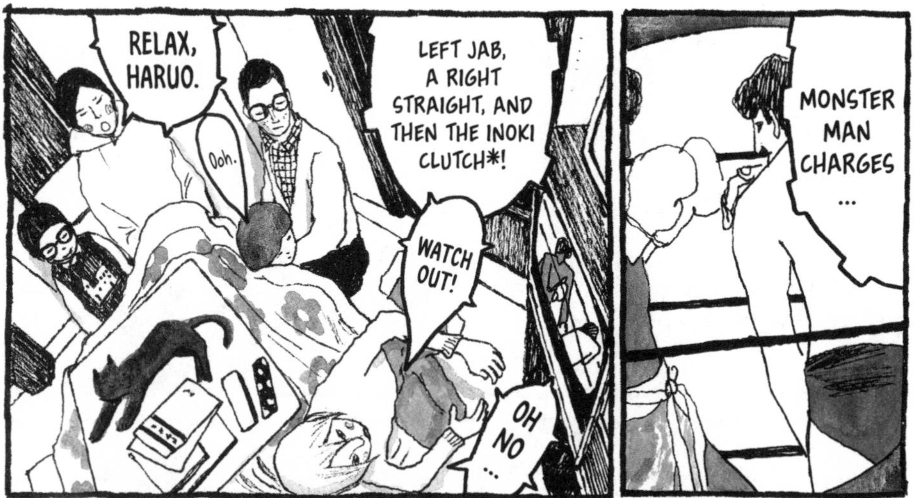
MONSTER MAN CHARGES ...
LEFT JAB, A RIGHT STRAIGHT, AND THEN THE INOKI CLUTCH*!
RELAX, HARUO.
Ooh.
WATCH OUT!
OH NO ...

*In 1977 and again in 1978, American martial arts fighter Everett "Monster Man" Eddy lost bouts to famed Japanese wrestler Antonio Inoki (both times by knockout).

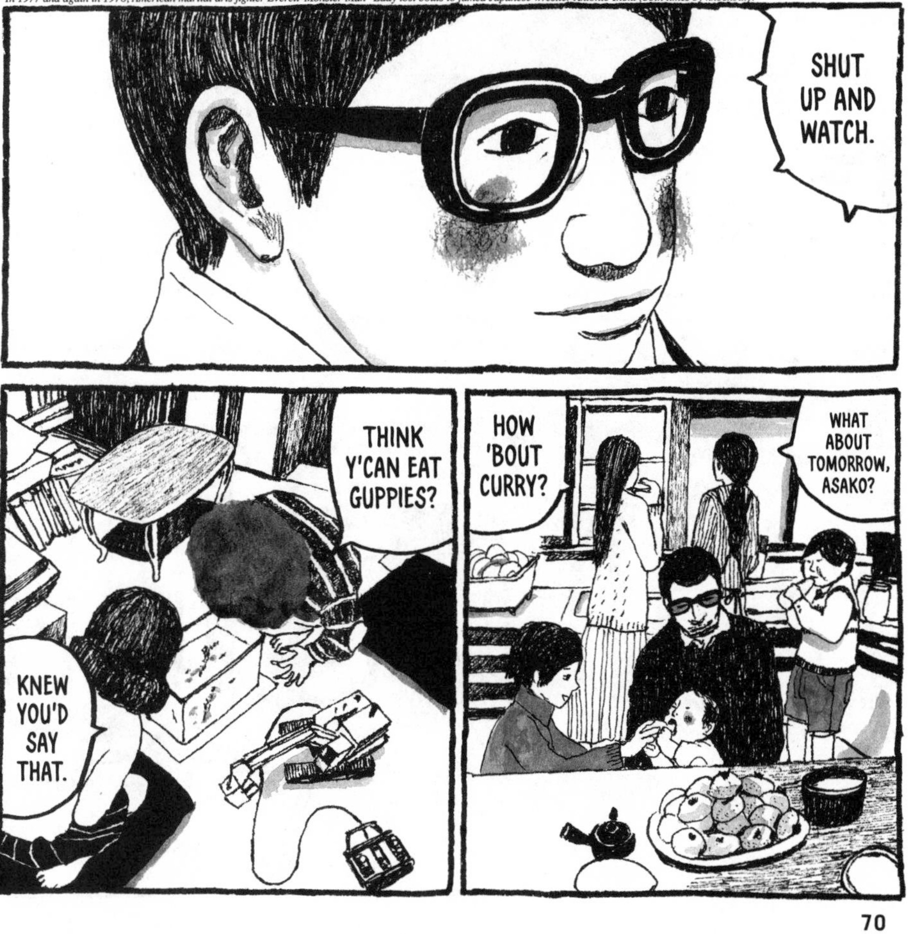
SHUT UP AND WATCH.
WHAT ABOUT TOMORROW, ASAKO?
HOW 'BOUT CURRY?
THINK Y'CAN EAT GUPPIES?
KNEW YOU'D SAY THAT.

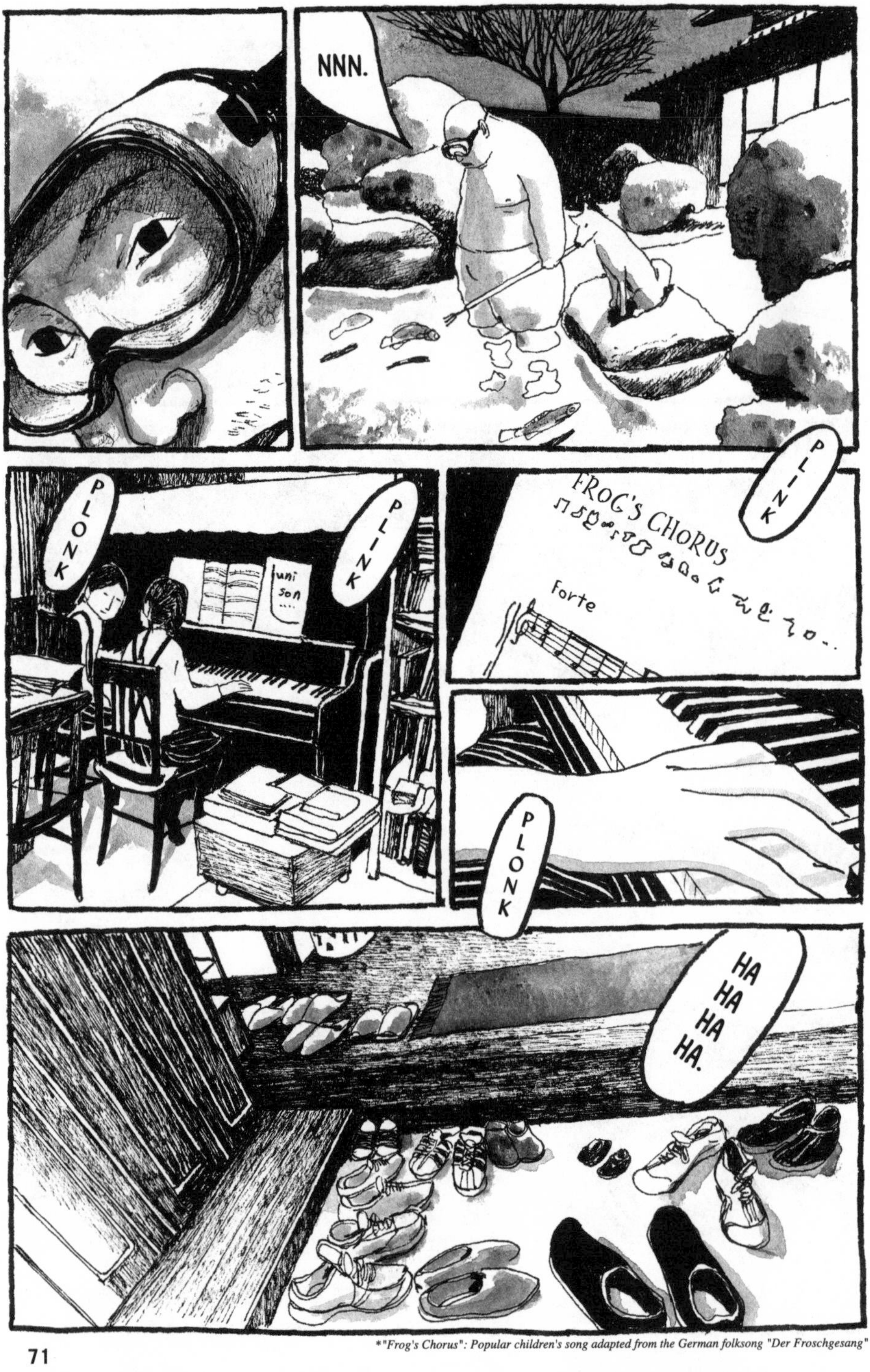
NNN.
PLINK
FROG'S CHORUS
Forte
PLONK
PLINK
PLONK
uni son ....
HA HA HA HA.

*"Frog's Chorus": Popular children's song adapted from the German folksong "Der Froschgesang"

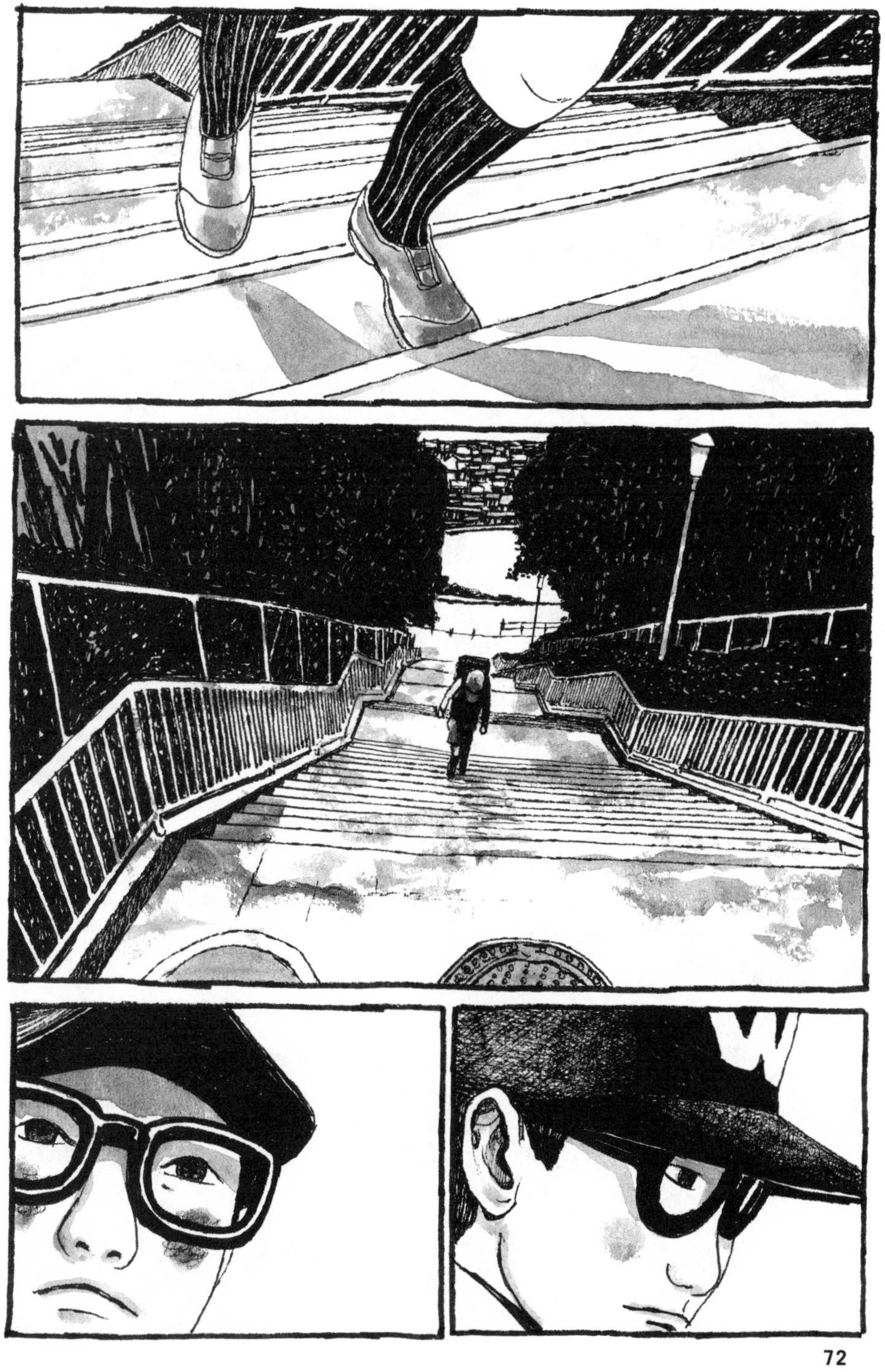

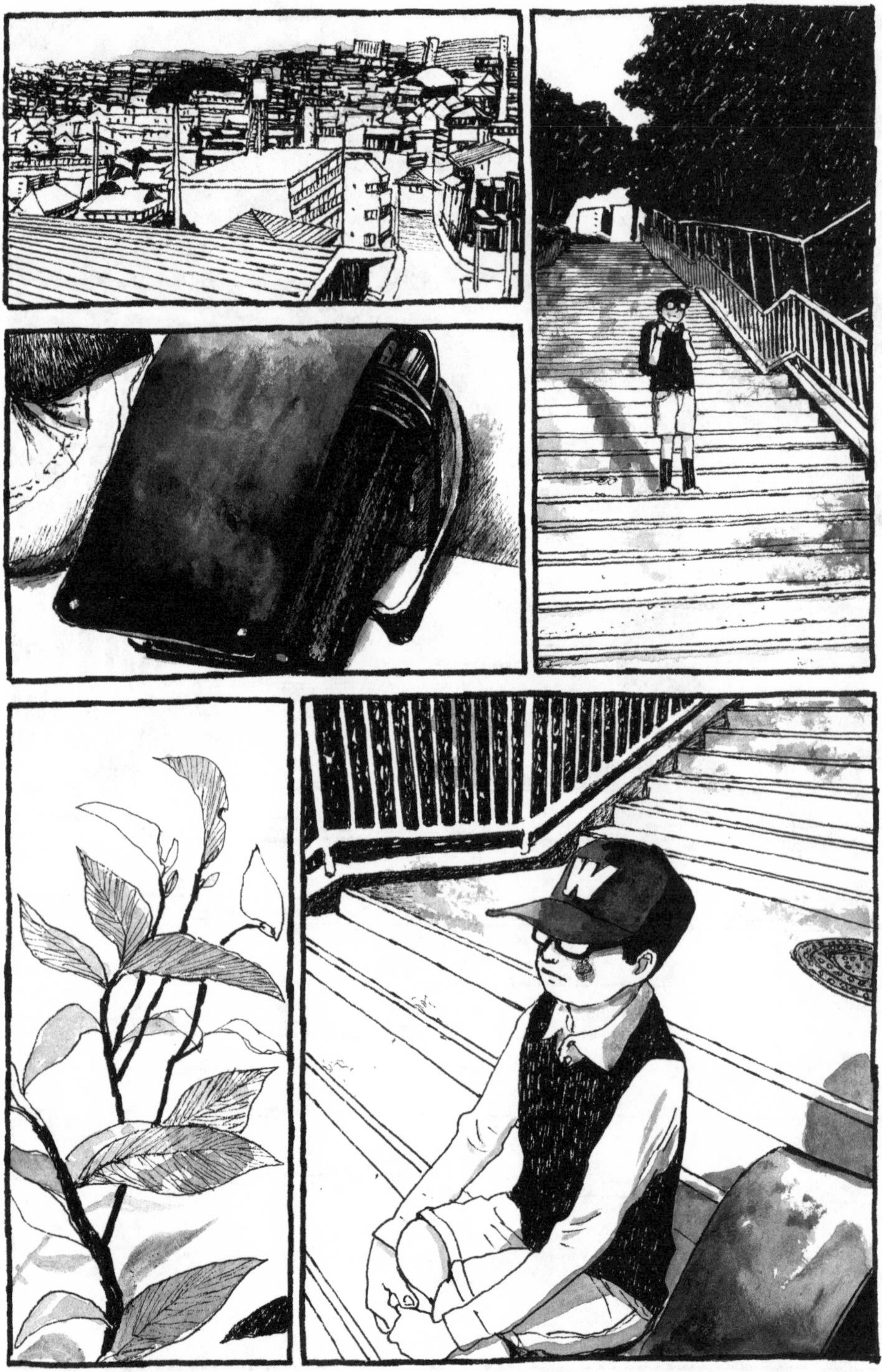

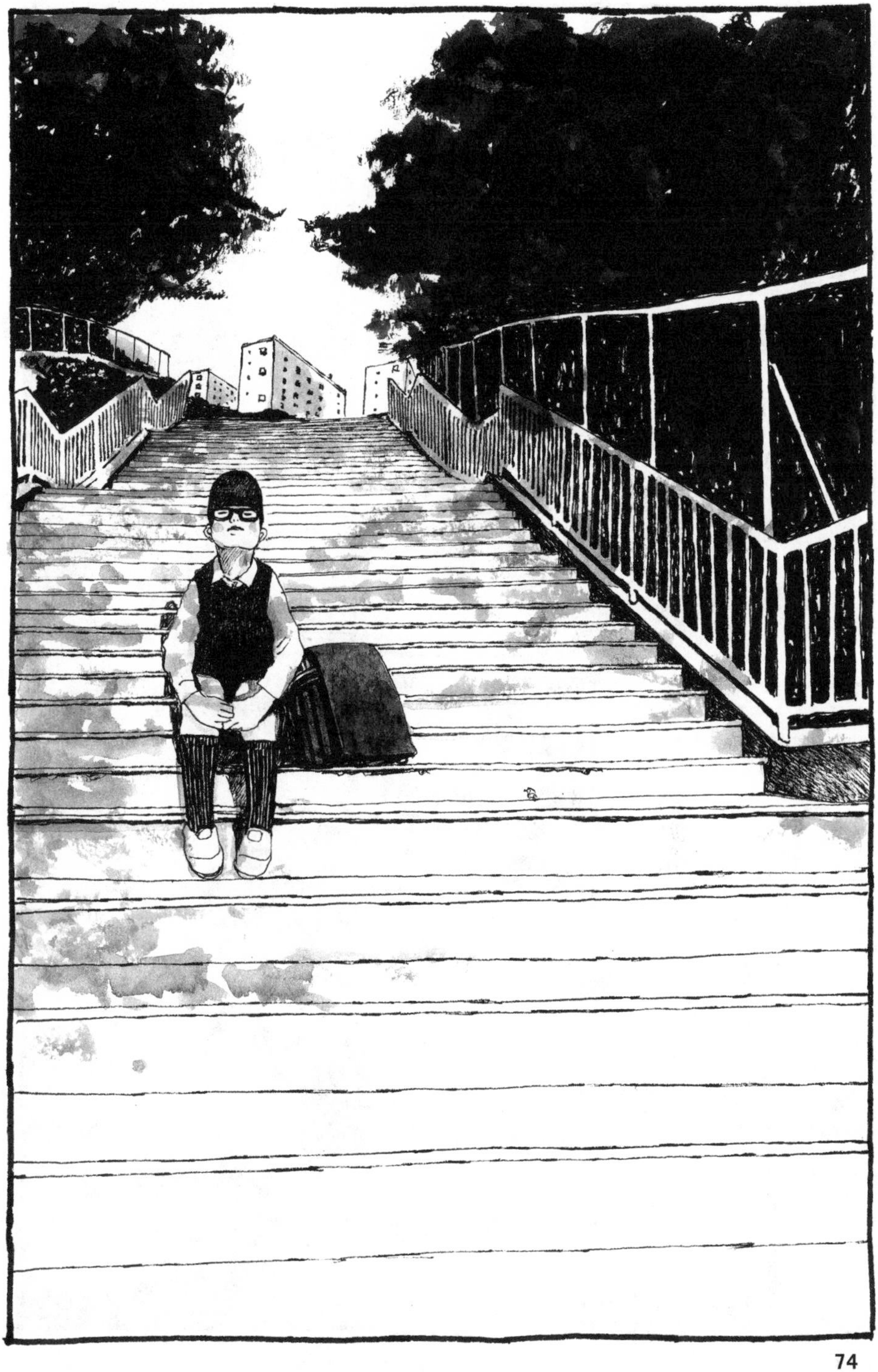

CHAPTER 9

"The sun
is great!
It comes
back every
morning."

"The earth's
goin' around
it, y'know."

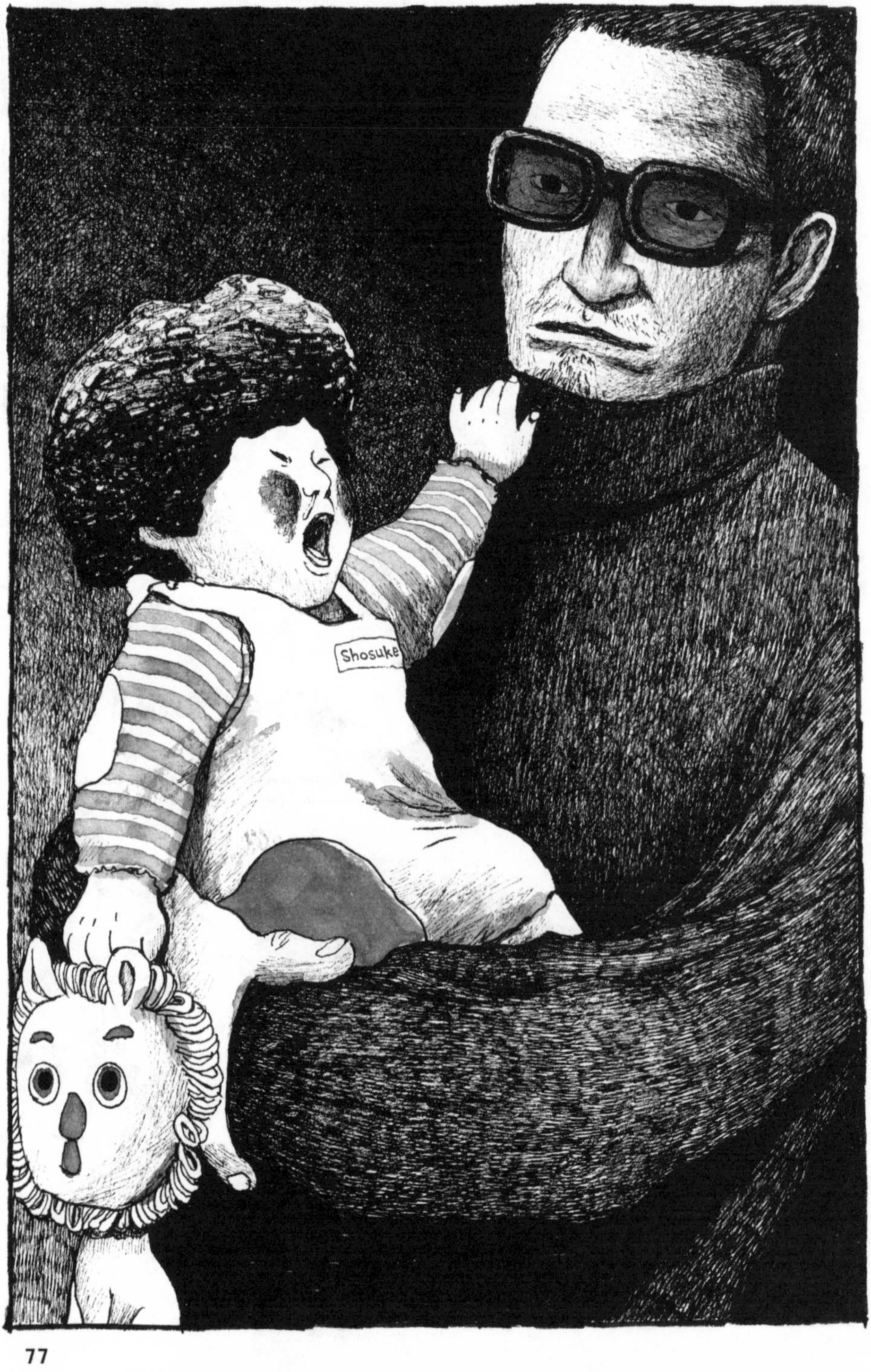
Shosuke

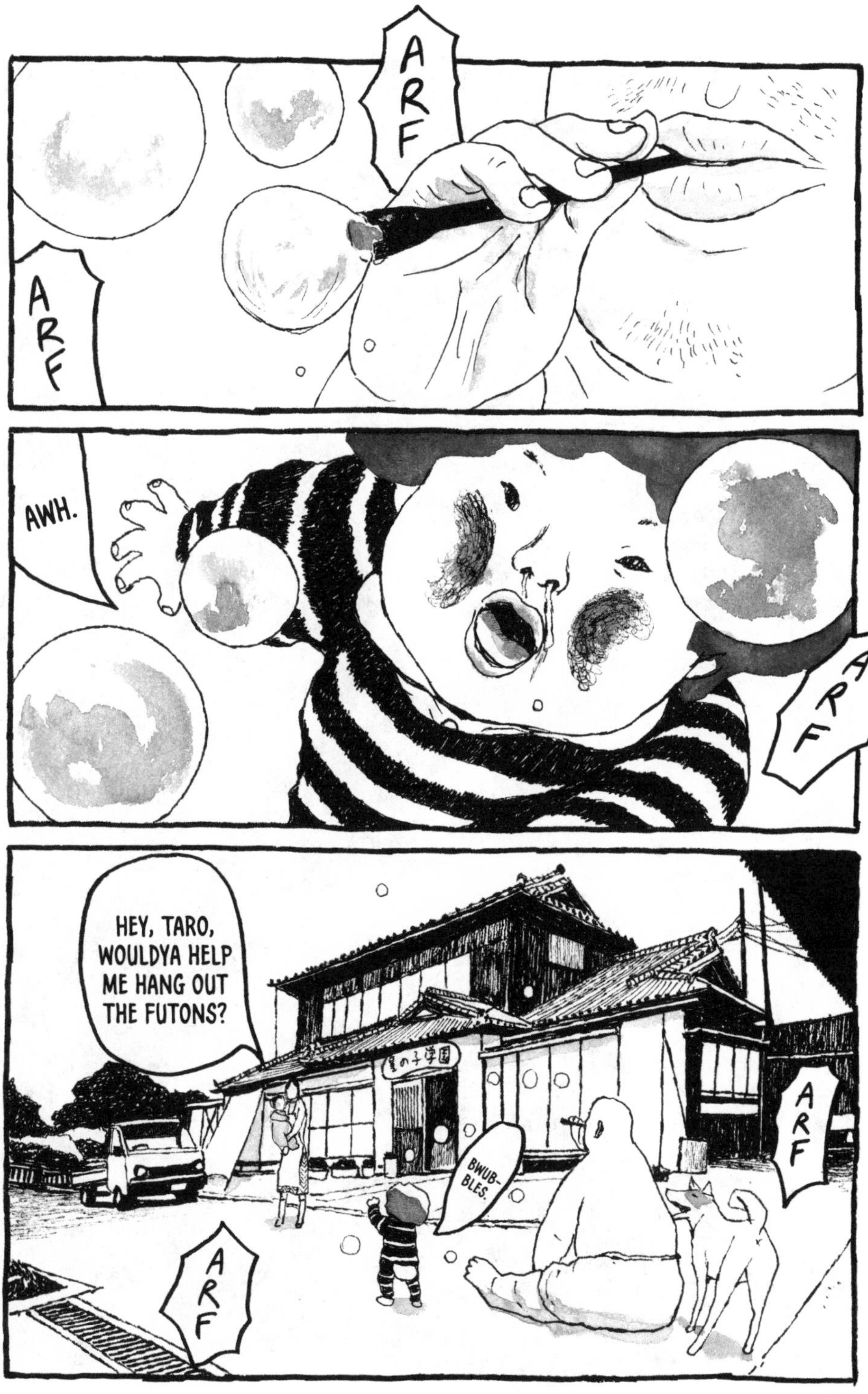
ARF
ARF
ARF
AWH.
ARF
HEY, TARO, WOULDYA HELP ME HANG OUT THE FUTONS?
BWUB-BLES.
ARF

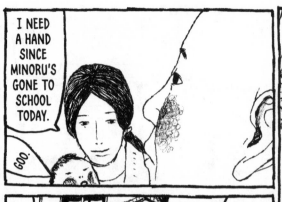

I NEED A HAND SINCE MINORU'S GONE TO SCHOOL TODAY.

GOO.

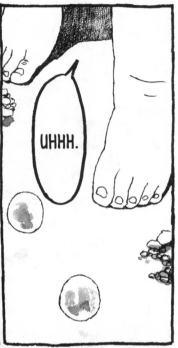

UHHH.

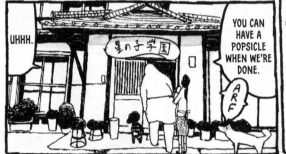

UHHH.

星の子学園

YOU CAN HAVE A POPSICLE WHEN WE'RE DONE.

ARF

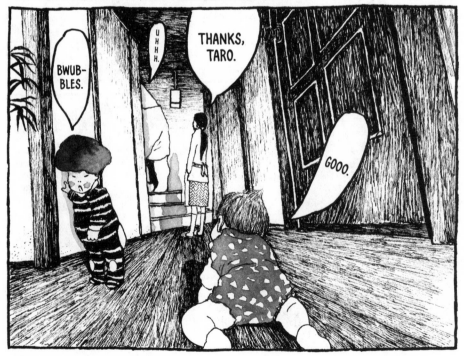

BWUB-BLES.

UHHH.

THANKS, TARO.

GOOO.

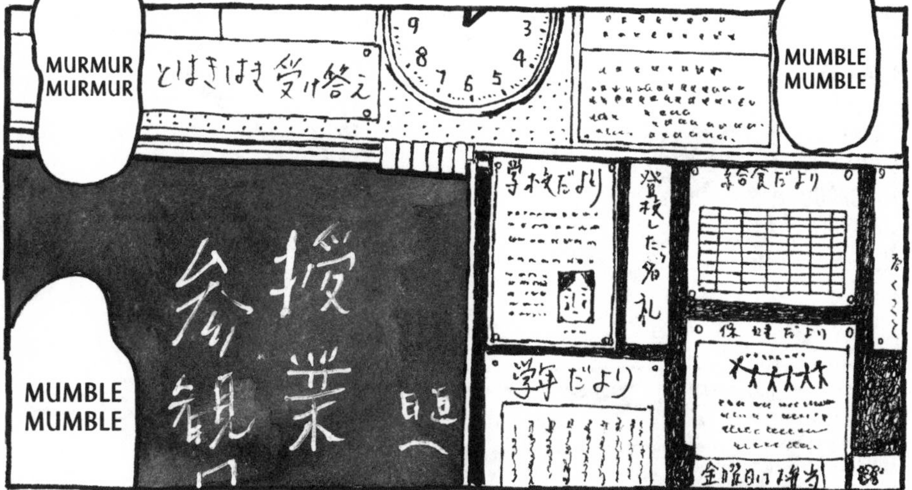
MUMBLE MUMBLE
MURMUR MURMUR
MUMBLE MUMBLE

*Chalkboard: Parents' Day Open House

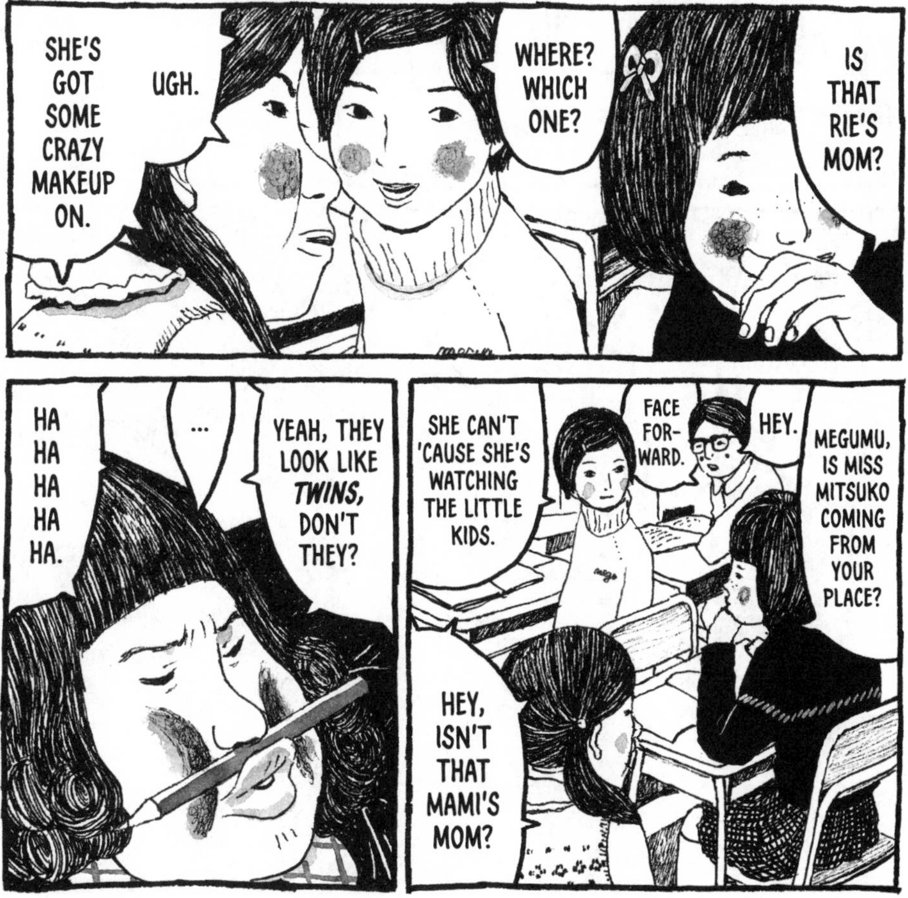
IS THAT RIE'S MOM?
WHERE? WHICH ONE?
UGH.
SHE'S GOT SOME CRAZY MAKEUP ON.
MEGUMU, IS MISS MITSUKO COMING FROM YOUR PLACE?
HEY.
FACE FOR-WARD.
SHE CAN'T 'CAUSE SHE'S WATCHING THE LITTLE KIDS.
HEY, ISN'T THAT MAMI'S MOM?
YEAH, THEY LOOK LIKE *TWINS,* DON'T THEY?
...
HA HA HA HA HA.

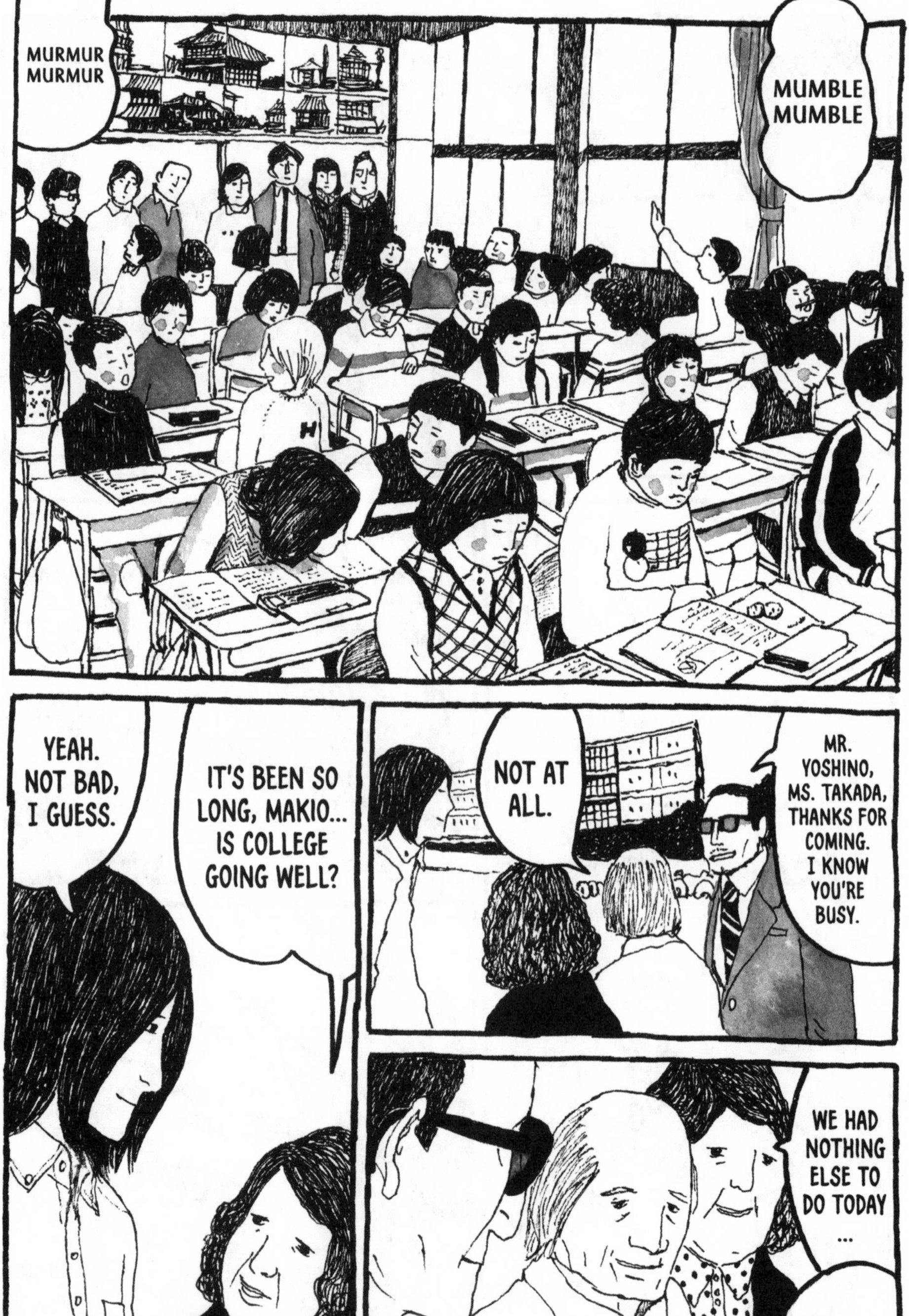
MUMBLE MUMBLE
MURMUR MURMUR
MR. YOSHINO, MS. TAKADA, THANKS FOR COMING. I KNOW YOU'RE BUSY.
NOT AT ALL.
WE HAD NOTHING ELSE TO DO TODAY ...
YUP.
IT'S BEEN SO LONG, MAKIO... IS COLLEGE GOING WELL?
YEAH. NOT BAD, I GUESS.

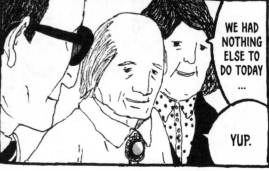

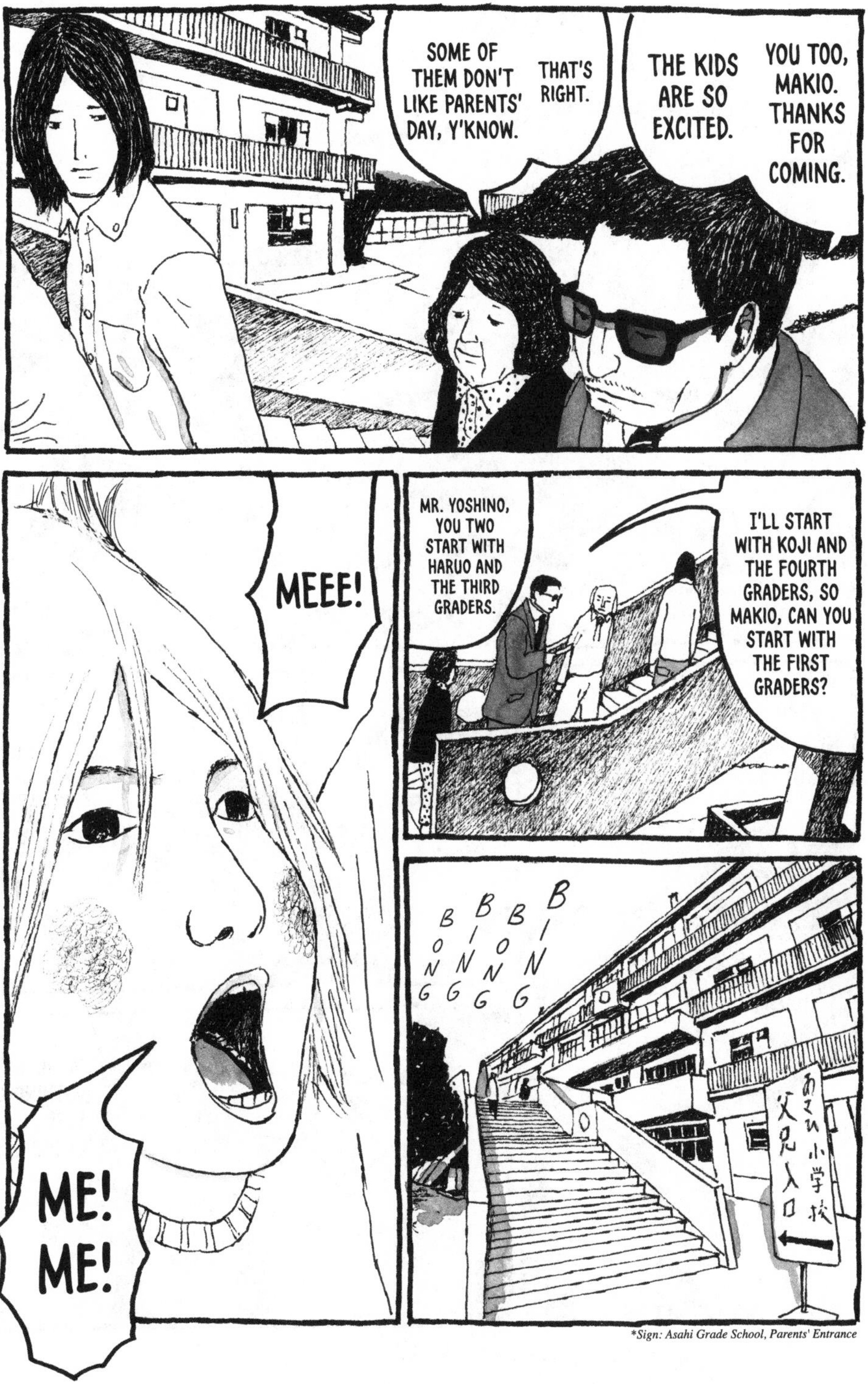
YOU TOO, MAKIO. THANKS FOR COMING.
THE KIDS ARE SO EXCITED.
THAT'S RIGHT.
SOME OF THEM DON'T LIKE PARENTS' DAY, Y'KNOW.
I'LL START WITH KOJI AND THE FOURTH GRADERS, SO MAKIO, CAN YOU START WITH THE FIRST GRADERS?
MR. YOSHINO, YOU TWO START WITH HARUO AND THE THIRD GRADERS.
BING
BONG
BING
BONG
あさひ小学校
父兄入口
MEEE!
ME! ME!

*Sign: Asahi Grade School, Parents' Entrance

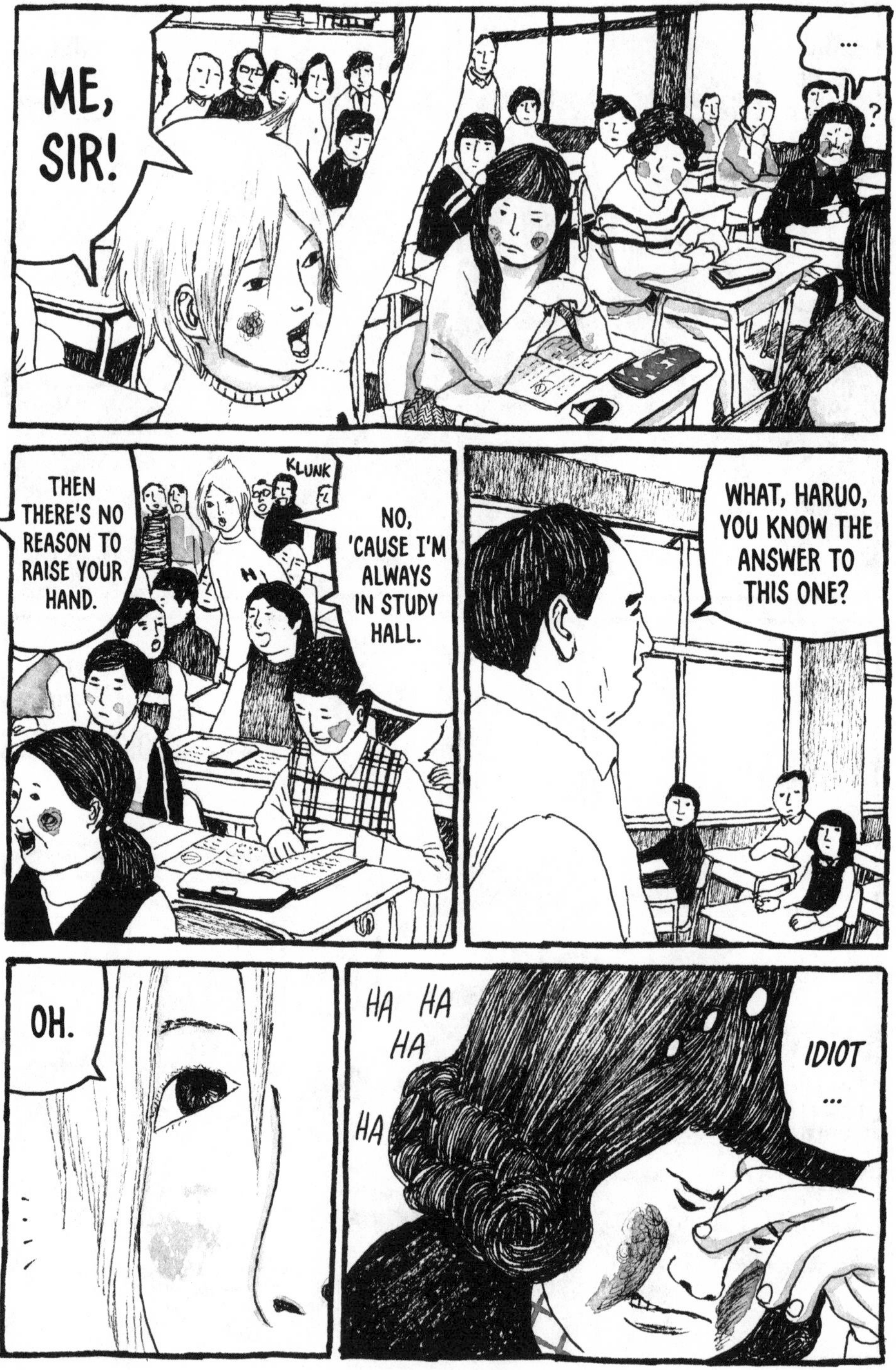
...
?
ME, SIR!
WHAT, HARUO, YOU KNOW THE ANSWER TO THIS ONE?
KLUNK
NO, 'CAUSE I'M ALWAYS IN STUDY HALL.
THEN THERE'S NO REASON TO RAISE YOUR HAND.
IDIOT ...
HA HA HA HA
OH.

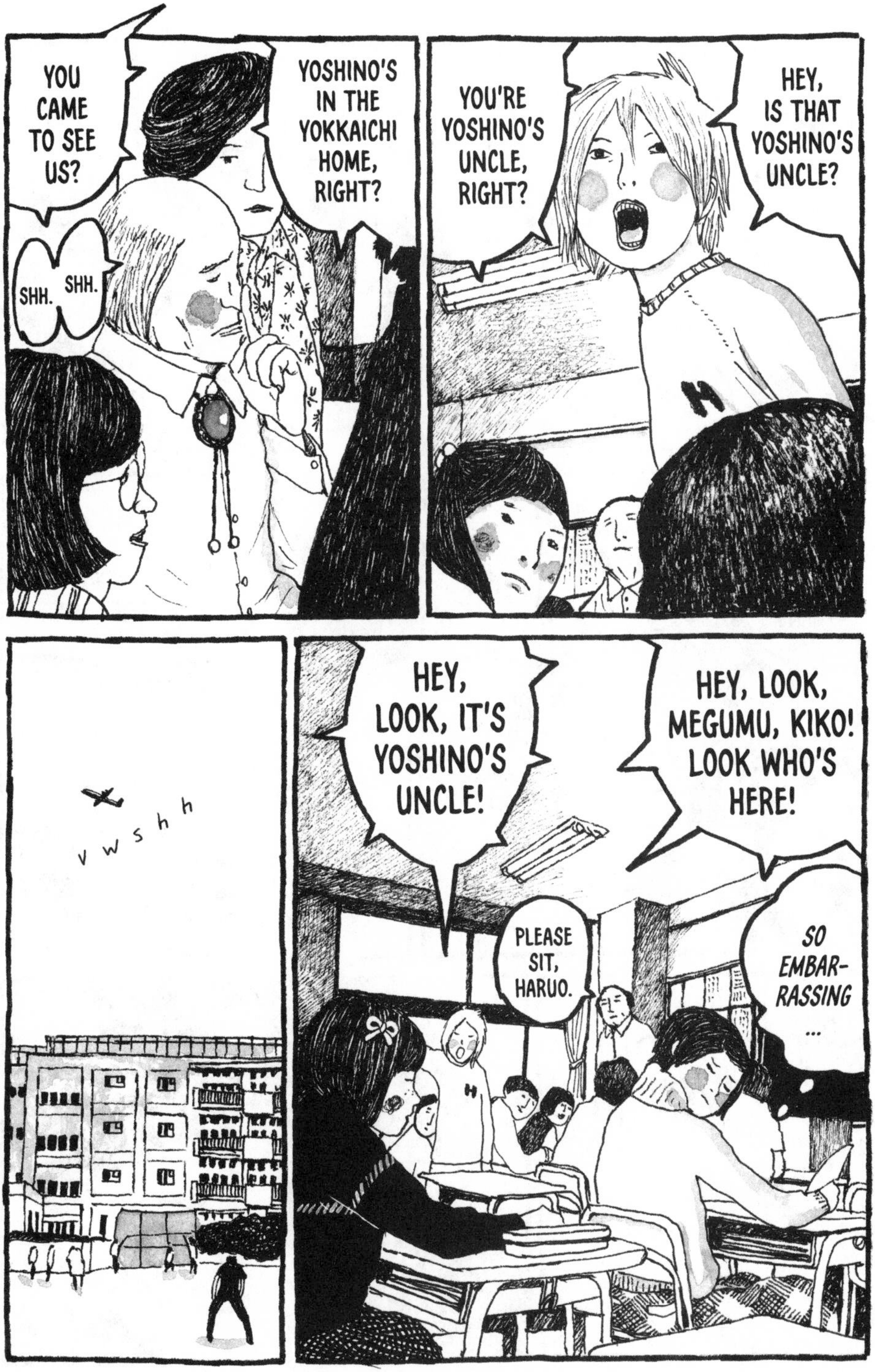
HEY, IS THAT YOSHINO'S UNCLE?
YOU'RE YOSHINO'S UNCLE, RIGHT?
YOSHINO'S IN THE YOKKAICHI HOME, RIGHT?
YOU CAME TO SEE US?
SHH. SHH.
HEY, LOOK, MEGUMU, KIKO! LOOK WHO'S HERE!
HEY, LOOK, IT'S YOSHINO'S UNCLE!
SO EMBARRASSING ...
PLEASE SIT, HARUO.
vwshh

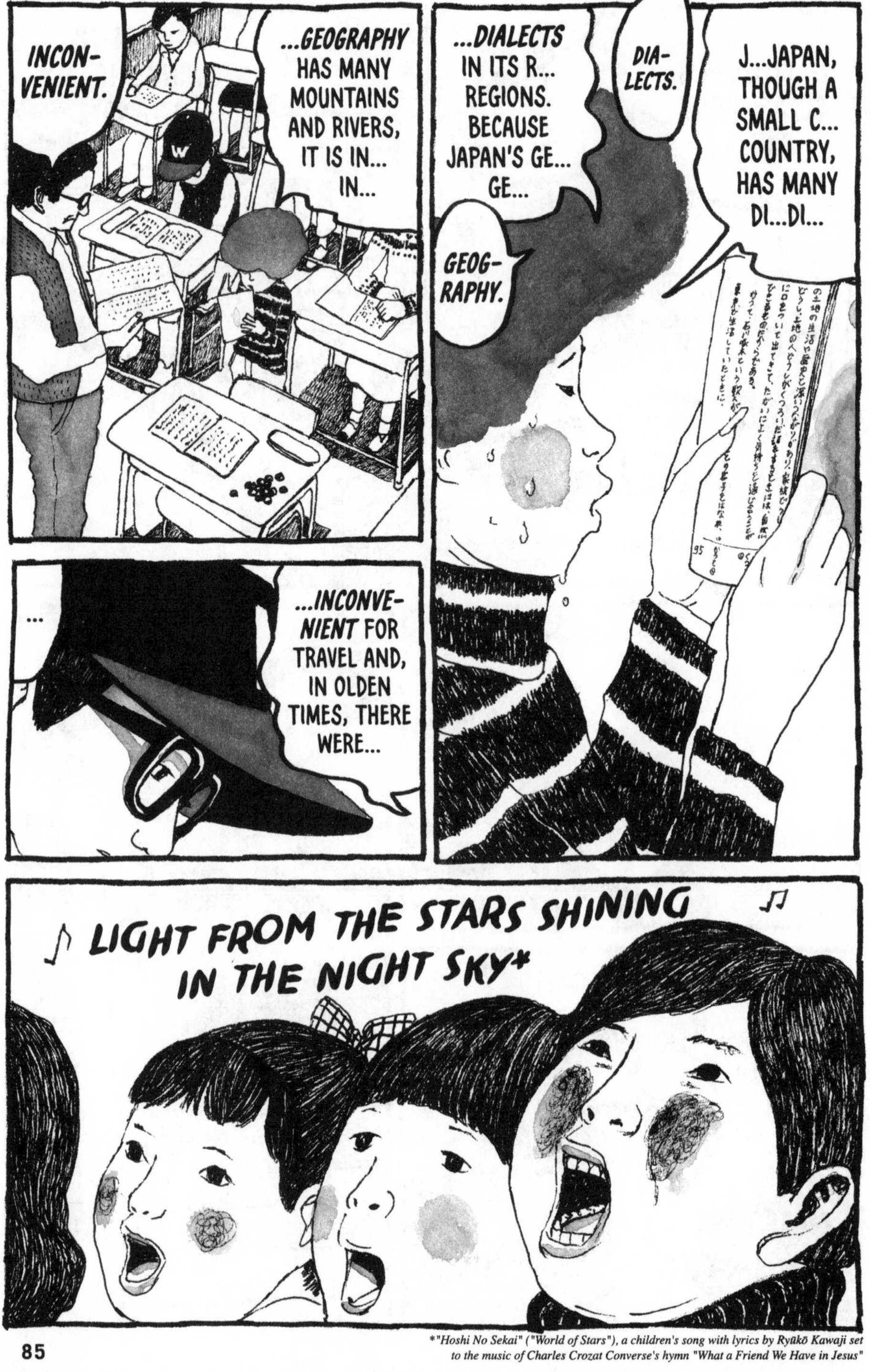
J...JAPAN, THOUGH A SMALL C... COUNTRY, HAS MANY DI...DI...
DIA-LECTS.
...DIALECTS IN ITS R... REGIONS. BECAUSE JAPAN'S GE... GE...
GEOG-RAPHY.
...GEOGRAPHY HAS MANY MOUNTAINS AND RIVERS, IT IS IN... IN...
INCON-VENIENT.
...INCONVE-NIENT FOR TRAVEL AND, IN OLDEN TIMES, THERE WERE...
...
♪ LIGHT FROM THE STARS SHINING IN THE NIGHT SKY* ♫

*"Hoshi No Sekai" ("World of Stars"), a children's song with lyrics by Ryūkō Kawaji set to the music of Charles Crozat Converse's hymn "What a Friend We Have in Jesus"

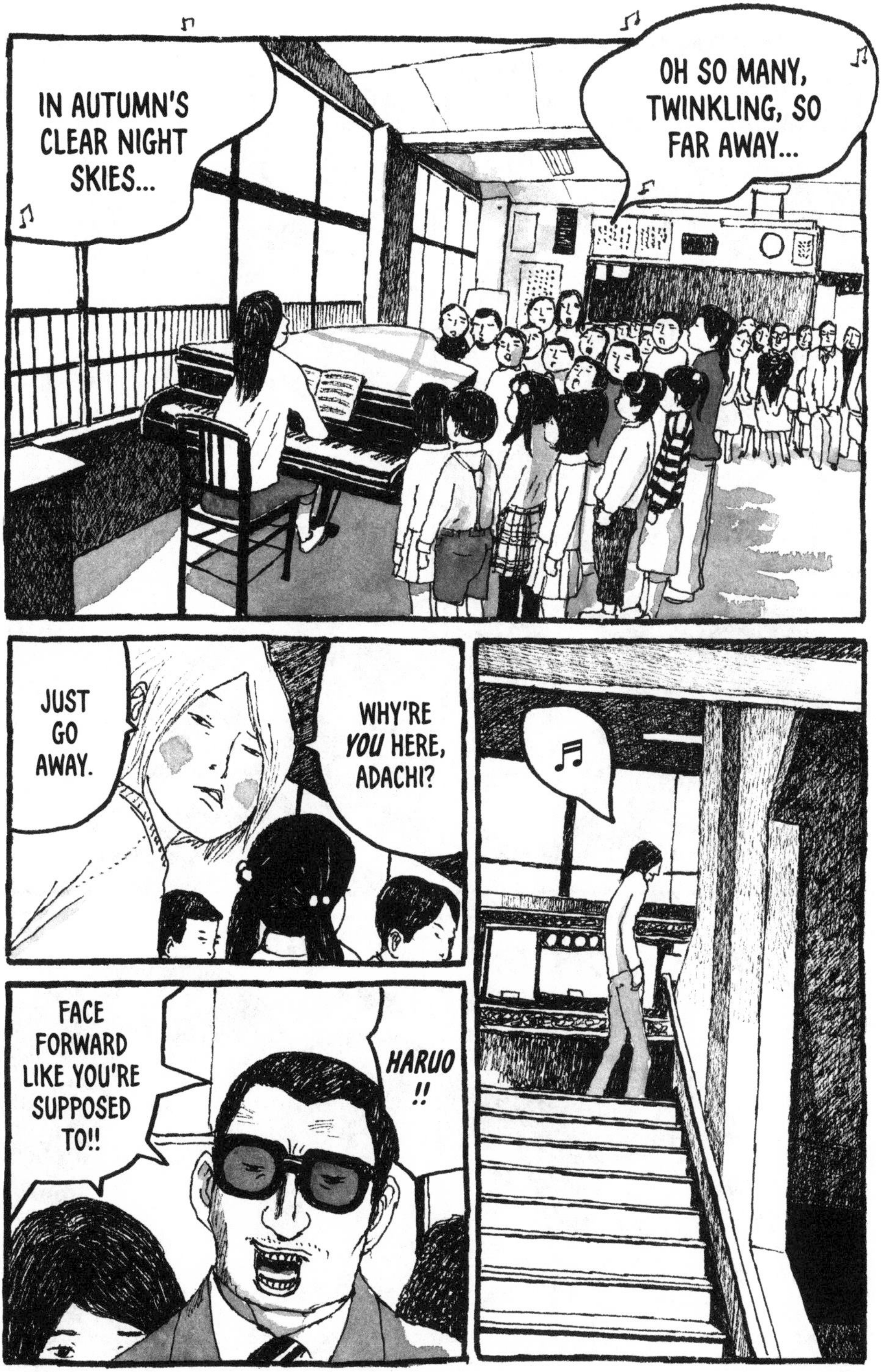
OH SO MANY, TWINKLING, SO FAR AWAY...
IN AUTUMN'S CLEAR NIGHT SKIES...
WHY'RE *YOU* HERE, ADACHI?
JUST GO AWAY.
HARUO!!
FACE FORWARD LIKE YOU'RE SUPPOSED TO!!

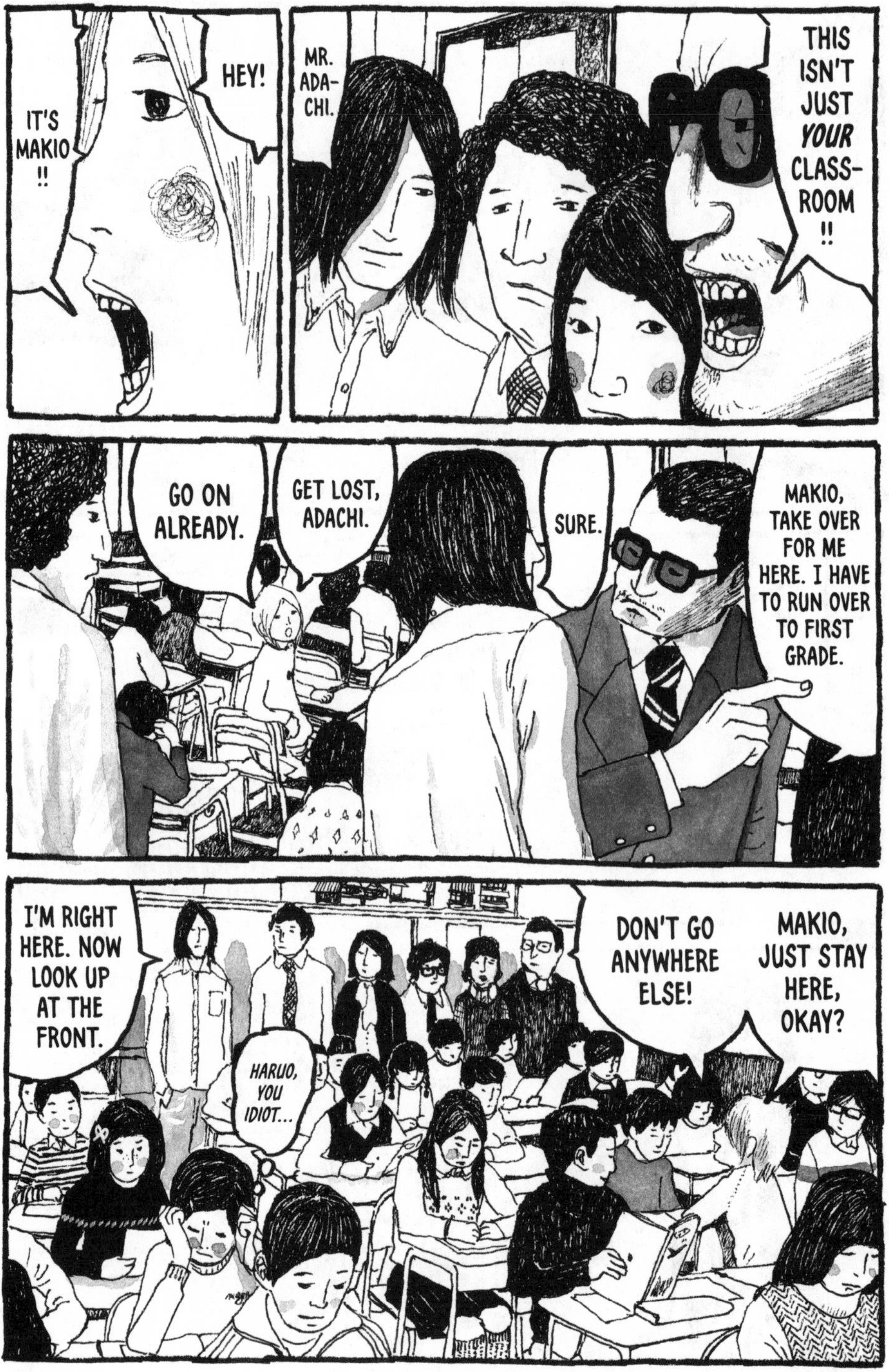
THIS ISN'T JUST *YOUR* CLASSROOM !!
MR. ADACHI.
HEY!
IT'S MAKIO !!
MAKIO, TAKE OVER FOR ME HERE. I HAVE TO RUN OVER TO FIRST GRADE.
SURE.
GET LOST, ADACHI.
GO ON ALREADY.
MAKIO, JUST STAY HERE, OKAY?
DON'T GO ANYWHERE ELSE!
HARUO, YOU IDIOT...
I'M RIGHT HERE. NOW LOOK UP AT THE FRONT.

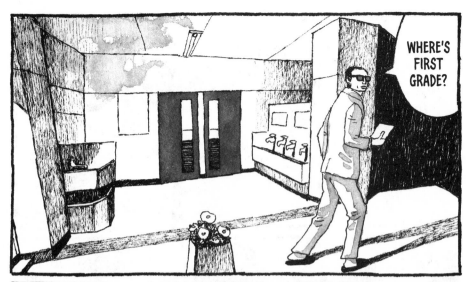

WHERE'S FIRST GRADE?

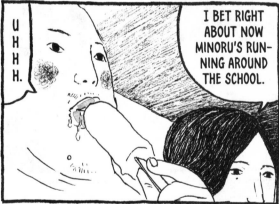

UHHH.

I BET RIGHT ABOUT NOW MINORU'S RUNNING AROUND THE SCHOOL.

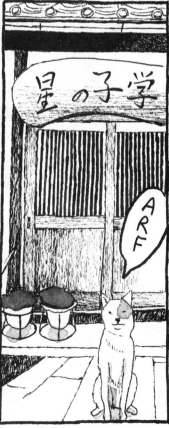

星の子学

ARF

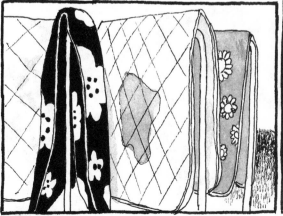

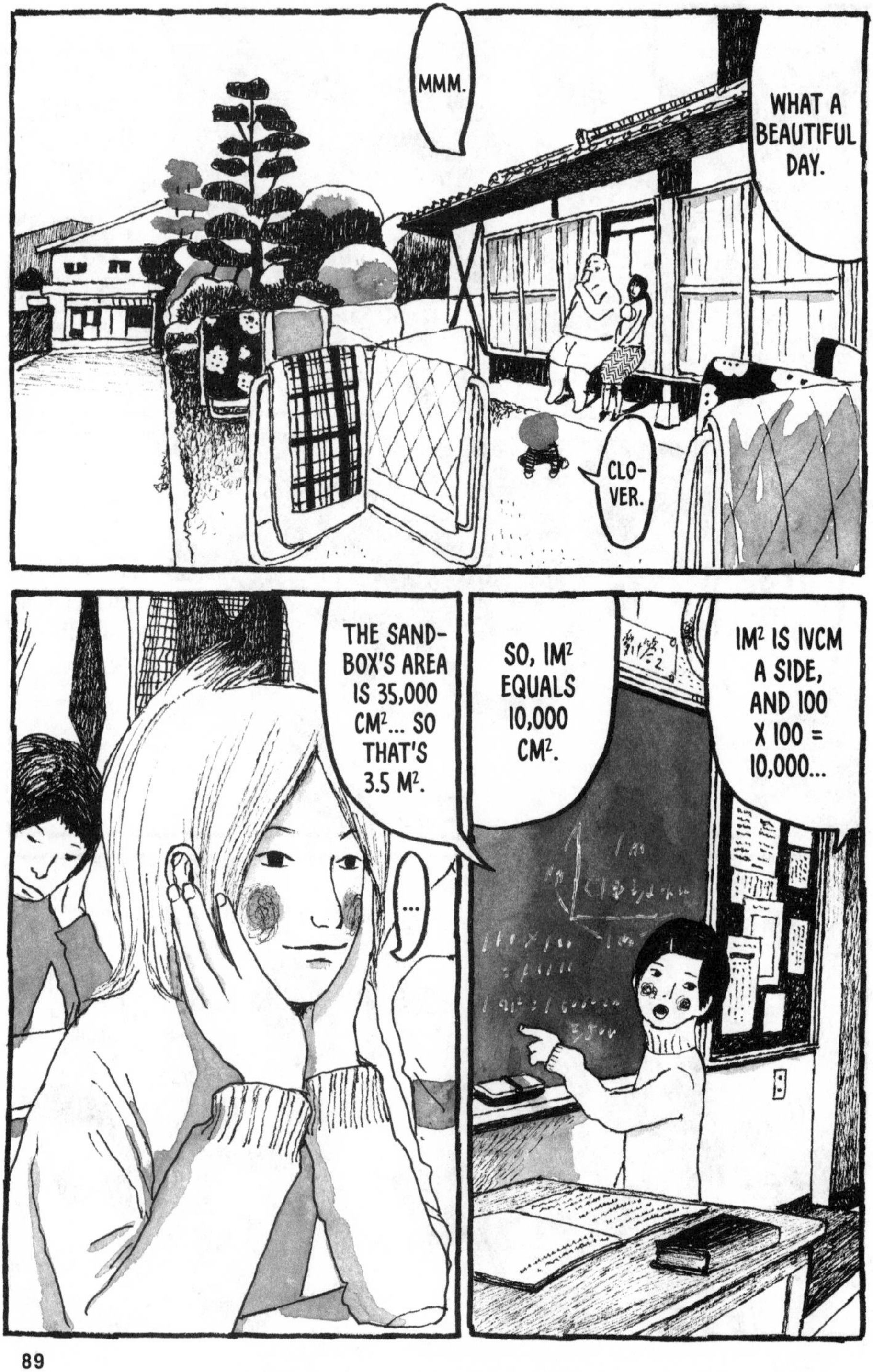
WHAT A BEAUTIFUL DAY.
MMM.
CLO-VER.
IM^2 IS IVCM A SIDE, AND 100 X 100 = 10,000...
SO, IM^2 EQUALS 10,000 CM^2.
THE SAND-BOX'S AREA IS 35,000 CM^2... SO THAT'S 3.5 M^2.
...

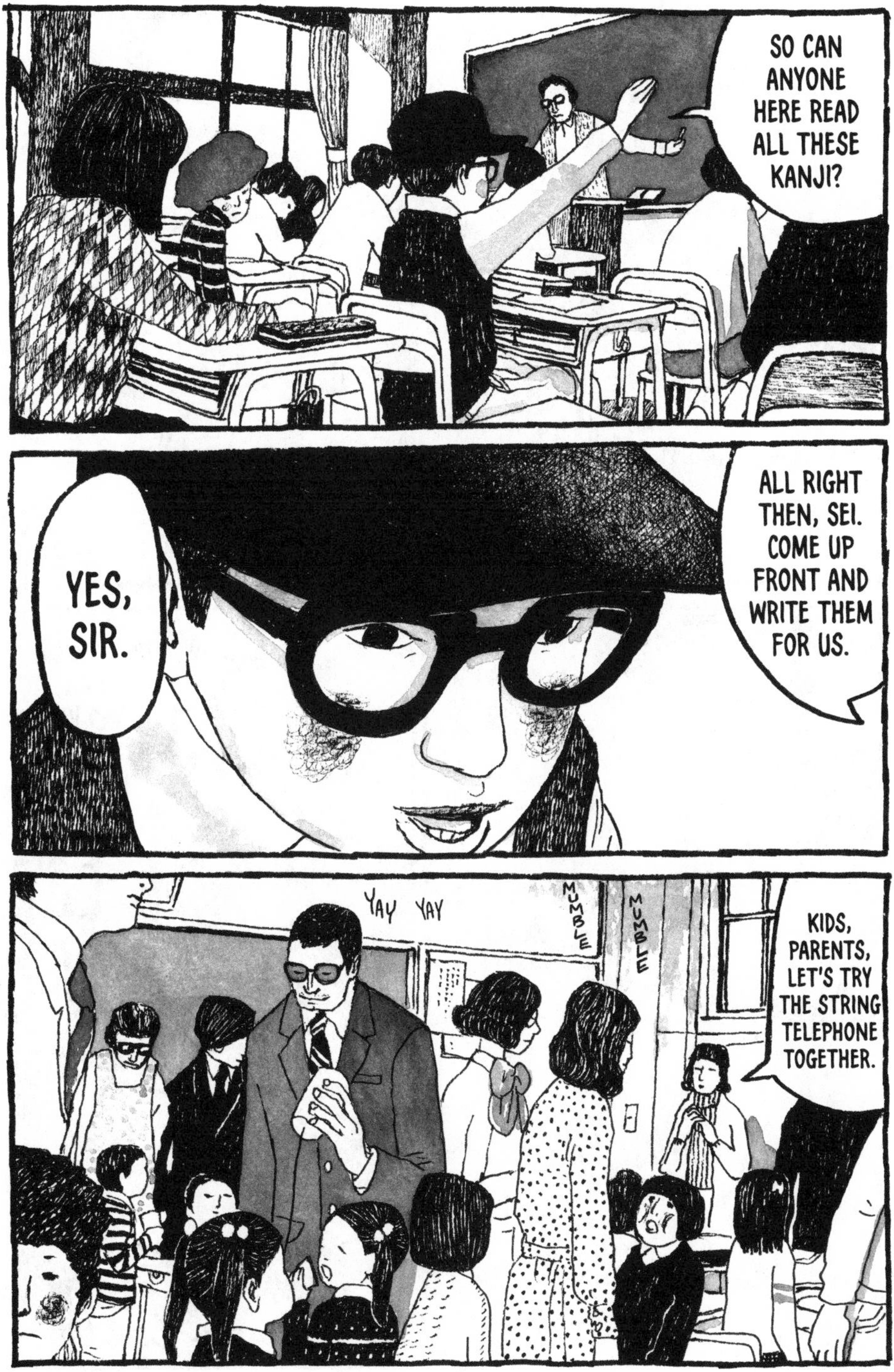
SO CAN ANYONE HERE READ ALL THESE KANJI?
ALL RIGHT THEN, SEI. COME UP FRONT AND WRITE THEM FOR US.
YES, SIR.
KIDS, PARENTS, LET'S TRY THE STRING TELEPHONE TOGETHER.
MUMBLE
MUMBLE
YAY YAY

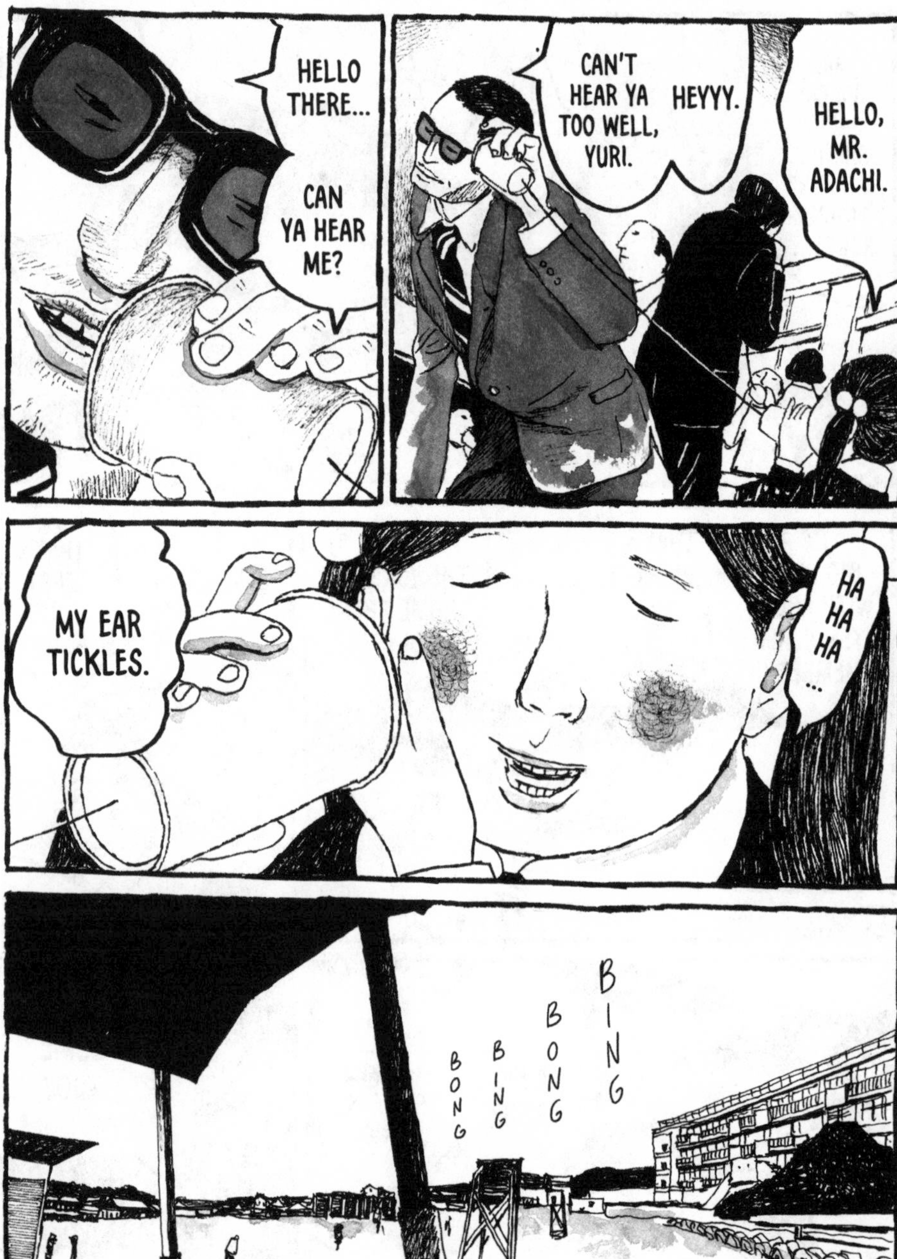
HELLO, MR. ADACHI.
HEYYY.
CAN'T HEAR YA TOO WELL, YURI.
HELLO THERE...
CAN YA HEAR ME?
HA HA HA ...
MY EAR TICKLES.
BING
BONG
BING
BONG

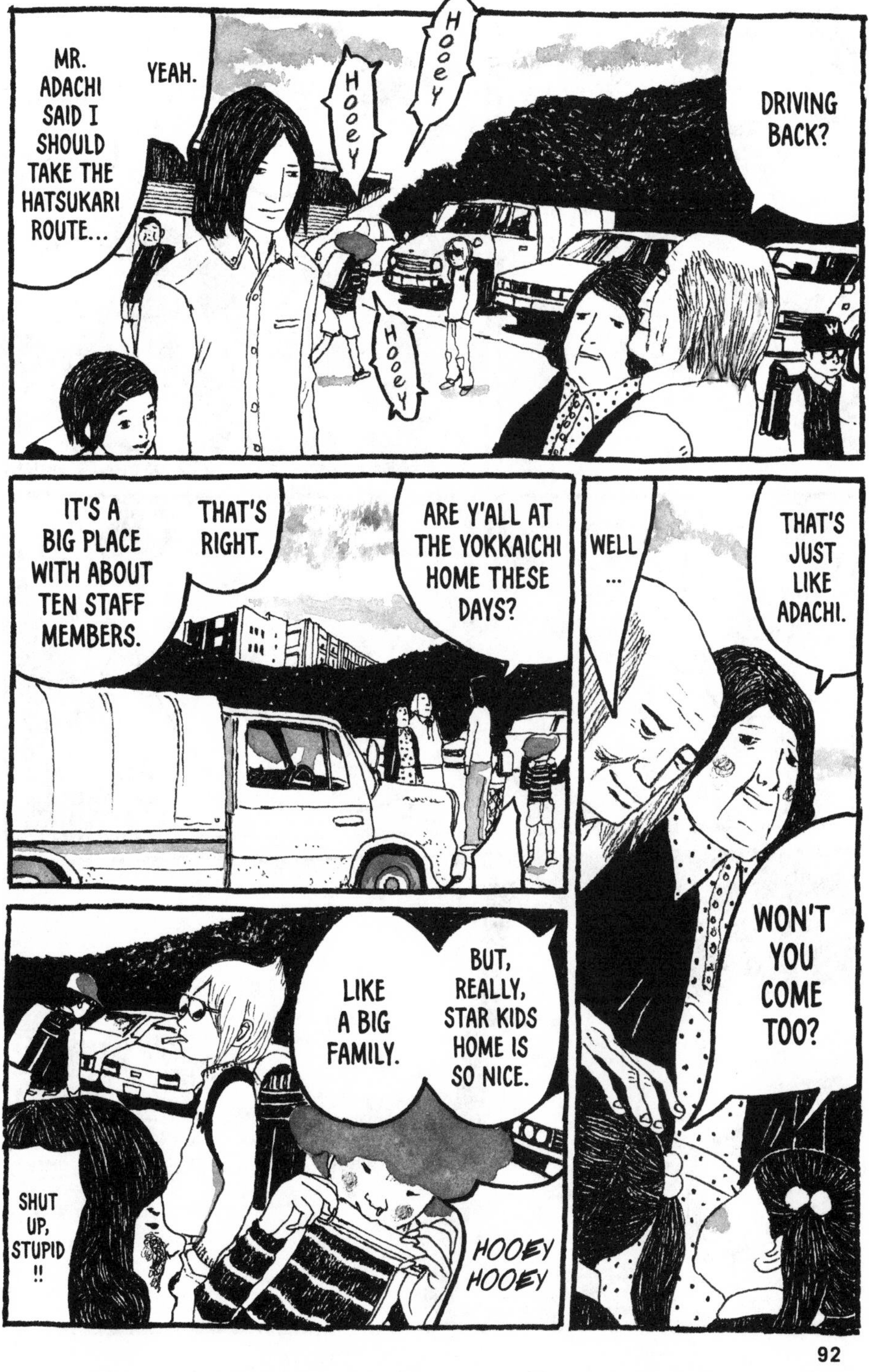
DRIVING BACK?
HOOEY
HOOEY
YEAH.
MR. ADACHI SAID I SHOULD TAKE THE HATSUKARI ROUTE...
HOOEY
THAT'S JUST LIKE ADACHI.
WELL...
WON'T YOU COME TOO?
ARE Y'ALL AT THE YOKKAICHI HOME THESE DAYS?
THAT'S RIGHT.
IT'S A BIG PLACE WITH ABOUT TEN STAFF MEMBERS.
BUT, REALLY, STAR KIDS HOME IS SO NICE.
LIKE A BIG FAMILY.
HOOEY HOOEY
SHUT UP, STUPID!!

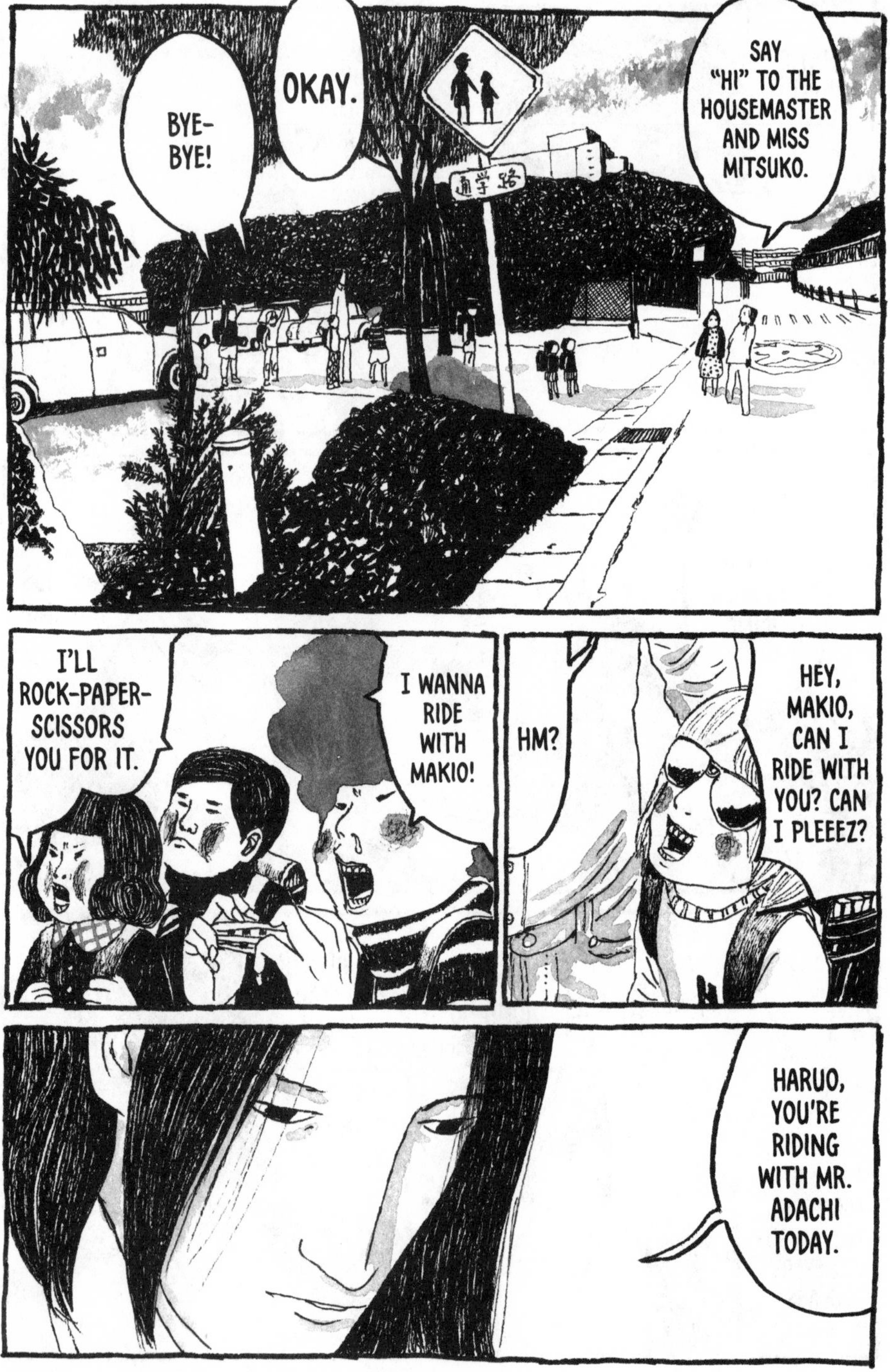
SAY "HI" TO THE HOUSEMASTER AND MISS MITSUKO.
OKAY.
通学路
BYE-BYE!
HEY, MAKIO, CAN I RIDE WITH YOU? CAN I PLEEEZ?
HM?
I WANNA RIDE WITH MAKIO!
I'LL ROCK-PAPER-SCISSORS YOU FOR IT.
HARUO, YOU'RE RIDING WITH MR. ADACHI TODAY.

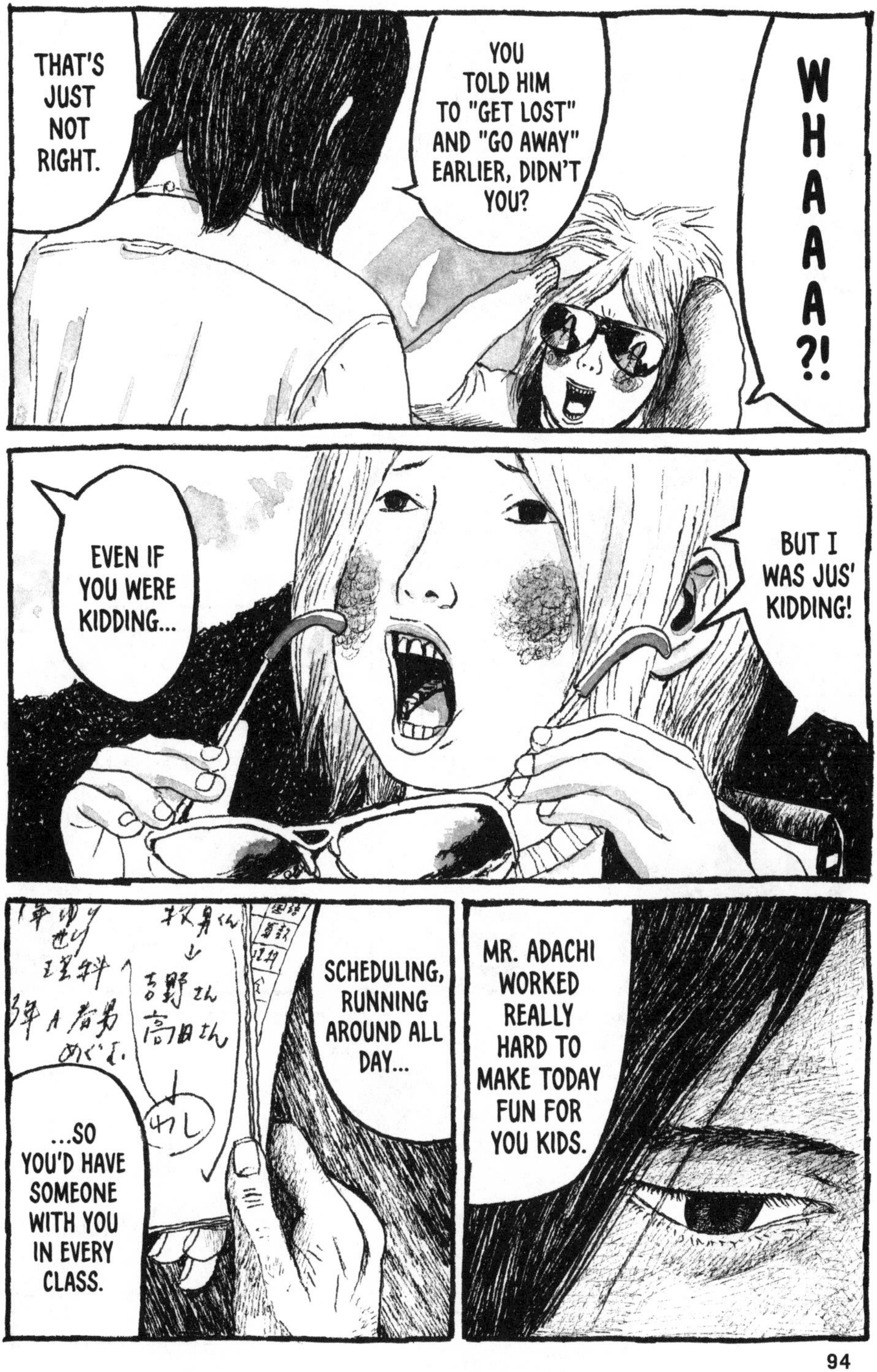
WHAAAA?!
YOU TOLD HIM TO "GET LOST" AND "GO AWAY" EARLIER, DIDN'T YOU?
THAT'S JUST NOT RIGHT.
BUT I WAS JUS' KIDDING!
EVEN IF YOU WERE KIDDING...
MR. ADACHI WORKED REALLY HARD TO MAKE TODAY FUN FOR YOU KIDS.
SCHEDULING, RUNNING AROUND ALL DAY...
...SO YOU'D HAVE SOMEONE WITH YOU IN EVERY CLASS.

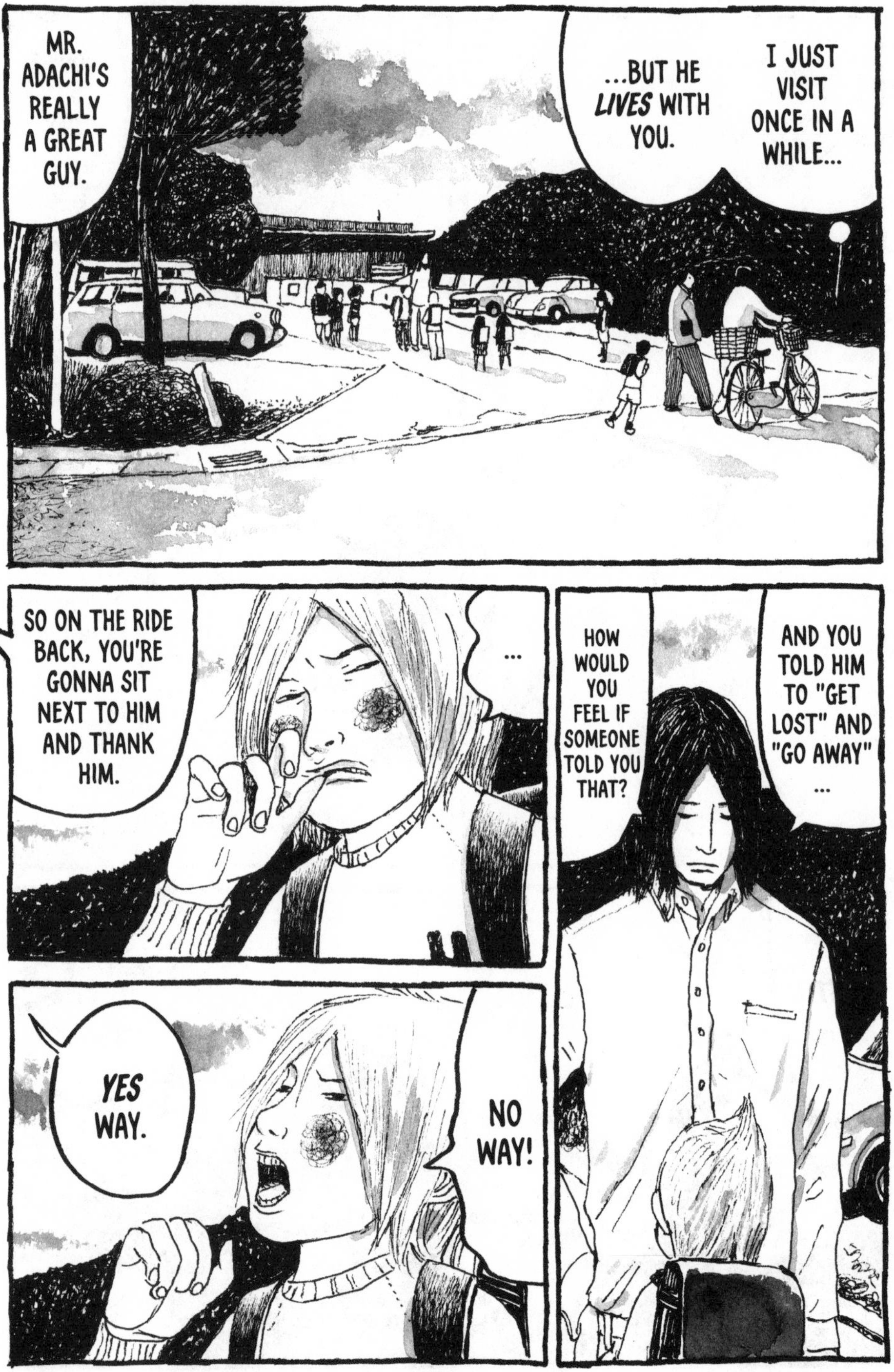
I JUST VISIT ONCE IN A WHILE...
...BUT HE *LIVES* WITH YOU.
MR. ADACHI'S REALLY A GREAT GUY.
AND YOU TOLD HIM TO "GET LOST" AND "GO AWAY" ...
HOW WOULD YOU FEEL IF SOMEONE TOLD YOU THAT?
...
SO ON THE RIDE BACK, YOU'RE GONNA SIT NEXT TO HIM AND THANK HIM.
NO WAY!
YES WAY.

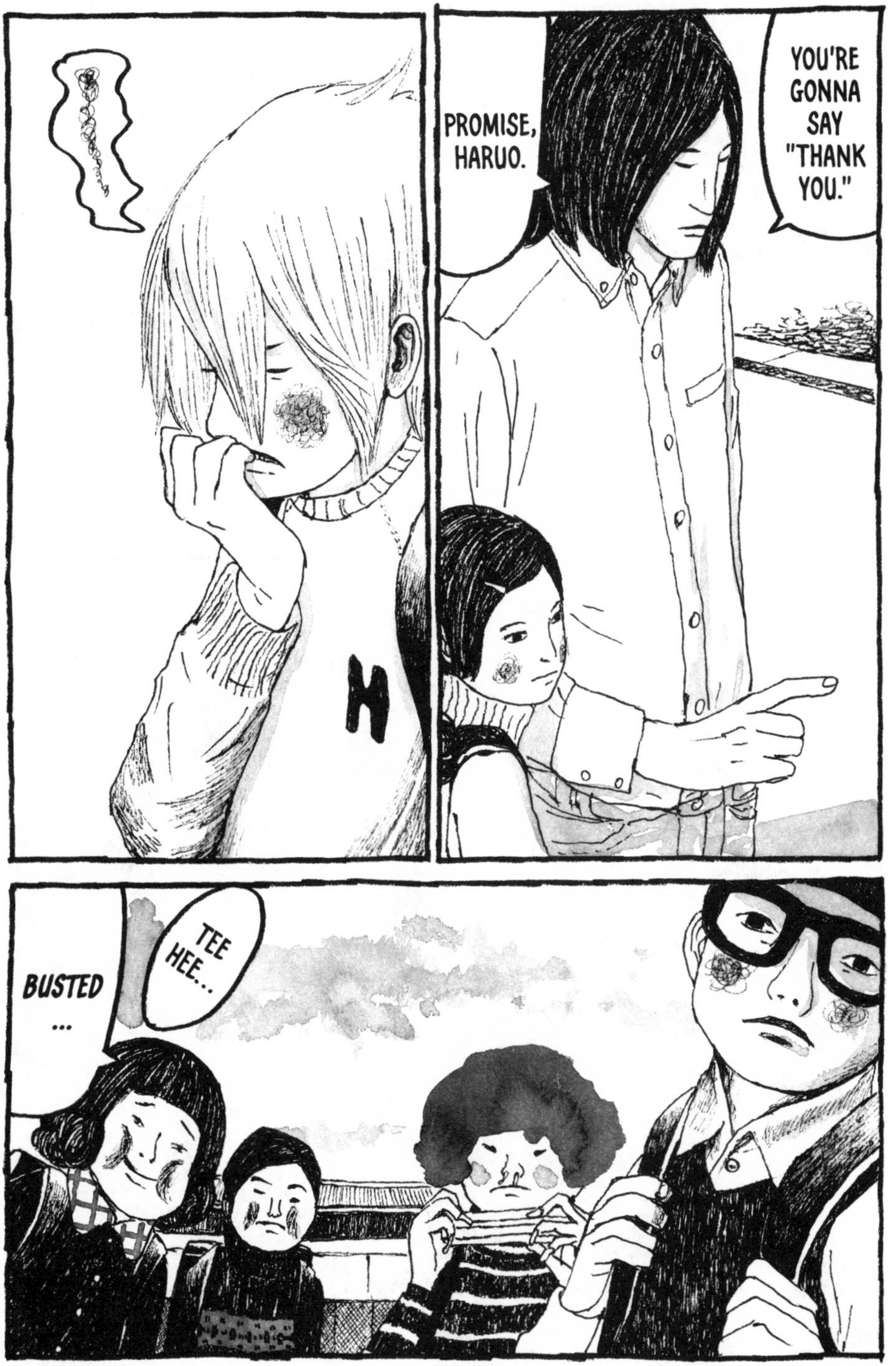
YOU'RE GONNA SAY "THANK YOU."
PROMISE, HARUO.
TEE HEE...
BUSTED ...

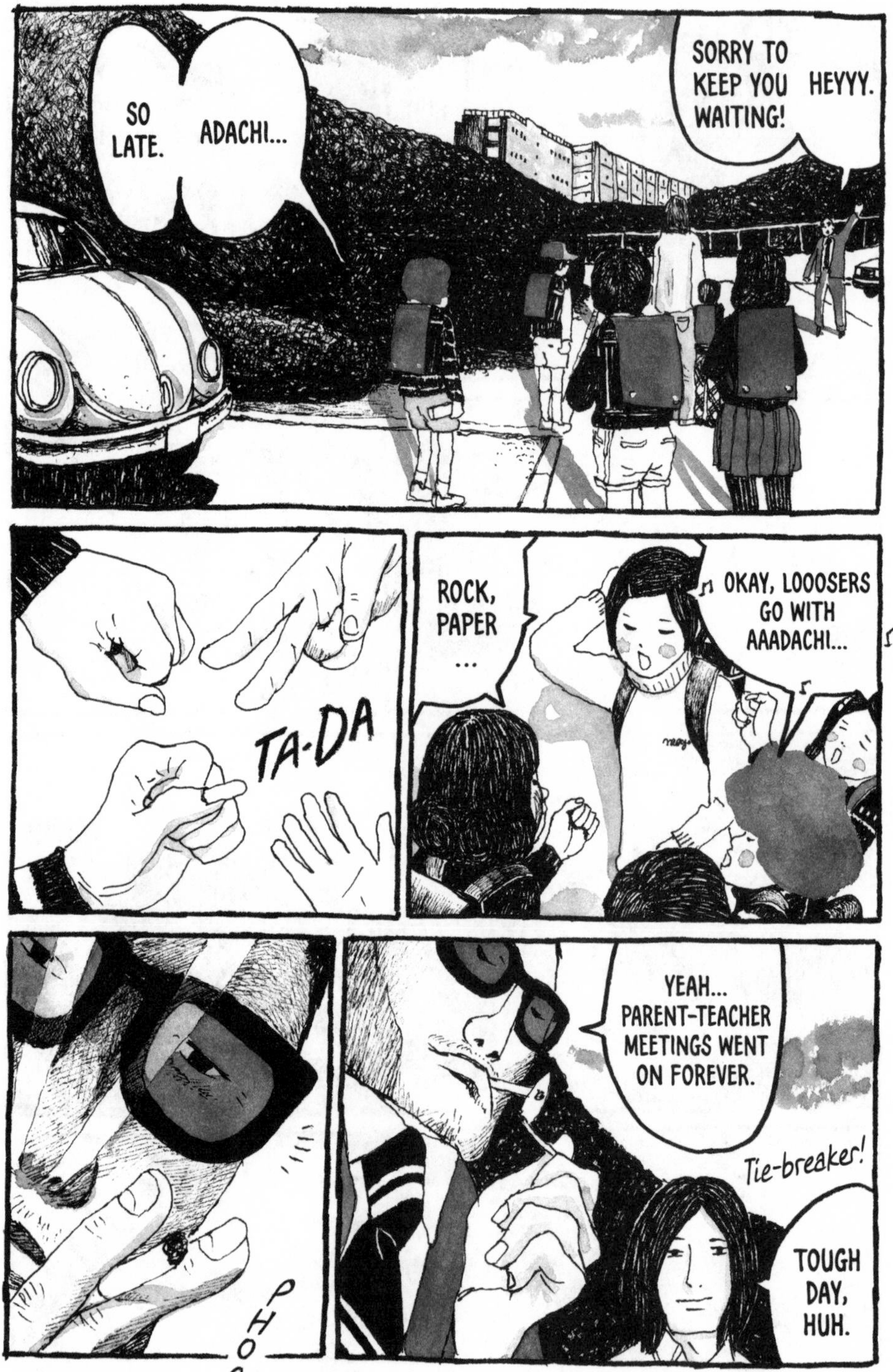
HEYYY.
SORRY TO KEEP YOU WAITING!
ADACHI...
SO LATE.
OKAY, LOOOSERS GO WITH AAADACHI...
ROCK, PAPER ...
TA-DA
YEAH... PARENT-TEACHER MEETINGS WENT ON FOREVER.
Tie-breaker!
TOUGH DAY, HUH.
PHOOO

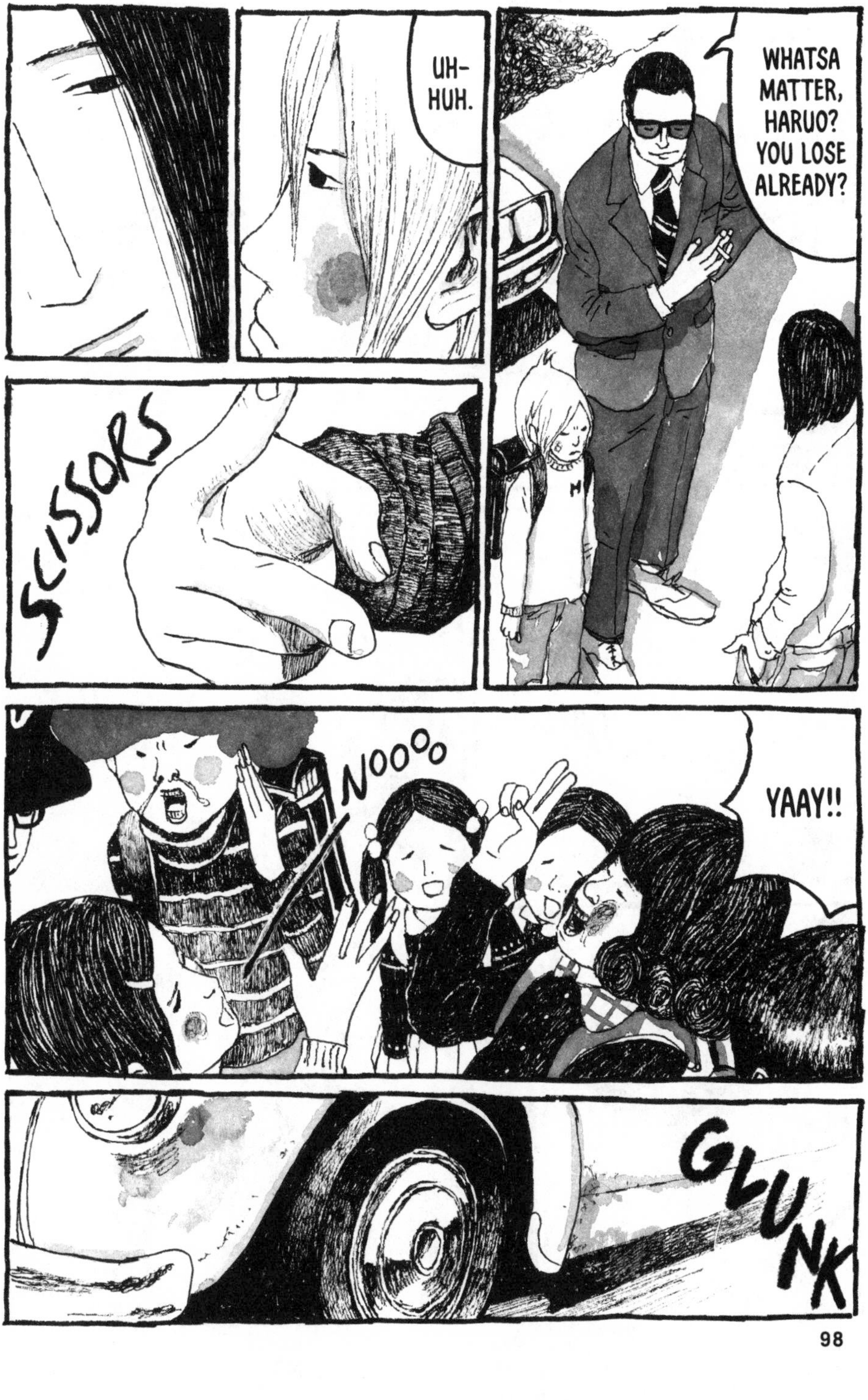
WHATSA MATTER, HARUO? YOU LOSE ALREADY?
UH-HUH.
SCISSORS
YAAY!!
NOOOO
GLUNK

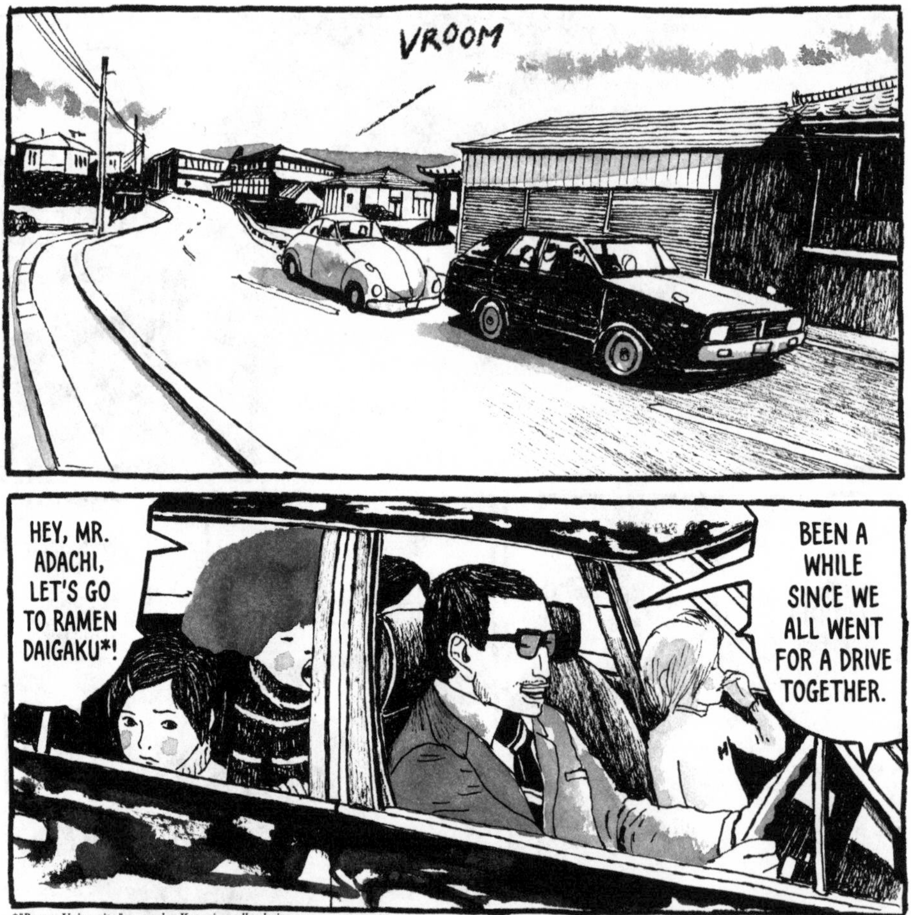
VROOM
BEEN A WHILE SINCE WE ALL WENT FOR A DRIVE TOGETHER.
HEY, MR. ADACHI, LET'S GO TO RAMEN DAIGAKU*!

*"Ramen University," a popular Kansai noodle chain

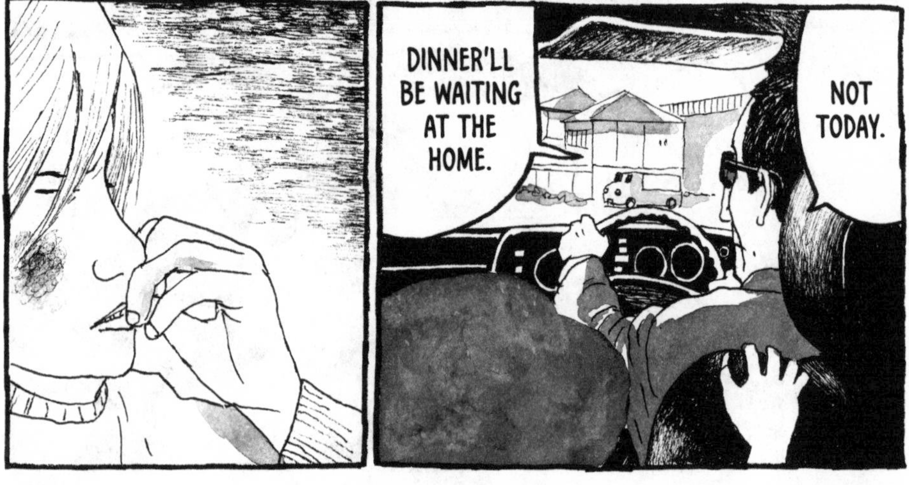
NOT TODAY.
DINNER'LL BE WAITING AT THE HOME.

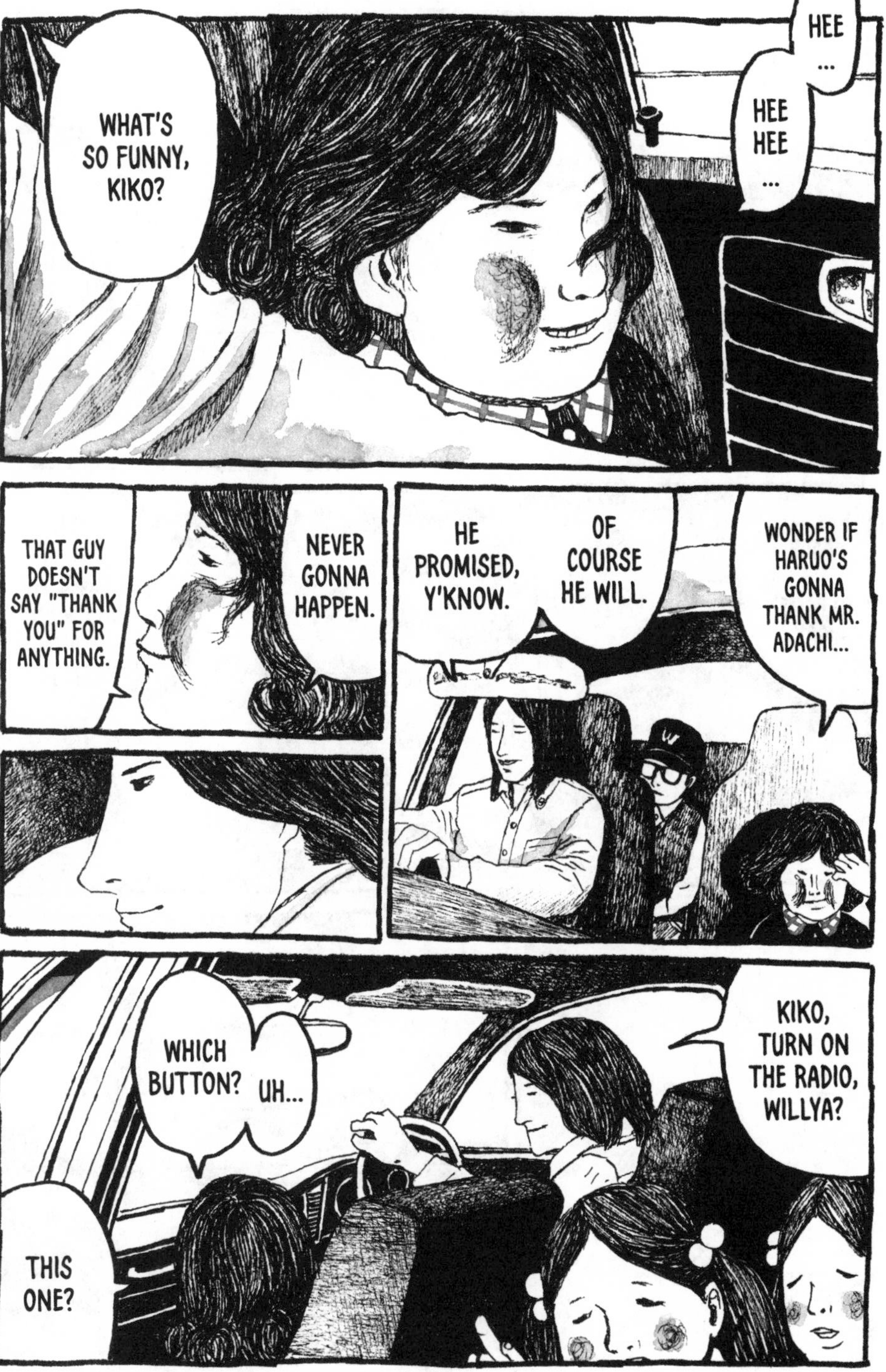
HEE ...
HEE HEE ...
WHAT'S SO FUNNY, KIKO?
WONDER IF HARUO'S GONNA THANK MR. ADACHI...
OF COURSE HE WILL.
HE PROMISED, Y'KNOW.
NEVER GONNA HAPPEN.
THAT GUY DOESN'T SAY "THANK YOU" FOR ANYTHING.
KIKO, TURN ON THE RADIO, WILLYA?
UH...
WHICH BUTTON?
THIS ONE?

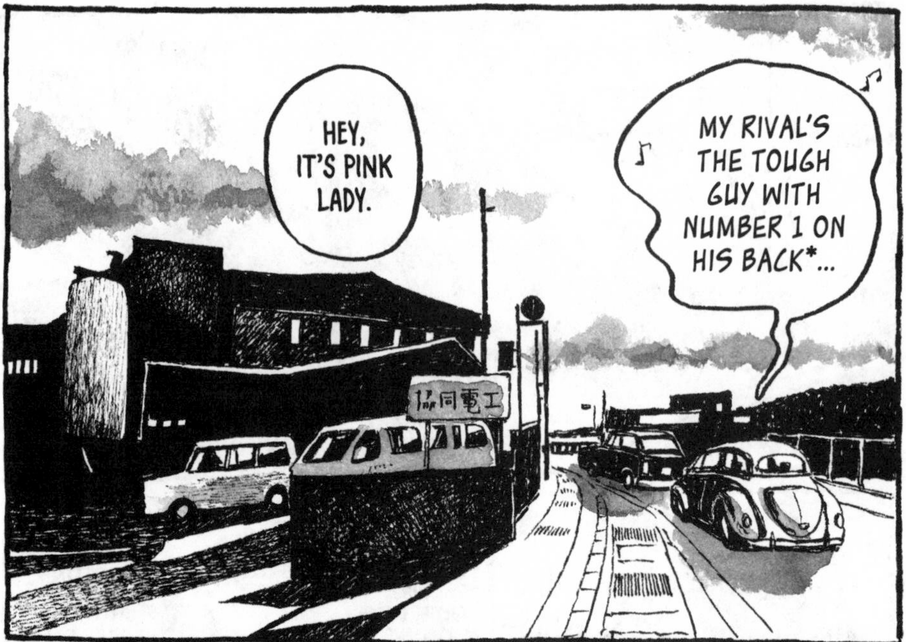
MY RIVAL'S THE TOUGH GUY WITH NUMBER 1 ON HIS BACK*...
HEY, IT'S PINK LADY.
協同電工

*From "Southpaw," a top-selling single from idol duo Pink Lady, 1978

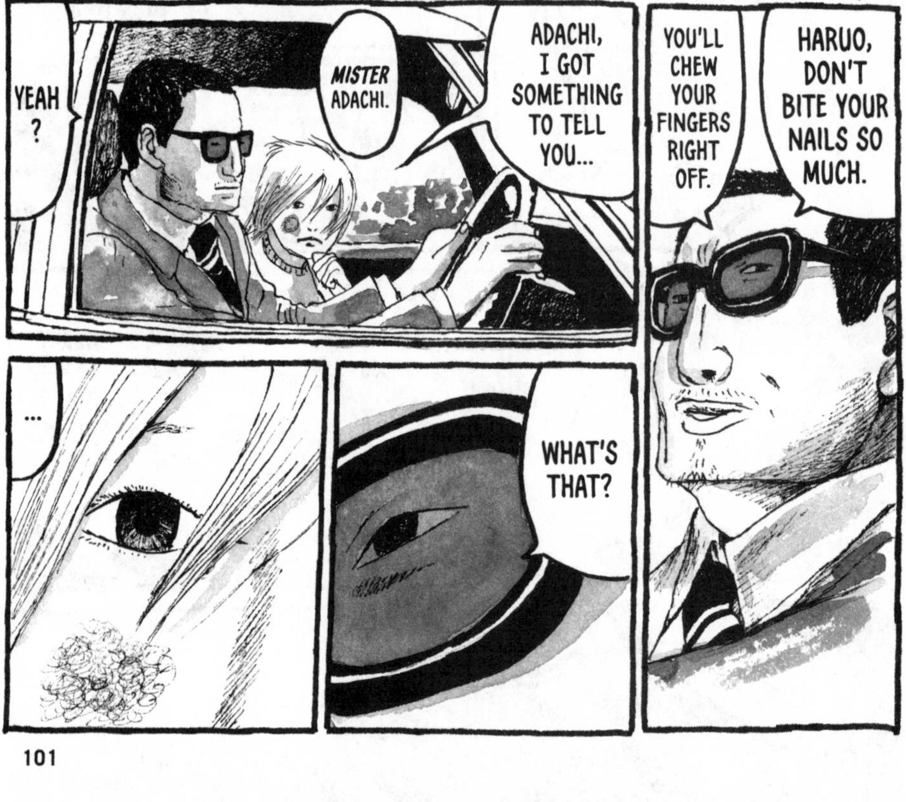
HARUO, DON'T BITE YOUR NAILS SO MUCH.
YOU'LL CHEW YOUR FINGERS RIGHT OFF.
ADACHI, I GOT SOMETHING TO TELL YOU...
MISTER ADACHI.
YEAH?
WHAT'S THAT?
...

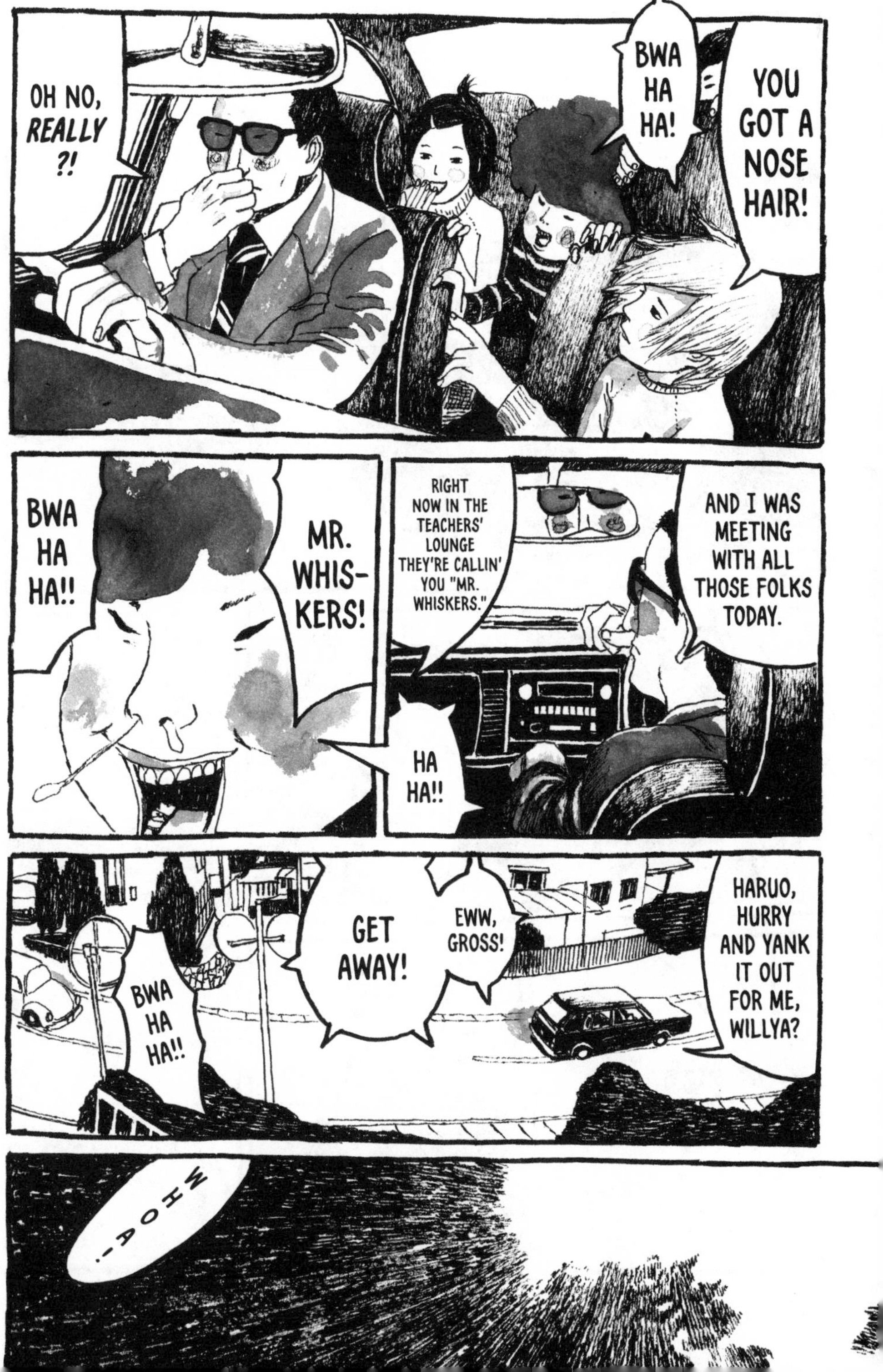
YOU GOT A NOSE HAIR!
BWA HA HA!
OH NO, *REALLY*?!
AND I WAS MEETING WITH ALL THOSE FOLKS TODAY.
RIGHT NOW IN THE TEACHERS' LOUNGE THEY'RE CALLIN' YOU "MR. WHISKERS."
HA HA!!
MR. WHIS-KERS!
BWA HA HA!!
HARUO, HURRY AND YANK IT OUT FOR ME, WILLYA?
EWW, GROSS!
GET AWAY!
BWA HA HA!!
WHOA-!

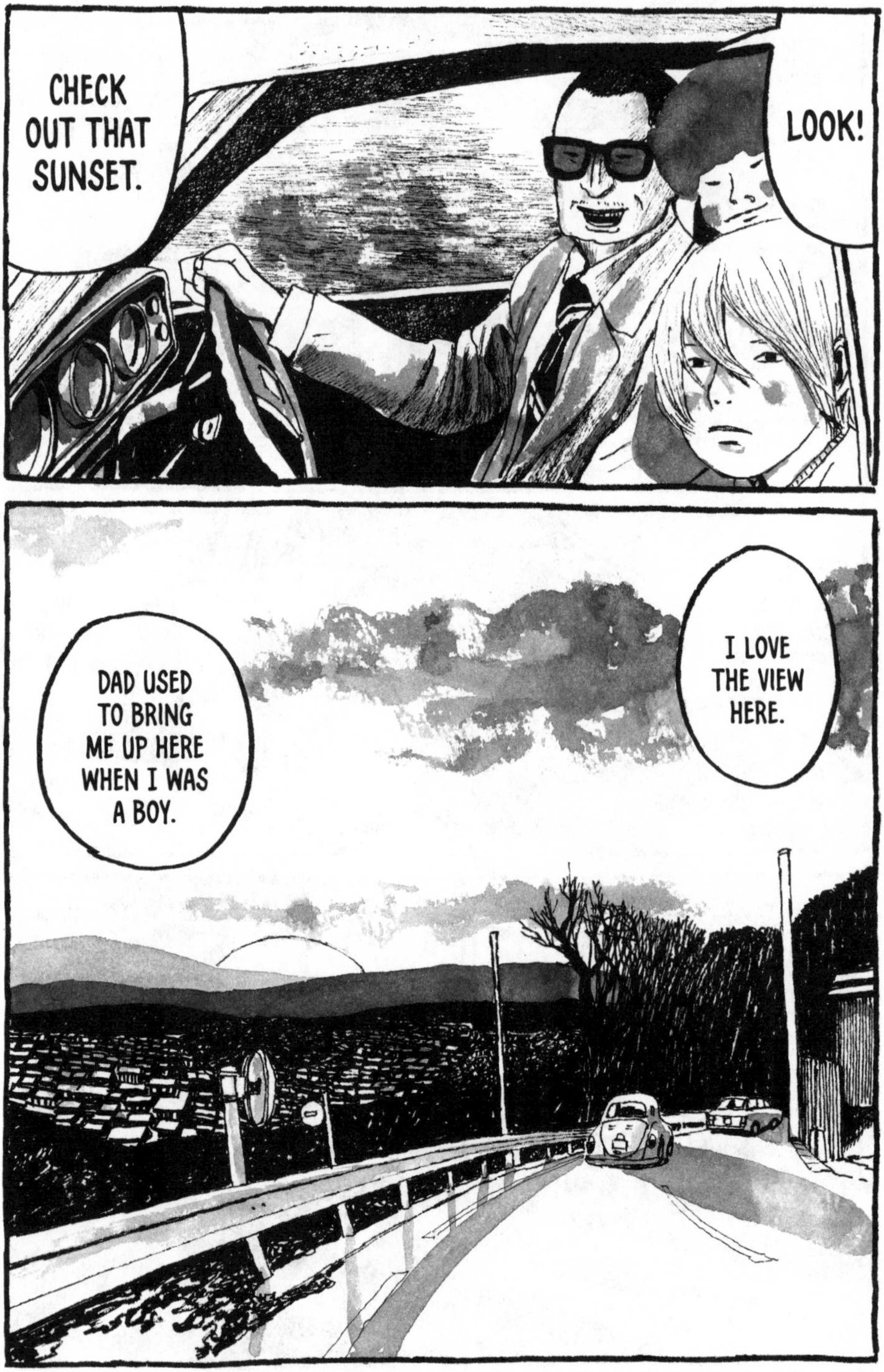
LOOK!
CHECK OUT THAT SUNSET.
I LOVE THE VIEW HERE.
DAD USED TO BRING ME UP HERE WHEN I WAS A BOY.

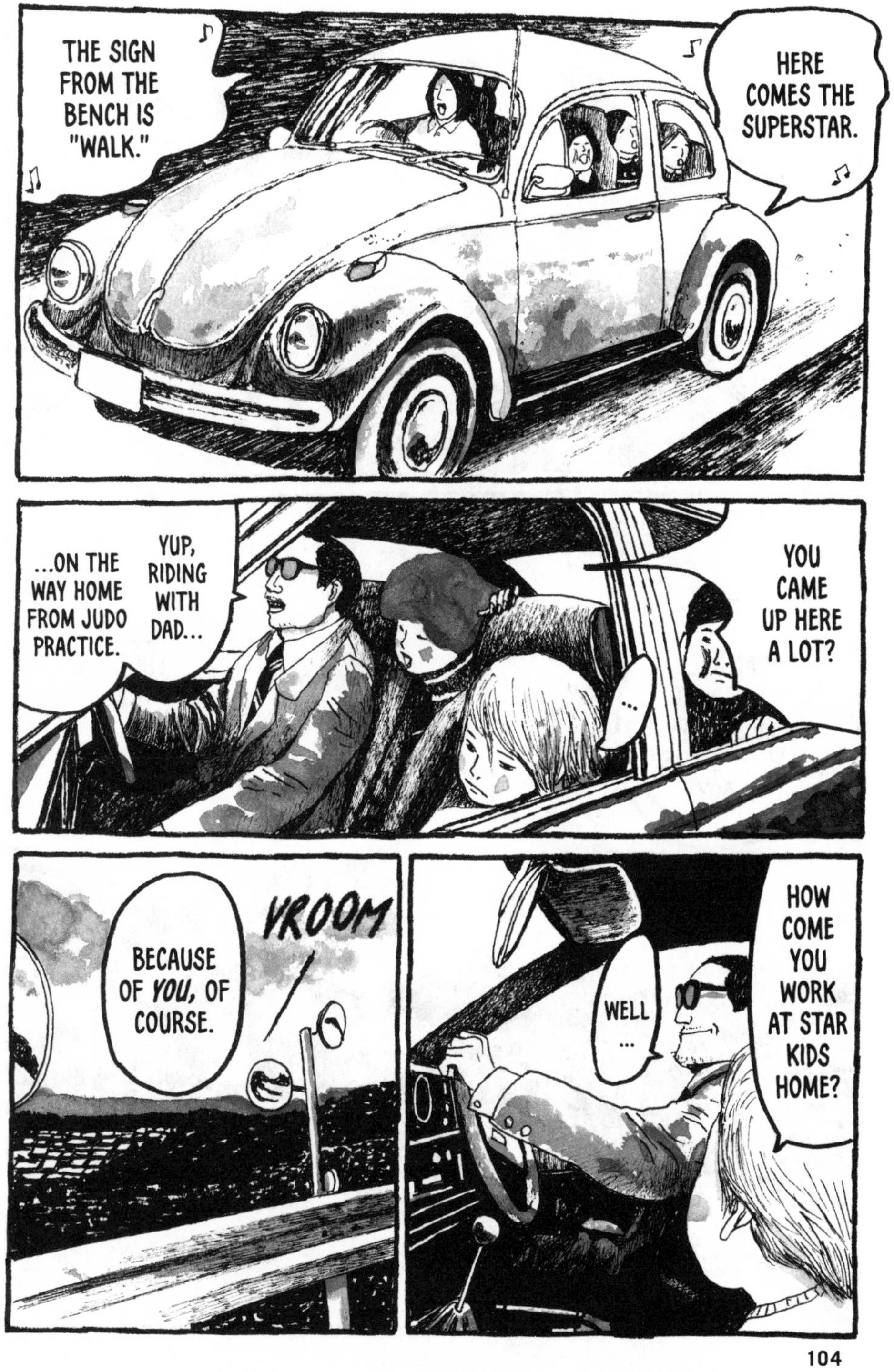
HERE COMES THE SUPERSTAR.
THE SIGN FROM THE BENCH IS "WALK."
YOU CAME UP HERE A LOT?
...
YUP, RIDING WITH DAD...
...ON THE WAY HOME FROM JUDO PRACTICE.
HOW COME YOU WORK AT STAR KIDS HOME?
WELL ...
VROOM
BECAUSE OF *YOU,* OF COURSE.

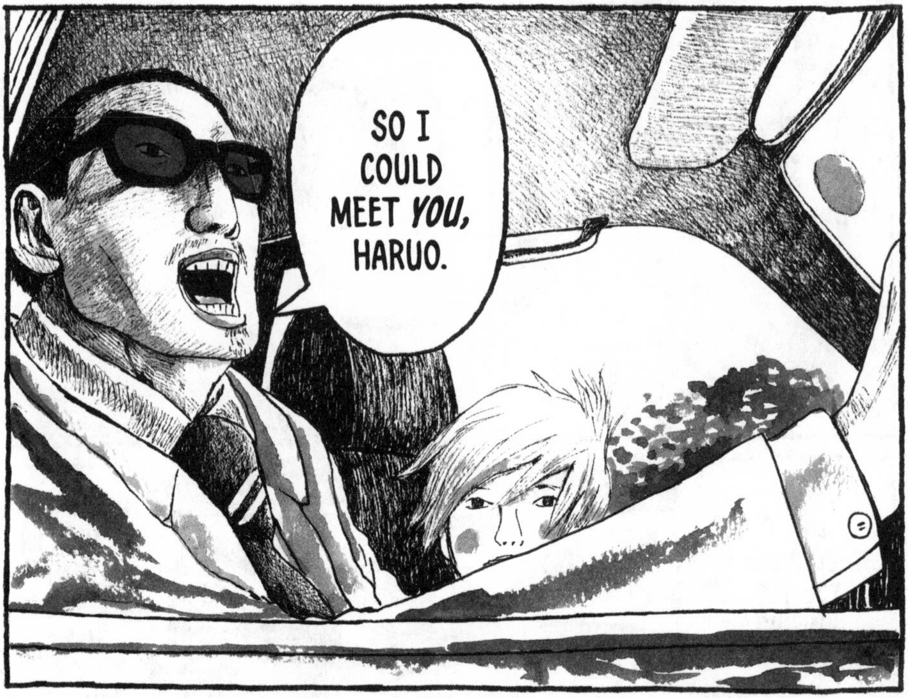
SO I COULD MEET *YOU*, HARUO.

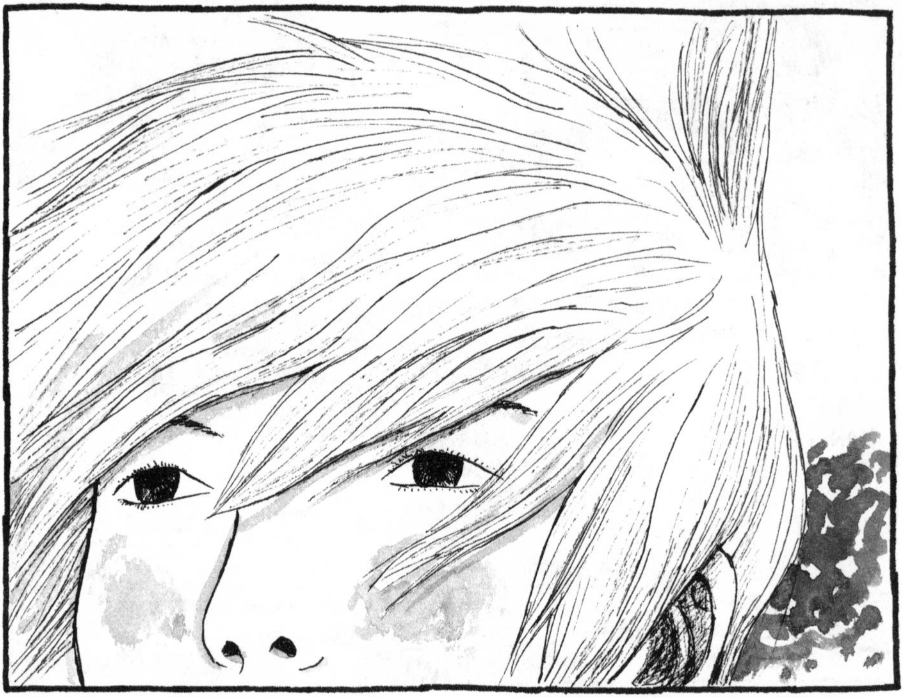

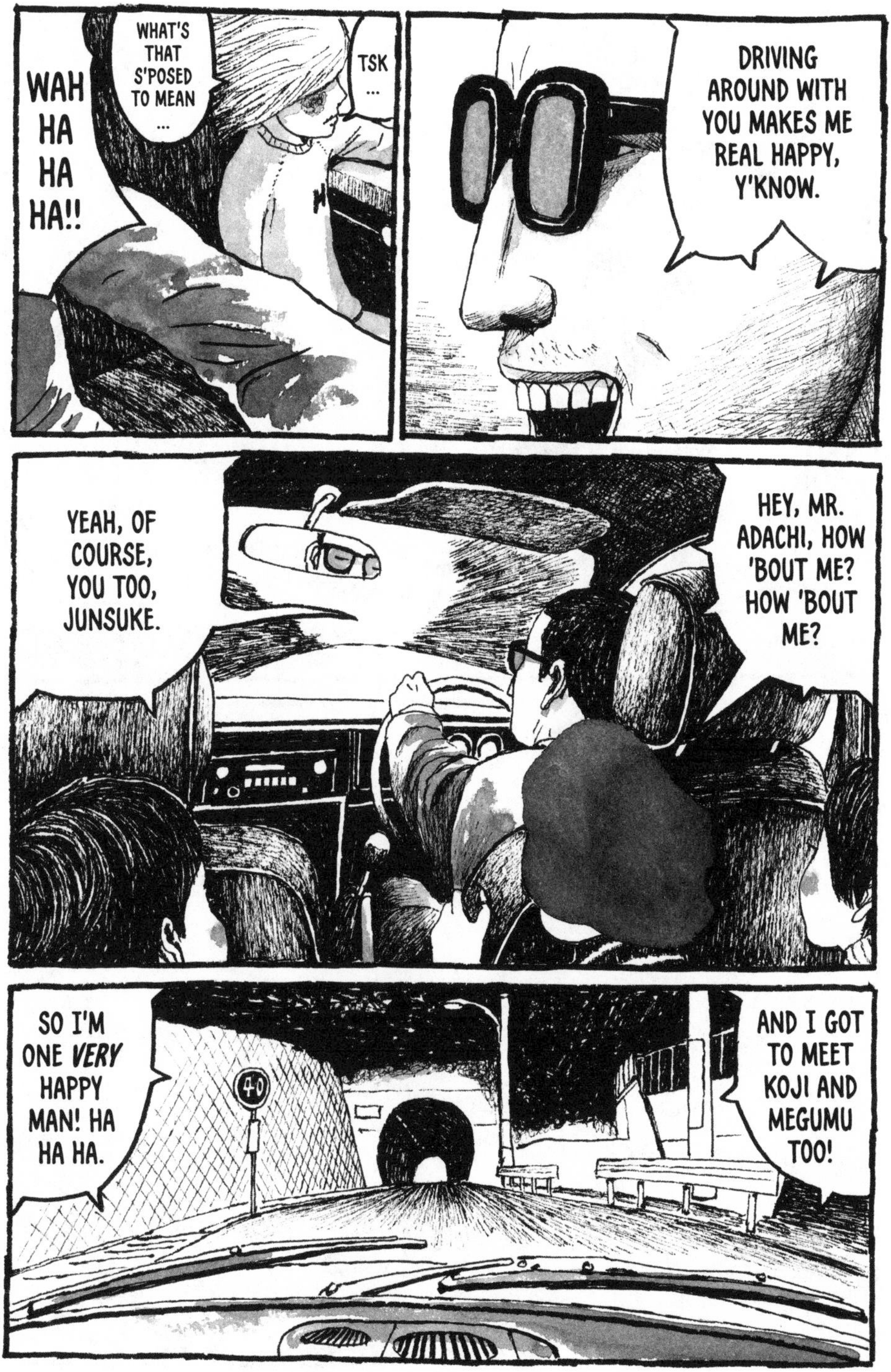
DRIVING AROUND WITH YOU MAKES ME REAL HAPPY, Y'KNOW.
TSK ...
WHAT'S THAT S'POSED TO MEAN ...
WAH HA HA HA!!
HEY, MR. ADACHI, HOW 'BOUT ME? HOW 'BOUT ME?
YEAH, OF COURSE, YOU TOO, JUNSUKE.
AND I GOT TO MEET KOJI AND MEGUMU TOO!
SO I'M ONE *VERY* HAPPY MAN! HA HA HA.
40

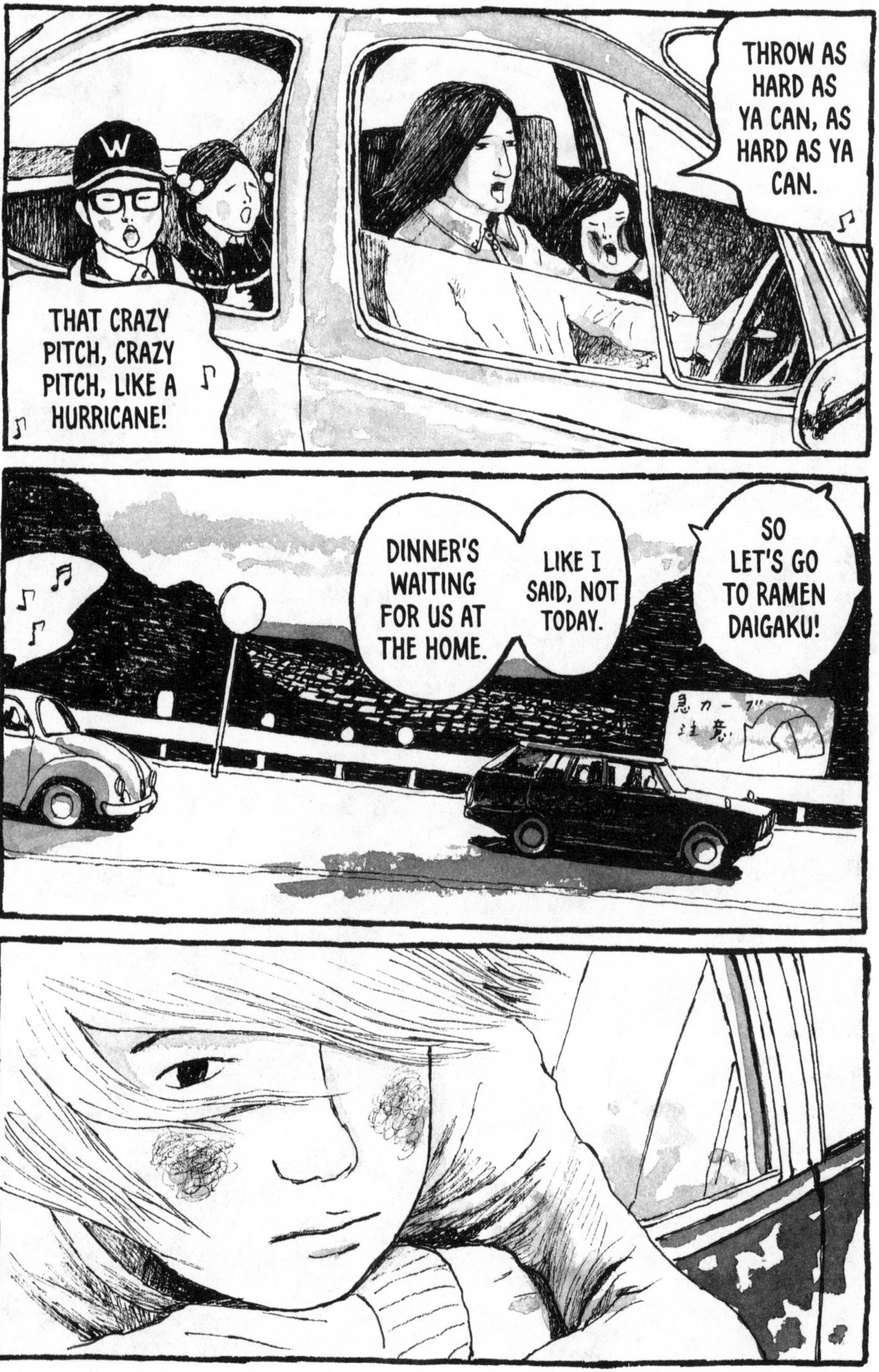
THROW AS HARD AS YA CAN, AS HARD AS YA CAN.
THAT CRAZY PITCH, CRAZY PITCH, LIKE A HURRICANE!
SO LET'S GO TO RAMEN DAIGAKU!
LIKE I SAID, NOT TODAY.
DINNER'S WAITING FOR US AT THE HOME.
急カーブ注意

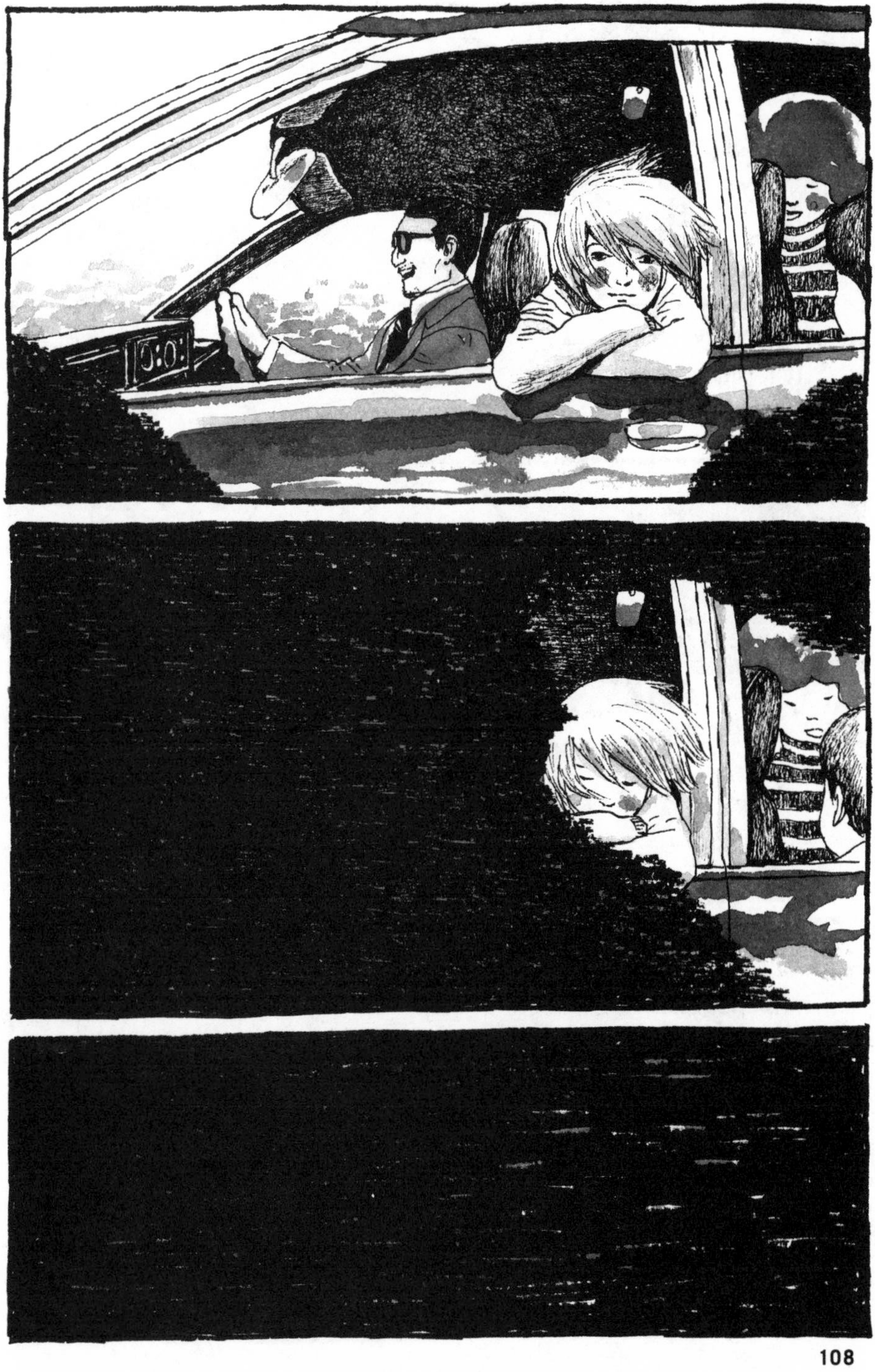

CHAPTER 10

"Humans
can fly if
they have
the guts."

"Okay,
so fly!"

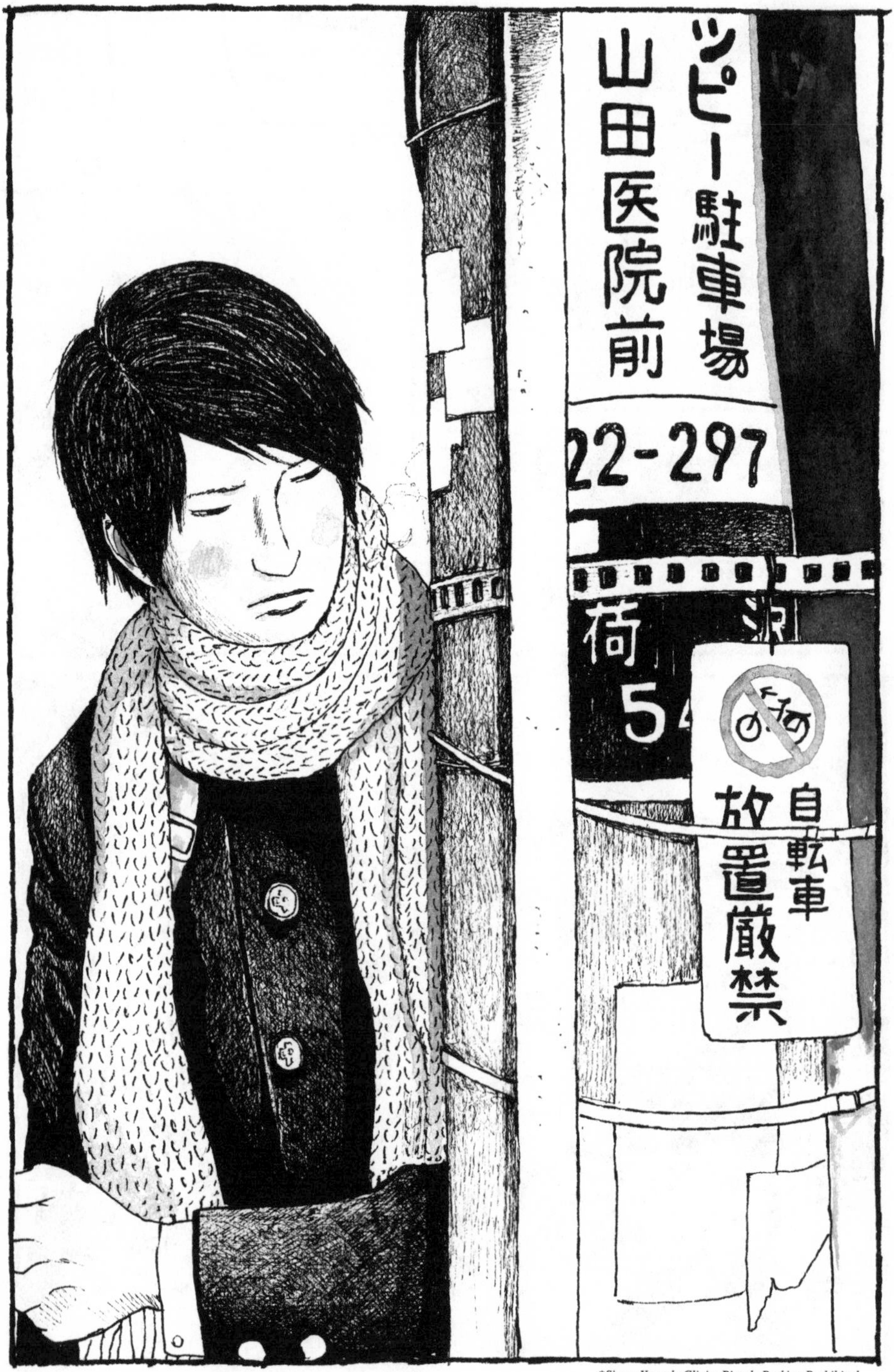
ッピー駐車場
山田医院前
22-297
荷
自転車
放置厳禁

Signs: Yamada Clinic; Bicycle Parking Prohibited

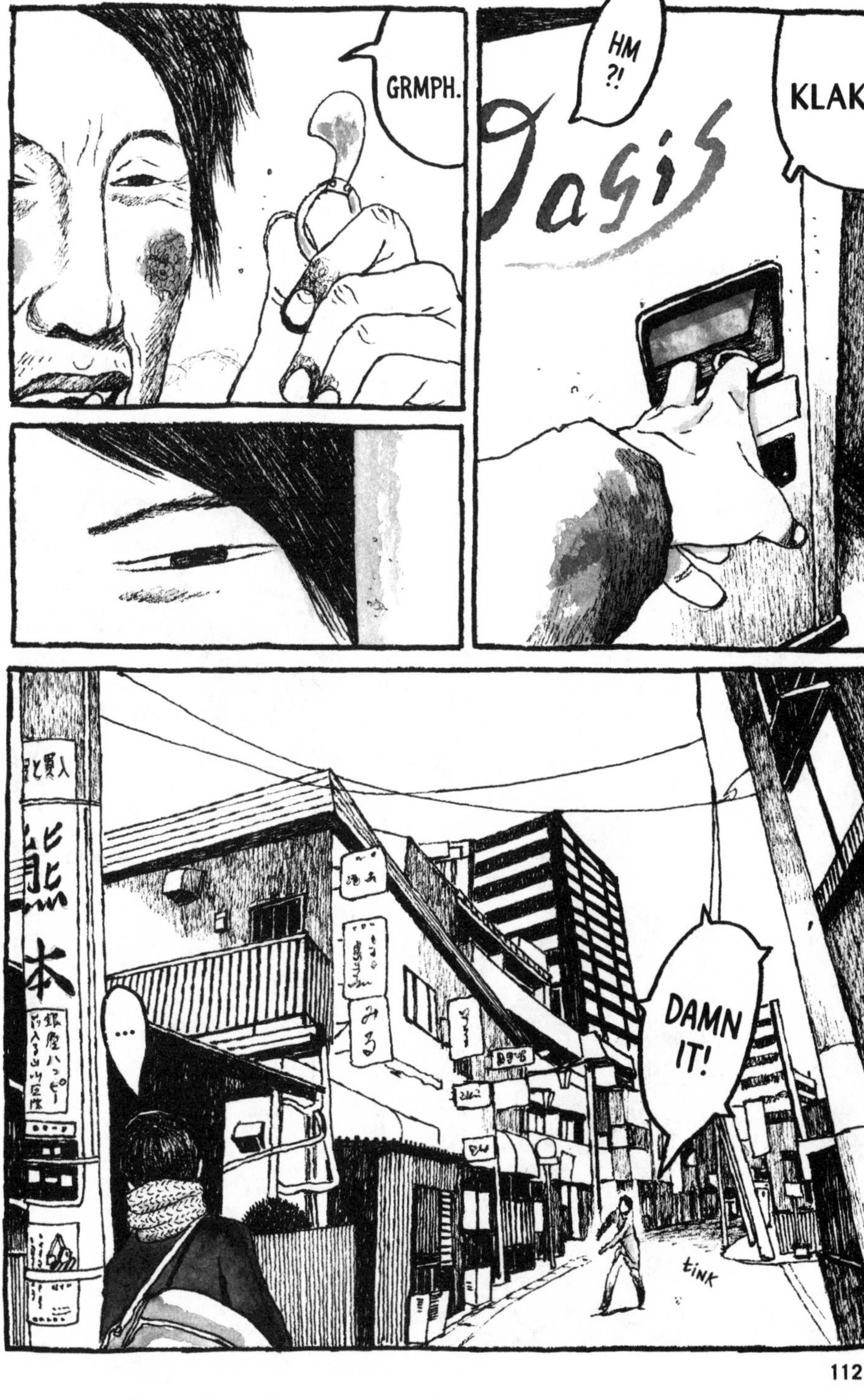
HM ?!
KLAK
Oasis
GRMPH.
DAMN IT!
...
tink

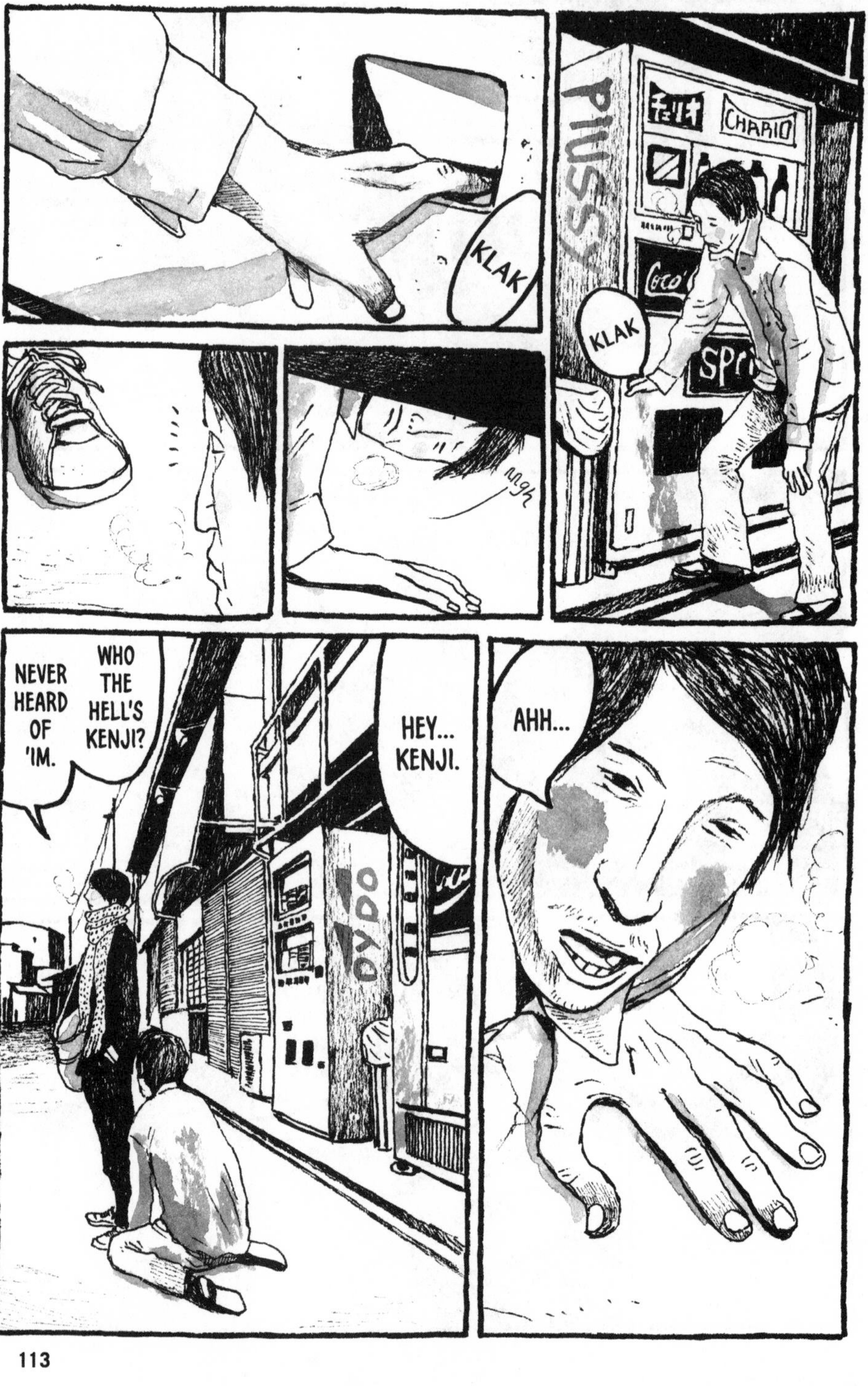
CHARIO
KLAK
KLAK
AHH...
HEY... KENJI.
WHO THE HELL'S KENJI?
NEVER HEARD OF 'IM.

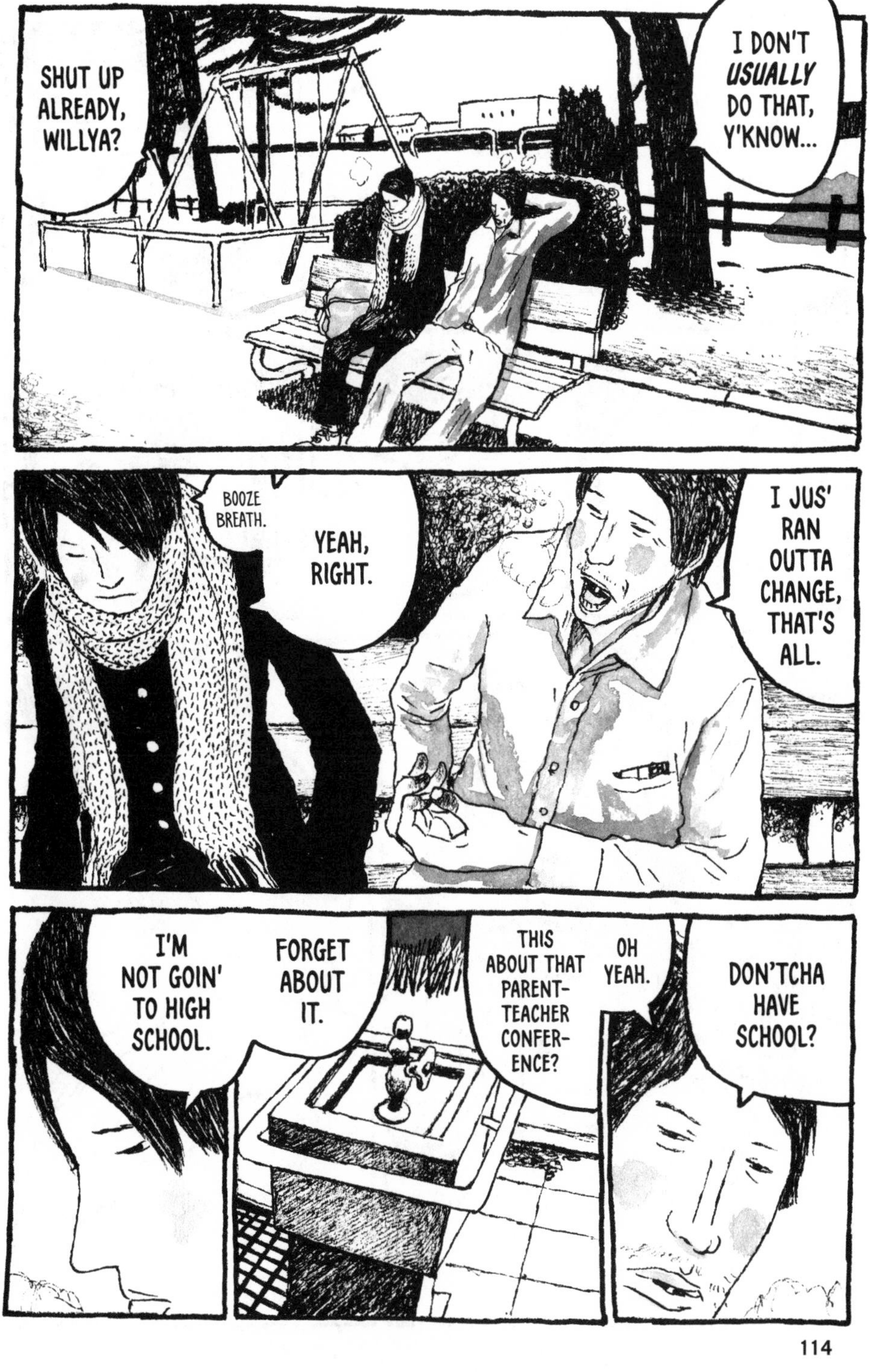
I DON'T *USUALLY* DO THAT, Y'KNOW...
SHUT UP ALREADY, WILLYA?
I JUS' RAN OUTTA CHANGE, THAT'S ALL.
YEAH, RIGHT.
BOOZE BREATH.
DON'TCHA HAVE SCHOOL?
OH YEAH.
THIS ABOUT THAT PARENT-TEACHER CONFERENCE?
FORGET ABOUT IT.
I'M NOT GOIN' TO HIGH SCHOOL.

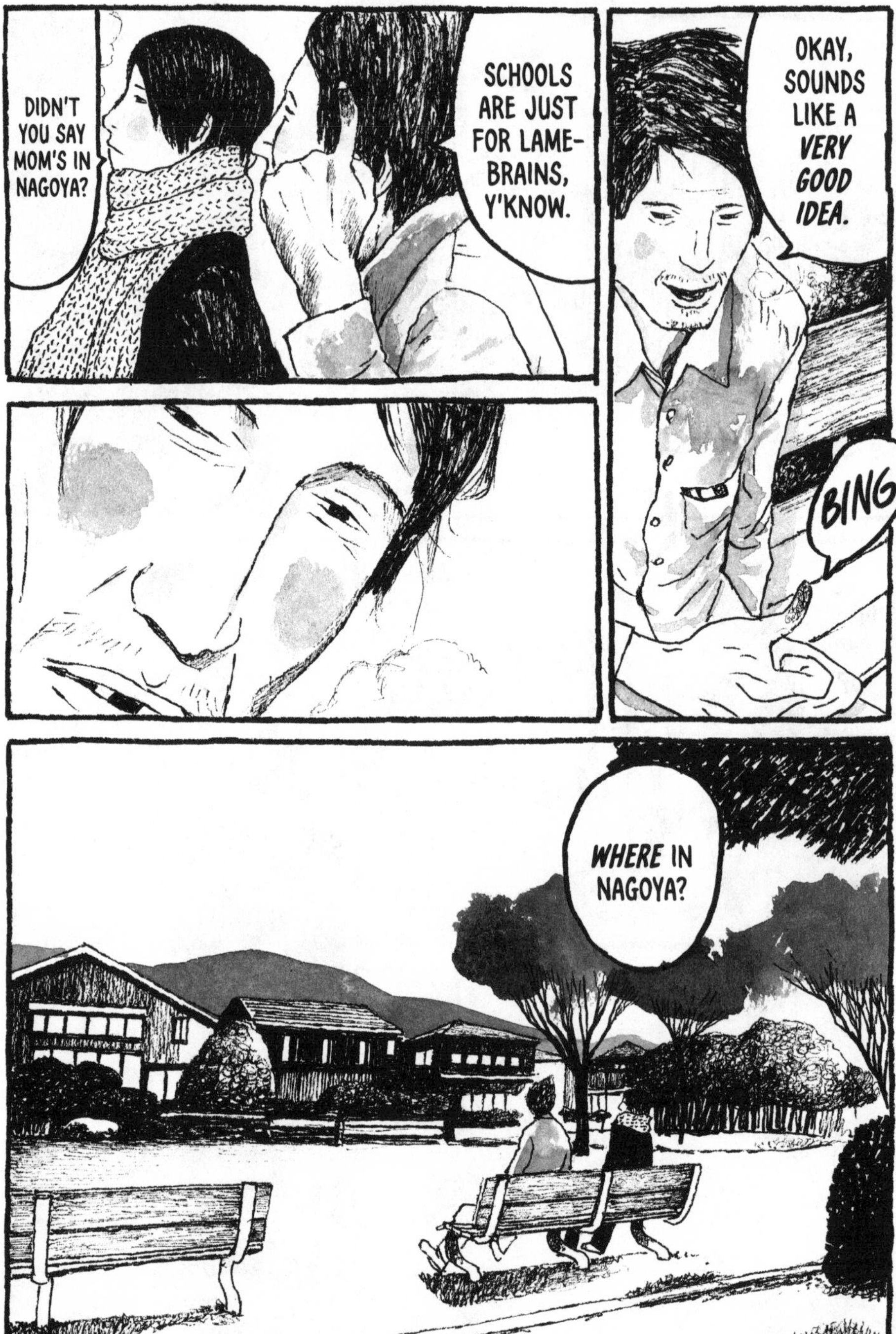
OKAY, SOUNDS LIKE A *VERY GOOD IDEA.*
BING
SCHOOLS ARE JUST FOR LAME-BRAINS, Y'KNOW.
DIDN'T YOU SAY MOM'S IN NAGOYA?
WHERE IN NAGOYA?

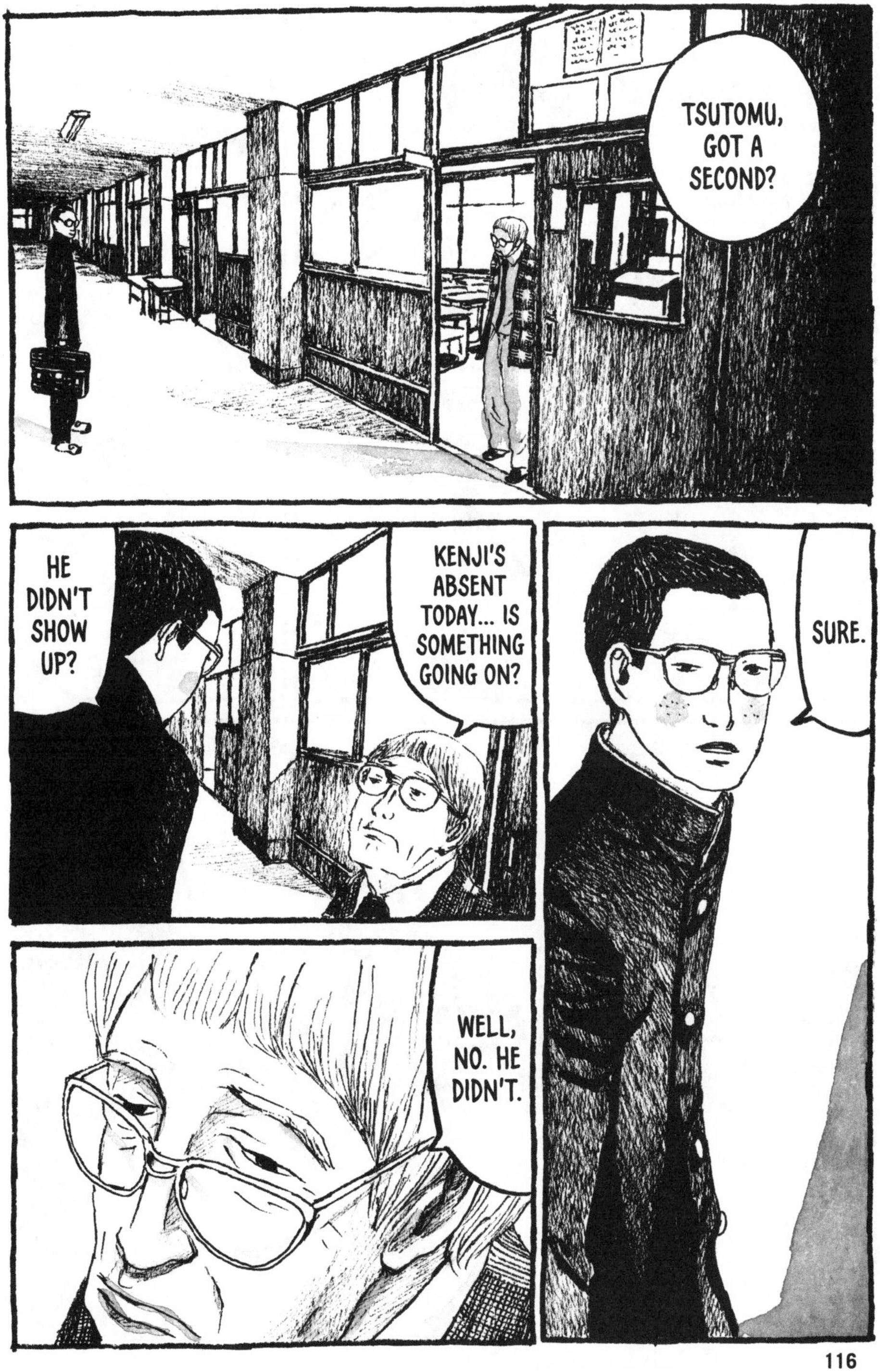
TSUTOMU, GOT A SECOND?
SURE.
KENJI'S ABSENT TODAY... IS SOMETHING GOING ON?
HE DIDN'T SHOW UP?
WELL, NO. HE DIDN'T.

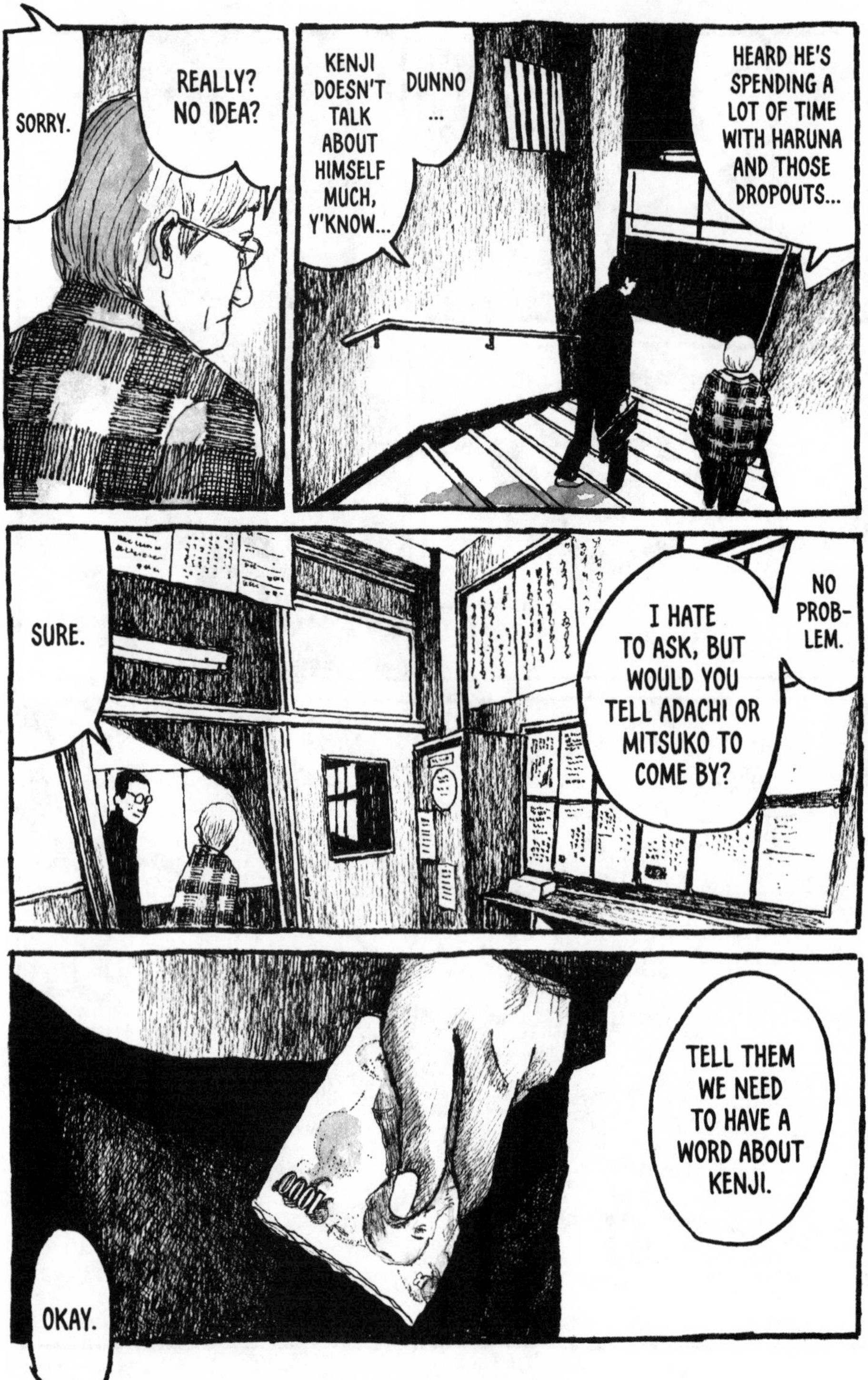
HEARD HE'S SPENDING A LOT OF TIME WITH HARUNA AND THOSE DROPOUTS...
DUNNO ...
KENJI DOESN'T TALK ABOUT HIMSELF MUCH, Y'KNOW...
REALLY? NO IDEA?
SORRY.
NO PROB-LEM.
I HATE TO ASK, BUT WOULD YOU TELL ADACHI OR MITSUKO TO COME BY?
SURE.
TELL THEM WE NEED TO HAVE A WORD ABOUT KENJI.
OKAY.

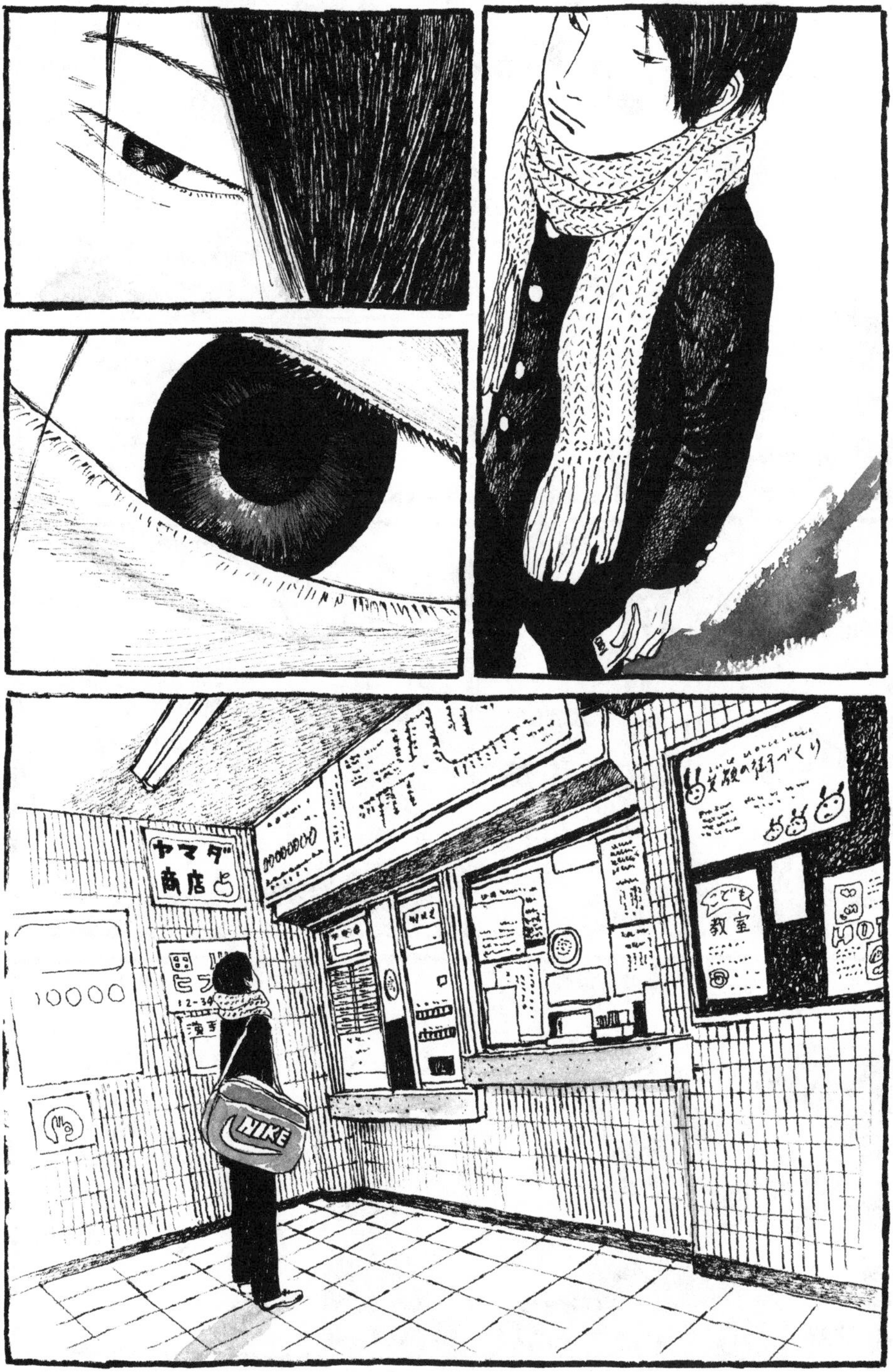
ヤマダ
商店
NIKE
こども
教室

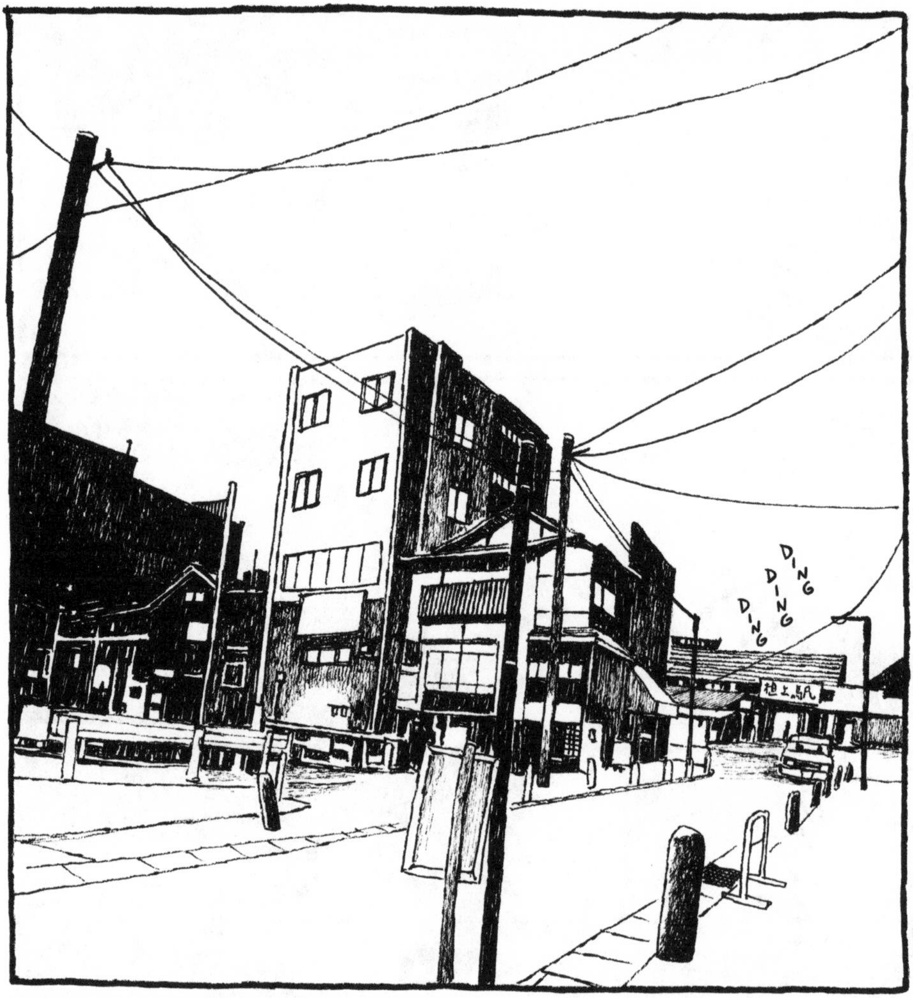
DING
DING
DING
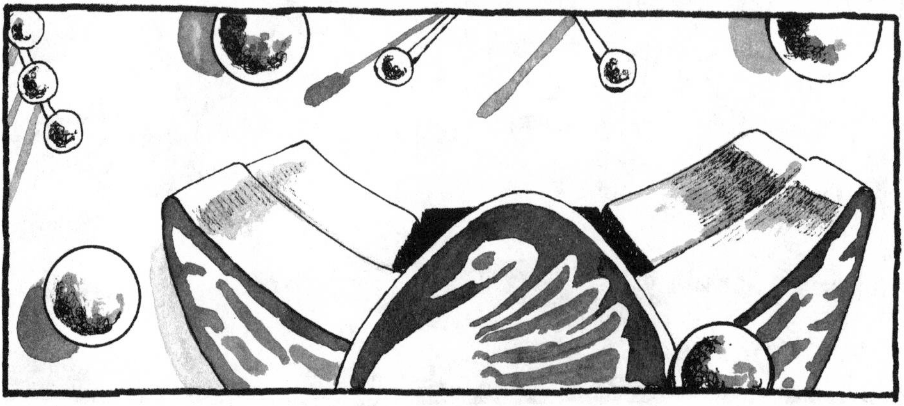

DRRM
CHING
DRMM
CHING
DRRM
CHING

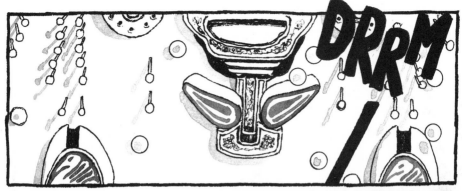

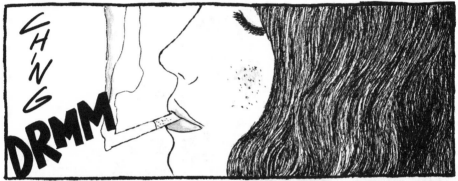

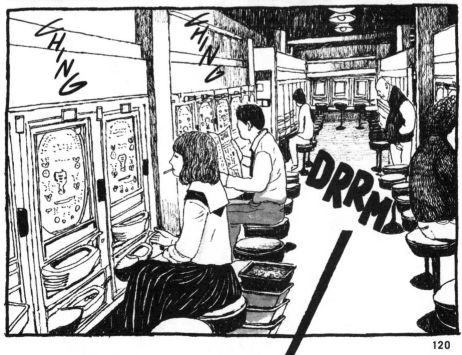

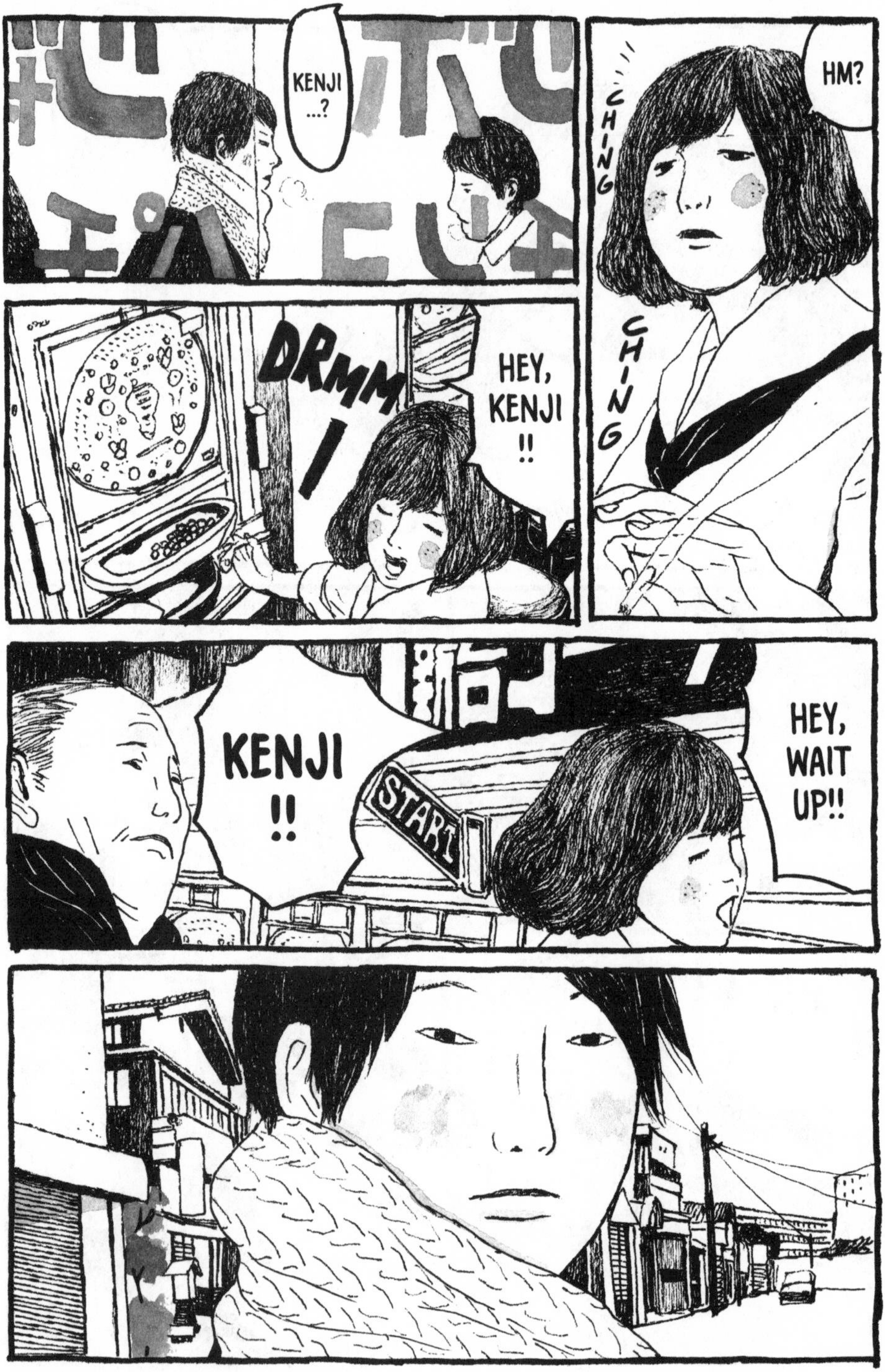
HM?
CHING
CHING
KENJI ...?
HEY, KENJI !!
DRMM
HEY, WAIT UP!!
KENJI !!
START

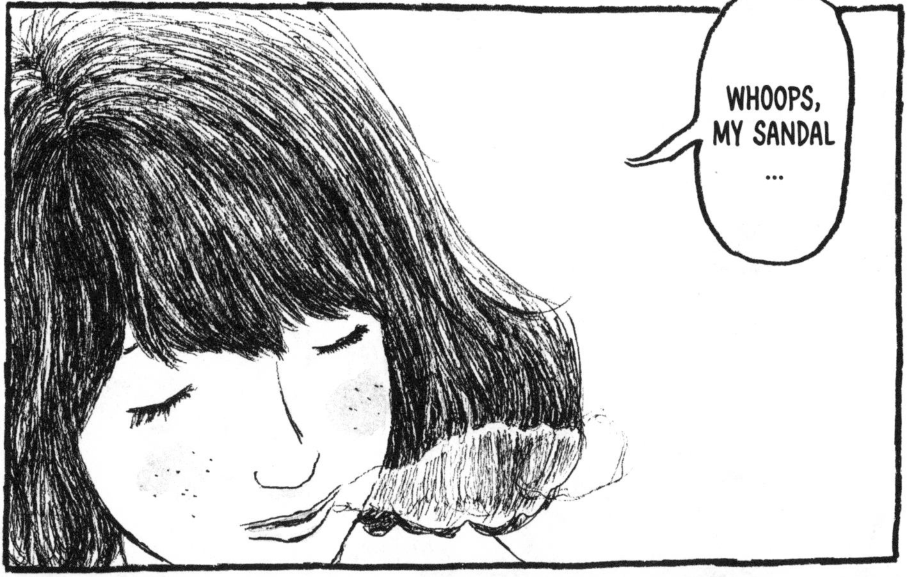
WHOOPS, MY SANDAL ...

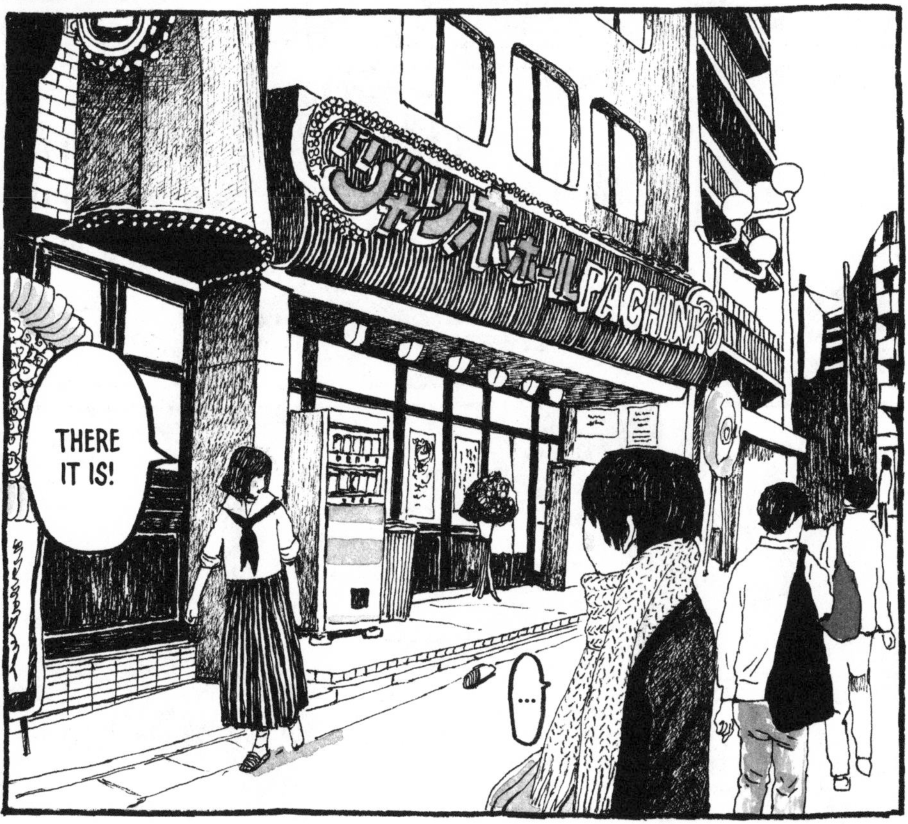
PACHINKO
THERE IT IS!
...

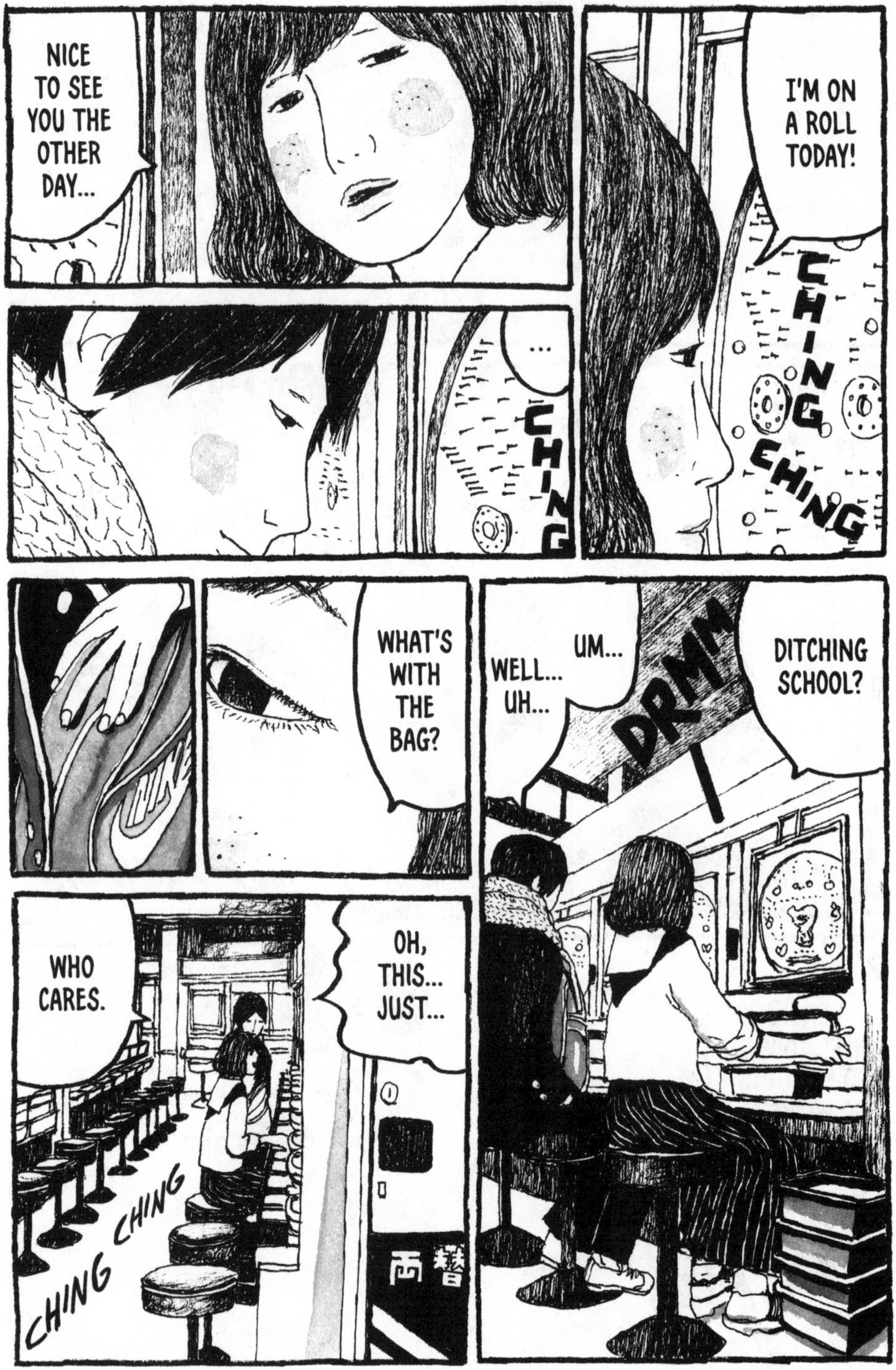

I'M ON A ROLL TODAY!
CHING
CHING
NICE TO SEE YOU THE OTHER DAY...
...
CHING
DITCHING SCHOOL?
UM...
WELL... UH...
DRMM
WHAT'S WITH THE BAG?
OH, THIS... JUST...
WHO CARES.
両替
CHING CHING

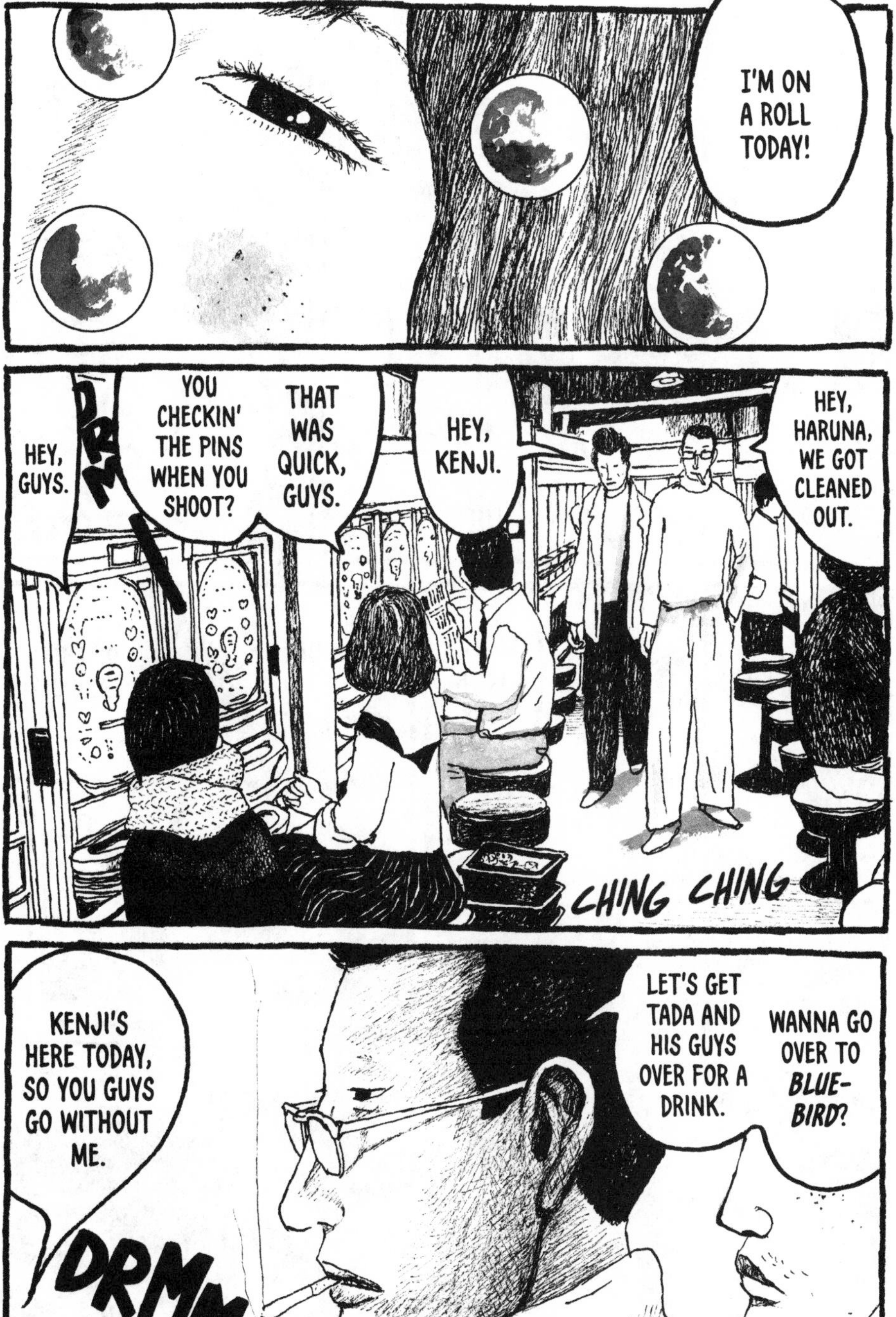
I'M ON A ROLL TODAY!
HEY, HARUNA, WE GOT CLEANED OUT.
HEY, KENJI.
THAT WAS QUICK, GUYS.
YOU CHECKIN' THE PINS WHEN YOU SHOOT?
DRM
HEY, GUYS.
CHING CHING
WANNA GO OVER TO *BLUE-BIRD*?
LET'S GET TADA AND HIS GUYS OVER FOR A DRINK.
KENJI'S HERE TODAY, SO YOU GUYS GO WITHOUT ME.
DRMM

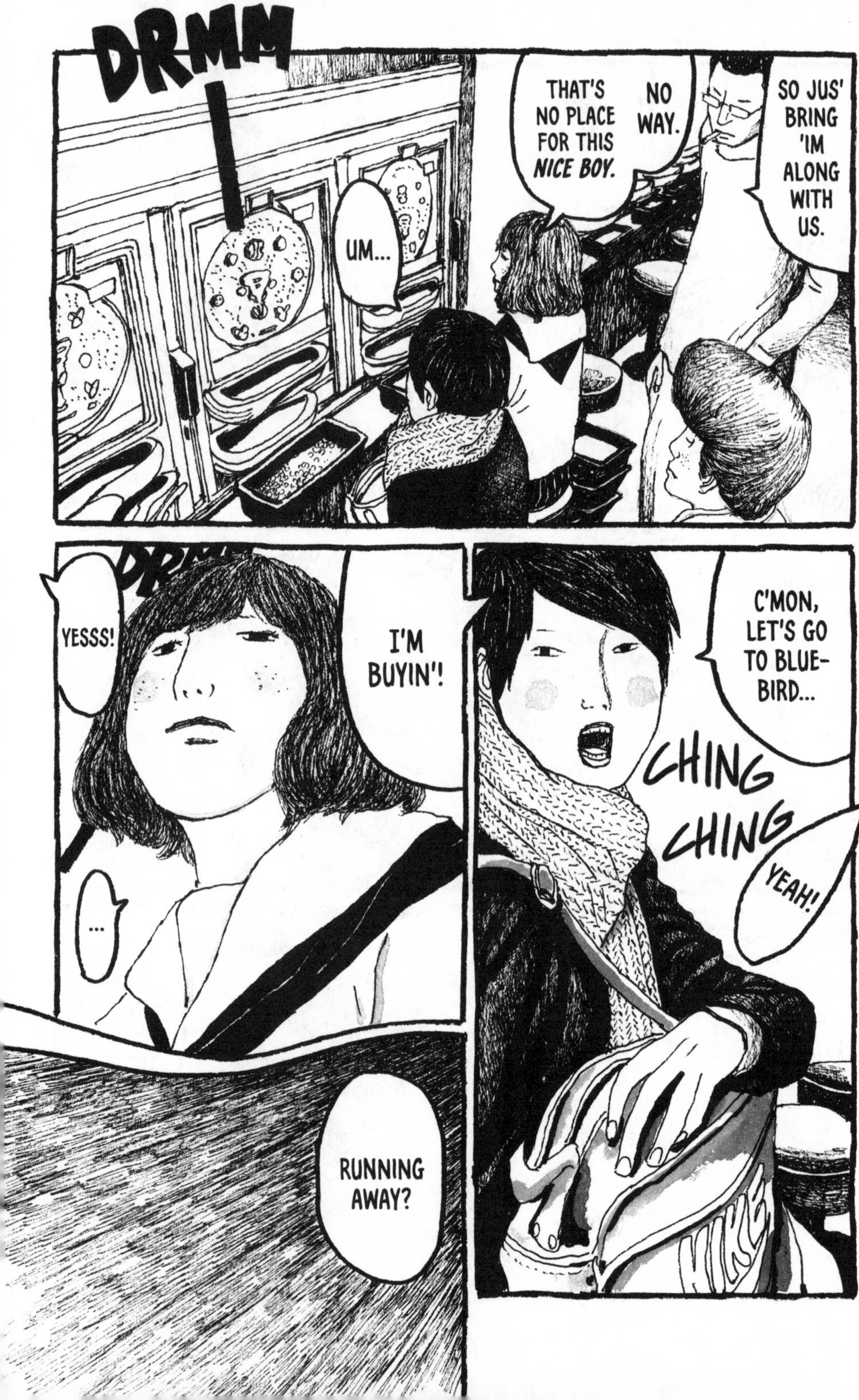
SO JUS' BRING 'IM ALONG WITH US.
NO WAY.
THAT'S NO PLACE FOR THIS *NICE BOY.*
DRMM
UM...
C'MON, LET'S GO TO BLUE-BIRD...
CHING CHING
YEAH!
I'M BUYIN'!
YESSS!
...
RUNNING AWAY?

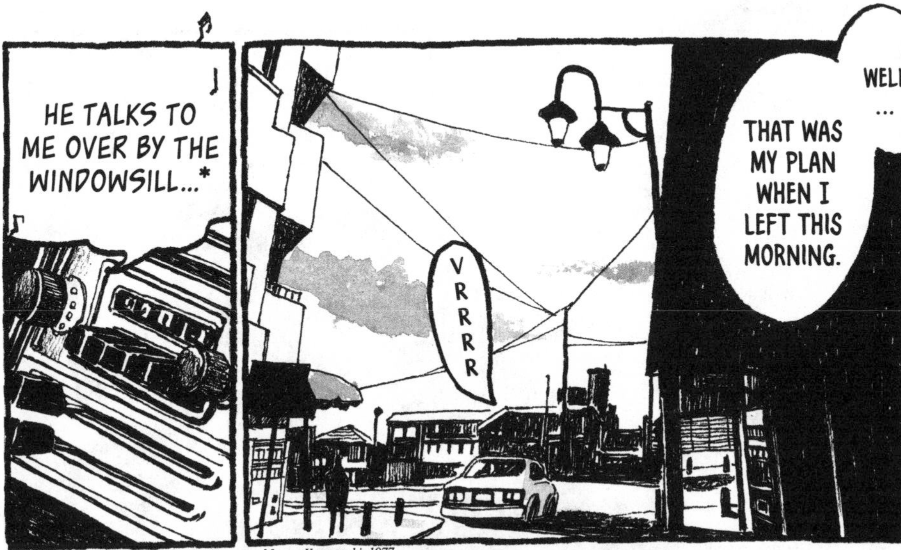
WELL ...
THAT WAS MY PLAN WHEN I LEFT THIS MORNING.
VRRRR
HE TALKS TO ME OVER BY THE WINDOWSILL...*

*"*Imitation Gold*," a hit single by singer-actress Momoe Yamaguchi, 1977

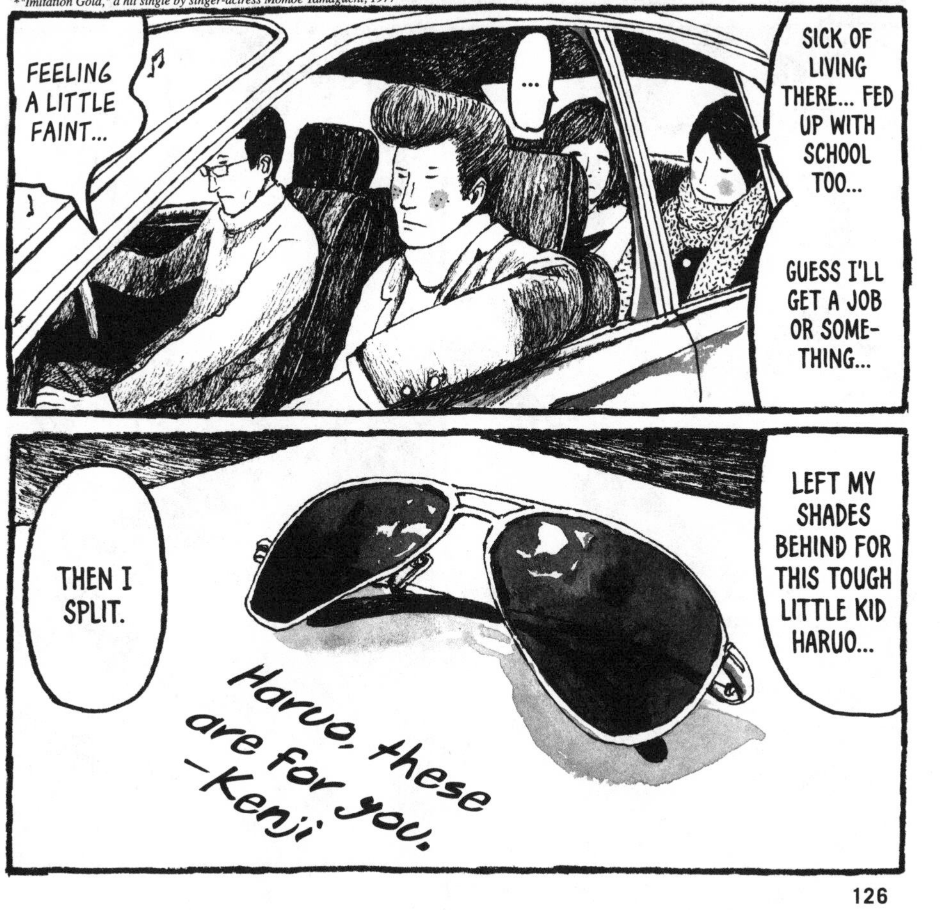
SICK OF LIVING THERE... FED UP WITH SCHOOL TOO...
GUESS I'LL GET A JOB OR SOME-THING...
...
FEELING A LITTLE FAINT...
LEFT MY SHADES BEHIND FOR THIS TOUGH LITTLE KID HARUO...
Haruo, these are for you. -Kenji
THEN I SPLIT.

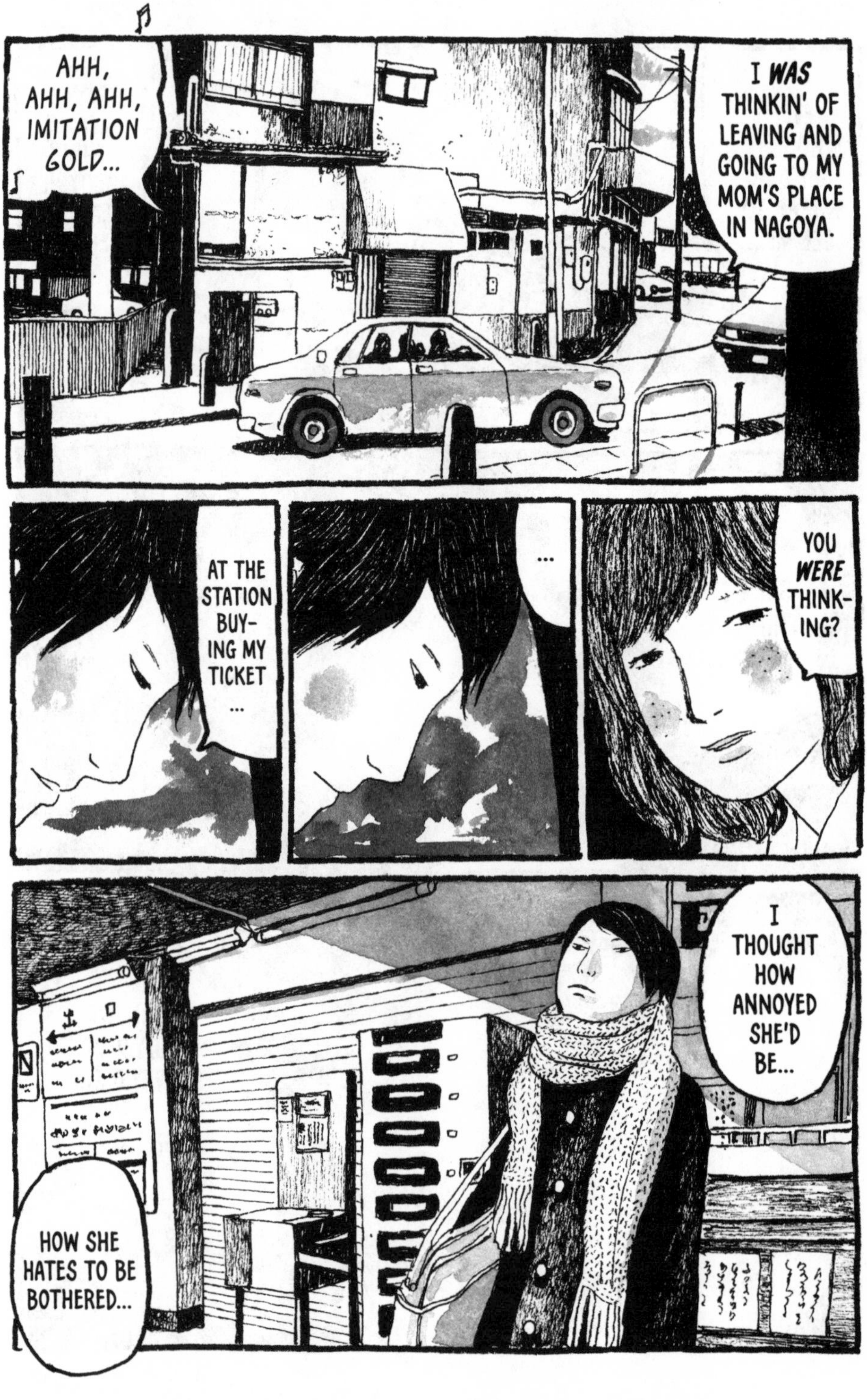
I WAS THINKIN' OF LEAVING AND GOING TO MY MOM'S PLACE IN NAGOYA.
AHH, AHH, AHH, IMITATION GOLD...
YOU WERE THINK-ING?
...
AT THE STATION BUY-ING MY TICKET ...
I THOUGHT HOW ANNOYED SHE'D BE...
HOW SHE HATES TO BE BOTHERED...

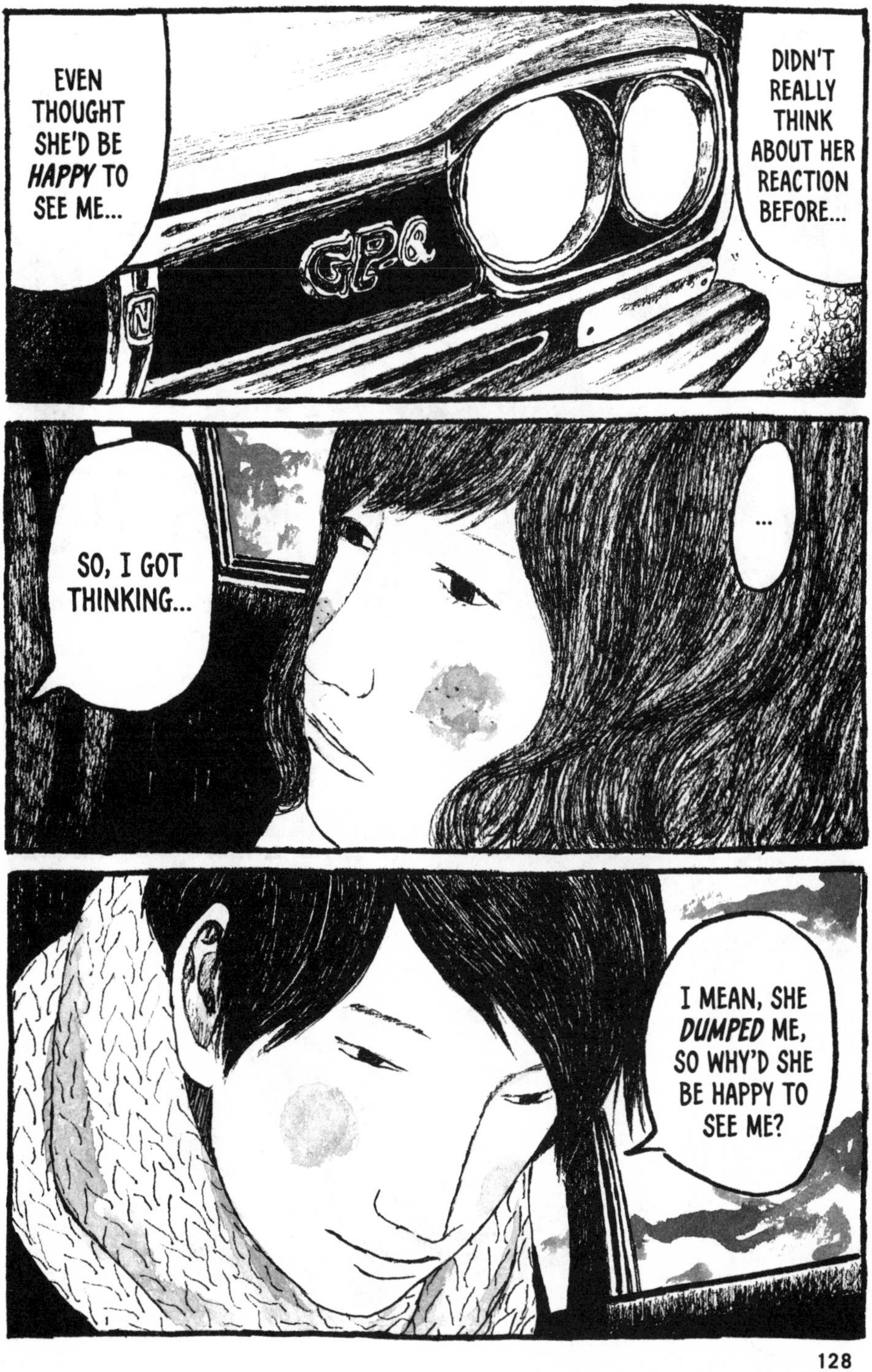
DIDN'T REALLY THINK ABOUT HER REACTION BEFORE...
EVEN THOUGHT SHE'D BE *HAPPY* TO SEE ME...
...
SO, I GOT THINKING...
I MEAN, SHE *DUMPED* ME, SO WHY'D SHE BE HAPPY TO SEE ME?

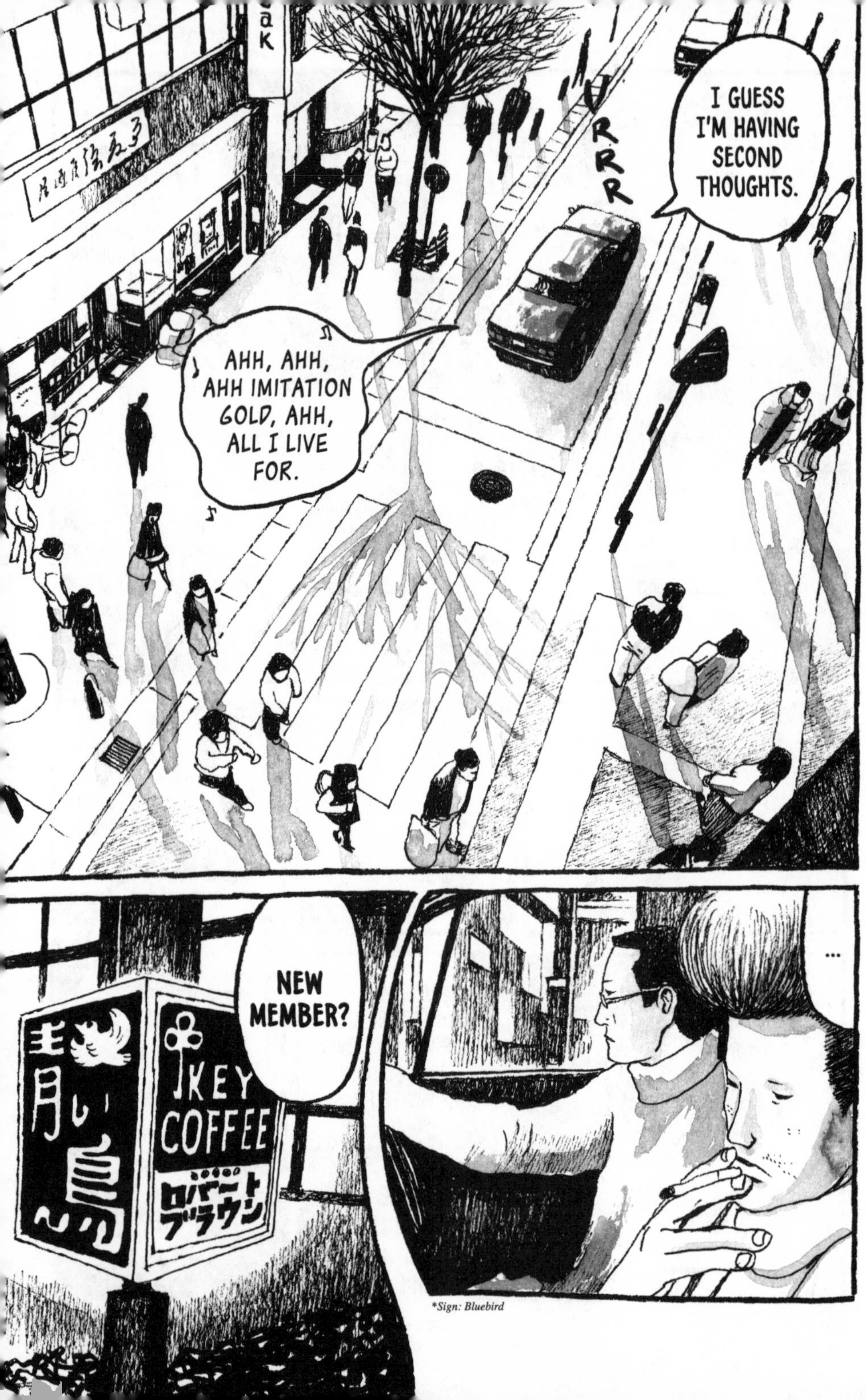
I GUESS I'M HAVING SECOND THOUGHTS.
RRR
AHH, AHH, AHH IMITATION GOLD, AHH, ALL I LIVE FOR.
...
NEW MEMBER?
青い鳥
KEY COFFEE
ロバートブラウン

*Sign: Bluebird

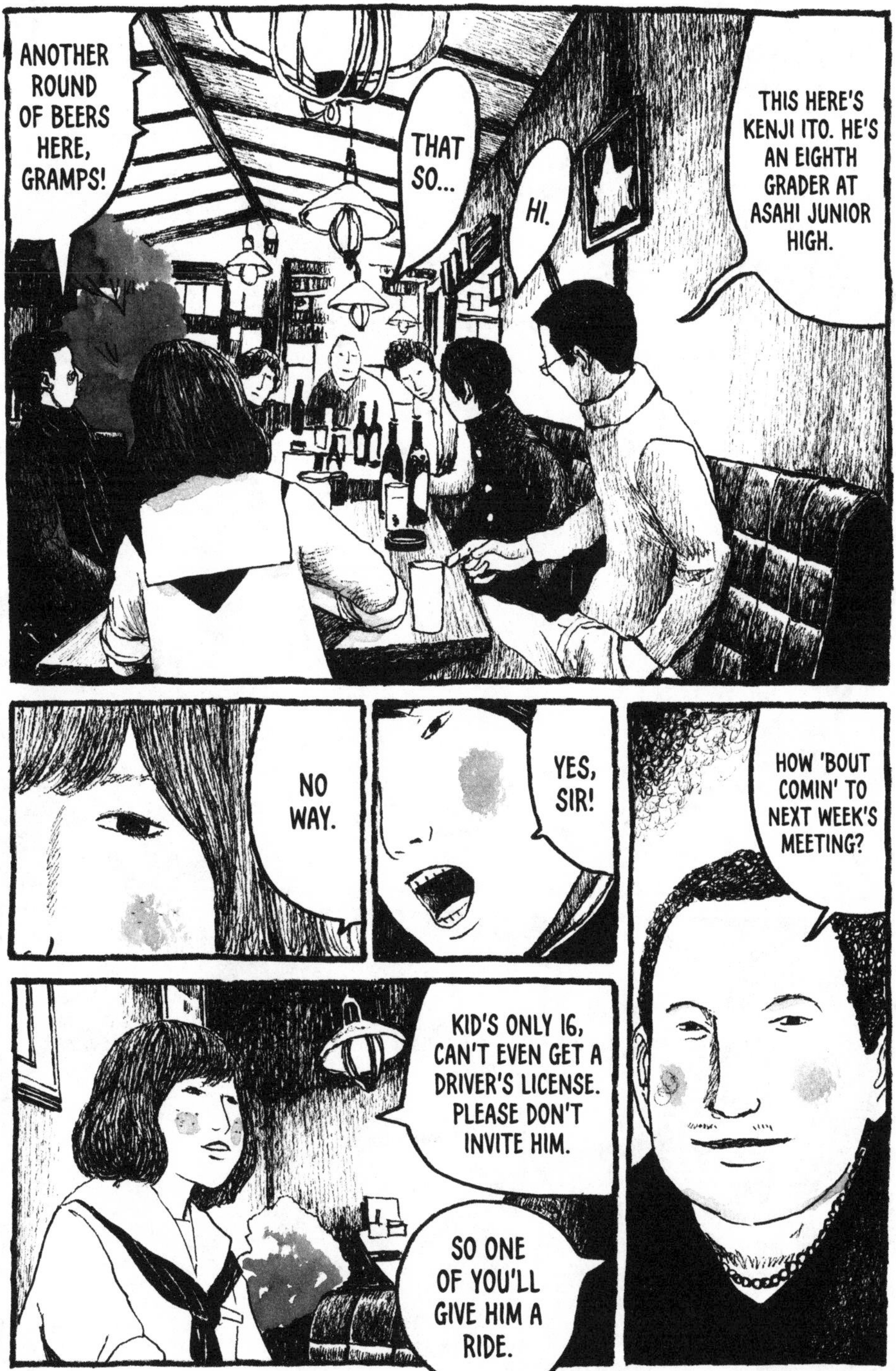
THIS HERE'S KENJI ITO. HE'S AN EIGHTH GRADER AT ASAHI JUNIOR HIGH.
HI.
THAT SO...
ANOTHER ROUND OF BEERS HERE, GRAMPS!
HOW 'BOUT COMIN' TO NEXT WEEK'S MEETING?
YES, SIR!
NO WAY.
KID'S ONLY 16, CAN'T EVEN GET A DRIVER'S LICENSE. PLEASE DON'T INVITE HIM.
SO ONE OF YOU'LL GIVE HIM A RIDE.

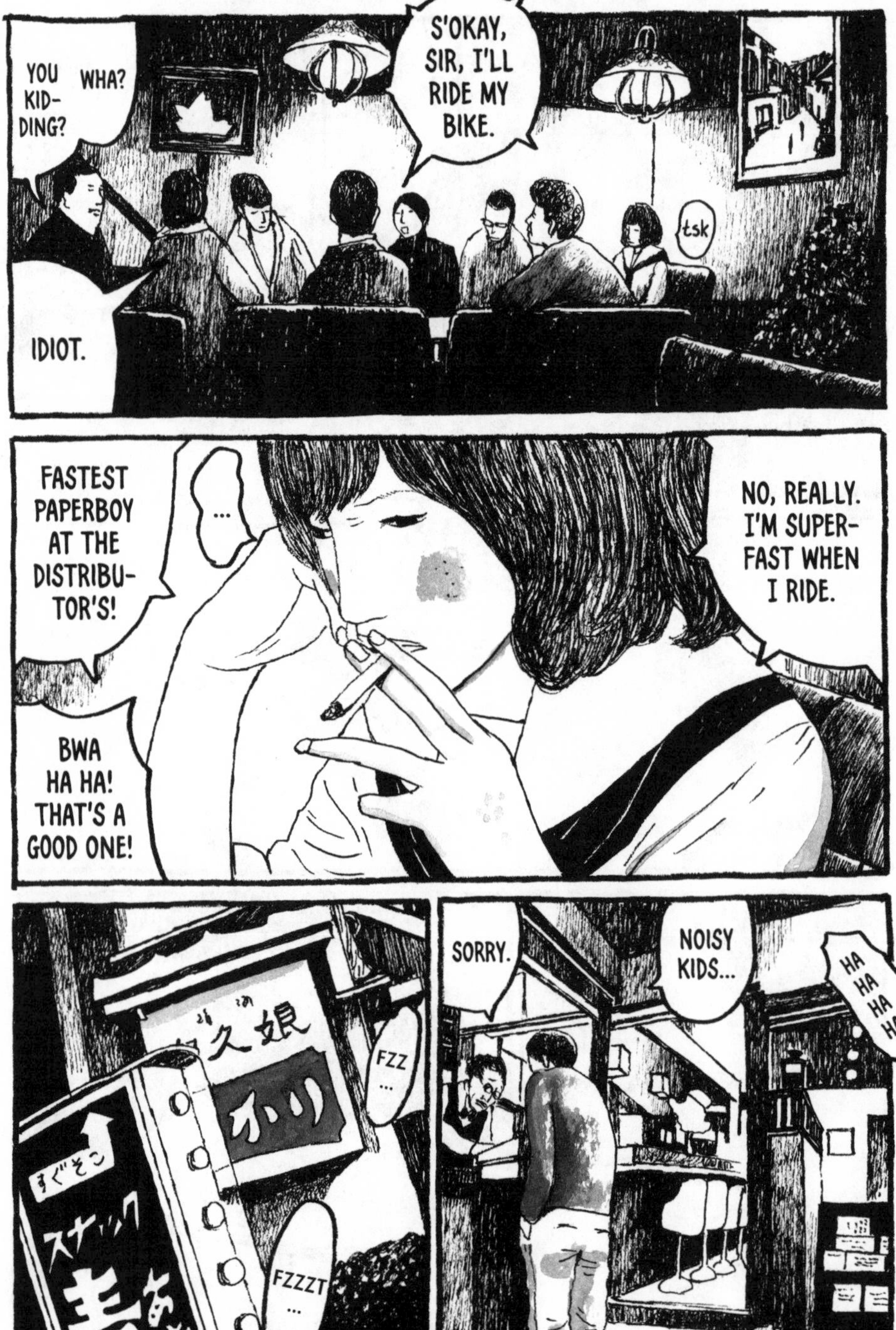
S'OKAY, SIR, I'LL RIDE MY BIKE.
WHA?
YOU KIDDING?
tsk
IDIOT.
NO, REALLY. I'M SUPER-FAST WHEN I RIDE.
...
FASTEST PAPERBOY AT THE DISTRIBUTOR'S!
BWA HA HA! THAT'S A GOOD ONE!
HA HA HA HA HA
NOISY KIDS...
SORRY.
FZZ...
FZZZT...
すぐそこ
スナック

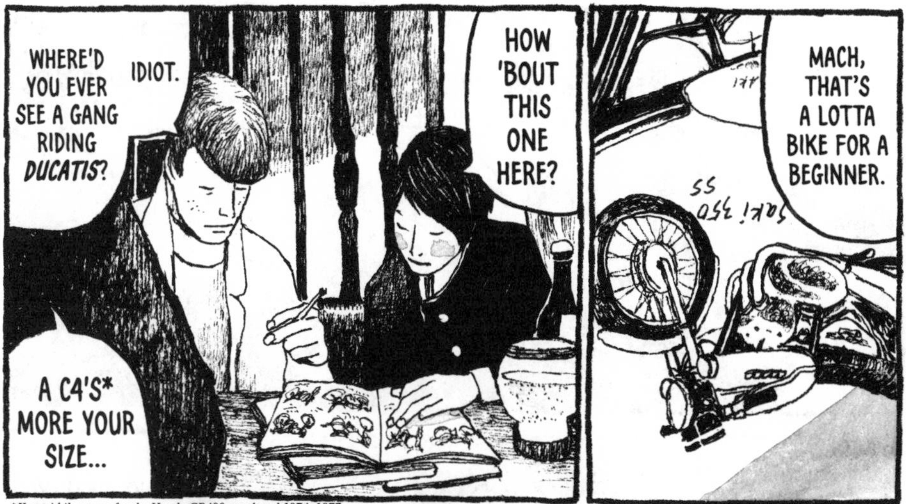
MACH, THAT'S A LOTTA BIKE FOR A BEGINNER.
HOW 'BOUT THIS ONE HERE?
IDIOT.
WHERE'D YOU EVER SEE A GANG RIDING *DUCATIS*?
A C4'S* MORE YOUR SIZE...

**Kansai biker term for the Honda CB400, produced 1974–1977*

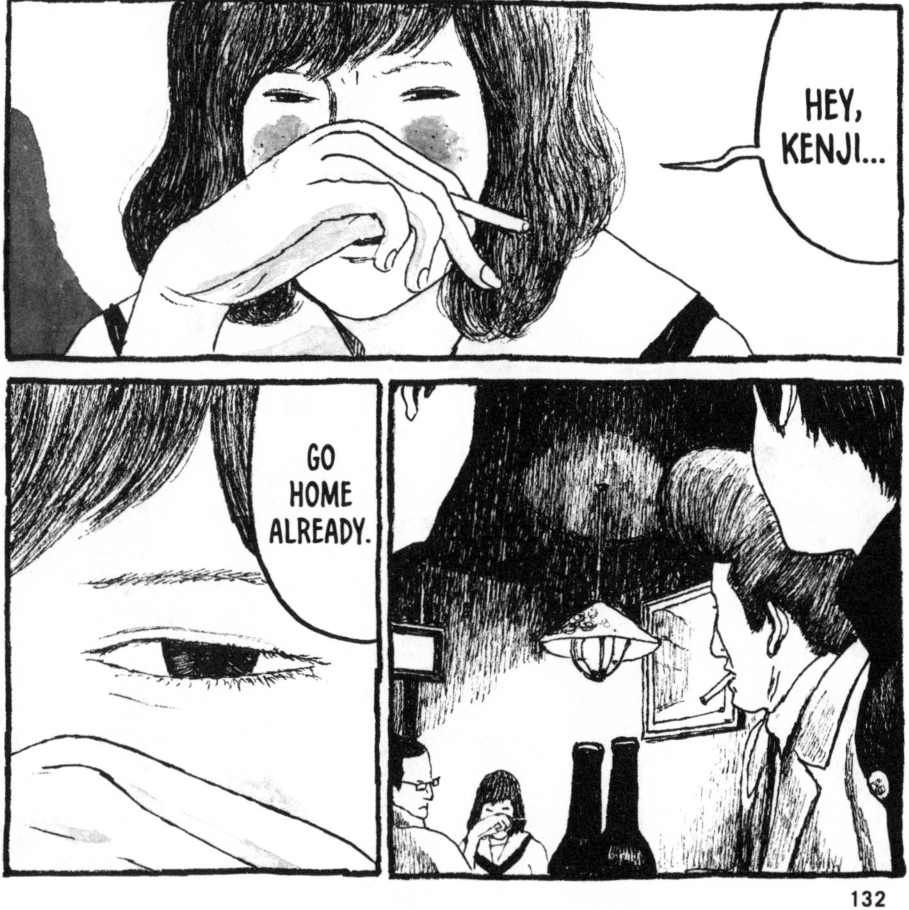
HEY, KENJI...
GO HOME ALREADY.

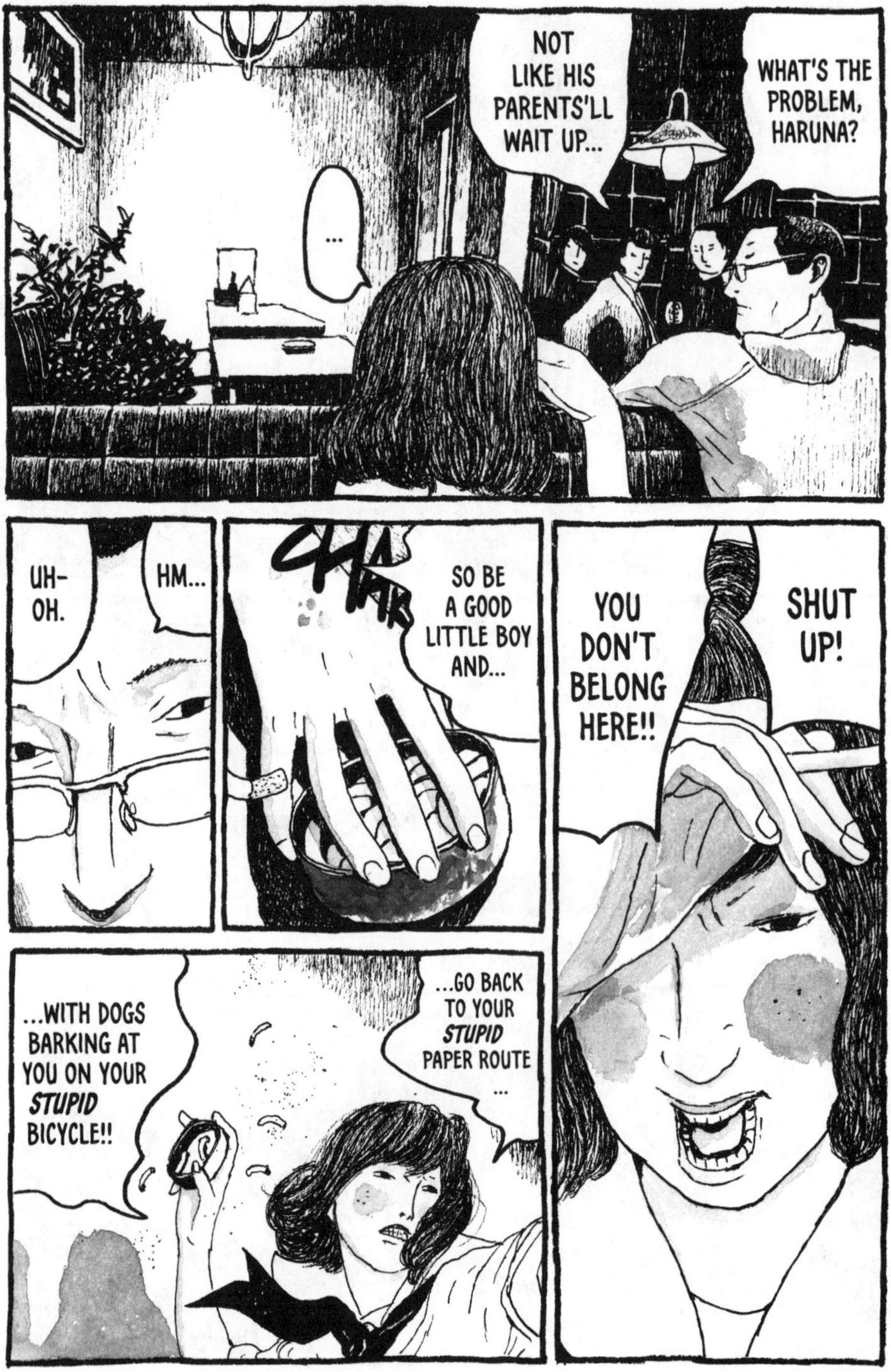
WHAT'S THE PROBLEM, HARUNA?
NOT LIKE HIS PARENTS'LL WAIT UP...
...
SHUT UP!
YOU DON'T BELONG HERE!!
SO BE A GOOD LITTLE BOY AND...
HM...
UH-OH.
...GO BACK TO YOUR *STUPID* PAPER ROUTE ...
...WITH DOGS BARKING AT YOU ON YOUR *STUPID* BICYCLE!!

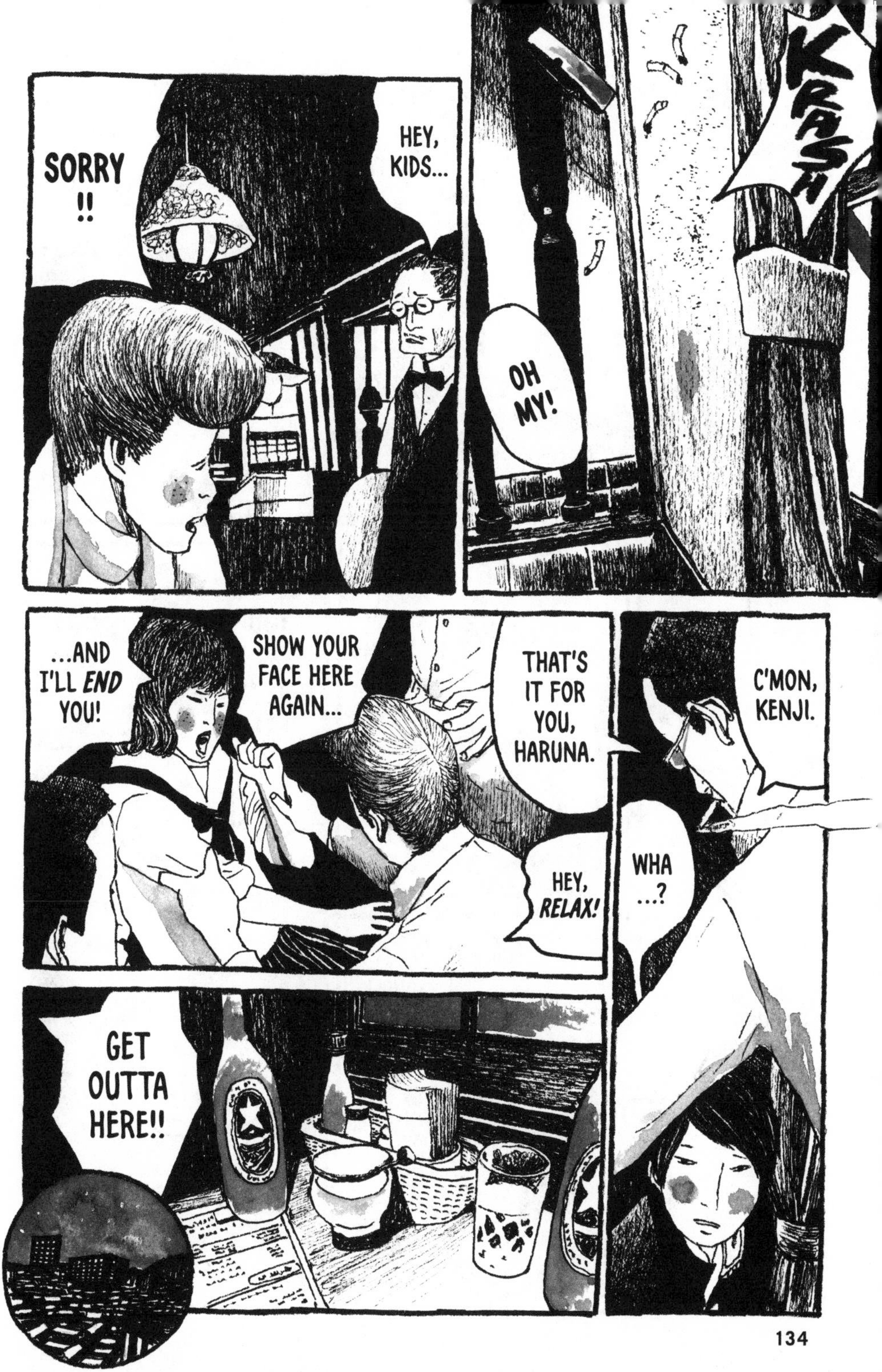
KRASH
OH MY!
HEY, KIDS...
SORRY !!
C'MON, KENJI.
WHA ...?
THAT'S IT FOR YOU, HARUNA.
SHOW YOUR FACE HERE AGAIN...
...AND I'LL *END* YOU!
HEY, *RELAX!*
GET OUTTA HERE!!

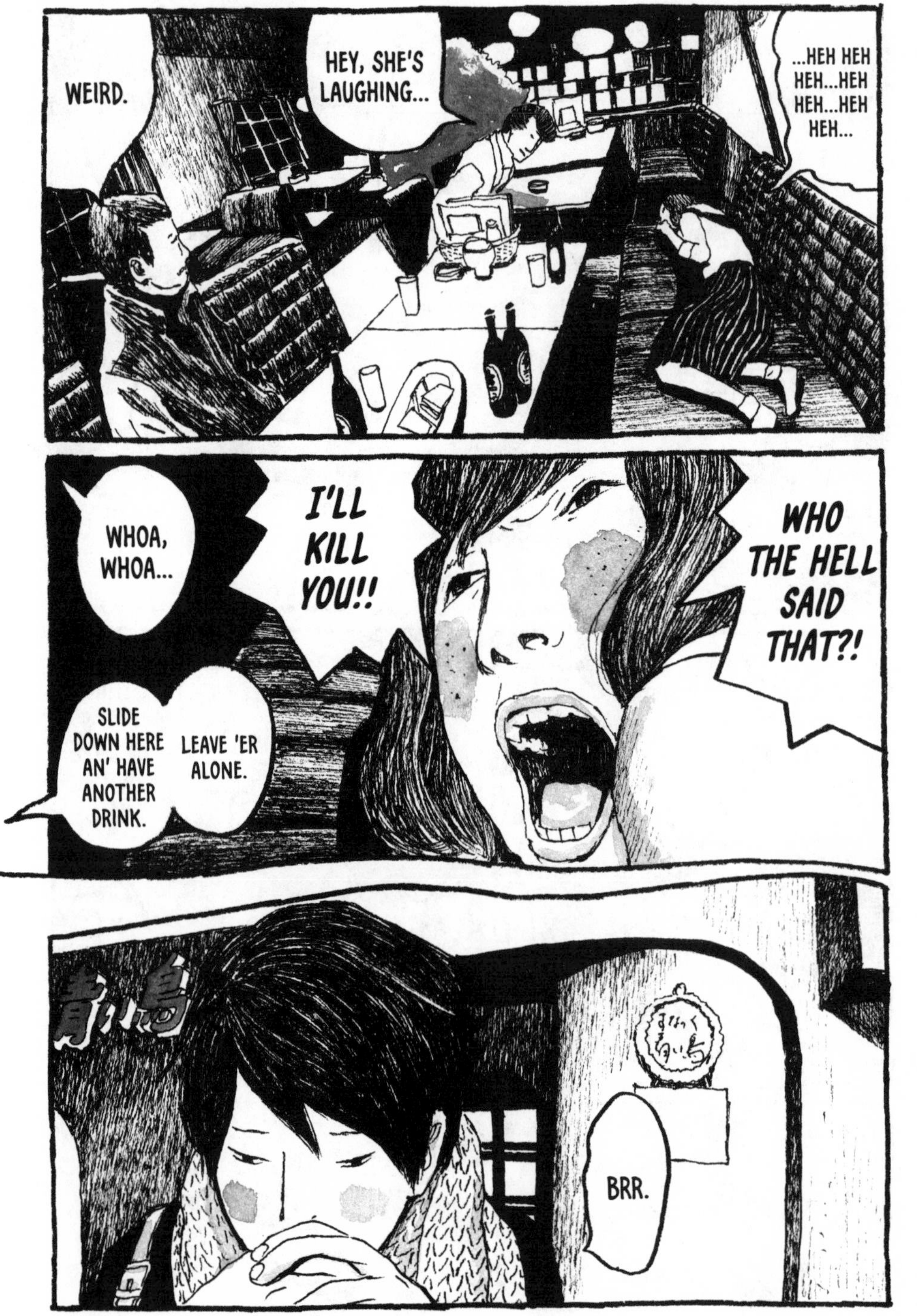
...HEH HEH HEH...HEH HEH...HEH HEH...
HEY, SHE'S LAUGHING...
WEIRD.
WHO THE HELL SAID THAT?!
I'LL KILL YOU!!
WHOA, WHOA...
LEAVE 'ER ALONE.
SLIDE DOWN HERE AN' HAVE ANOTHER DRINK.
BRR.
青い鳥

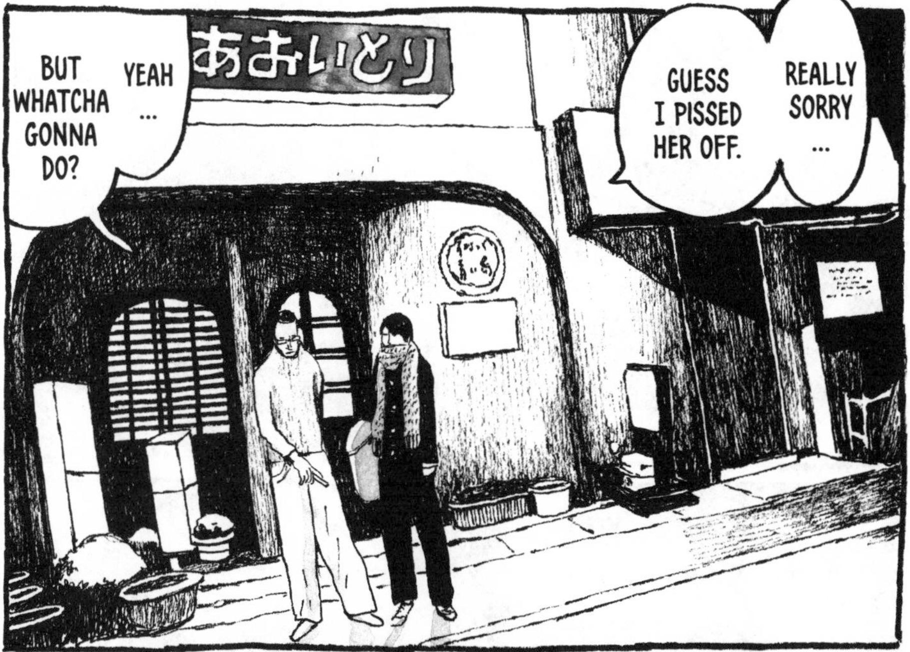
あおいとり
REALLY SORRY ...
GUESS I PISSED HER OFF.
YEAH ...
BUT WHATCHA GONNA DO?

Sign: Bluebird

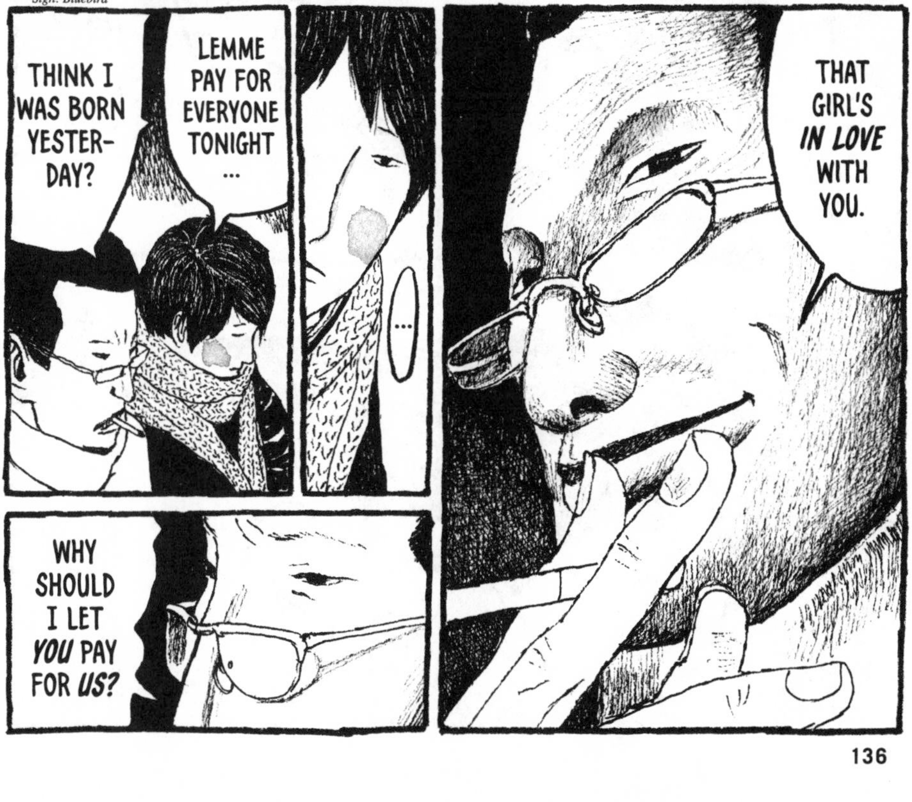
THAT GIRL'S *IN LOVE* WITH YOU.
...
LEMME PAY FOR EVERYONE TONIGHT ...
THINK I WAS BORN YESTER-DAY?
WHY SHOULD I LET *YOU* PAY FOR *US?*

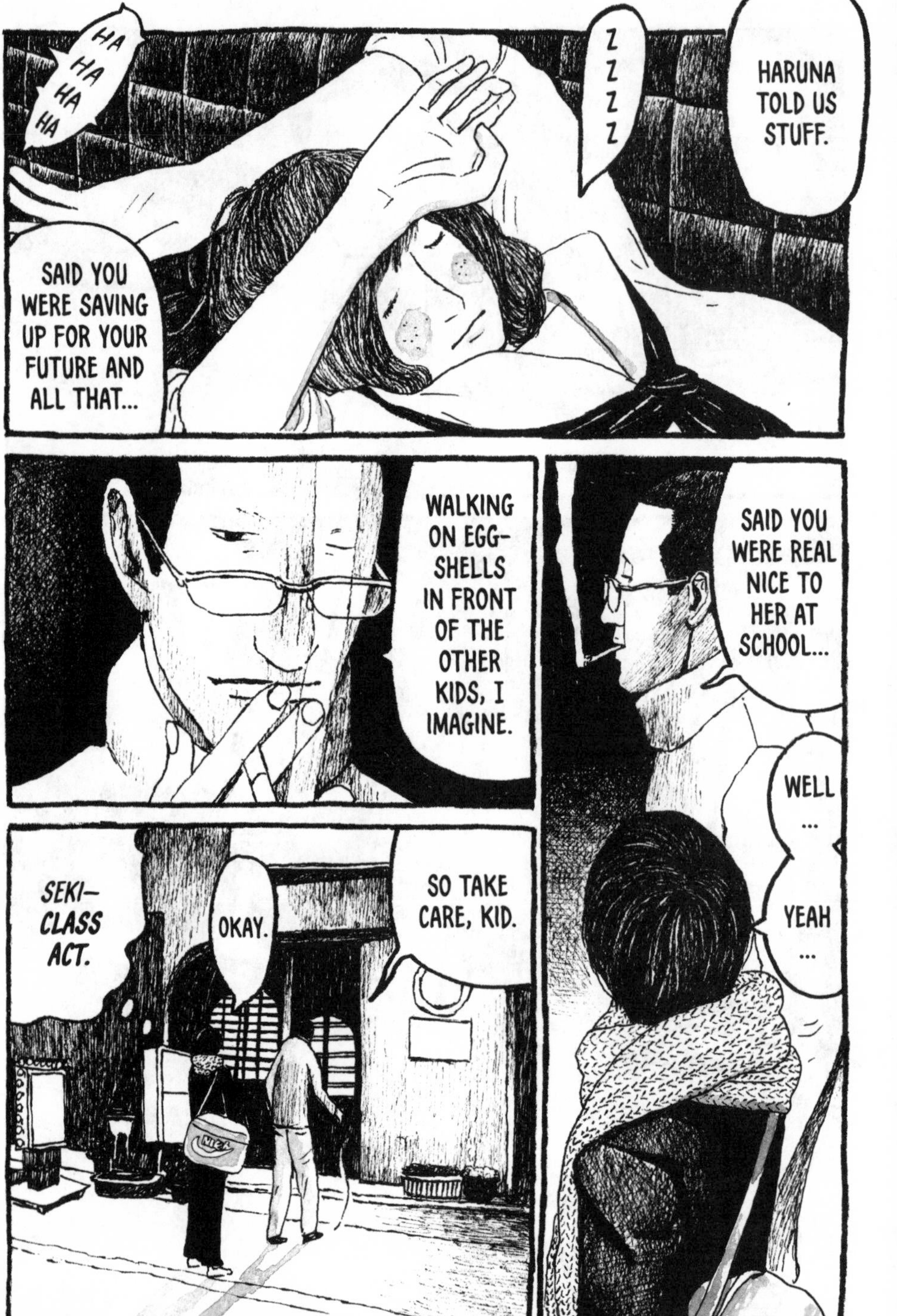
HARUNA TOLD US STUFF.
Z Z Z
HA HA HA HA
SAID YOU WERE SAVING UP FOR YOUR FUTURE AND ALL THAT...
SAID YOU WERE REAL NICE TO HER AT SCHOOL...
WELL ...
YEAH ...
WALKING ON EGG-SHELLS IN FRONT OF THE OTHER KIDS, I IMAGINE.
SO TAKE CARE, KID.
OKAY.
SEKI— CLASS ACT.

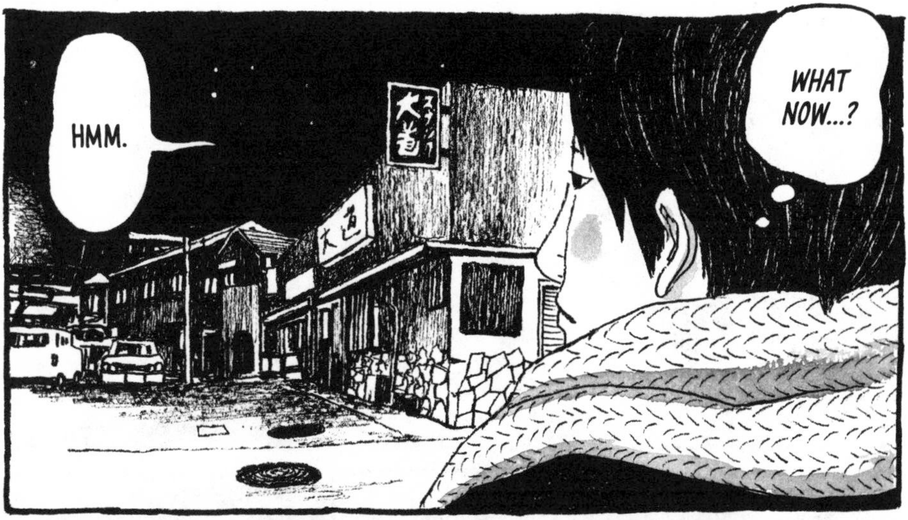
WHAT NOW...?
HMM.
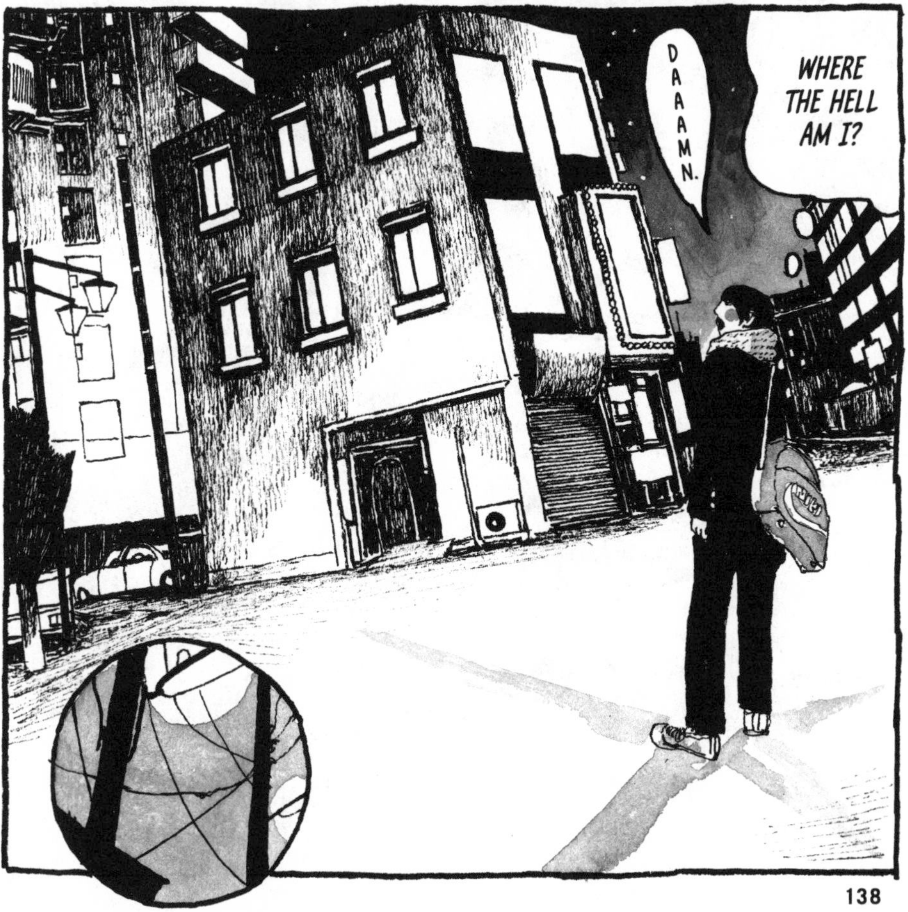
WHERE THE HELL AM I?
DAAAMN.

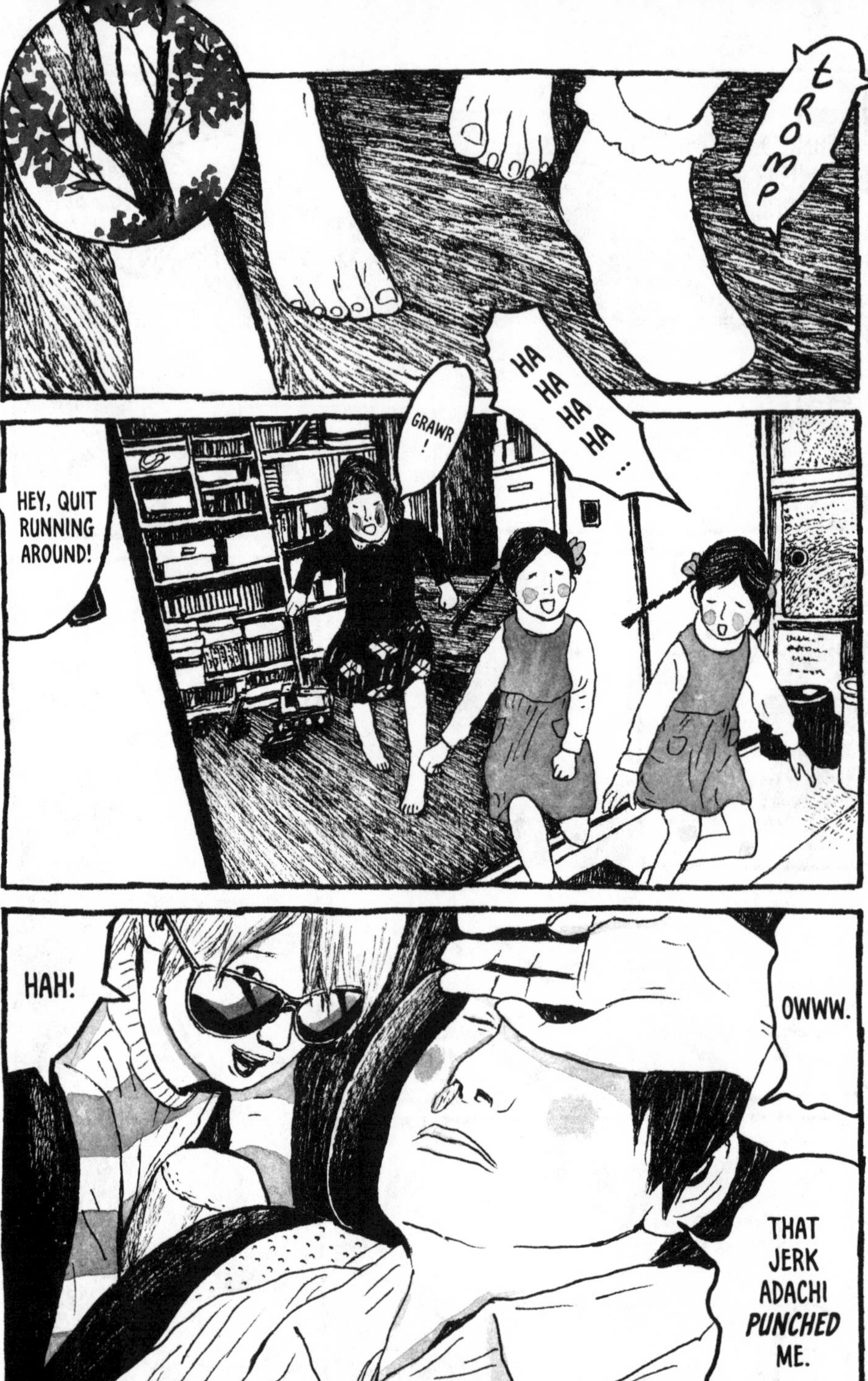
tromp
HA HA HA HA ...
GRAWR!
HEY, QUIT RUNNING AROUND!
OWWW.
HAH!
THAT JERK ADACHI *PUNCHED* ME.

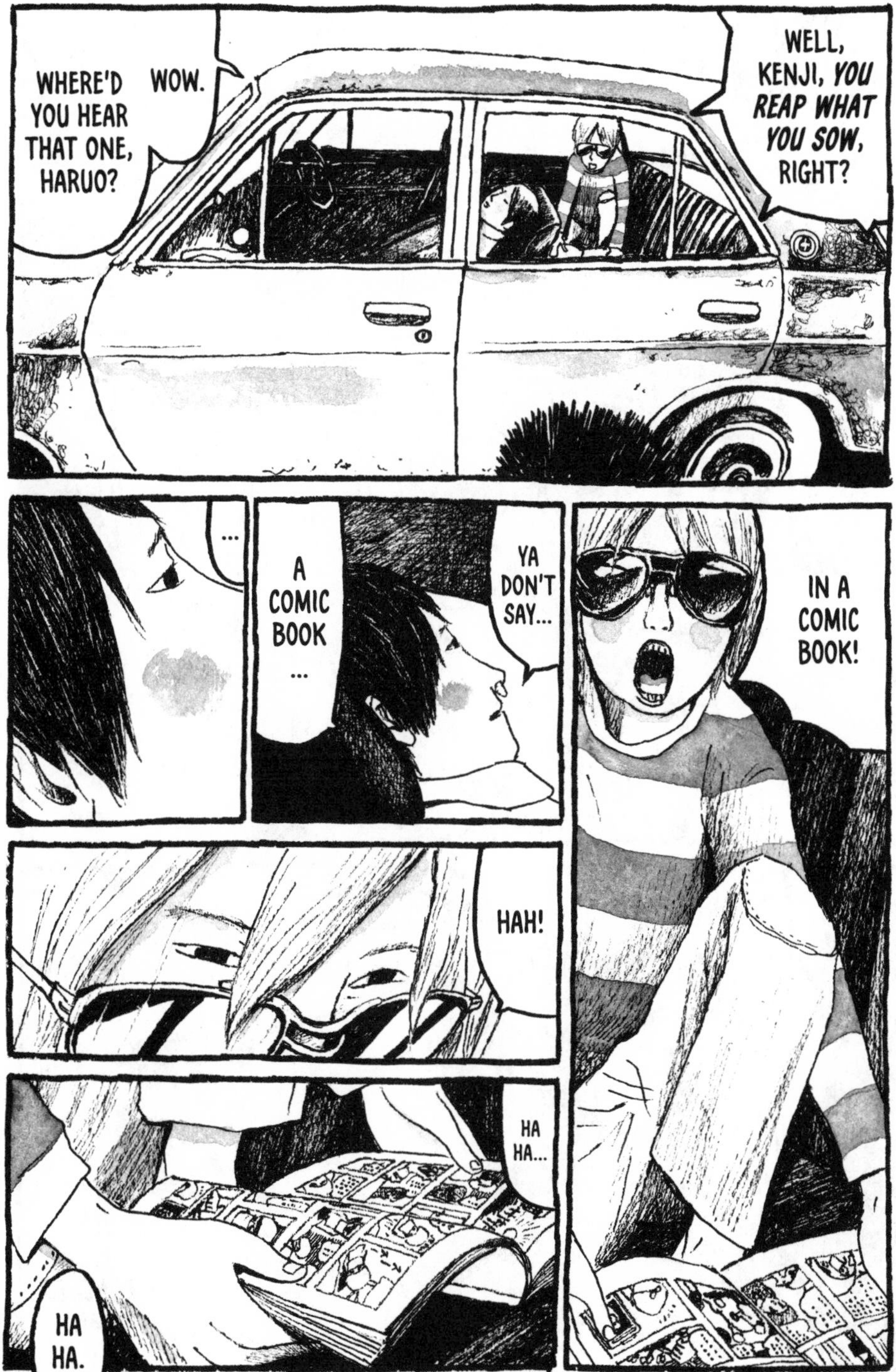
WELL, KENJI, *YOU REAP WHAT YOU SOW,* RIGHT?
WOW.
WHERE'D YOU HEAR THAT ONE, HARUO?
IN A COMIC BOOK!
YA DON'T SAY...
A COMIC BOOK ...
...
HAH!
HA HA...
HA HA.

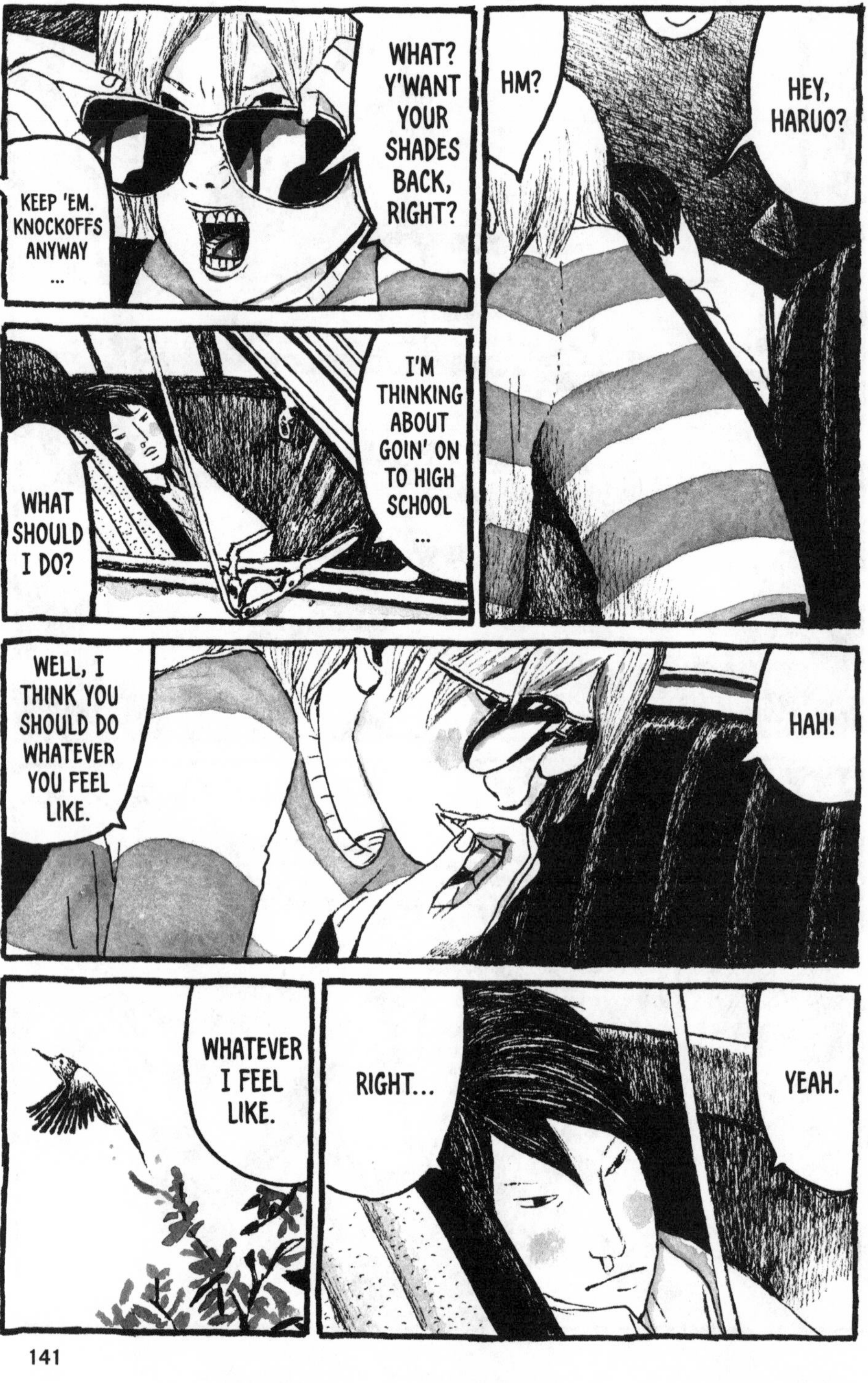
HEY, HARUO?
HM?
WHAT? Y'WANT YOUR SHADES BACK, RIGHT?
KEEP 'EM. KNOCKOFFS ANYWAY ...
I'M THINKING ABOUT GOIN' ON TO HIGH SCHOOL ...
WHAT SHOULD I DO?
HAH!
WELL, I THINK YOU SHOULD DO WHATEVER YOU FEEL LIKE.
YEAH.
RIGHT...
WHATEVER I FEEL LIKE.

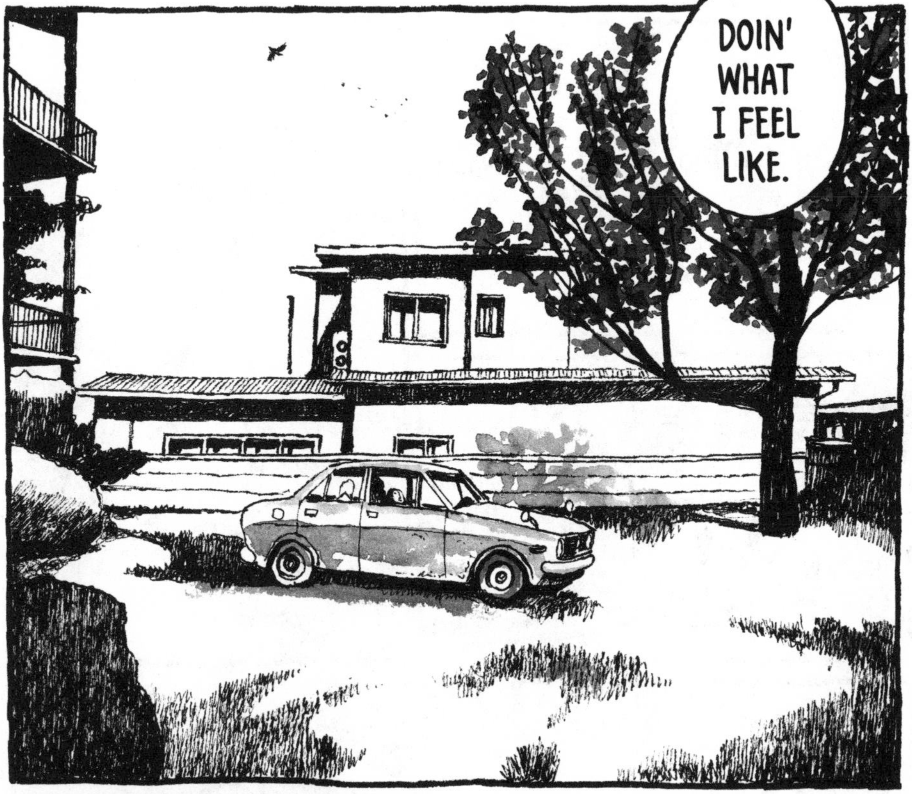
DOIN' WHAT I FEEL LIKE.
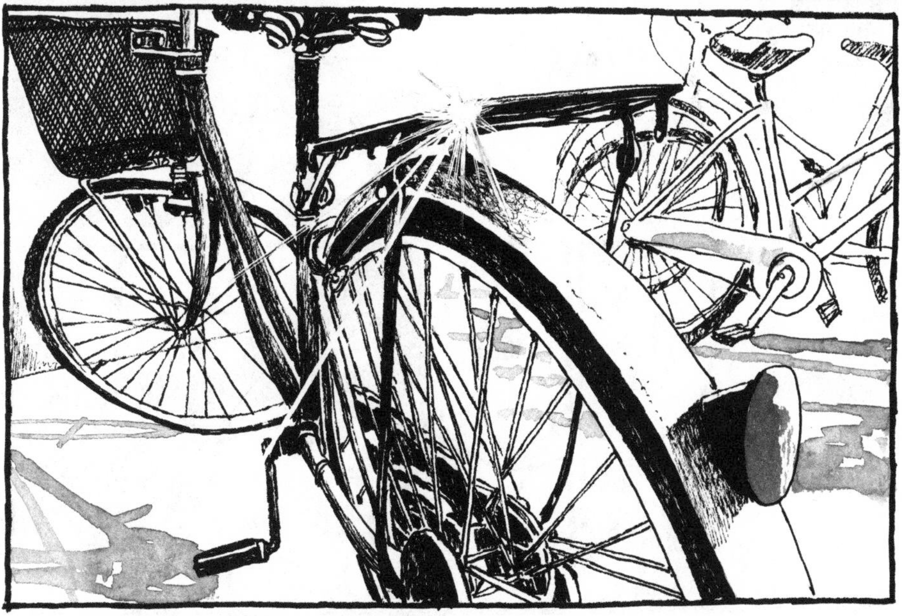

CHAPTER 11

"I wanna
see her as
much as I
don't wanna
see her."

"Well, I
do wanna
see her!"

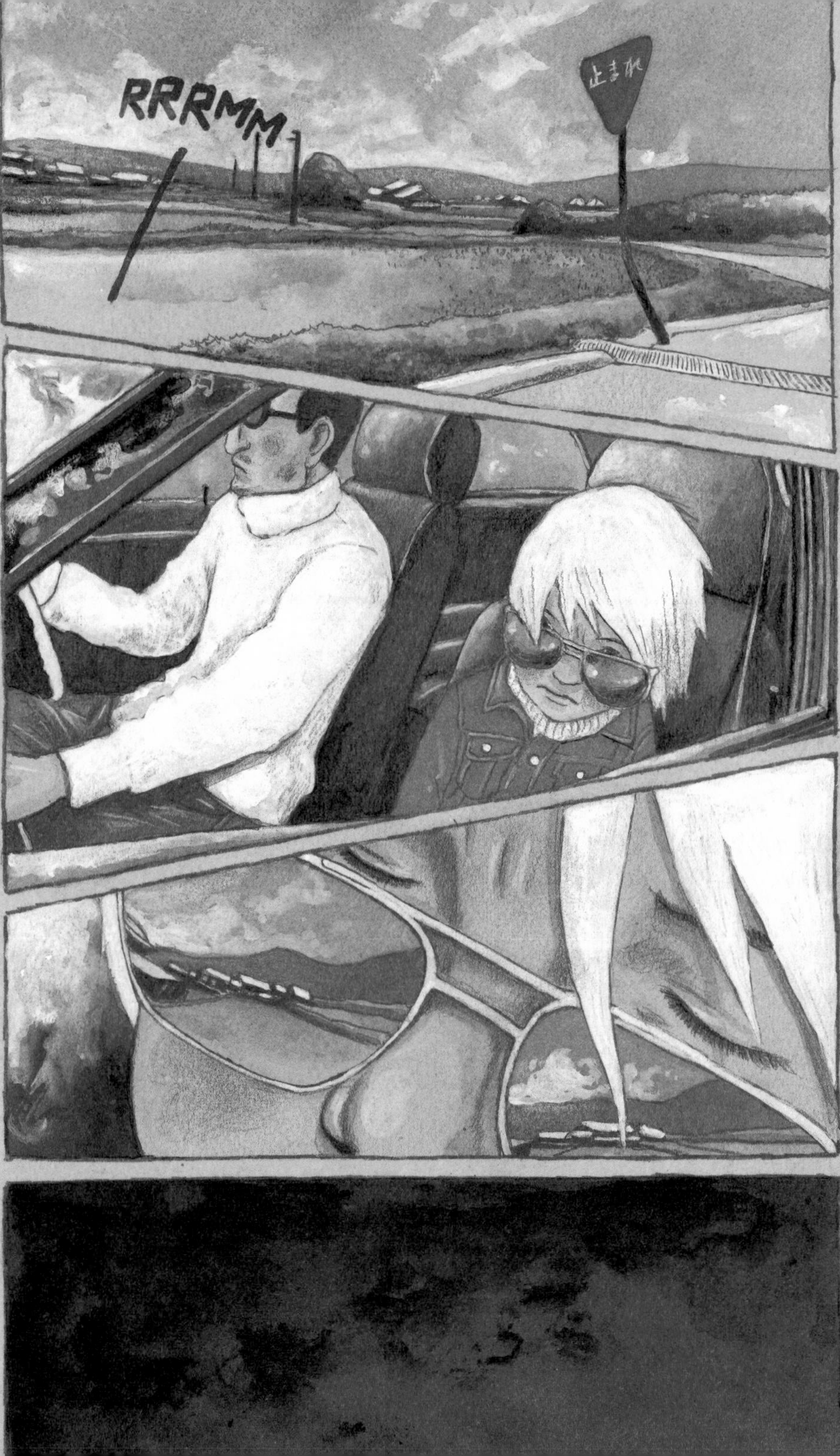
止まれ
RRRMM

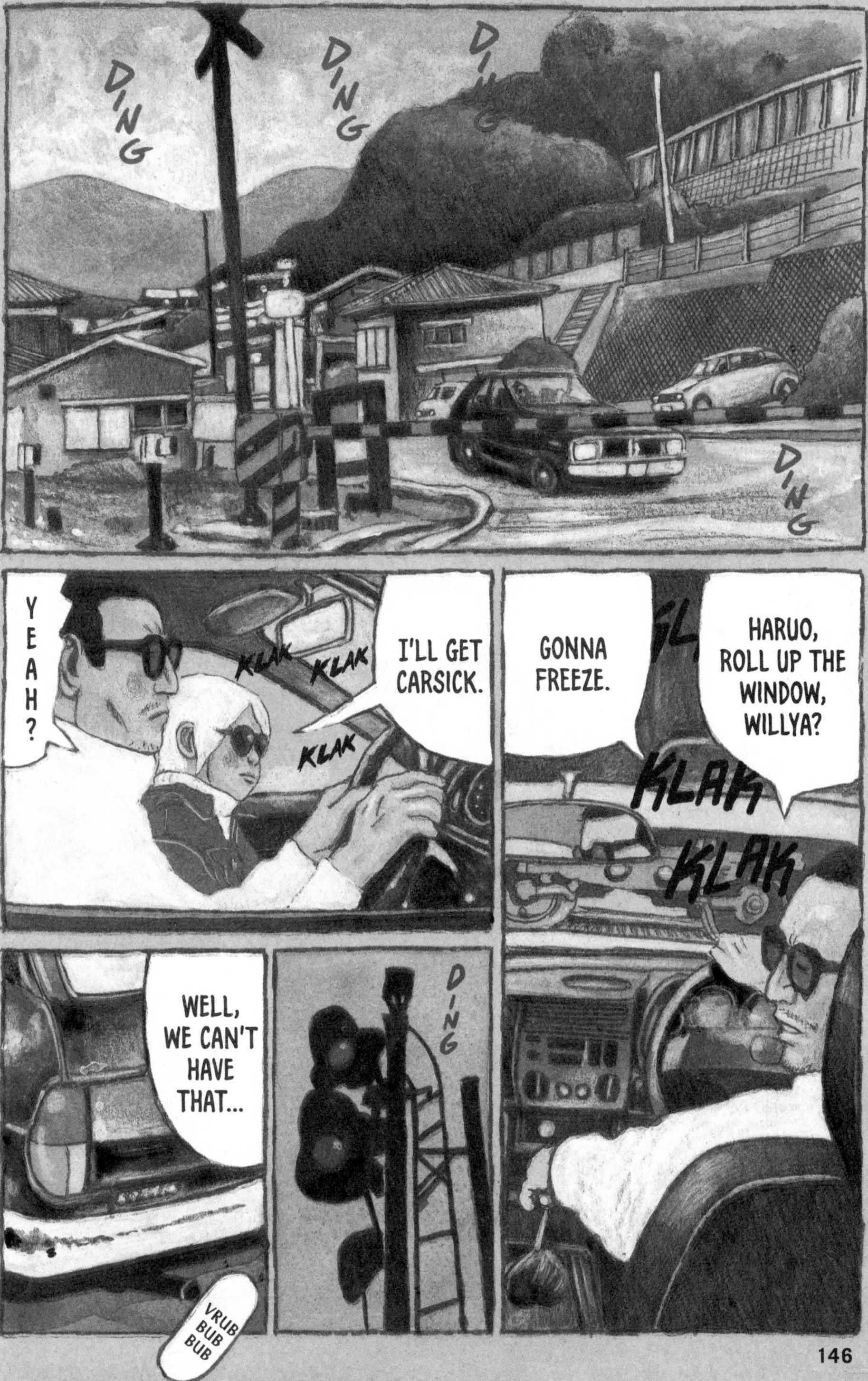
DING
DING
DING
DING
HARUO, ROLL UP THE WINDOW, WILLYA?
GONNA FREEZE.
KLAK
KLAK
I'LL GET CARSICK.
KLAK
KLAK
KLAK
YEAH?
DING
WELL, WE CAN'T HAVE THAT...
VRUB BUB BUB

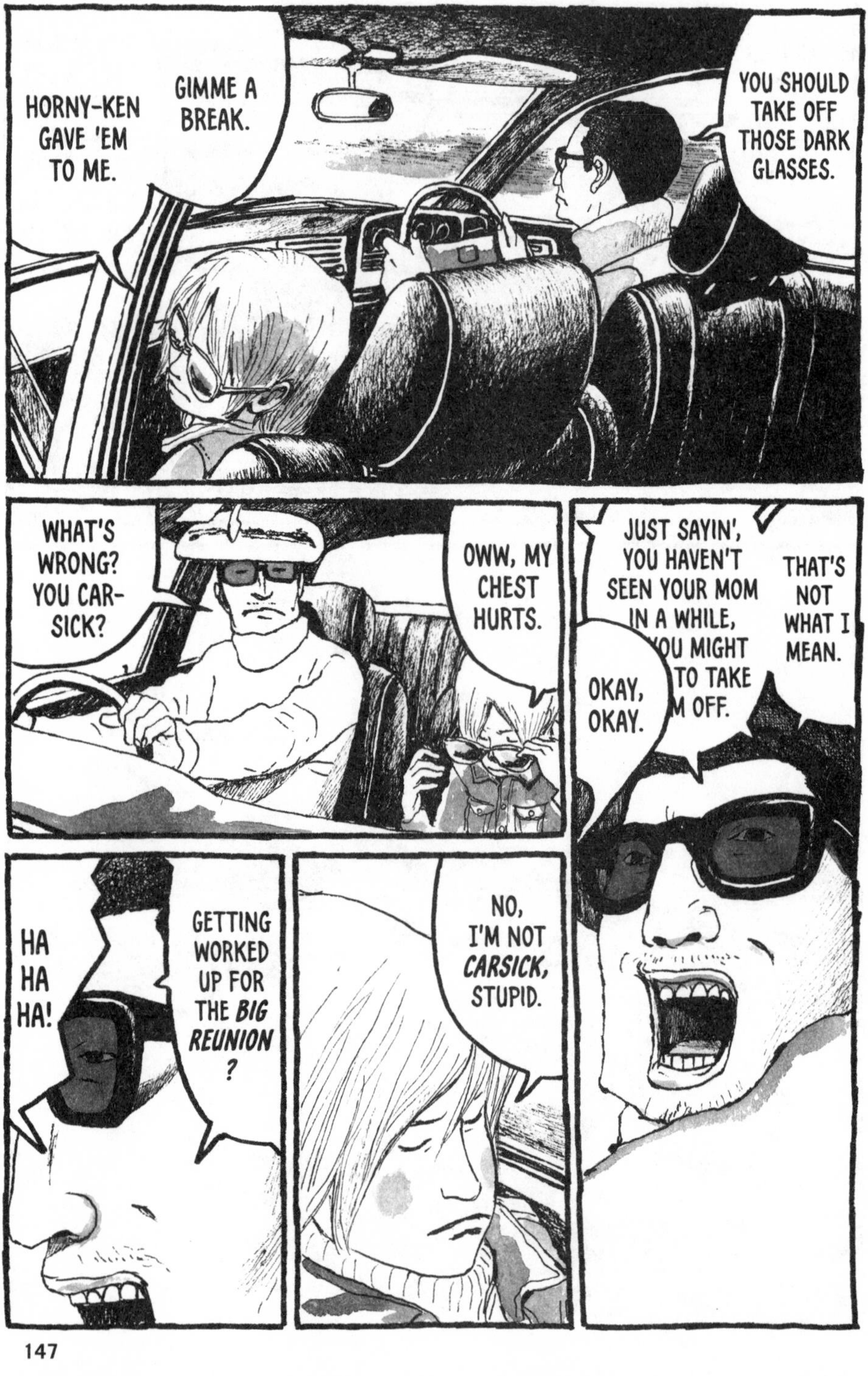
YOU SHOULD TAKE OFF THOSE DARK GLASSES.
GIMME A BREAK.
HORNY-KEN GAVE 'EM TO ME.
THAT'S NOT WHAT I MEAN.
JUST SAYIN', YOU HAVEN'T SEEN YOUR MOM IN A WHILE, ... YOU MIGHT ... TO TAKE ... M OFF.
OKAY, OKAY.
OWW, MY CHEST HURTS.
WHAT'S WRONG? YOU CAR-SICK?
NO, I'M NOT *CARSICK,* STUPID.
GETTING WORKED UP FOR THE *BIG REUNION* ?
HA HA HA!

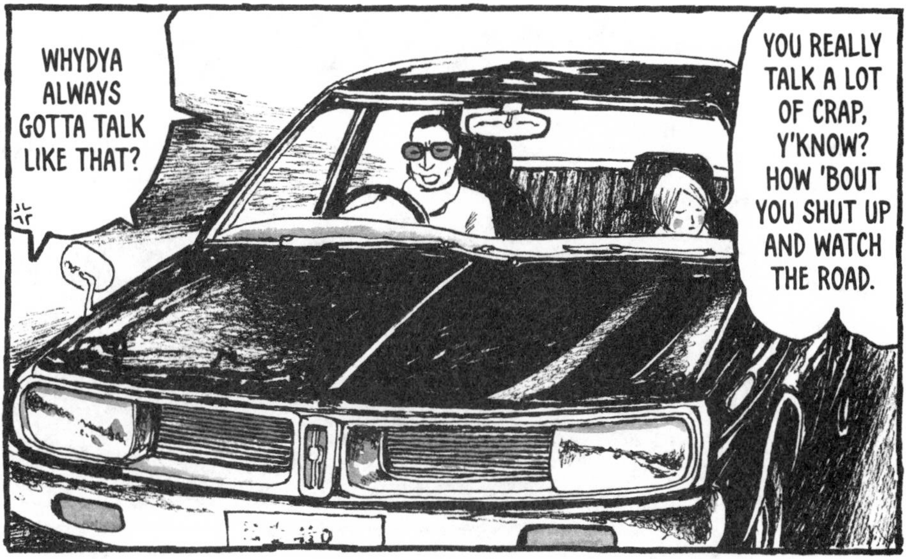
YOU REALLY TALK A LOT OF CRAP, Y'KNOW? HOW 'BOUT YOU SHUT UP AND WATCH THE ROAD.
WHYDYA ALWAYS GOTTA TALK LIKE THAT?
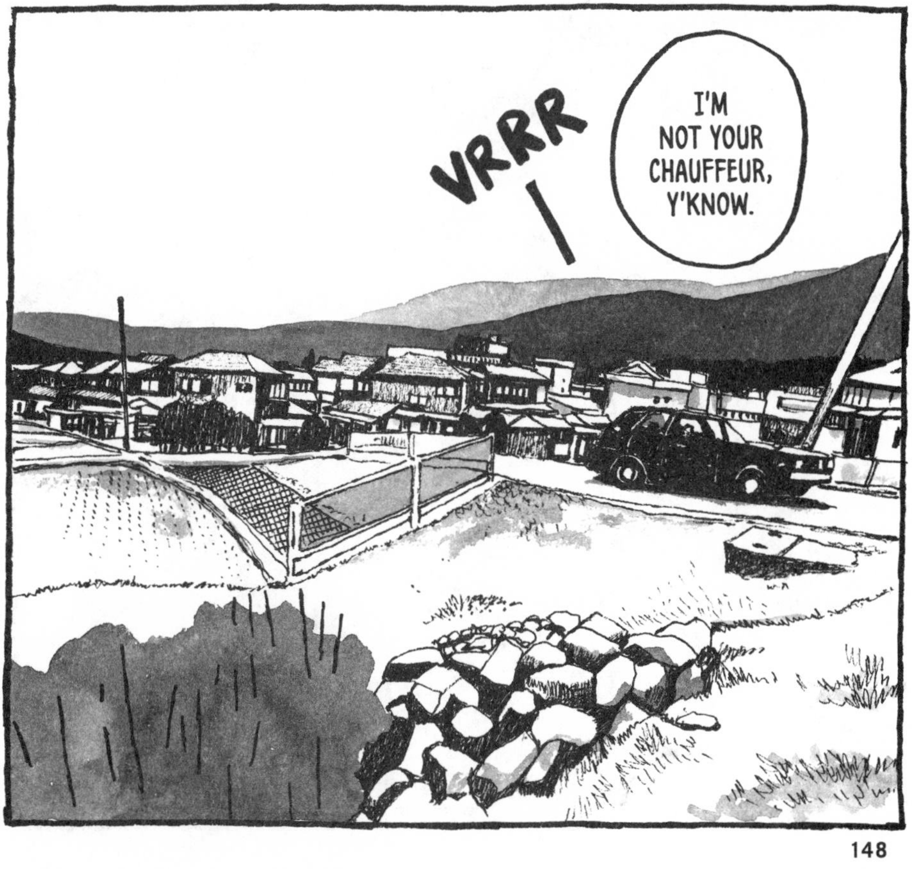
I'M NOT YOUR CHAUFFEUR, Y'KNOW.
VRRR

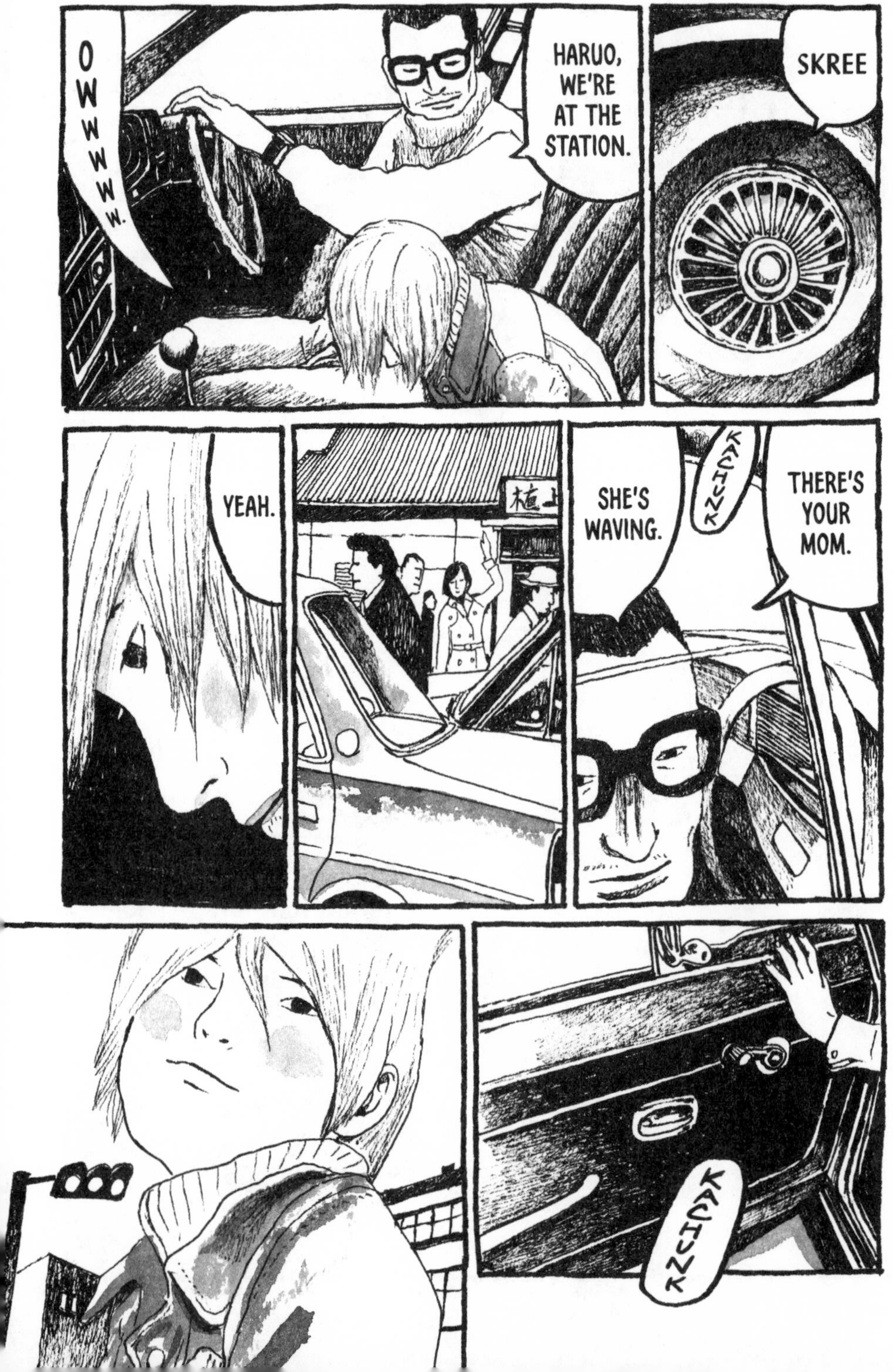
SKREE
HARUO, WE'RE AT THE STATION.
OWWWWWW.
THERE'S YOUR MOM.
KACHUNK
SHE'S WAVING.
YEAH.
KACHUNK

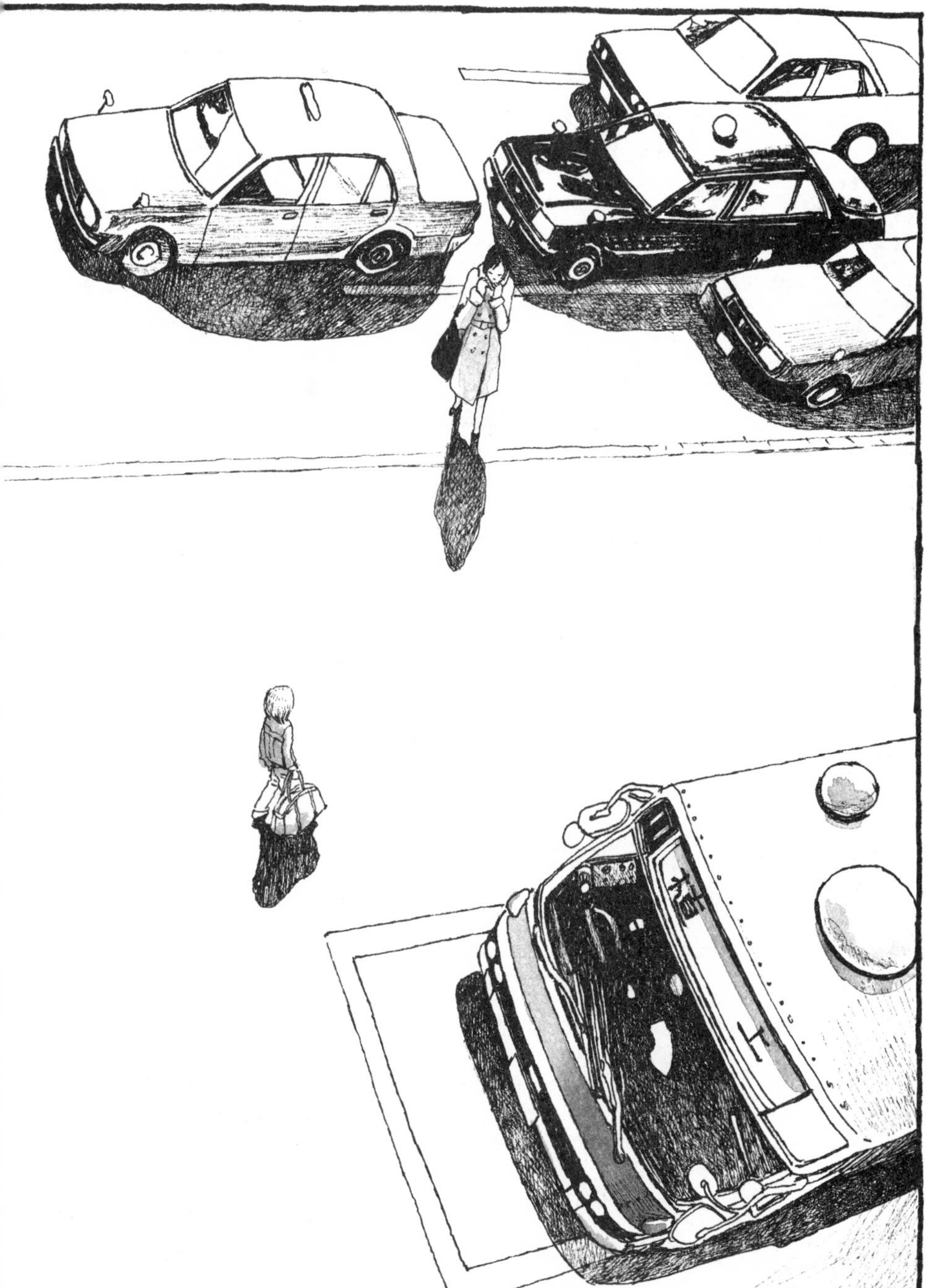

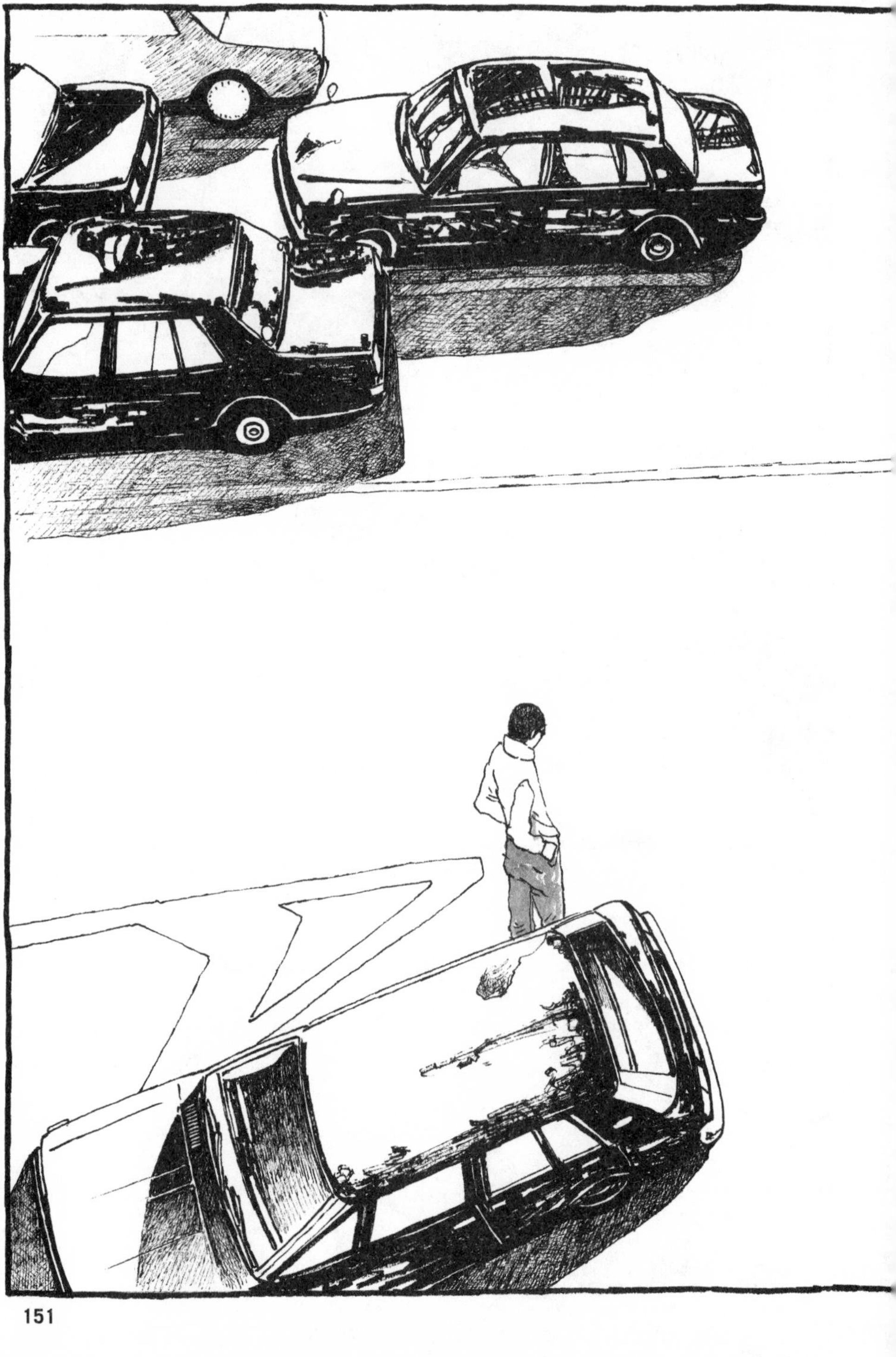

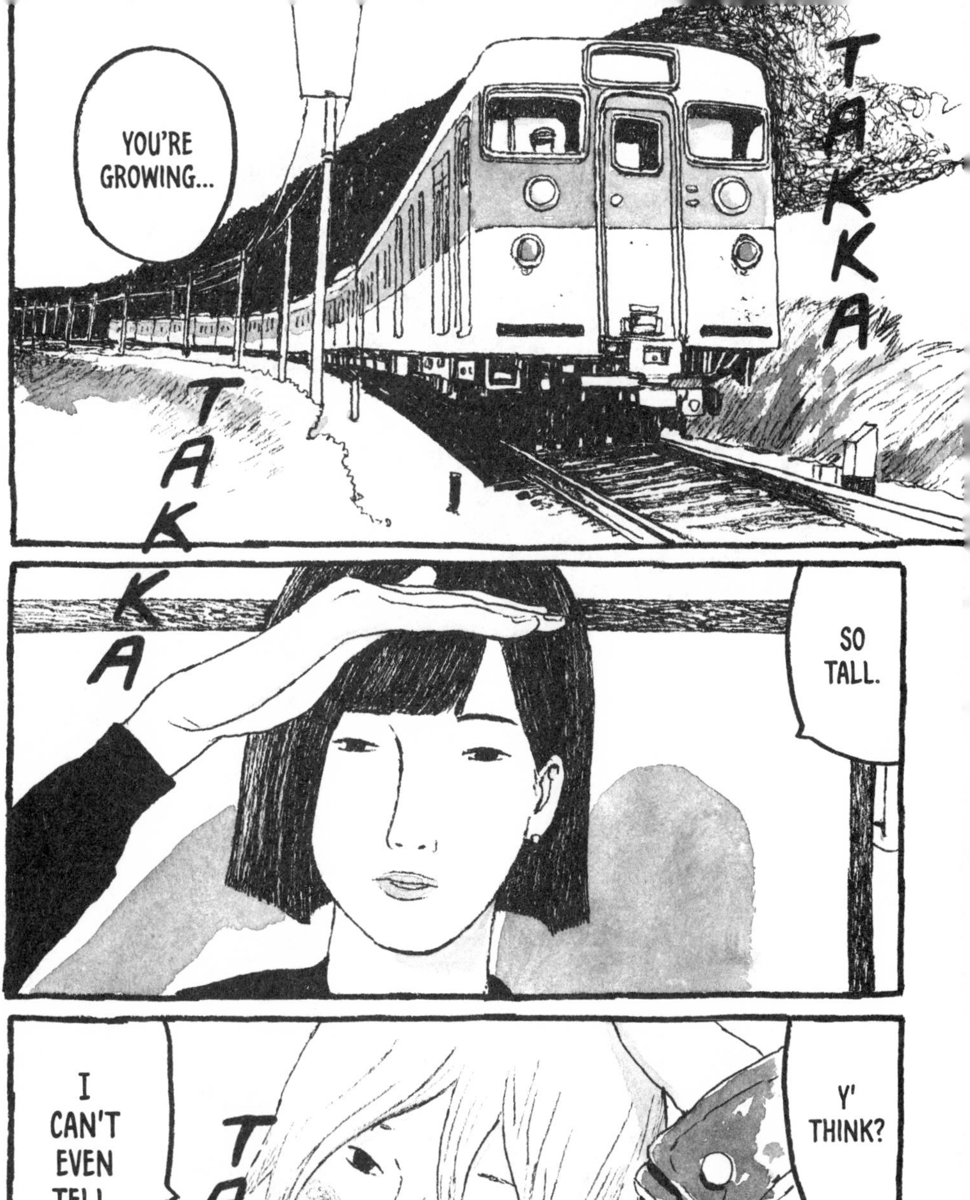
TAKA
YOU'RE GROWING...
TAKKA
SO TALL.
Y' THINK?
TAKKA
I CAN'T EVEN TELL.

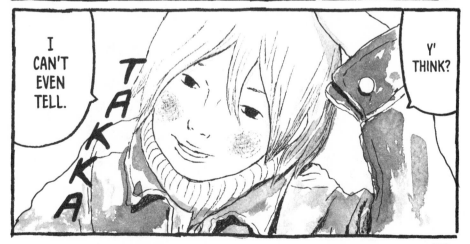

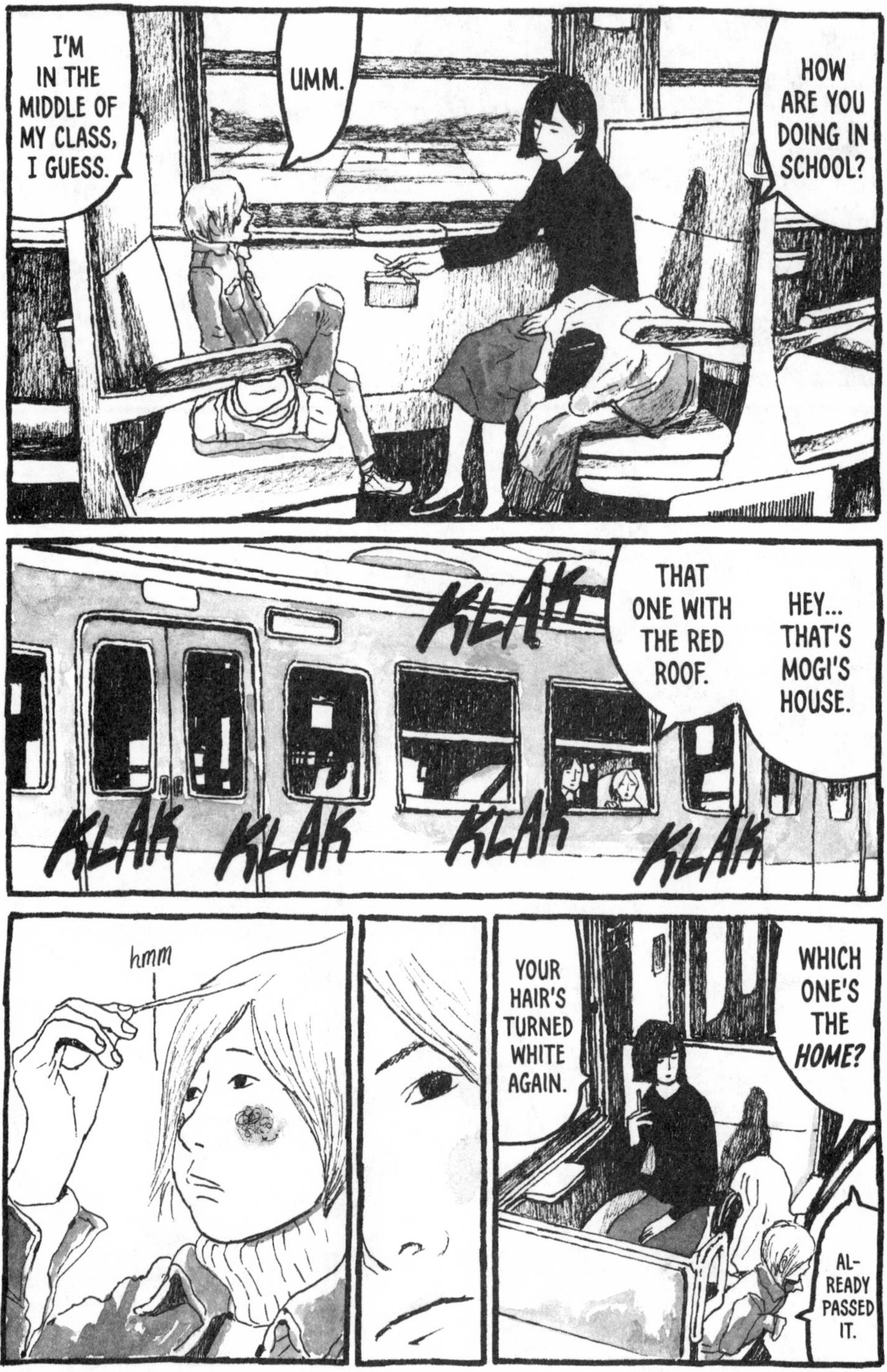
HOW ARE YOU DOING IN SCHOOL?
UMM.
I'M IN THE MIDDLE OF MY CLASS, I GUESS.
HEY... THAT'S MOGI'S HOUSE.
THAT ONE WITH THE RED ROOF.
KLAK
KLAK
KLAK
KLAK
KLAK
WHICH ONE'S THE *HOME?*
YOUR HAIR'S TURNED WHITE AGAIN.
AL-READY PASSED IT.
hmm

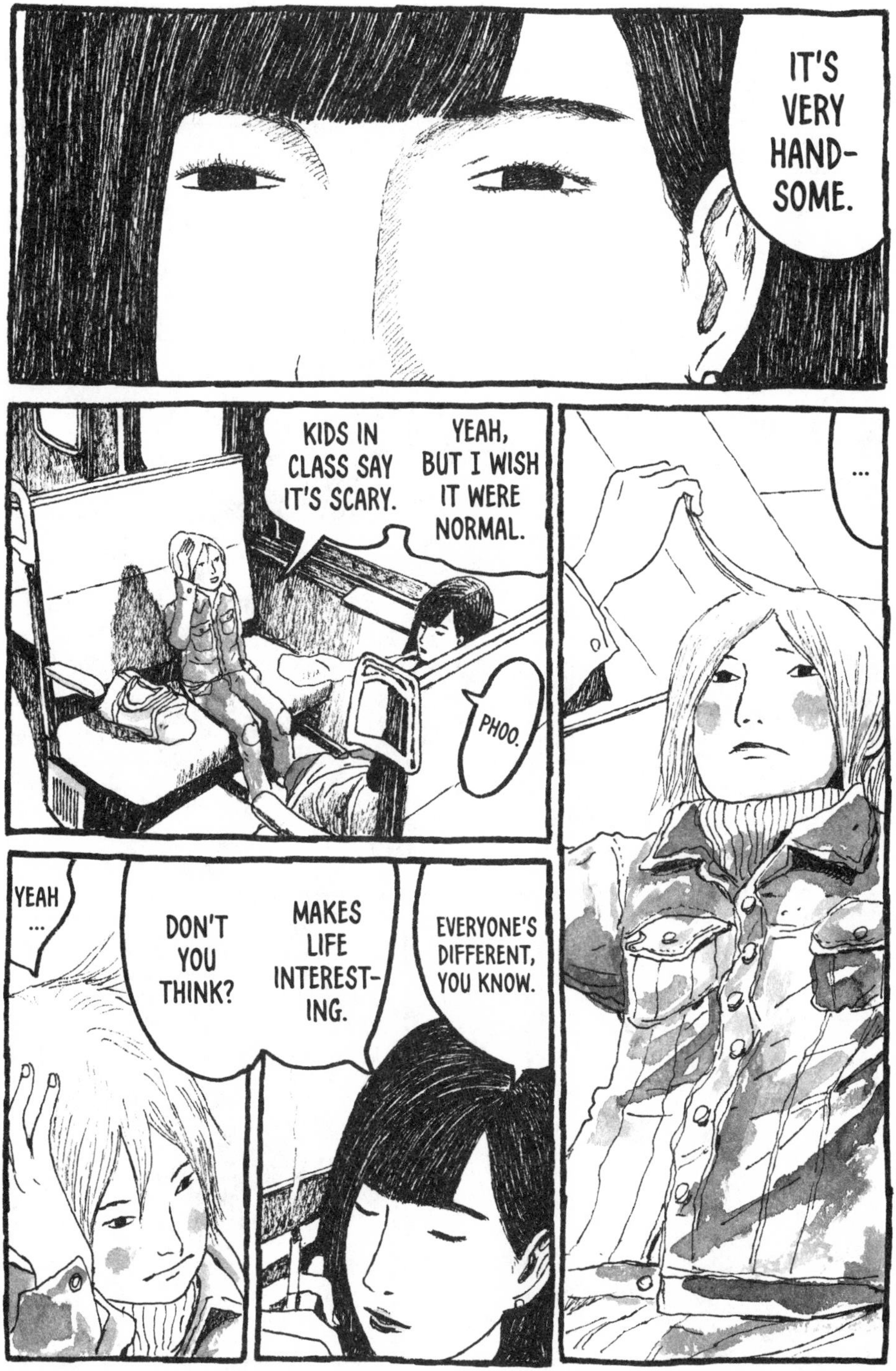
IT'S VERY HAND-SOME.
...
YEAH, BUT I WISH IT WERE NORMAL.
KIDS IN CLASS SAY IT'S SCARY.
PHOO.
EVERYONE'S DIFFERENT, YOU KNOW.
MAKES LIFE INTEREST-ING.
DON'T YOU THINK?
YEAH ...

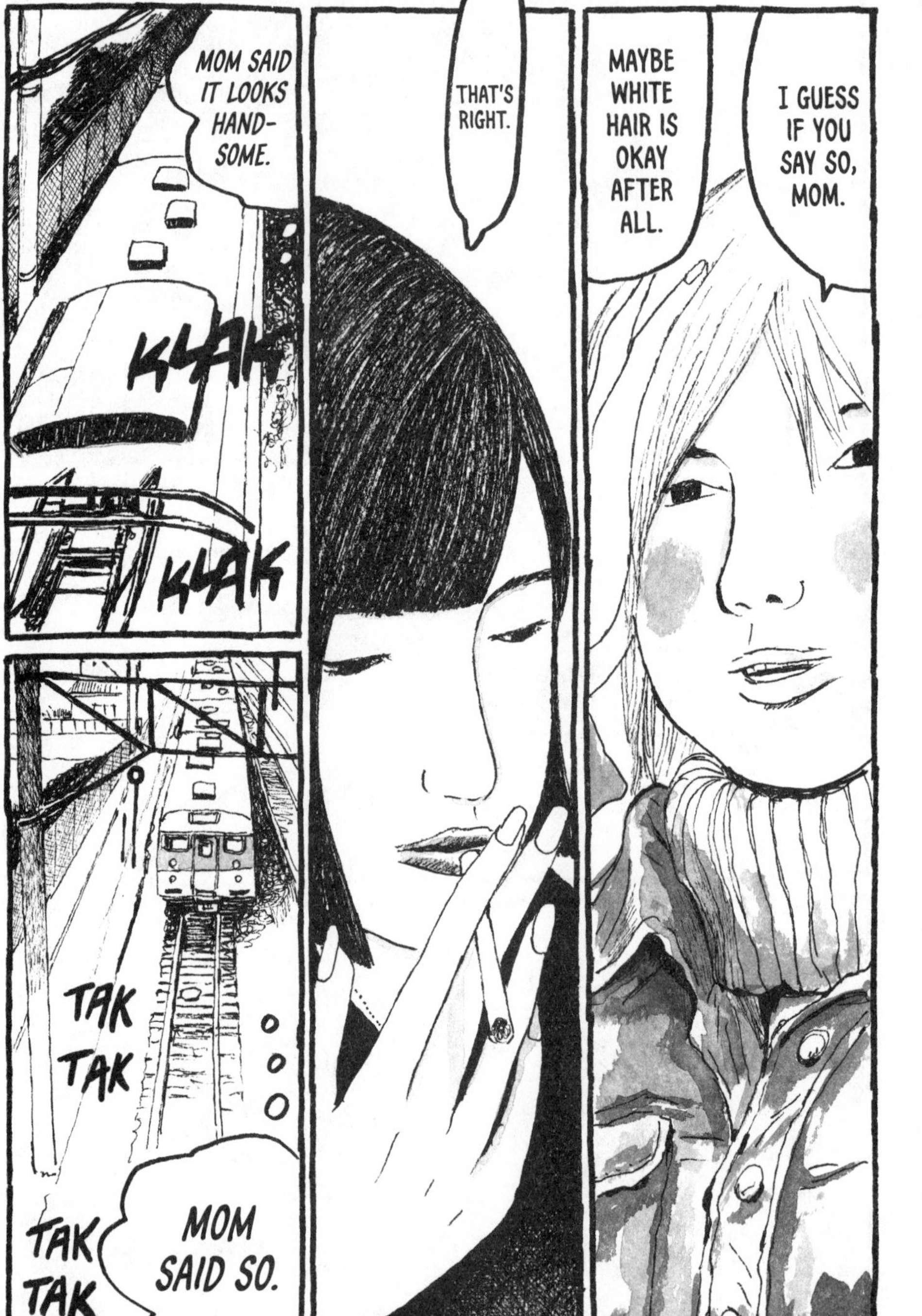
I GUESS IF YOU SAY SO, MOM.
MAYBE WHITE HAIR IS OKAY AFTER ALL.
THAT'S RIGHT.
MOM SAID IT LOOKS HAND-SOME.
KLAK
KLAK
TAK TAK
TAK TAK
MOM SAID SO.

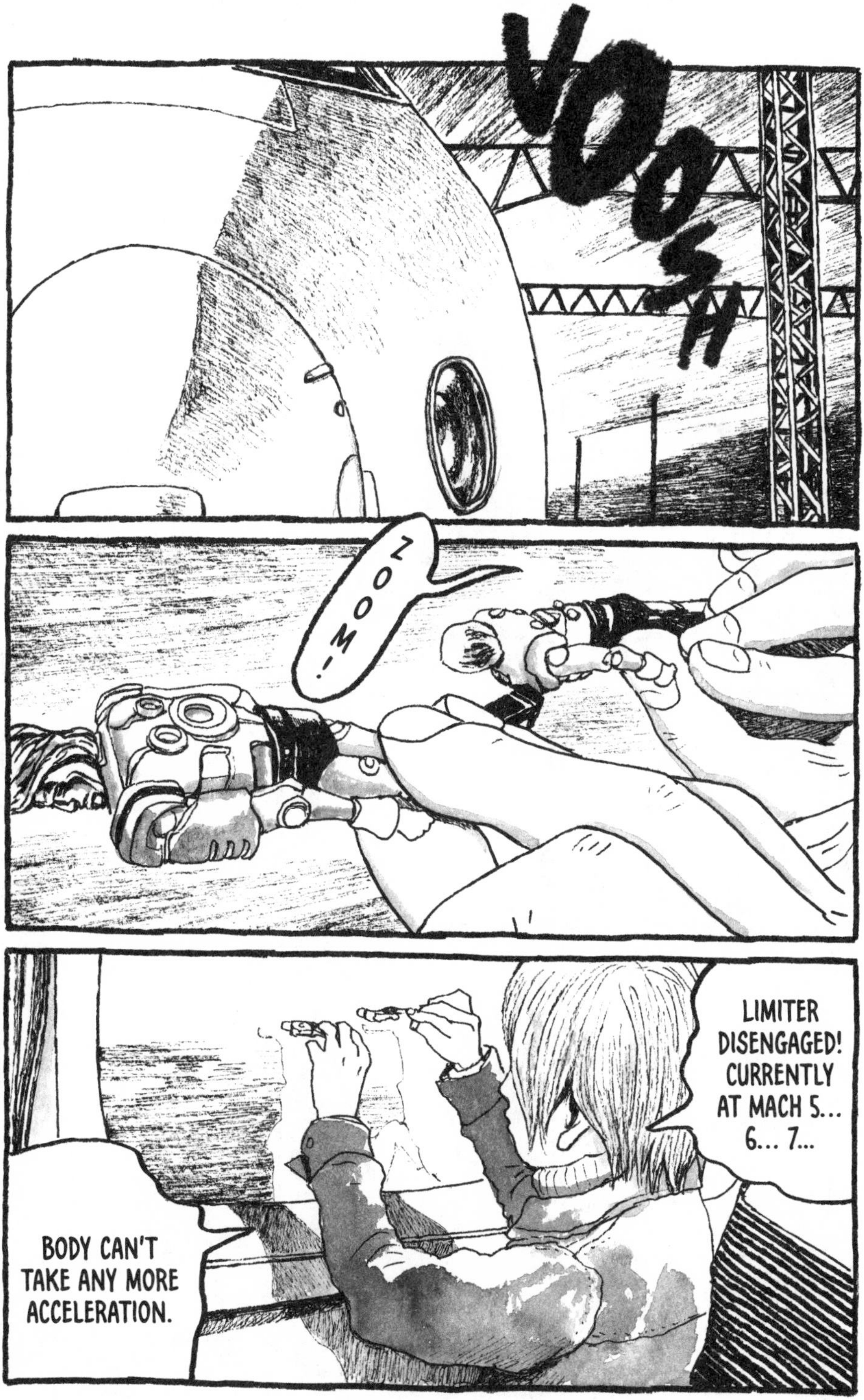
VOOSH
ZOOM!
LIMITER DISENGAGED! CURRENTLY AT MACH 5... 6... 7...
BODY CAN'T TAKE ANY MORE ACCELERATION.

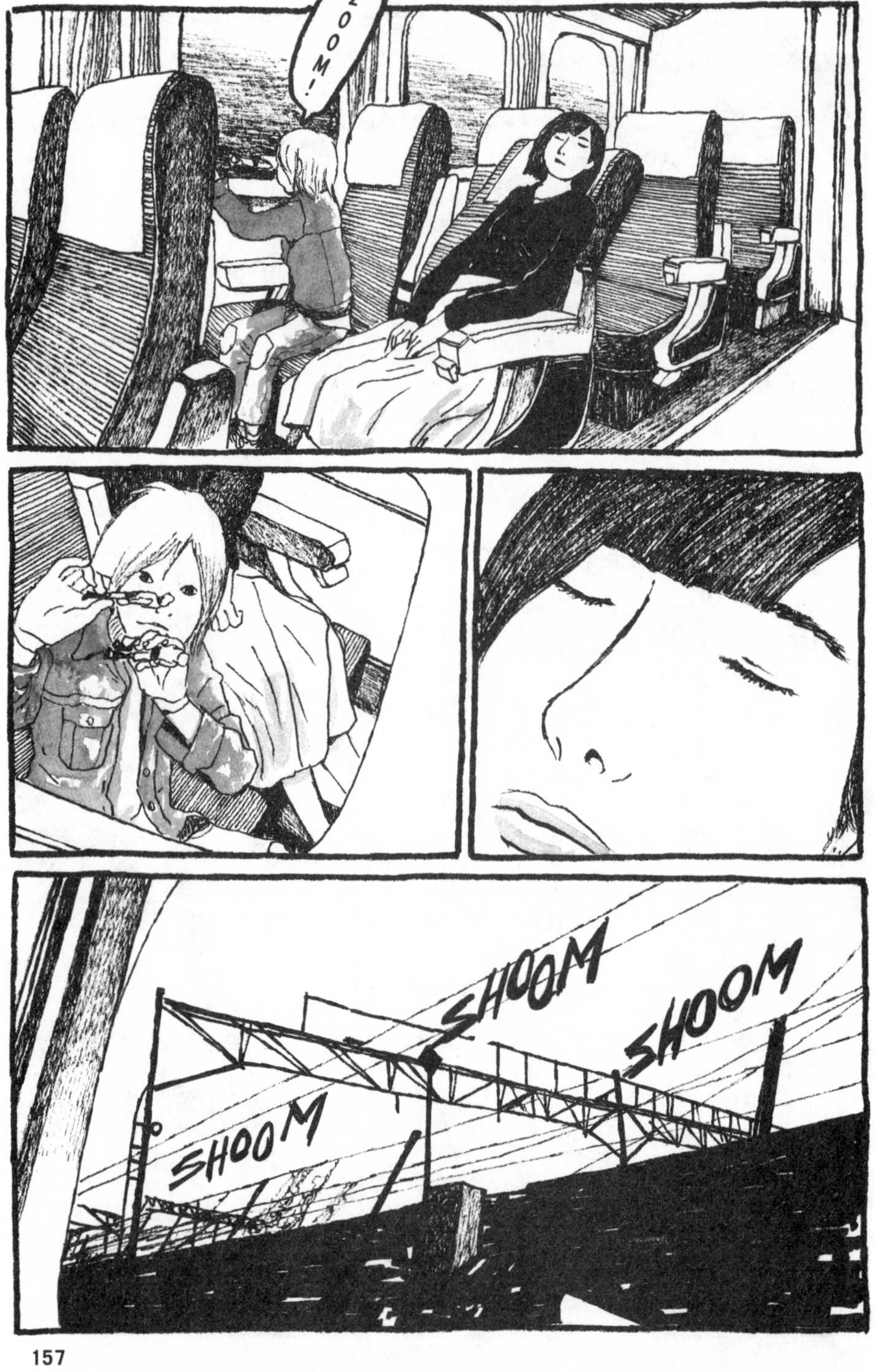
ZOOM!
SHOOM
SHOOM
SHOOM

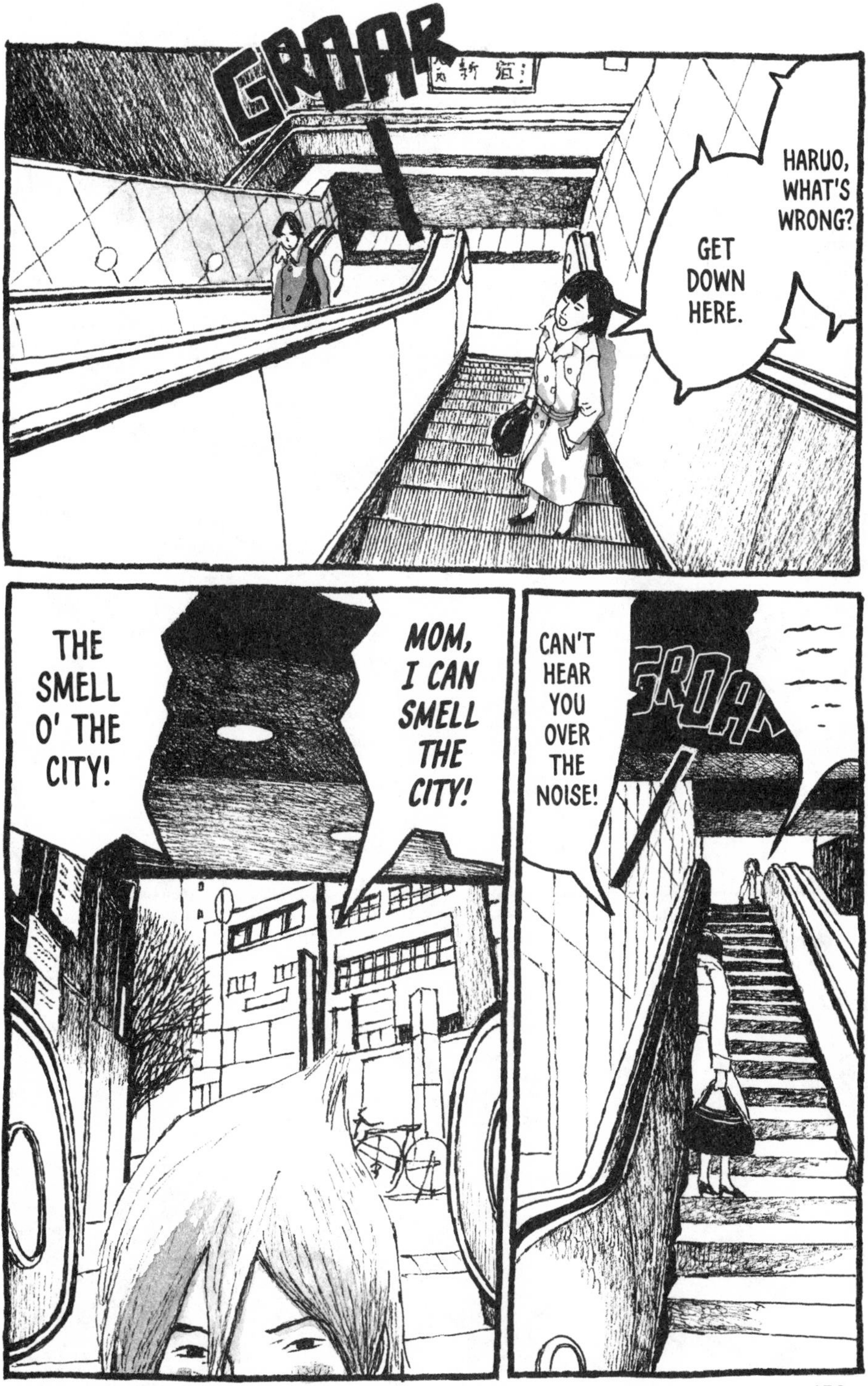
GROAR
HARUO, WHAT'S WRONG?
GET DOWN HERE.
CAN'T HEAR YOU OVER THE NOISE!
GROAR
MOM, I CAN SMELL THE CITY!
THE SMELL O' THE CITY!

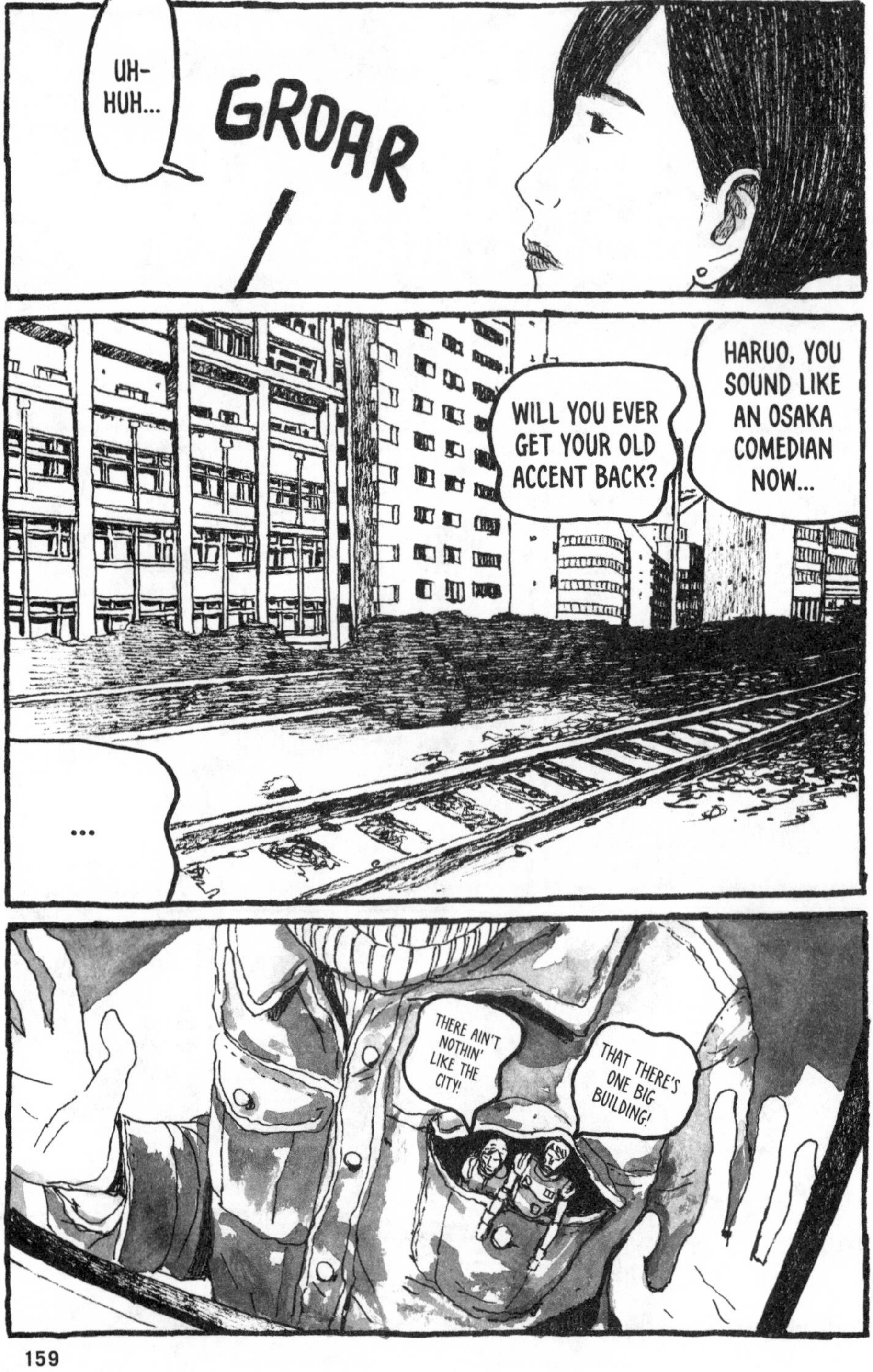
GROAR
UH-HUH...
HARUO, YOU SOUND LIKE AN OSAKA COMEDIAN NOW...
WILL YOU EVER GET YOUR OLD ACCENT BACK?
...
THAT THERE'S ONE BIG BUILDING!
THERE AIN'T NOTHIN' LIKE THE CITY!

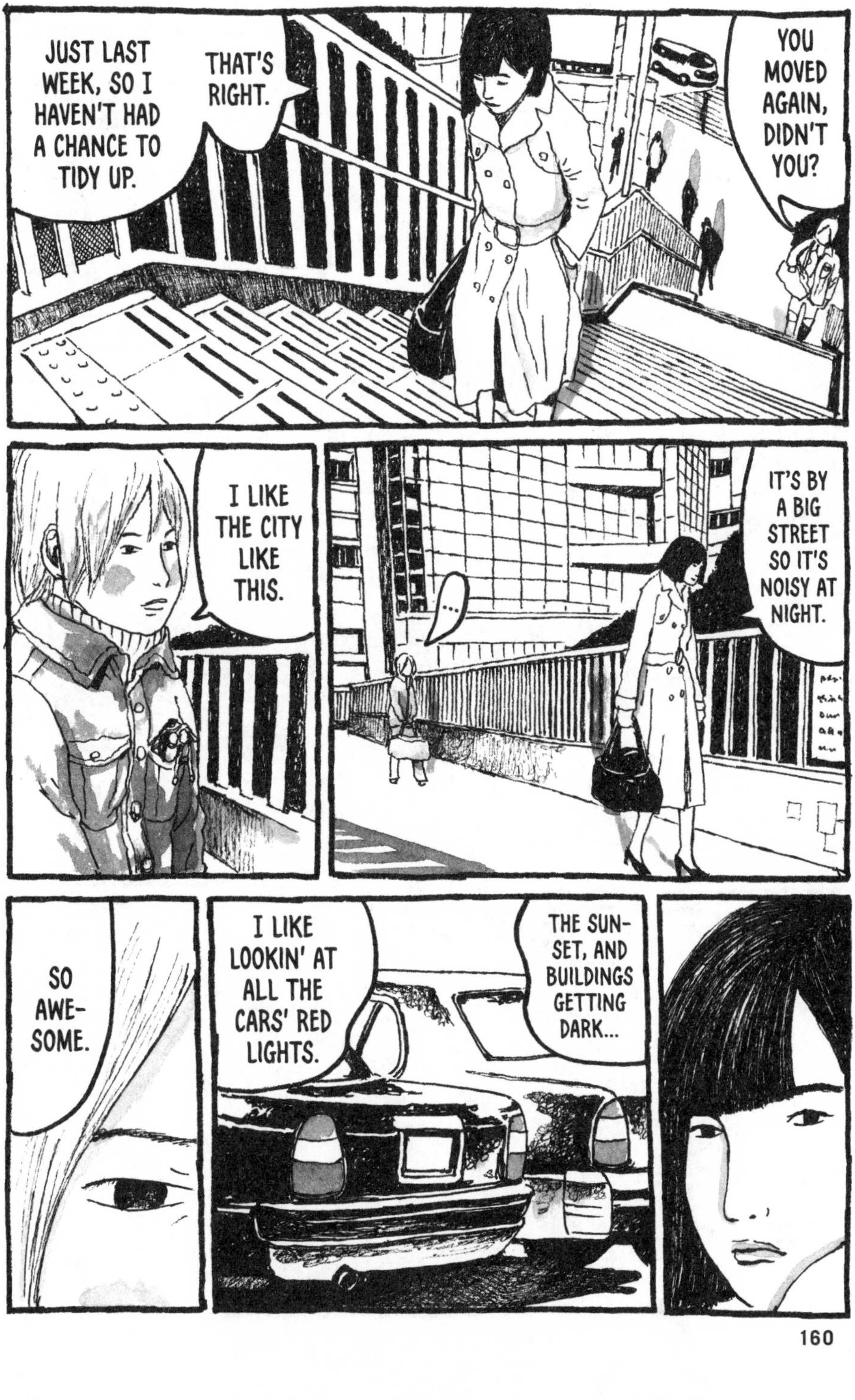
YOU MOVED AGAIN, DIDN'T YOU?
THAT'S RIGHT.
JUST LAST WEEK, SO I HAVEN'T HAD A CHANCE TO TIDY UP.
IT'S BY A BIG STREET SO IT'S NOISY AT NIGHT.
...
I LIKE THE CITY LIKE THIS.
THE SUN-SET, AND BUILDINGS GETTING DARK...
I LIKE LOOKIN' AT ALL THE CARS' RED LIGHTS.
SO AWE-SOME.

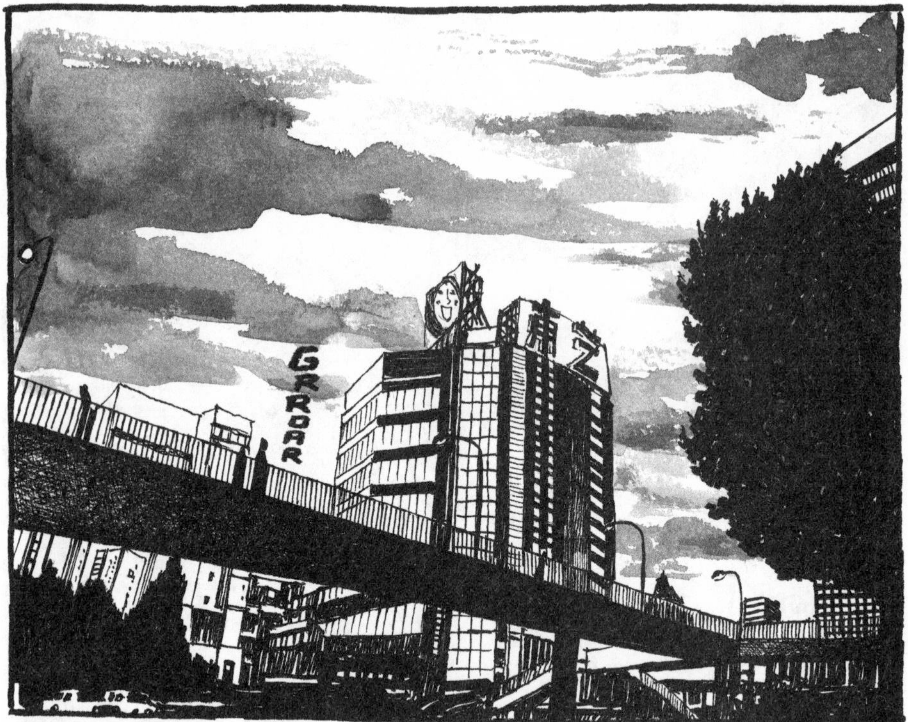
GRROAR
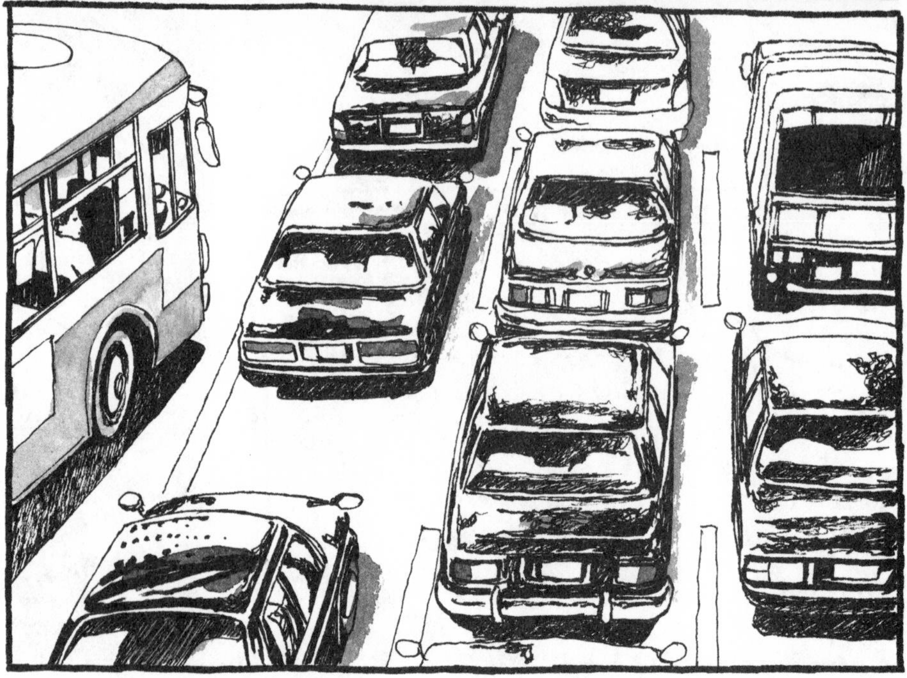

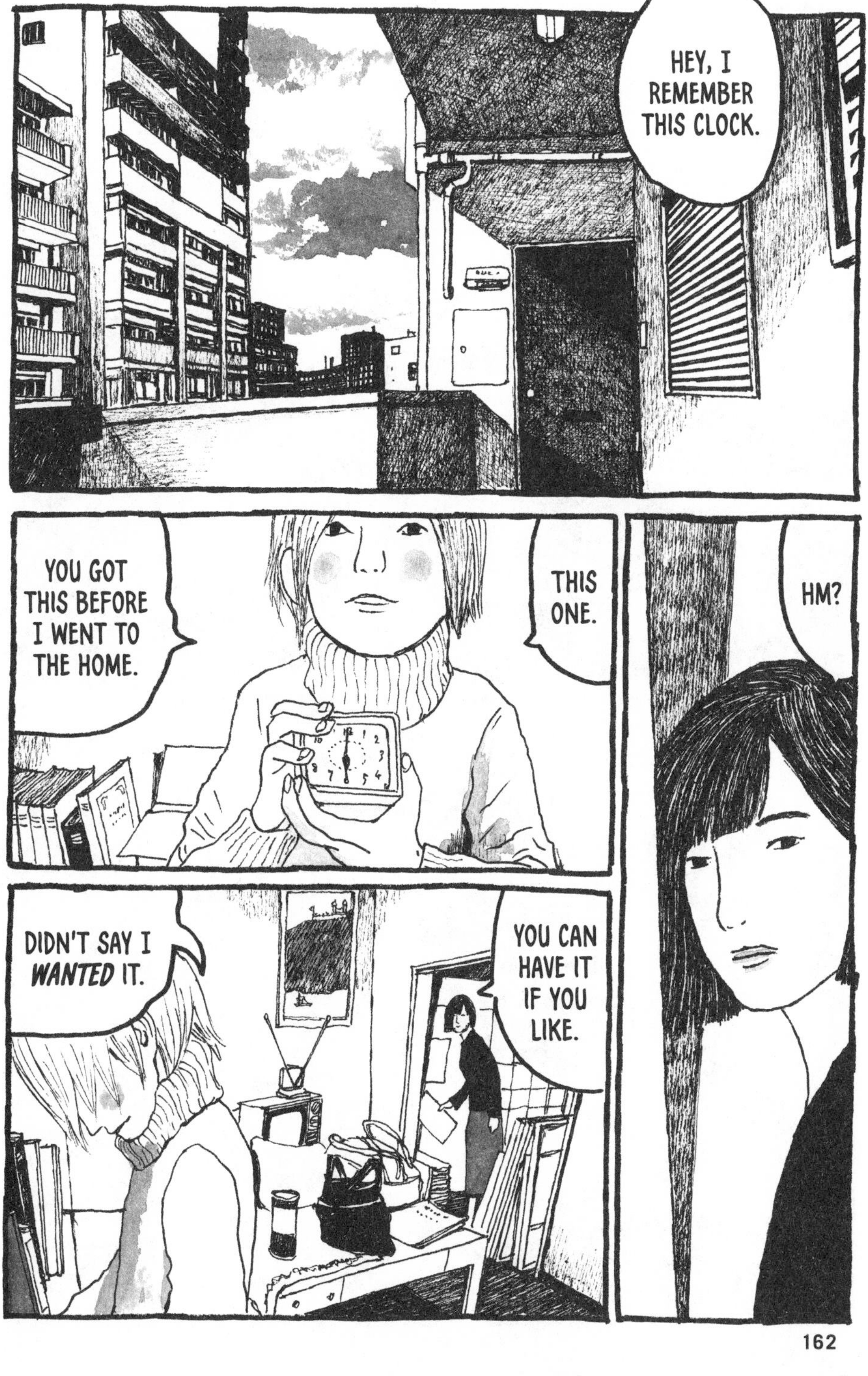
HEY, I REMEMBER THIS CLOCK.
HM?
THIS ONE.
YOU GOT THIS BEFORE I WENT TO THE HOME.
YOU CAN HAVE IT IF YOU LIKE.
DIDN'T SAY I *WANTED* IT.

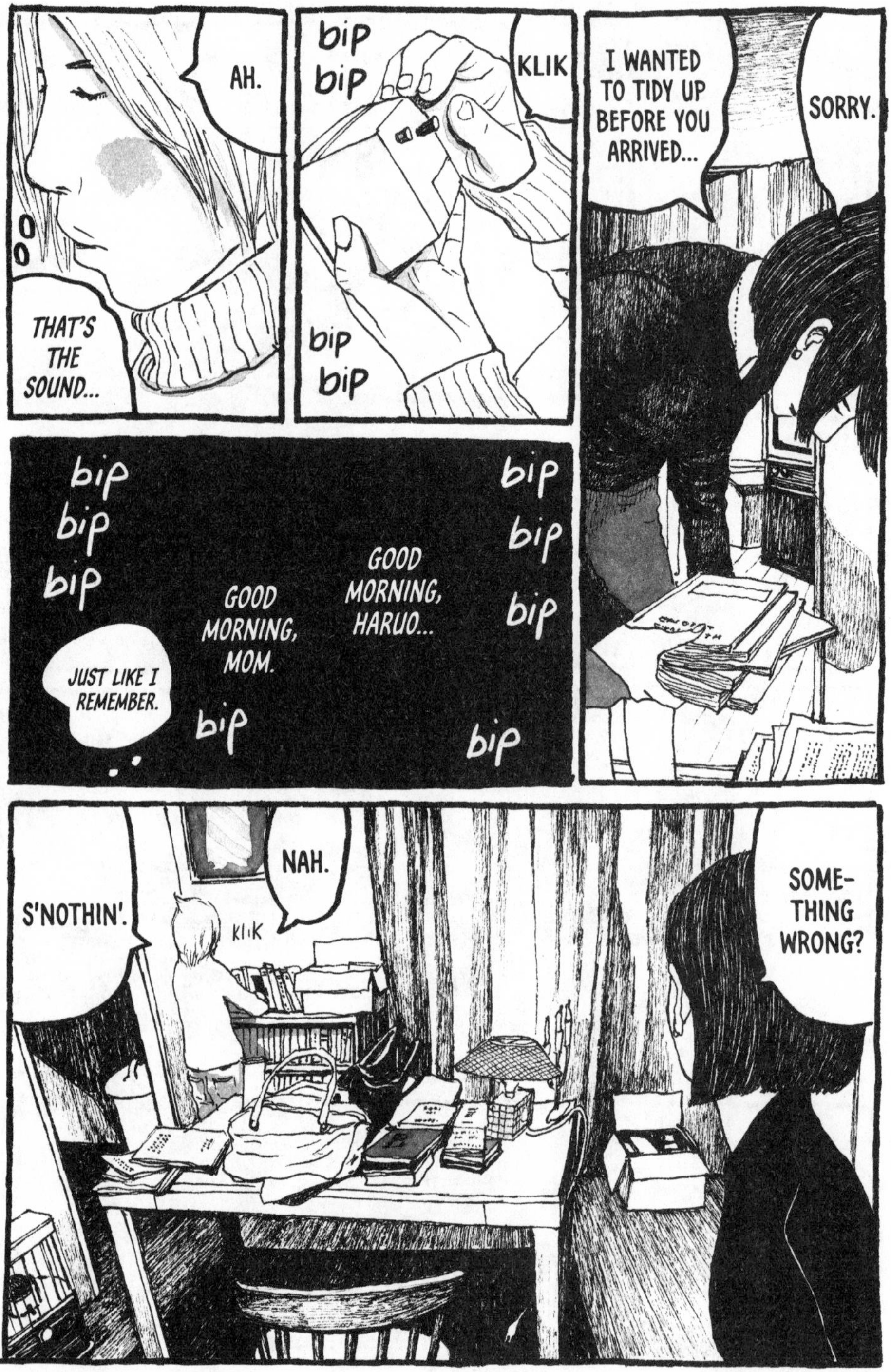
SORRY.
I WANTED TO TIDY UP BEFORE YOU ARRIVED...
KLIK
bip bip
bip bip
AH.
THAT'S THE SOUND...
bip bip bip
GOOD MORNING, HARUO...
GOOD MORNING, MOM.
bip
bip bip bip
bip
JUST LIKE I REMEMBER.
SOME-THING WRONG?
NAH.
KLIK
S'NOTHIN'.

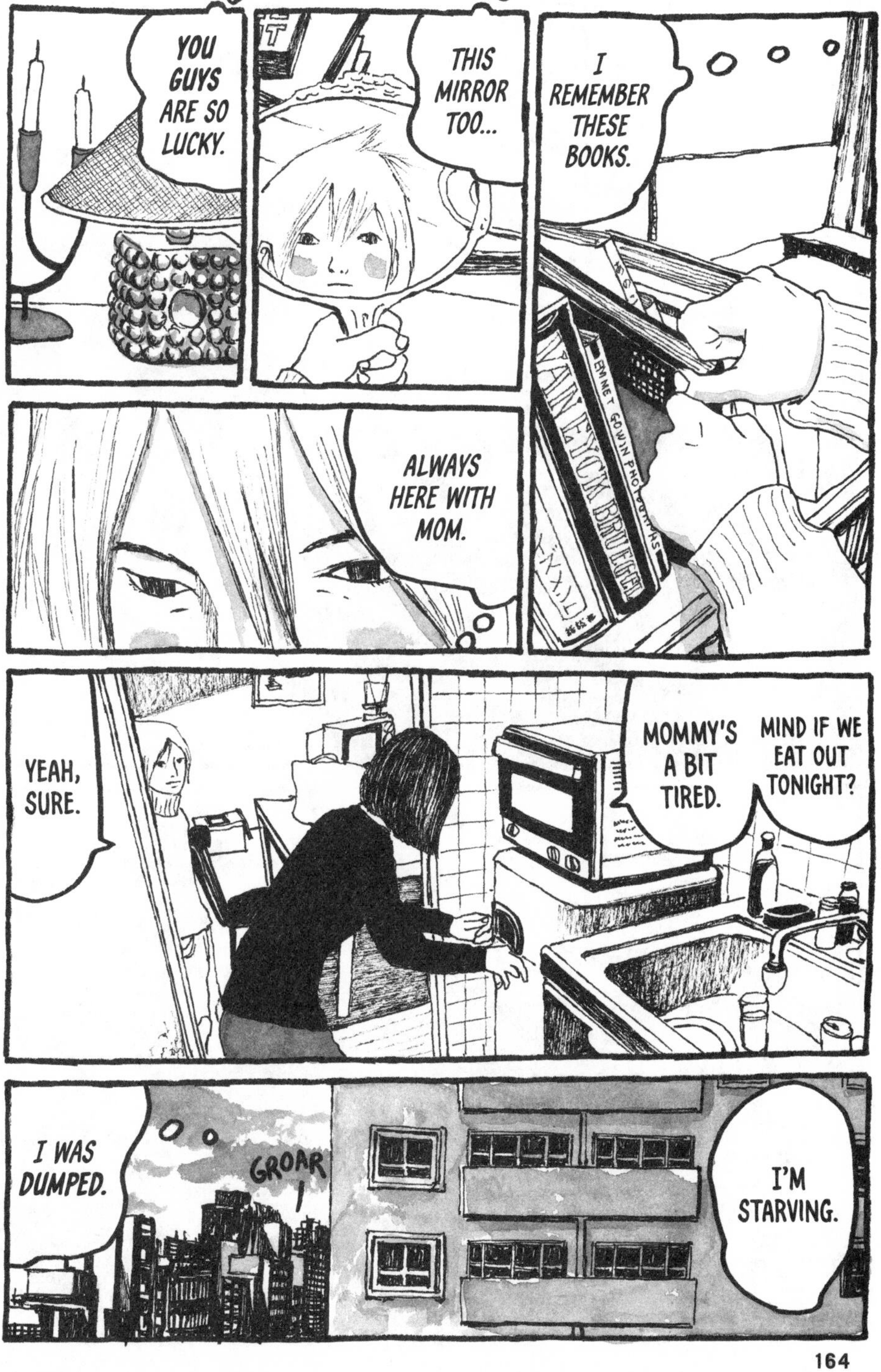
I REMEMBER THESE BOOKS.
VAN EYCK BRUEGEL
EMMET GOWIN PHOTOGRAPHS
THIS MIRROR TOO...
YOU GUYS ARE SO LUCKY.
ALWAYS HERE WITH MOM.
MIND IF WE EAT OUT TONIGHT?
MOMMY'S A BIT TIRED.
YEAH, SURE.
I'M STARVING.
GROAR
I WAS DUMPED.

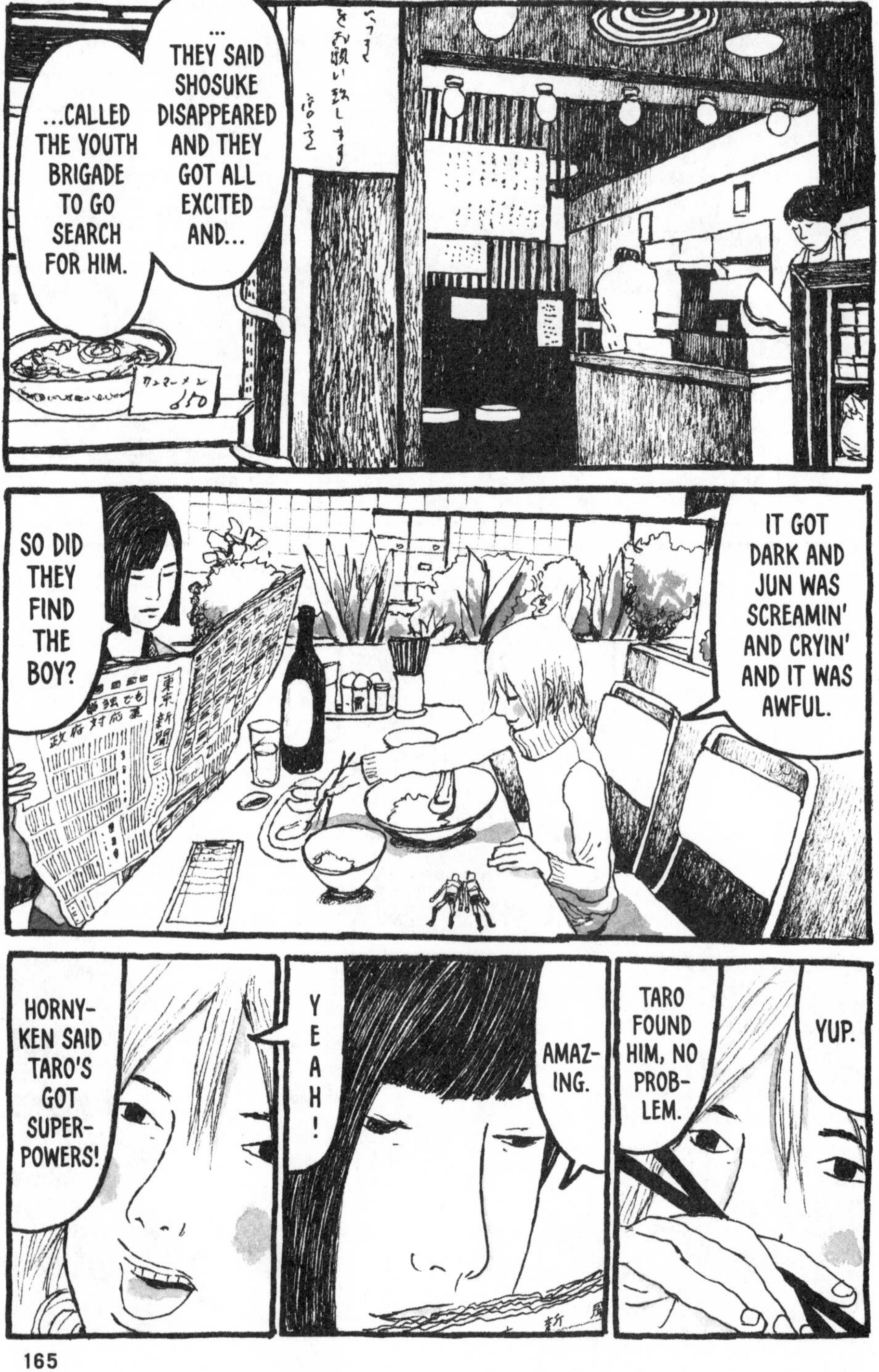
...THEY SAID SHOSUKE DISAPPEARED AND THEY GOT ALL EXCITED AND...
...CALLED THE YOUTH BRIGADE TO GO SEARCH FOR HIM.
IT GOT DARK AND JUN WAS SCREAMIN' AND CRYIN' AND IT WAS AWFUL.
SO DID THEY FIND THE BOY?
東京新聞
YUP.
TARO FOUND HIM, NO PROB-LEM.
AMAZ-ING.
YEAH!
HORNY-KEN SAID TARO'S GOT SUPER-POWERS!

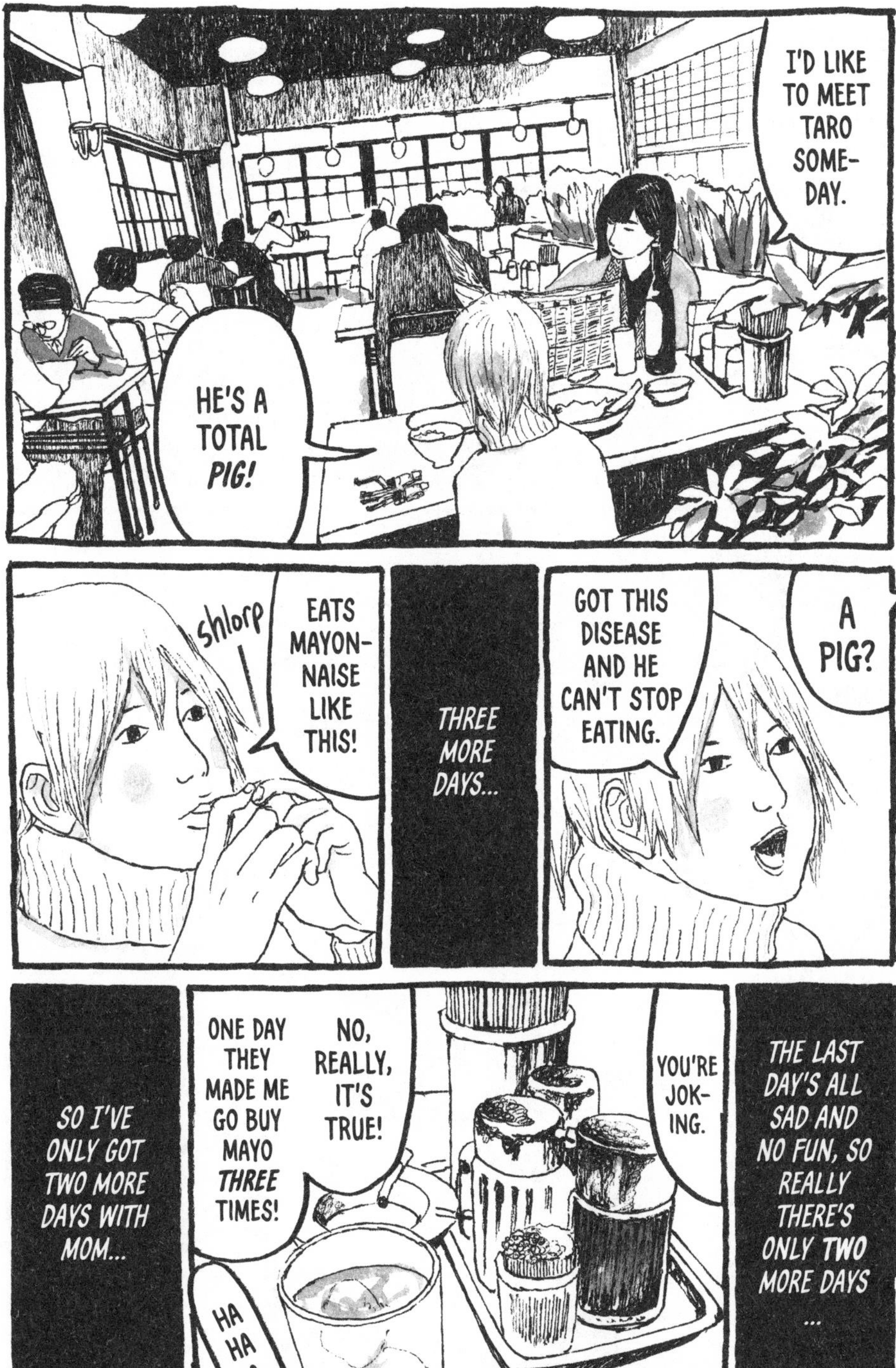
I'D LIKE TO MEET TARO SOME-DAY.
HE'S A TOTAL PIG!
A PIG?
GOT THIS DISEASE AND HE CAN'T STOP EATING.
THREE MORE DAYS...
EATS MAYON-NAISE LIKE THIS!
shlorp
THE LAST DAY'S ALL SAD AND NO FUN, SO REALLY THERE'S ONLY TWO MORE DAYS ...
YOU'RE JOK-ING.
NO, REALLY, IT'S TRUE!
ONE DAY THEY MADE ME GO BUY MAYO THREE TIMES!
HA HA HA.
SO I'VE ONLY GOT TWO MORE DAYS WITH MOM...

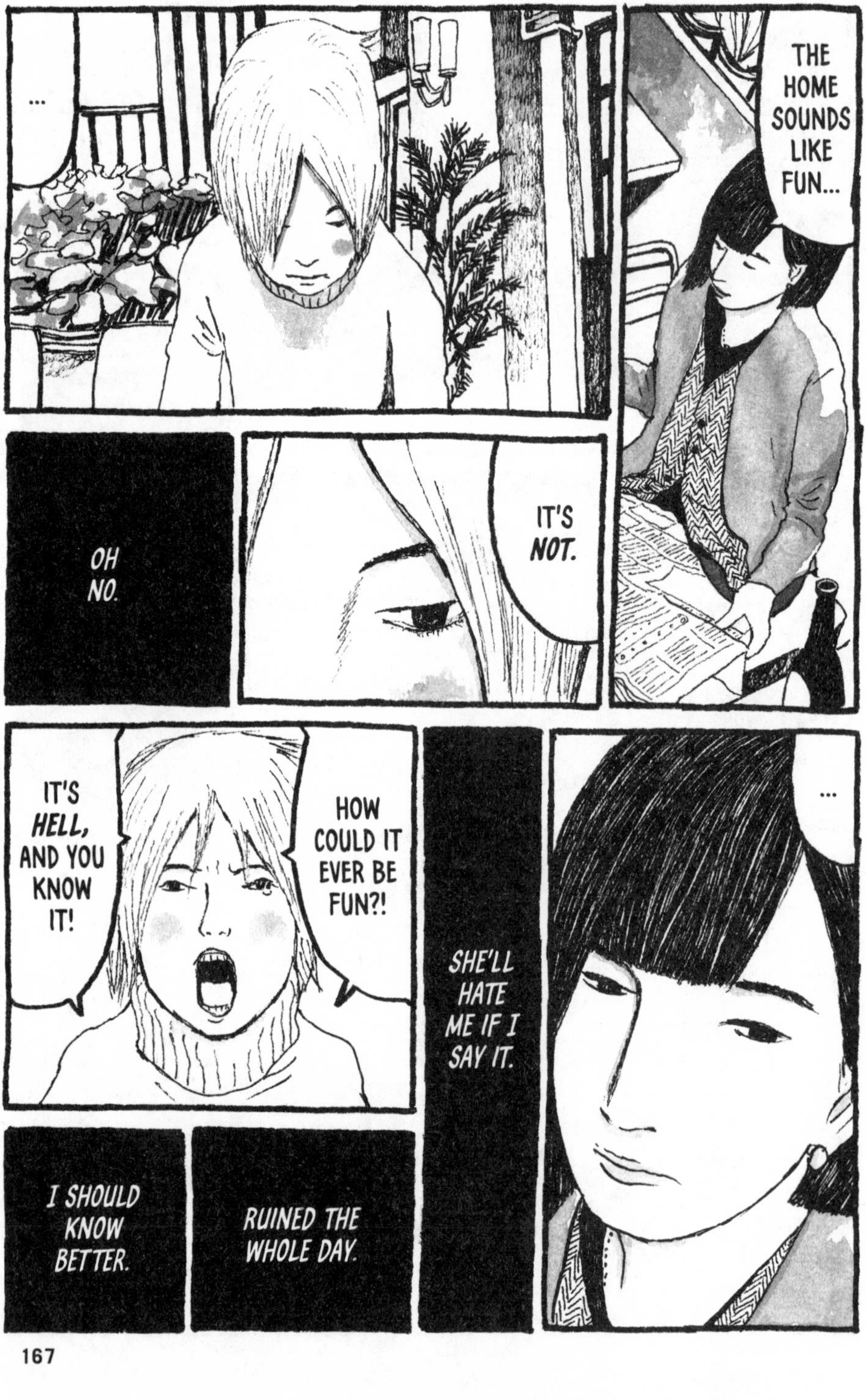
THE HOME SOUNDS LIKE FUN...
...
IT'S *NOT.*
OH NO.
...
SHE'LL HATE ME IF I SAY IT.
HOW COULD IT EVER BE FUN?!
IT'S *HELL,* AND YOU KNOW IT!
RUINED THE WHOLE DAY.
I SHOULD KNOW BETTER.

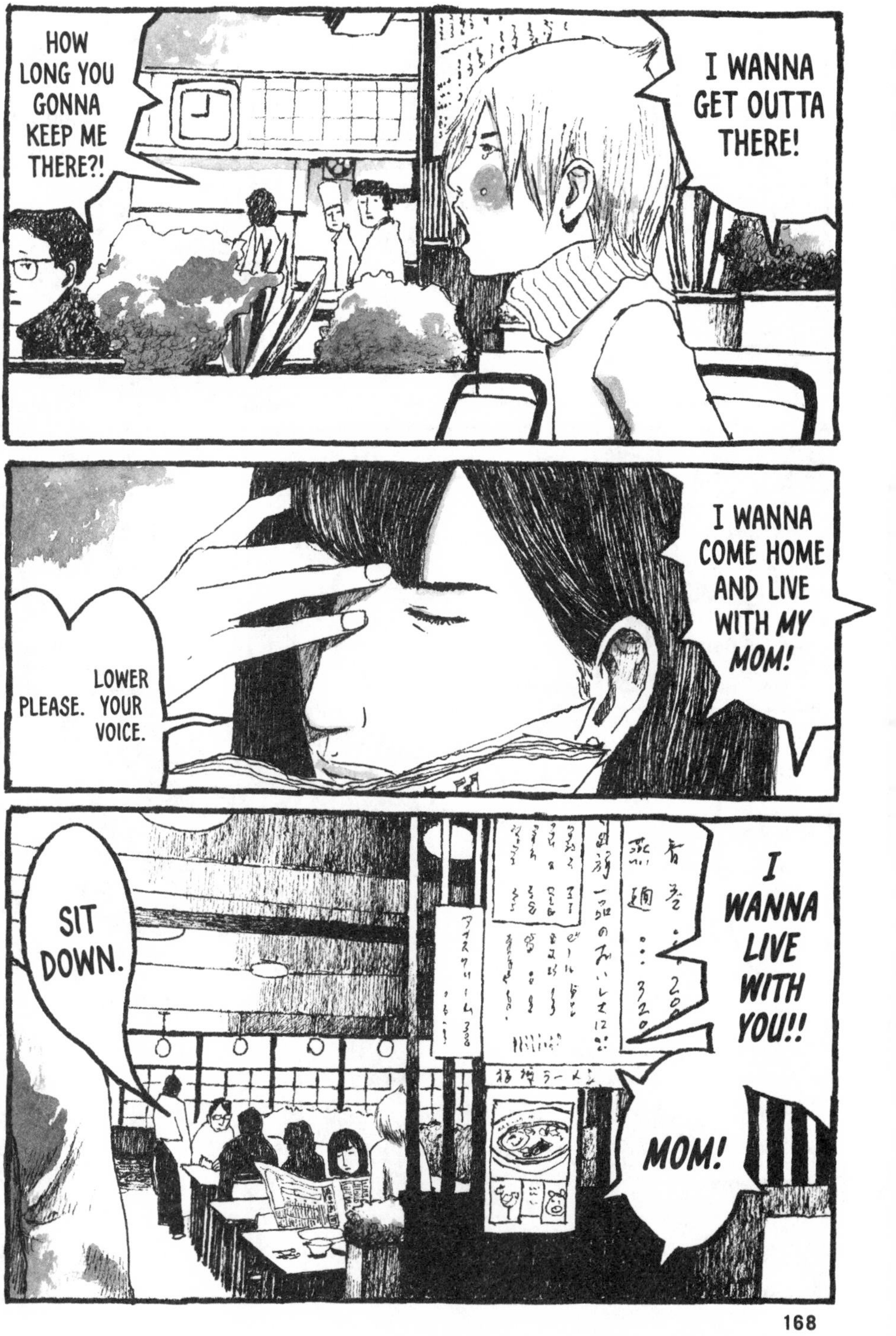
I WANNA GET OUTTA THERE!
HOW LONG YOU GONNA KEEP ME THERE?!
I WANNA COME HOME AND LIVE WITH *MY MOM!*
LOWER YOUR VOICE.
PLEASE.
I WANNA LIVE WITH YOU!!
MOM!
SIT DOWN.

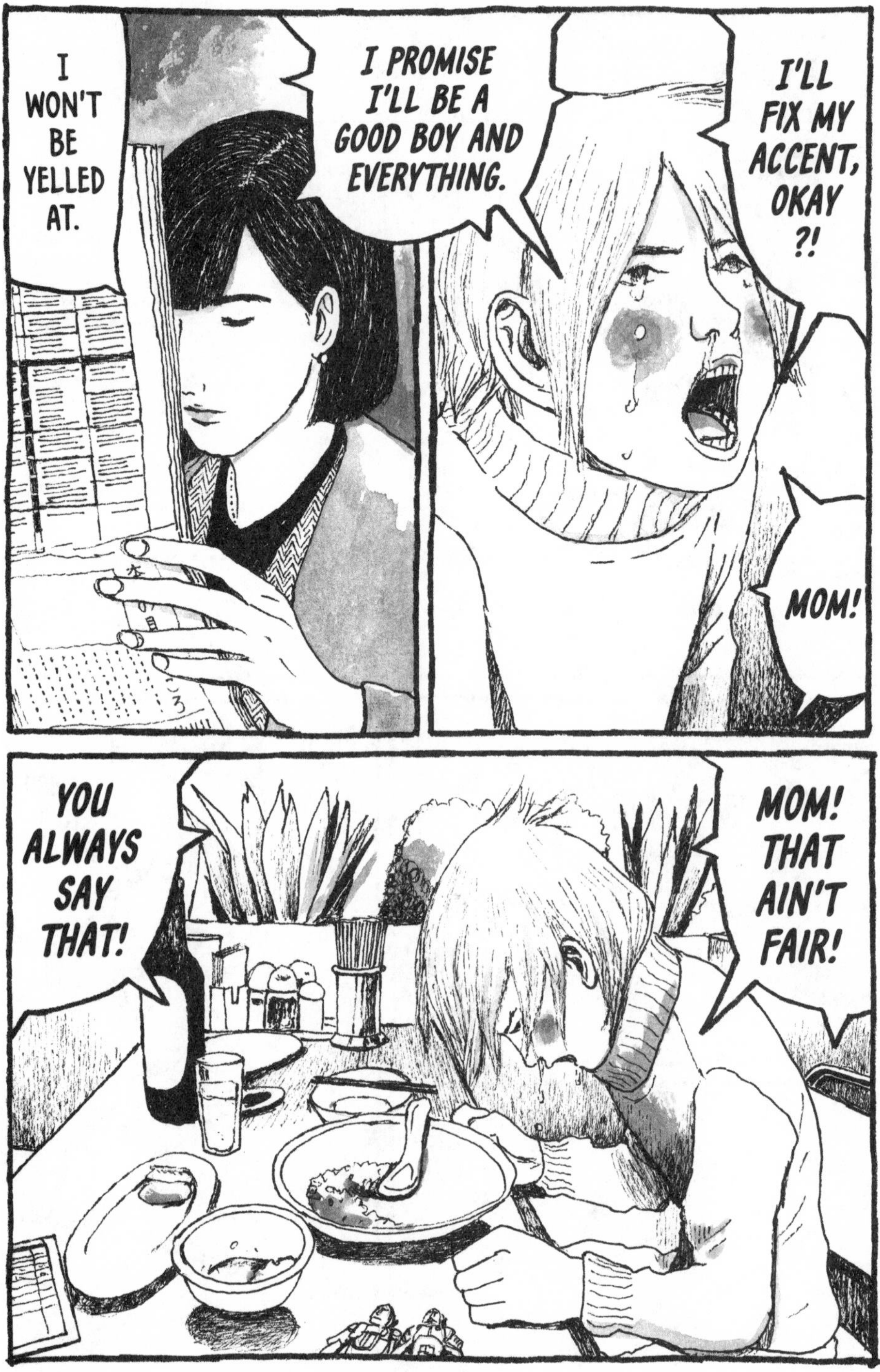
I'LL FIX MY ACCENT, OKAY?!
MOM!
I PROMISE I'LL BE A GOOD BOY AND EVERYTHING.
I WON'T BE YELLED AT.
MOM! THAT AIN'T FAIR!
YOU ALWAYS SAY THAT!

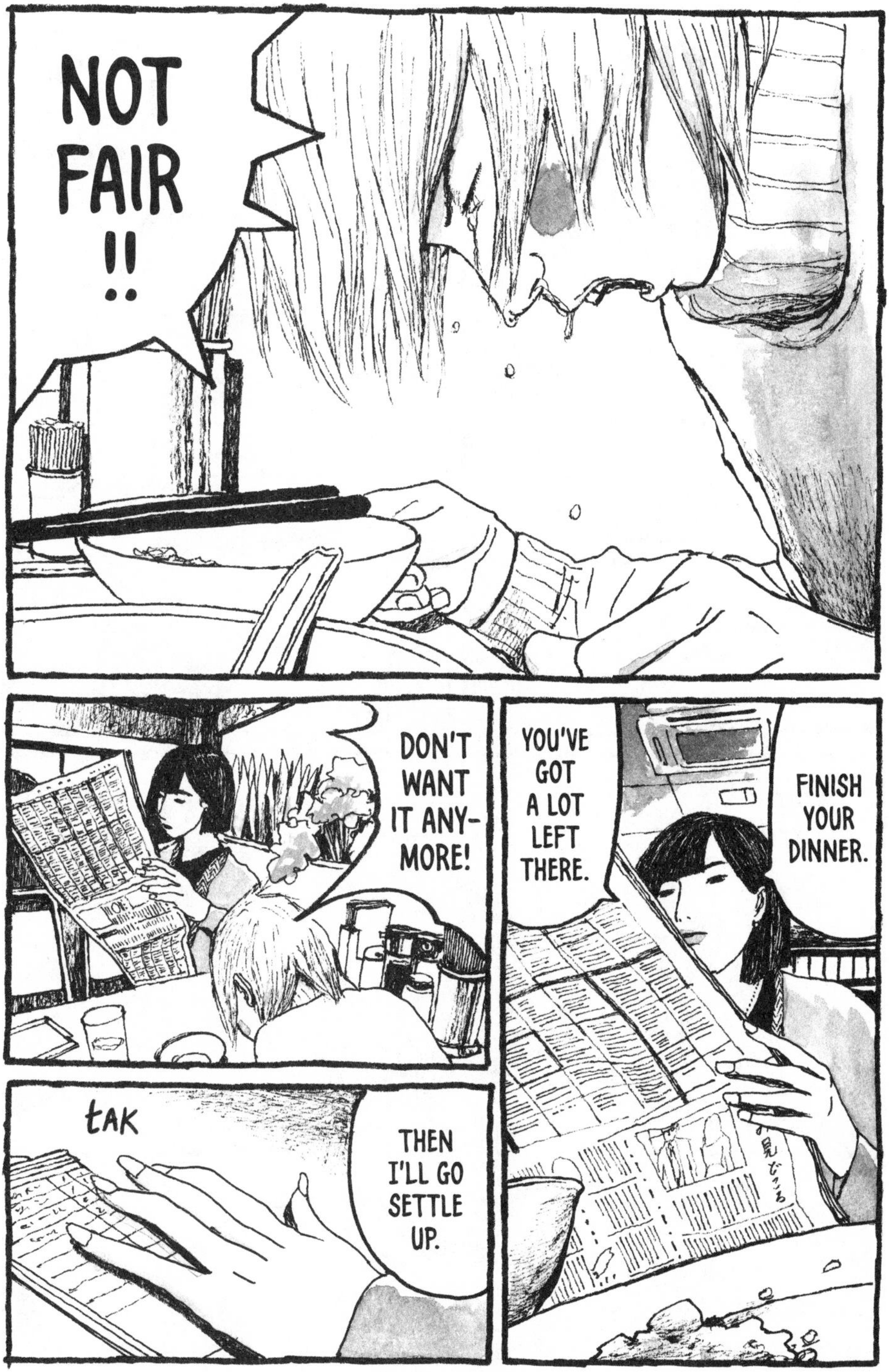
NOT FAIR!!
FINISH YOUR DINNER.
YOU'VE GOT A LOT LEFT THERE.
DON'T WANT IT ANY-MORE!
tak
THEN I'LL GO SETTLE UP.

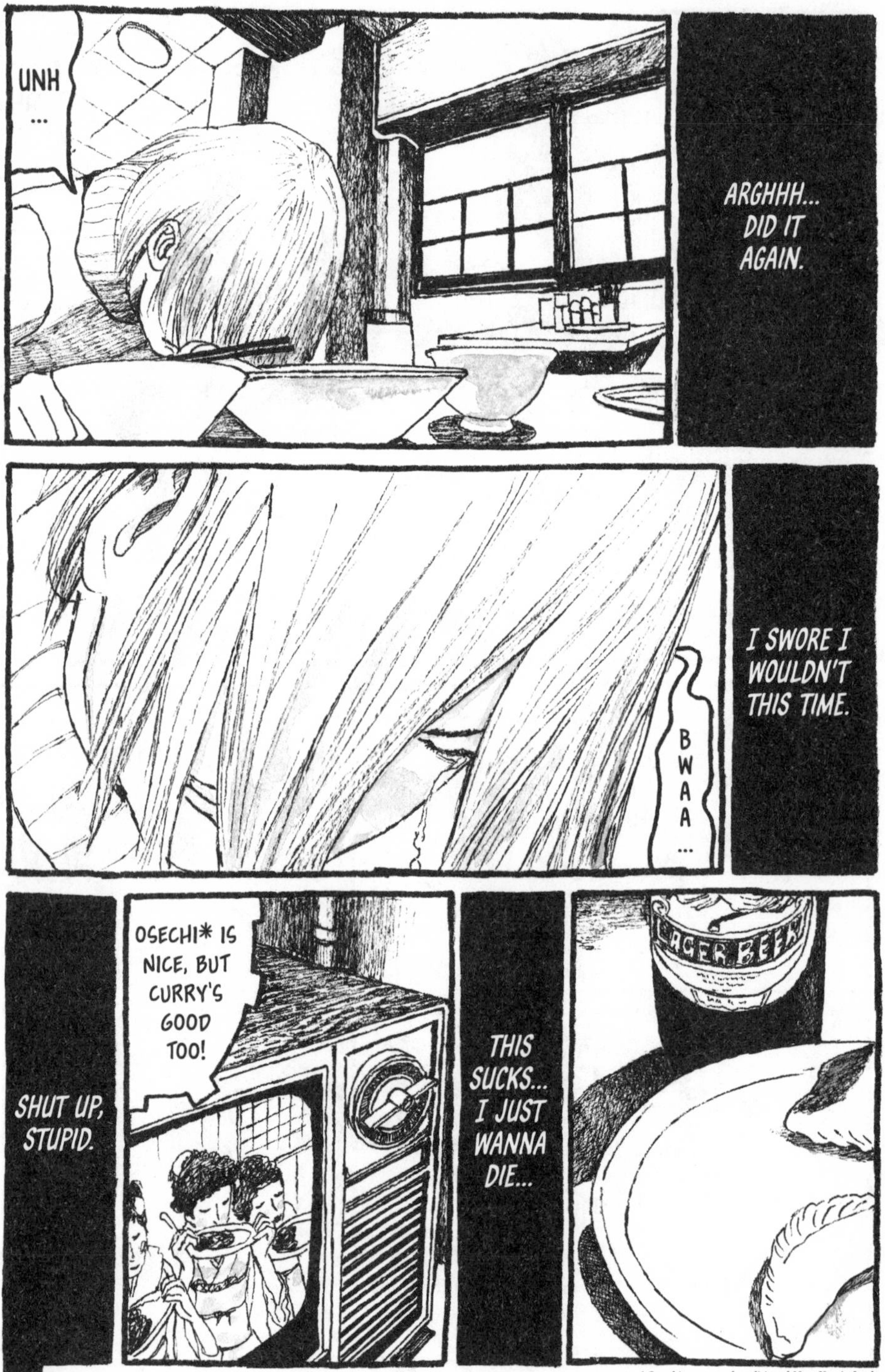
ARGHHH... DID IT AGAIN.
UNH ...
I SWORE I WOULDN'T THIS TIME.
BWAA ...
LAGER BEER
THIS SUCKS... I JUST WANNA DIE...
OSECHI* IS NICE, BUT CURRY'S GOOD TOO!
SHUT UP, STUPID.

*Osechi = a set of traditional New Year's foods

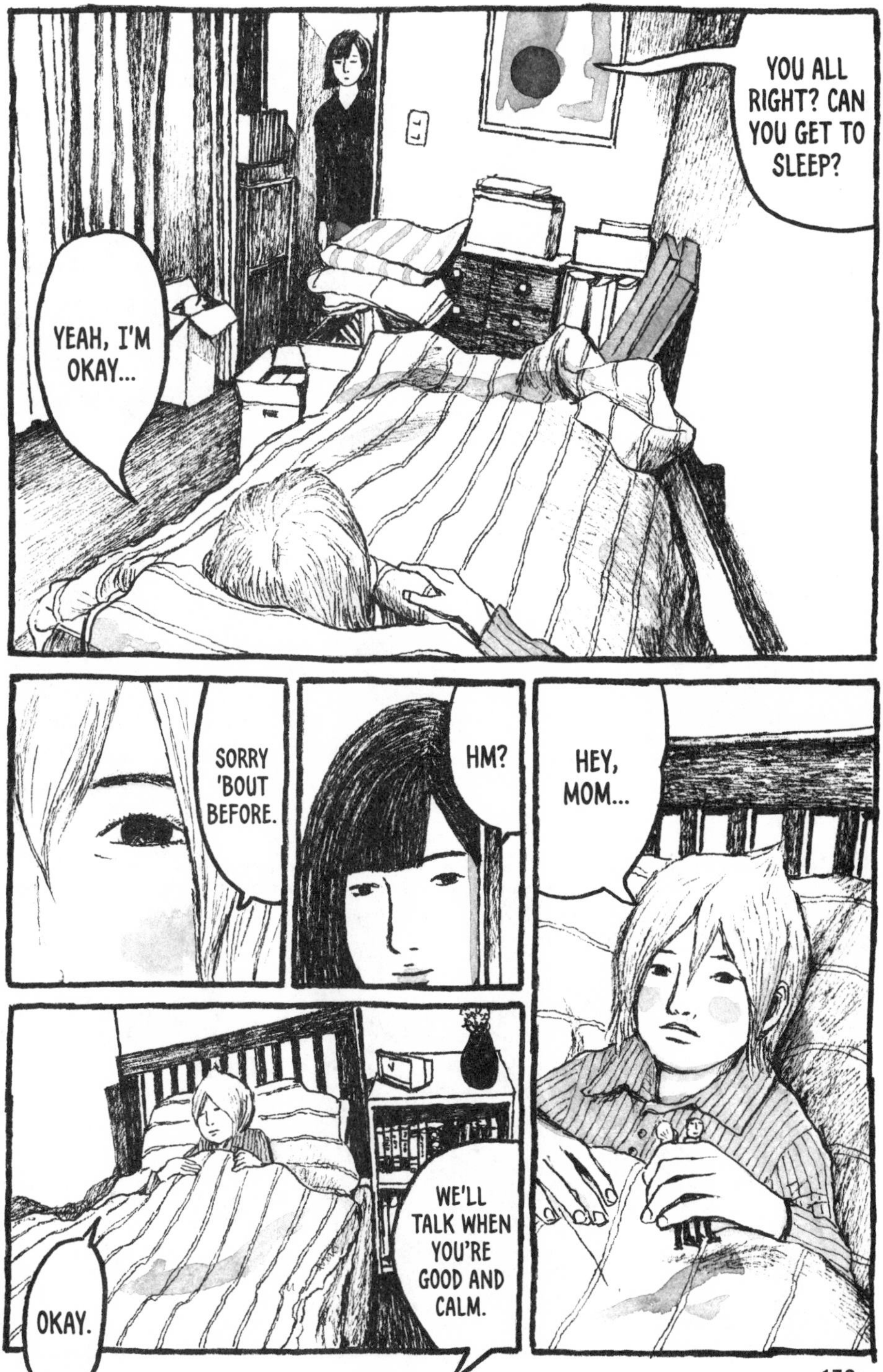
YOU ALL RIGHT? CAN YOU GET TO SLEEP?
YEAH, I'M OKAY...
HEY, MOM...
HM?
SORRY 'BOUT BEFORE.
WE'LL TALK WHEN YOU'RE GOOD AND CALM.
OKAY.

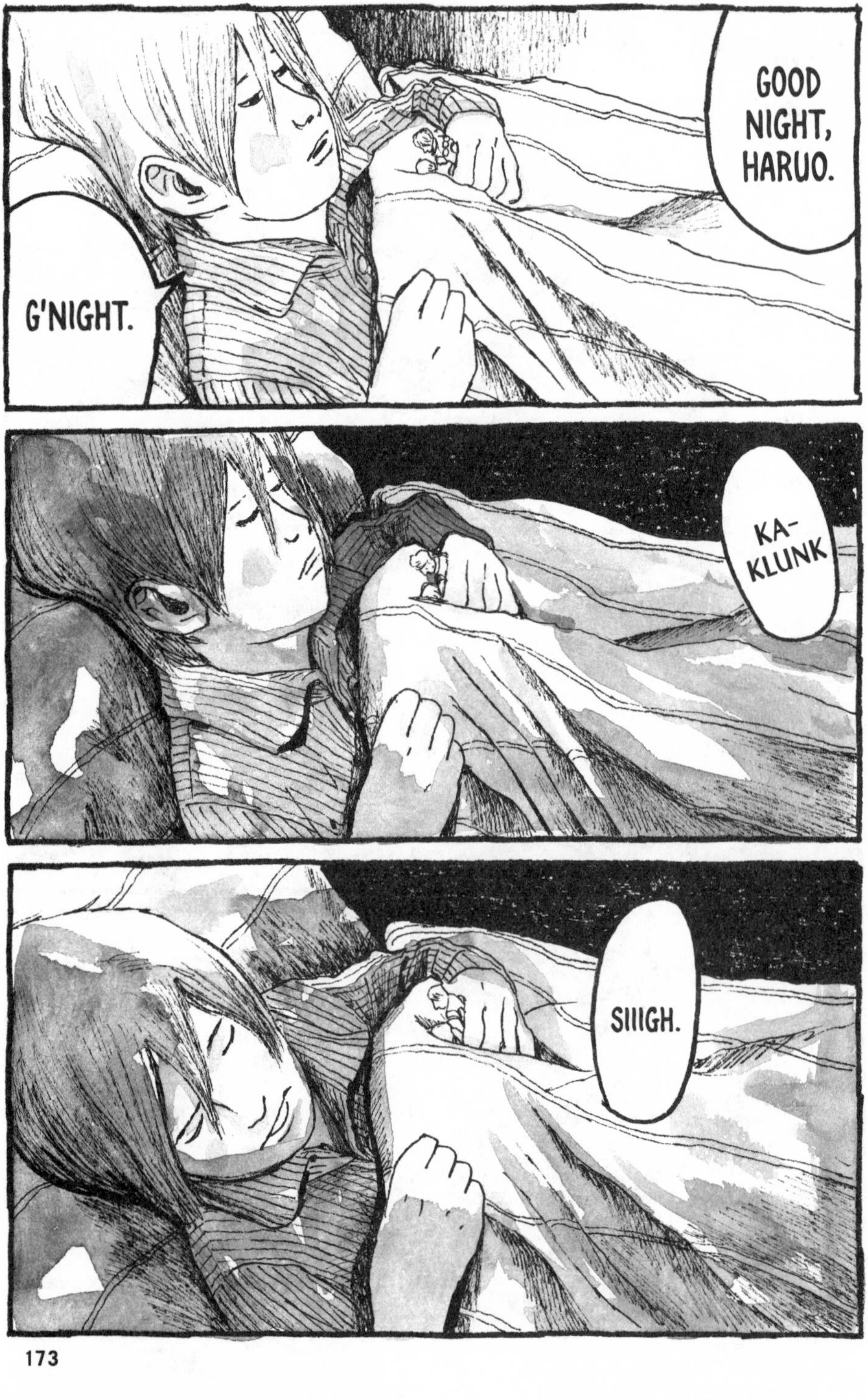
GOOD NIGHT, HARUO.
G'NIGHT.
KA-KLUNK
SIIIGH.

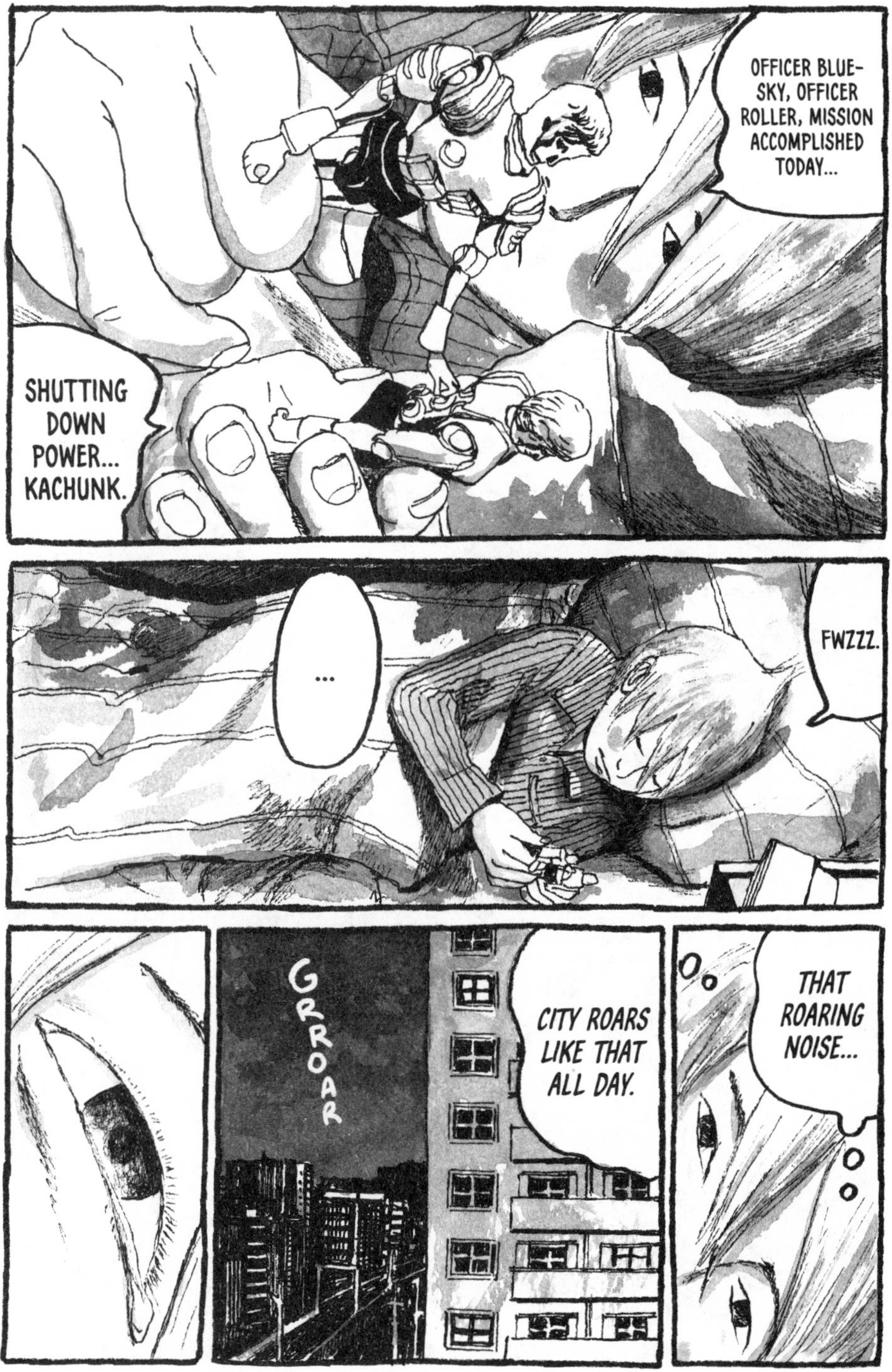

OFFICER BLUE-SKY, OFFICER ROLLER, MISSION ACCOMPLISHED TODAY...
SHUTTING DOWN POWER... KACHUNK.
FWZZZ.
...
THAT ROARING NOISE...
CITY ROARS LIKE THAT ALL DAY.
GRROAR

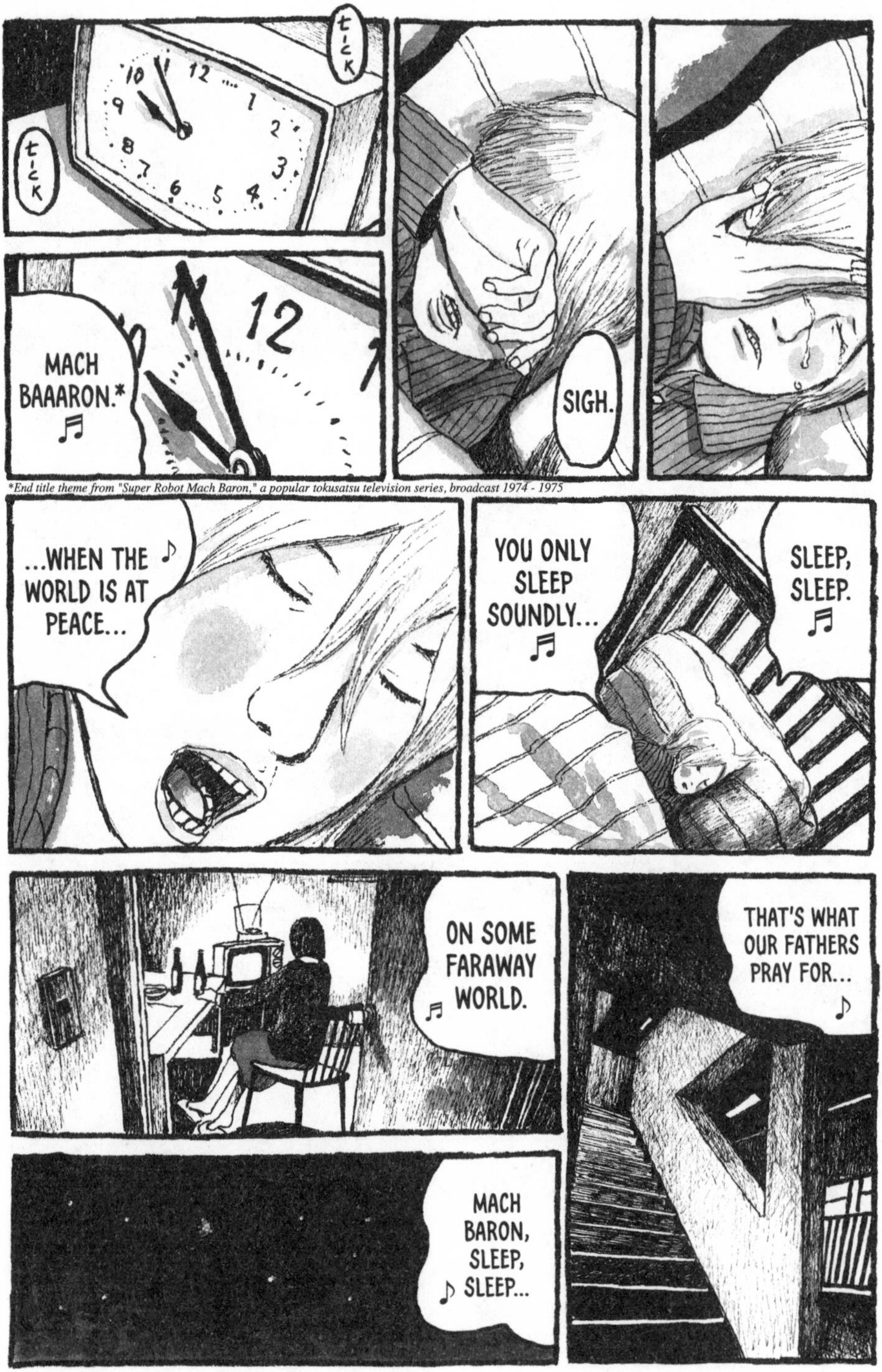
SIGH.
tick
tick
MACH BAAARON.*
SLEEP, SLEEP.
YOU ONLY SLEEP SOUNDLY...
...WHEN THE WORLD IS AT PEACE...
THAT'S WHAT OUR FATHERS PRAY FOR...
ON SOME FARAWAY WORLD.
MACH BARON, SLEEP, SLEEP...

*End title theme from "Super Robot Mach Baron," a popular tokusatsu television series, broadcast 1974 - 1975

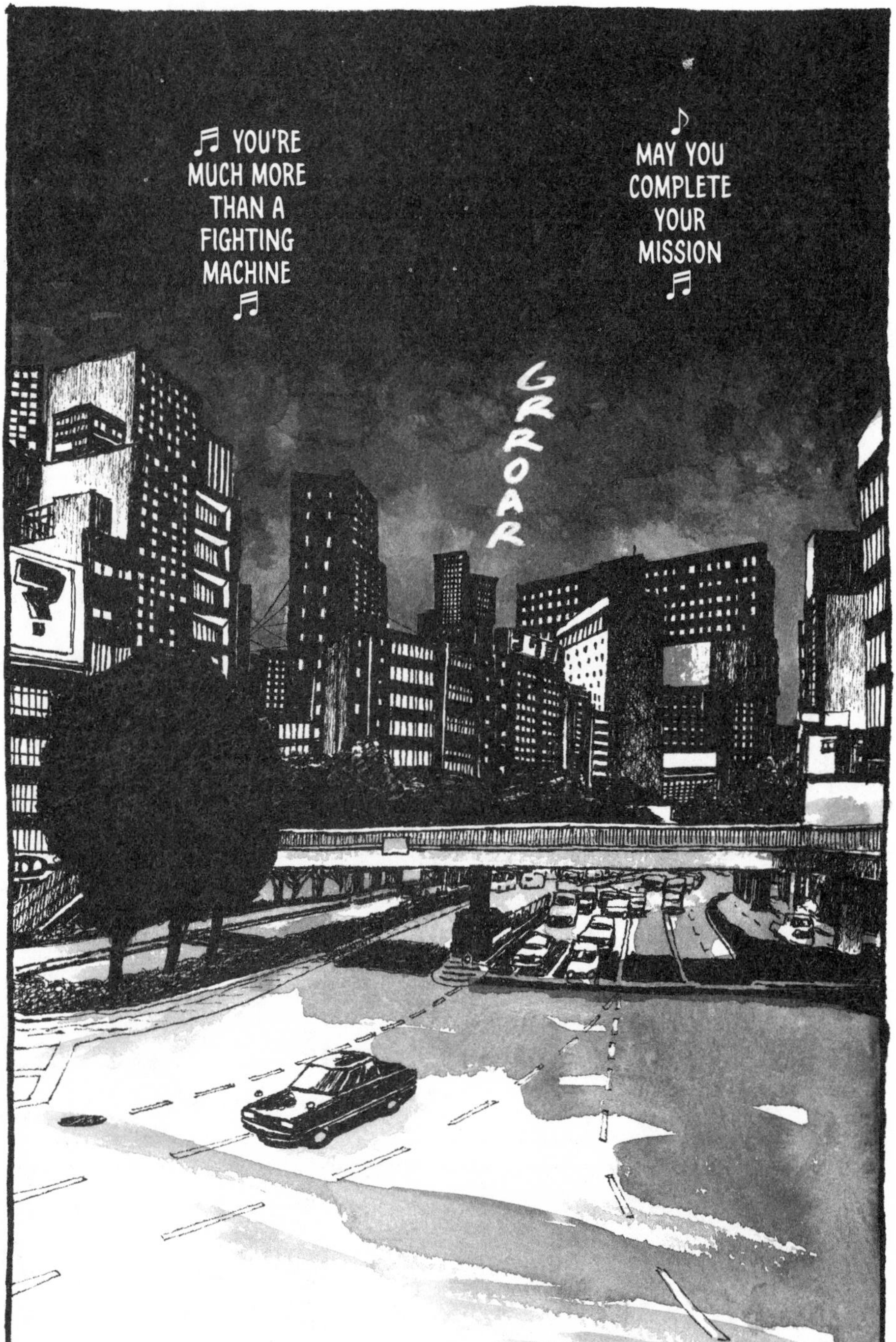
♪ MAY YOU COMPLETE YOUR MISSION ♬
♬ YOU'RE MUCH MORE THAN A FIGHTING MACHINE ♬
GRROAR

CHAPTER 12

"The city always seems angry."

"Like it's shoutin' 'HEY!' or somethin'?"

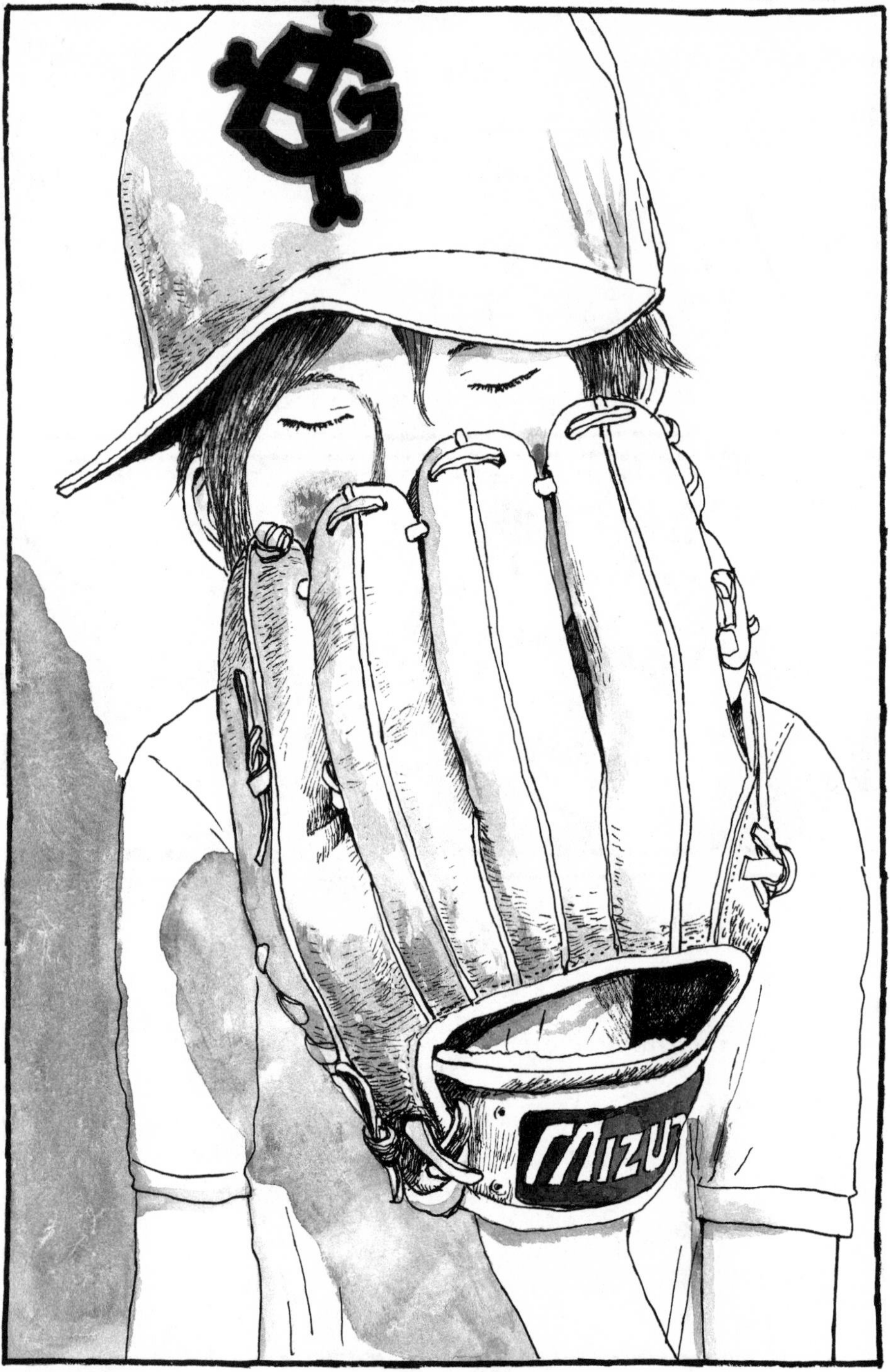
MIZUN

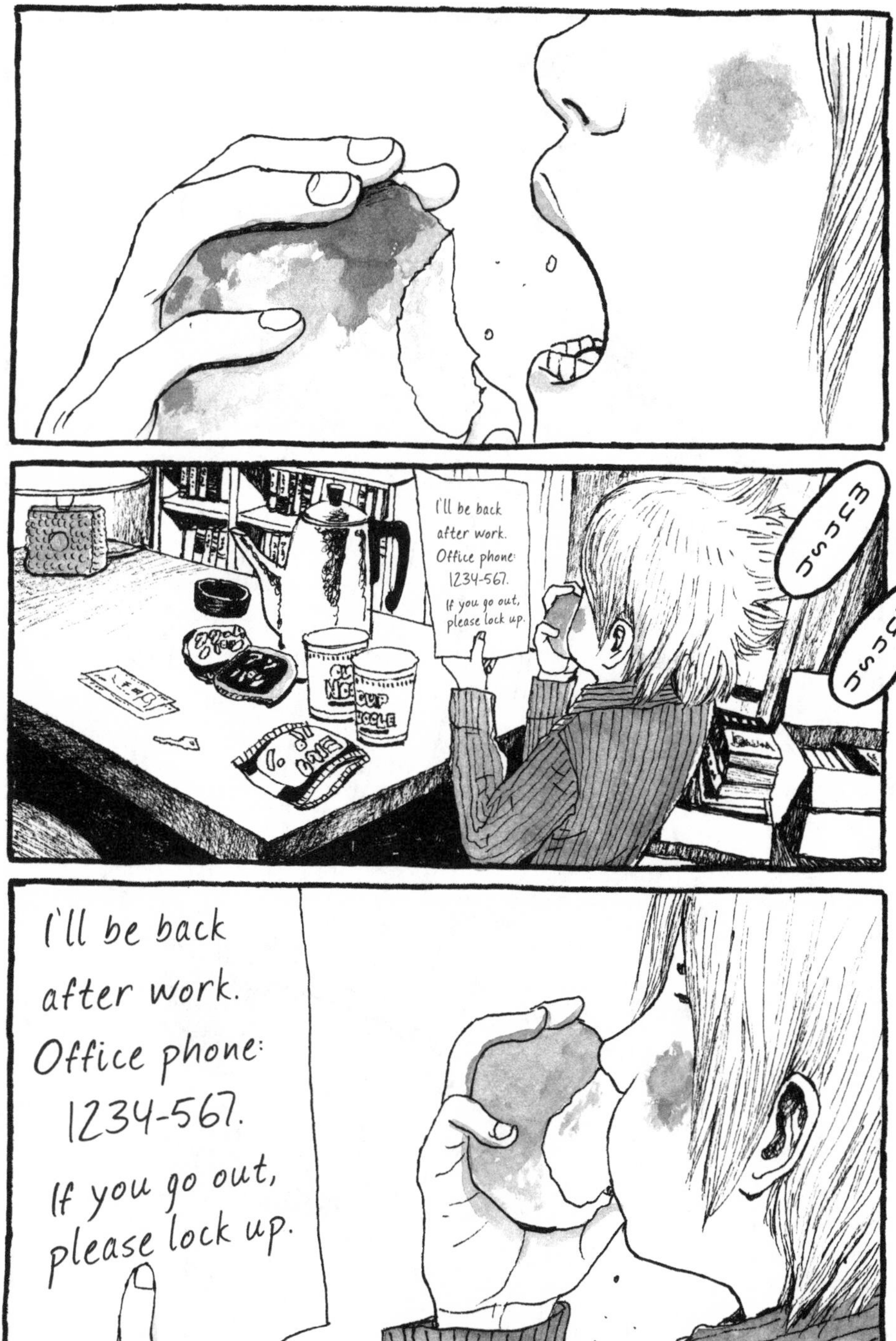
I'll be back after work. Office phone: 1234-567. If you go out, please lock up.
I'll be back after work. Office phone: 1234-567. If you go out, please lock up.

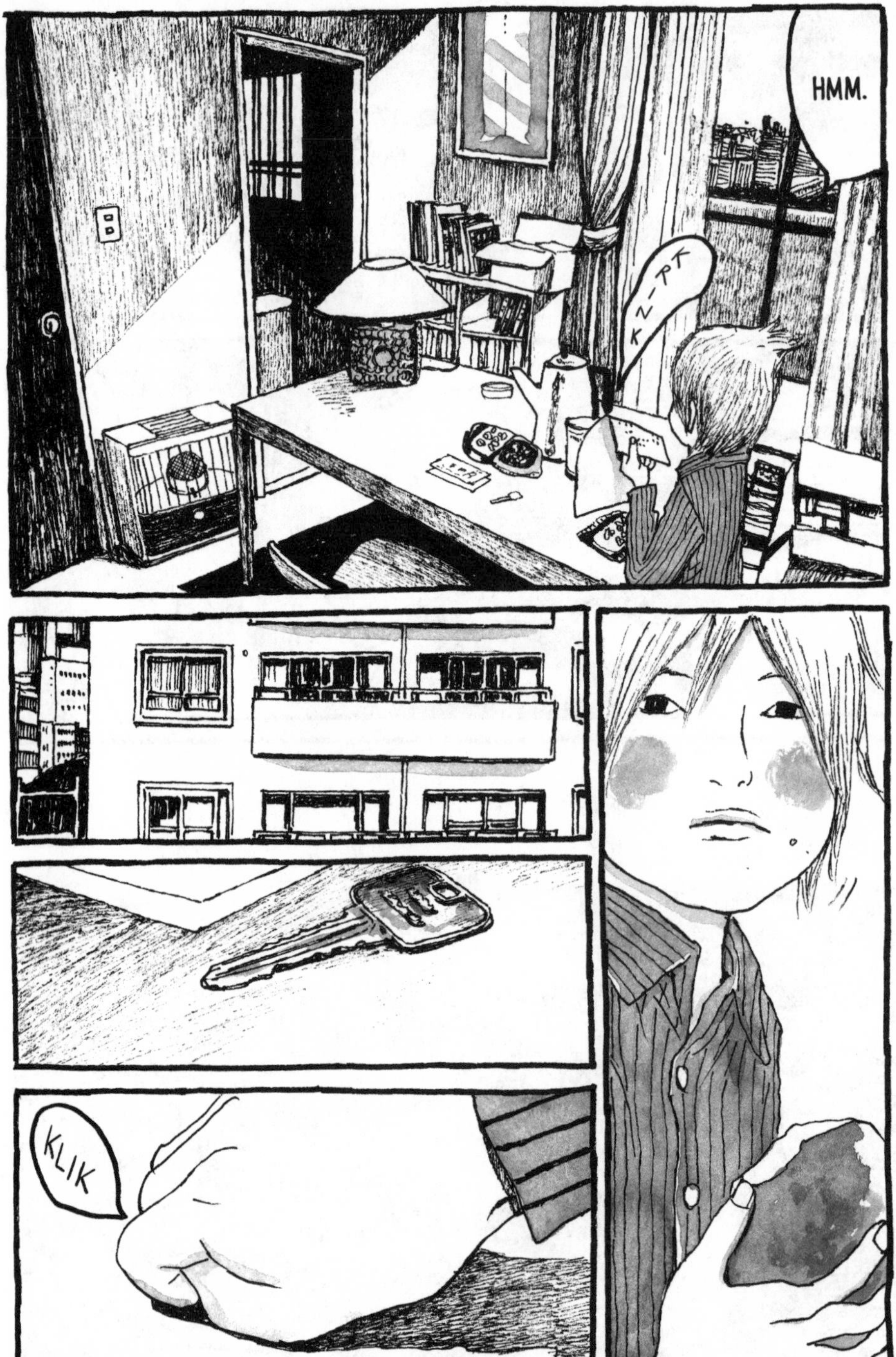
HMM.
KNIRK
KLIK

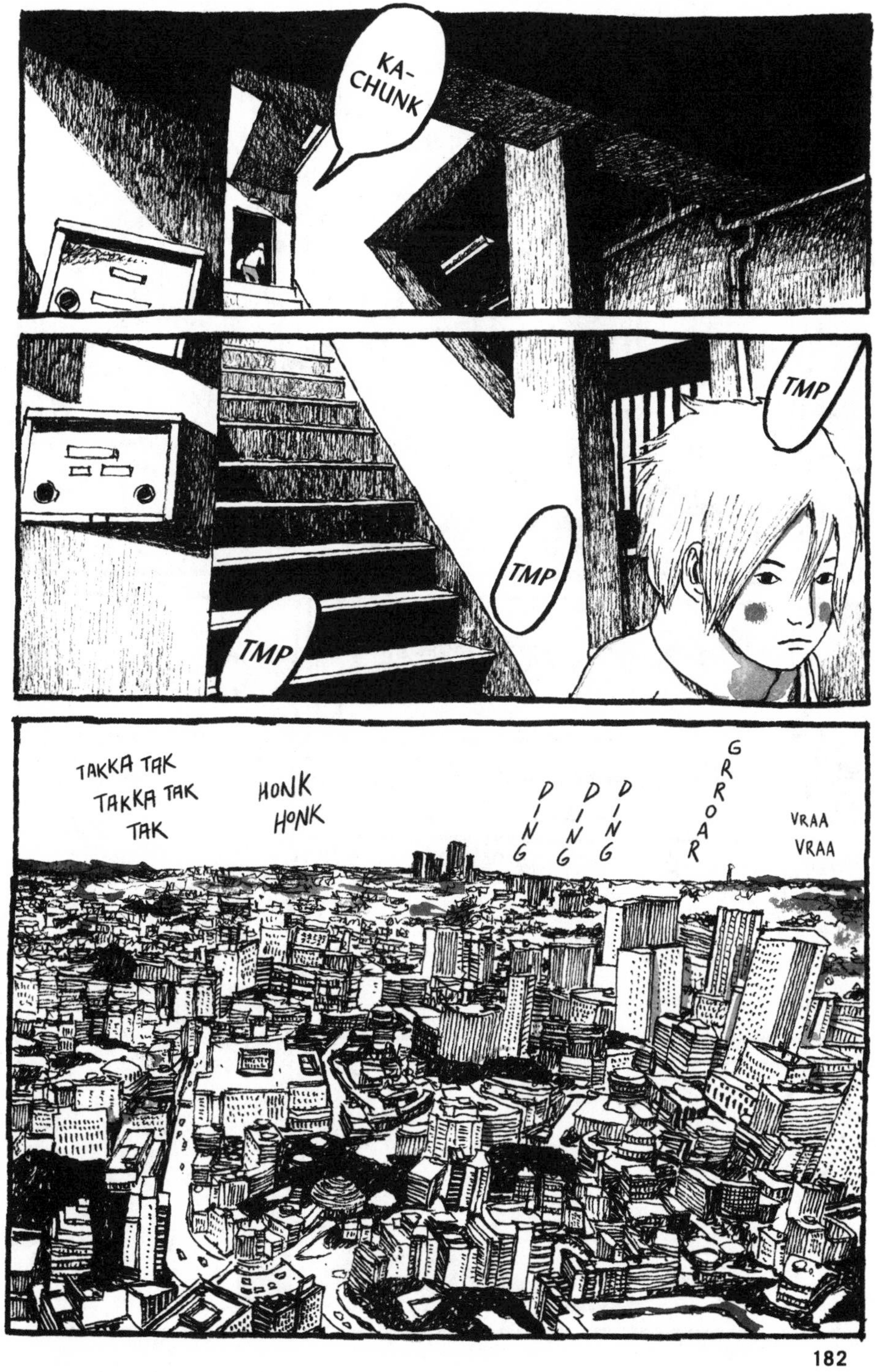
KA-CHUNK
TMP
TMP
TMP
VRAA VRAA
GRROAR
DING
DING
DING
HONK HONK
TAKKA TAK TAKKA TAK TAK

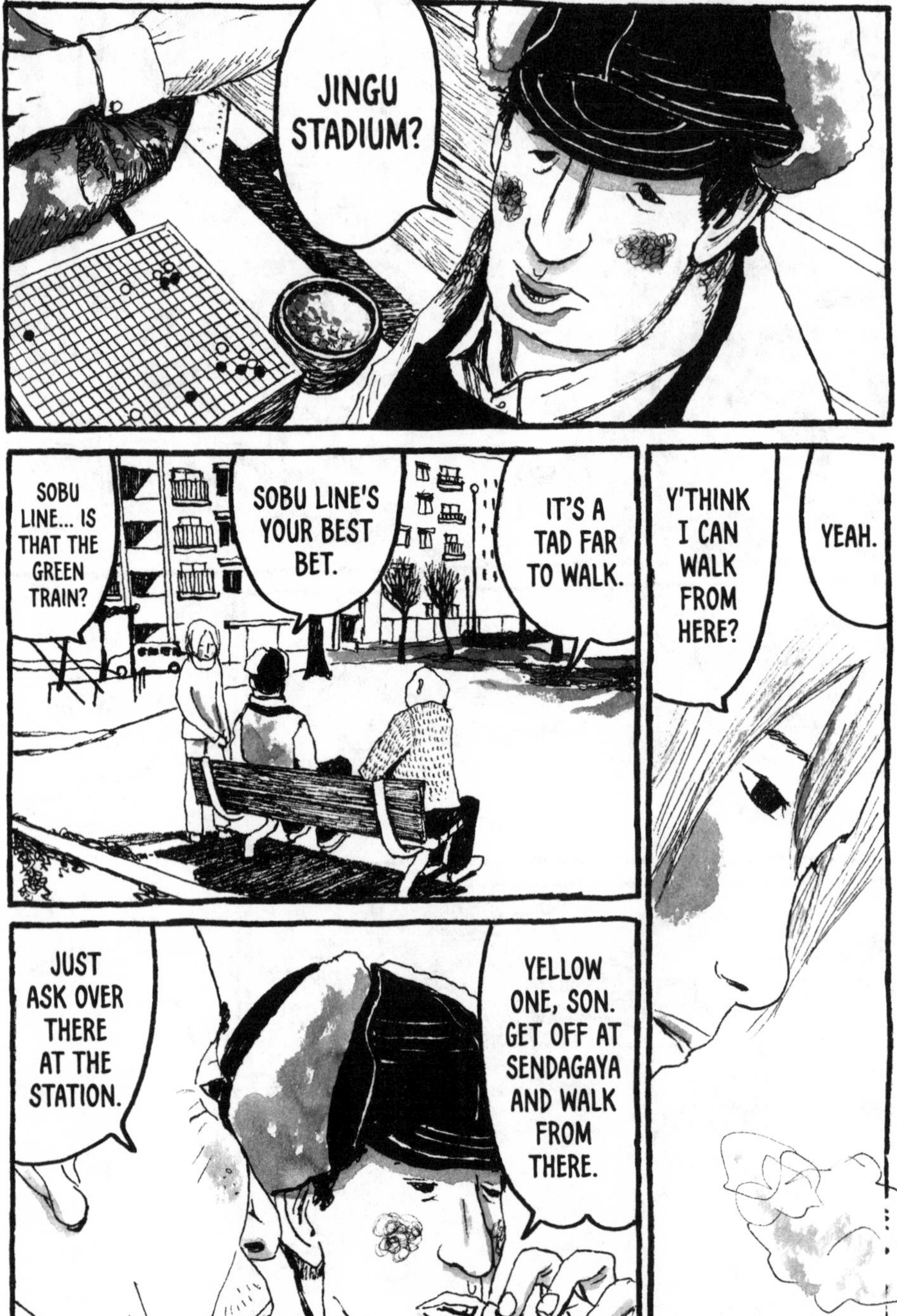
JINGU STADIUM?
YEAH.
Y'THINK I CAN WALK FROM HERE?
...
IT'S A TAD FAR TO WALK.
SOBU LINE'S YOUR BEST BET.
SOBU LINE... IS THAT THE GREEN TRAIN?
YELLOW ONE, SON. GET OFF AT SENDAGAYA AND WALK FROM THERE.
JUST ASK OVER THERE AT THE STATION.

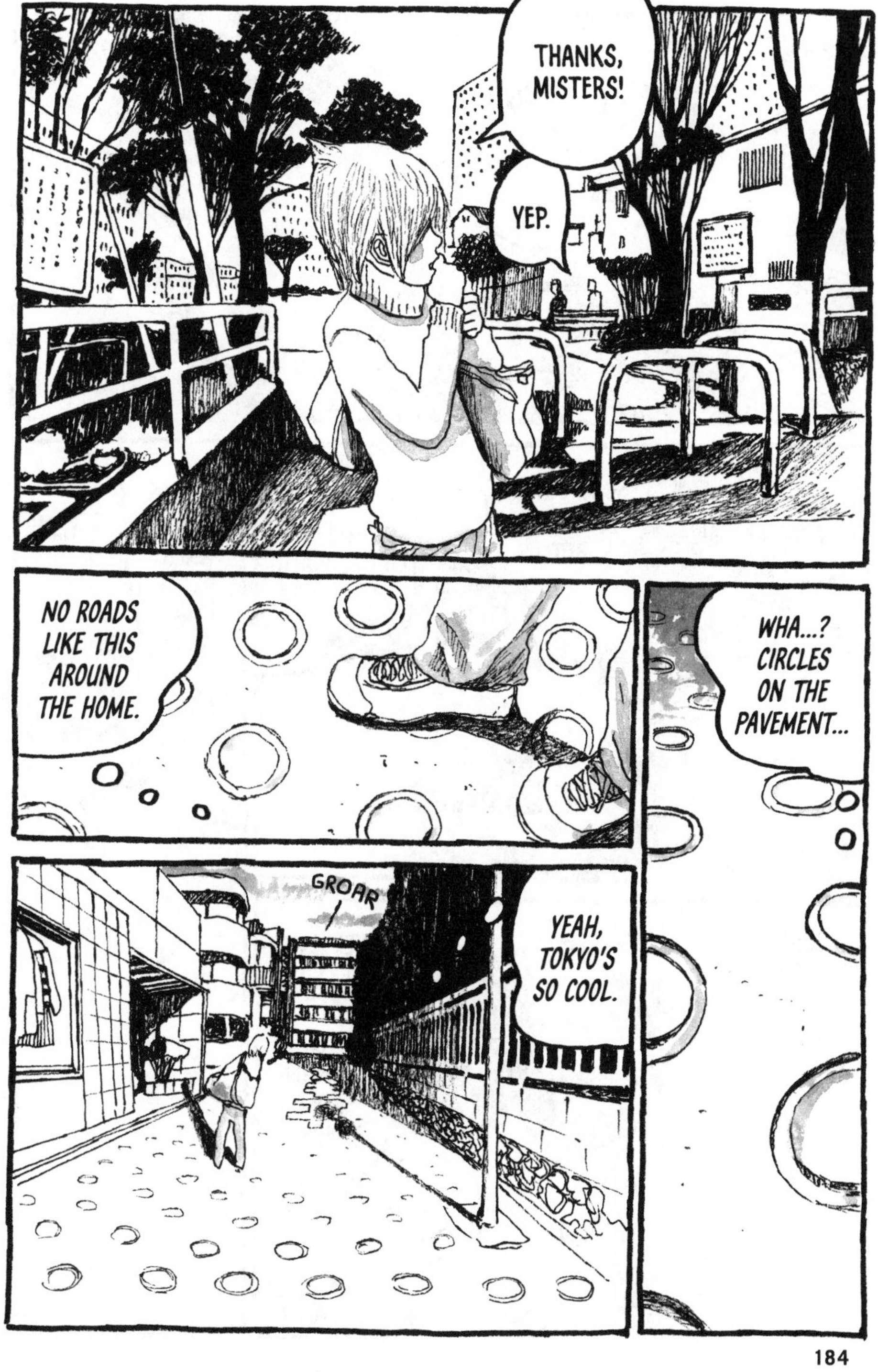
THANKS, MISTERS!
YEP.
WHA...? CIRCLES ON THE PAVEMENT...
NO ROADS LIKE THIS AROUND THE HOME.
YEAH, TOKYO'S SO COOL.
GROAR

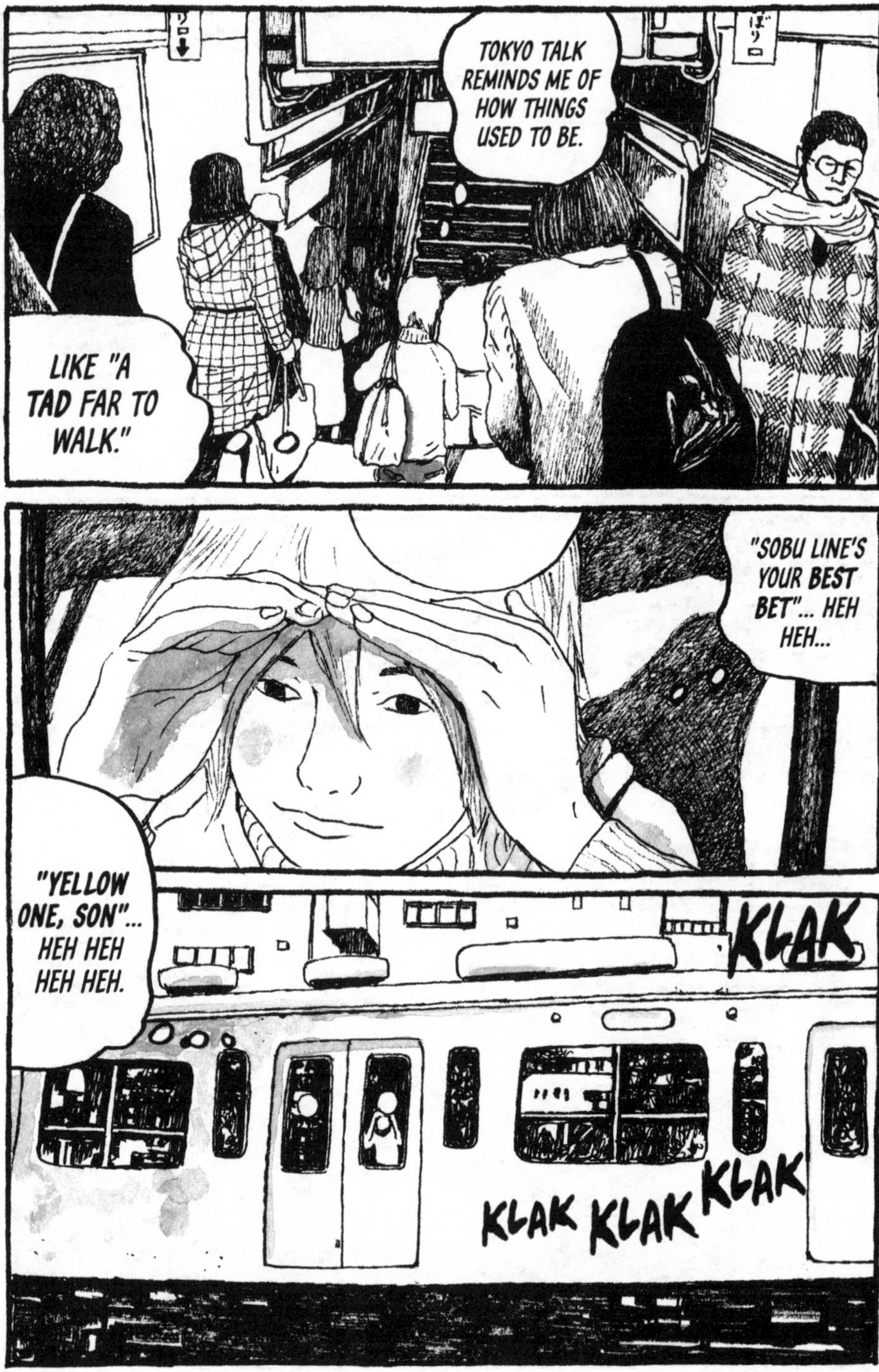
TOKYO TALK REMINDS ME OF HOW THINGS USED TO BE.
LIKE "A TAD FAR TO WALK."
"SOBU LINE'S YOUR BEST BET"... HEH HEH...
"YELLOW ONE, SON"... HEH HEH HEH HEH.
KLAK
KLAK KLAK KLAK

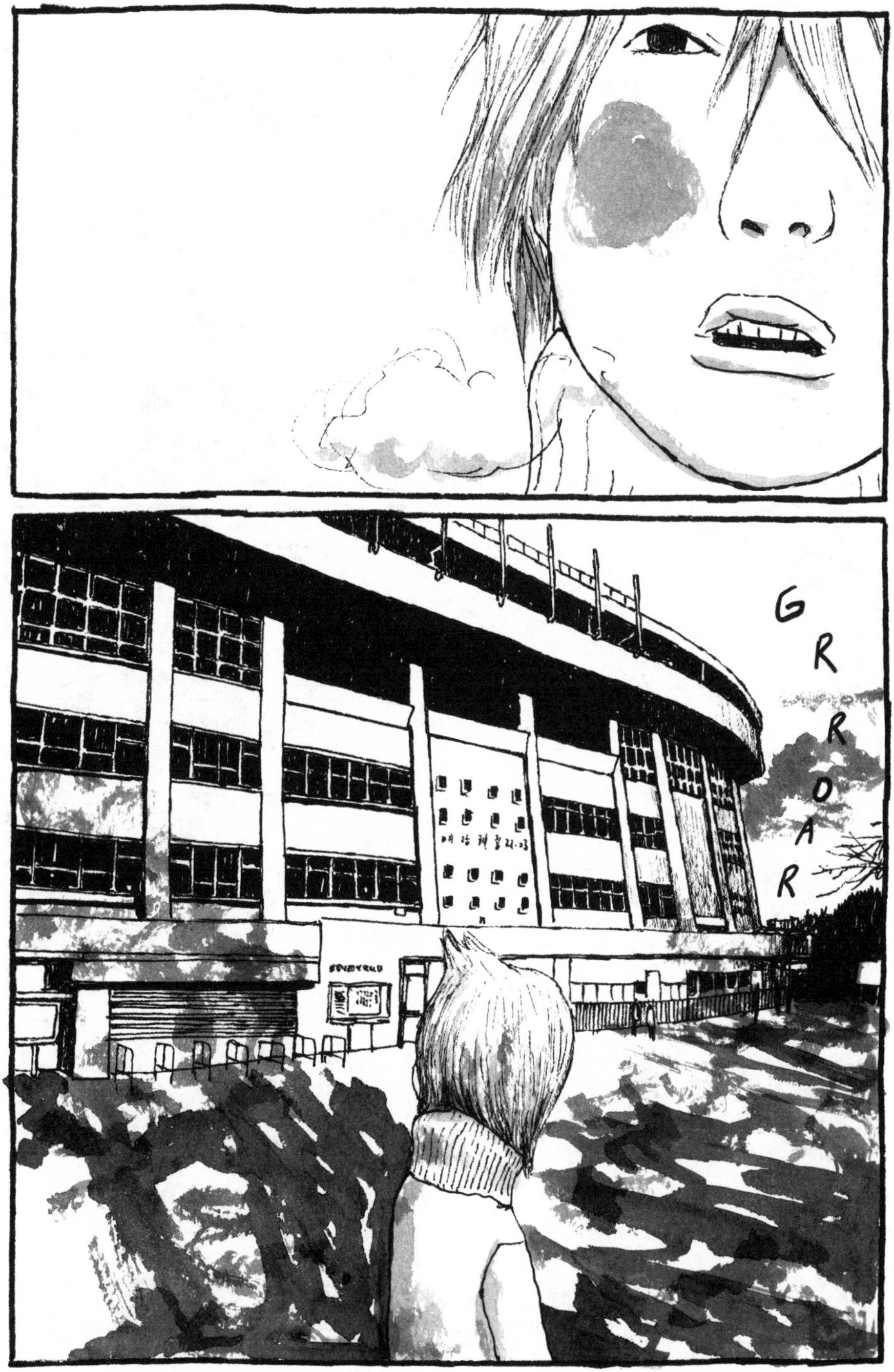
GRROAR

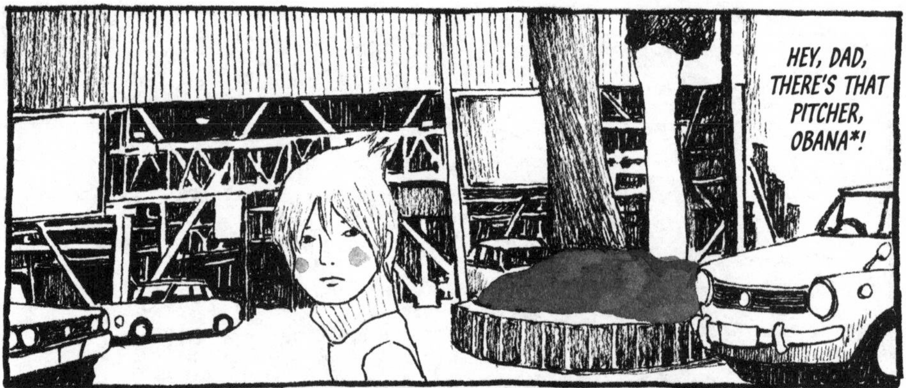
HEY, DAD, THERE'S THAT PITCHER, OBANA*!

*Takao Obana, starting pitcher for the Yakult Swallows, 1978 – 1991

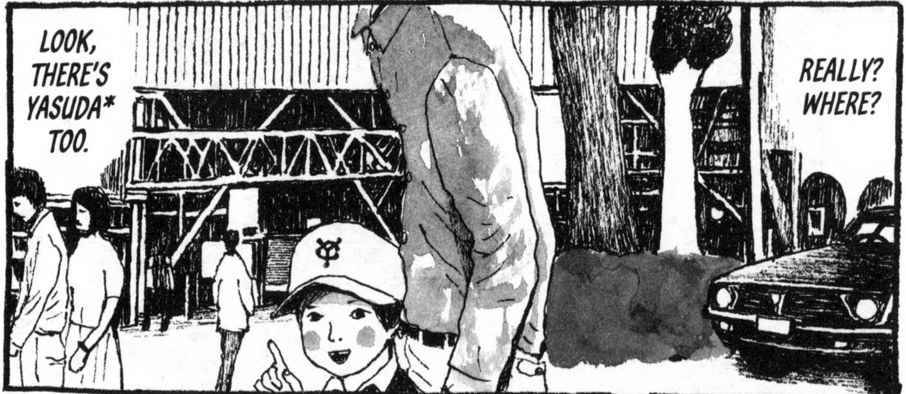
REALLY? WHERE?
LOOK, THERE'S YASUDA* TOO.

*Takeshi Yasuda, veteran southpaw pitcher for the Yakult Swallows, 1972–1981

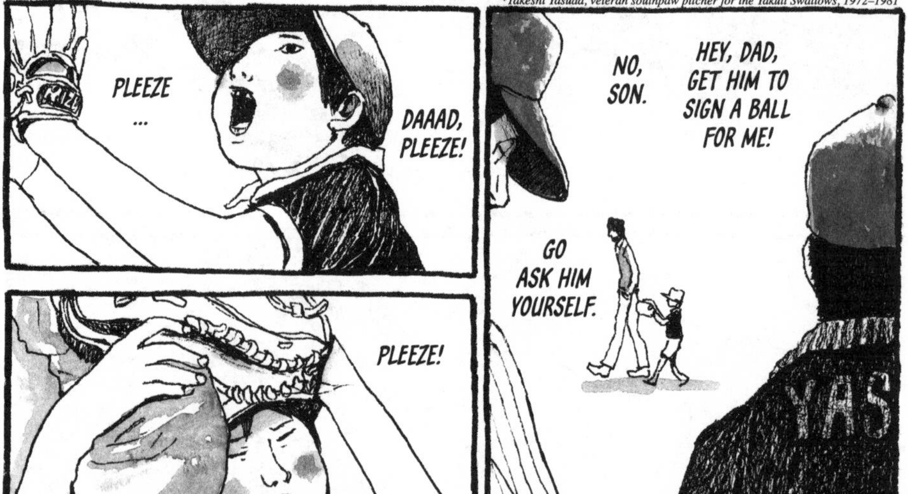
HEY, DAD, GET HIM TO SIGN A BALL FOR ME!
NO, SON.
GO ASK HIM YOURSELF.
YAS
DAAAD, PLEEZE!
PLEEZE ...
PLEEZE!

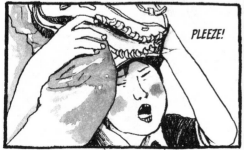

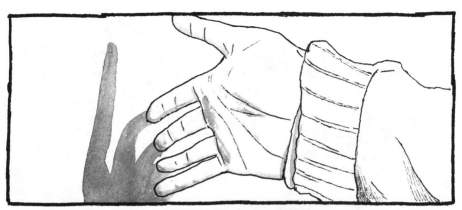

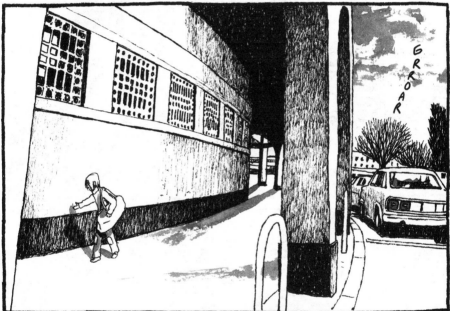

GRROAR

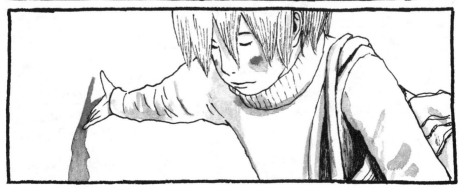

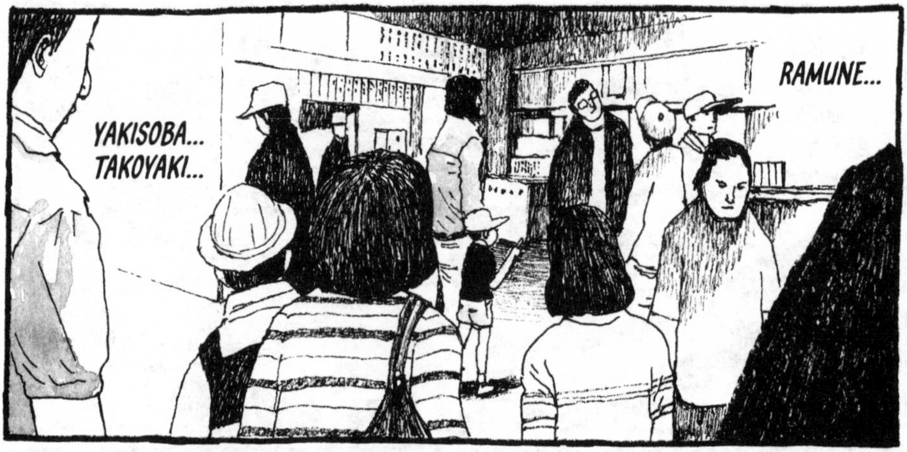
RAMUNE...
YAKISOBA... TAKOYAKI...

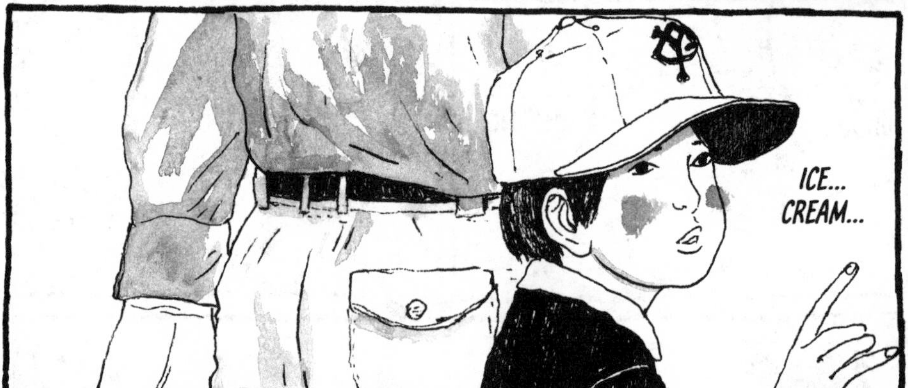
ICE... CREAM...

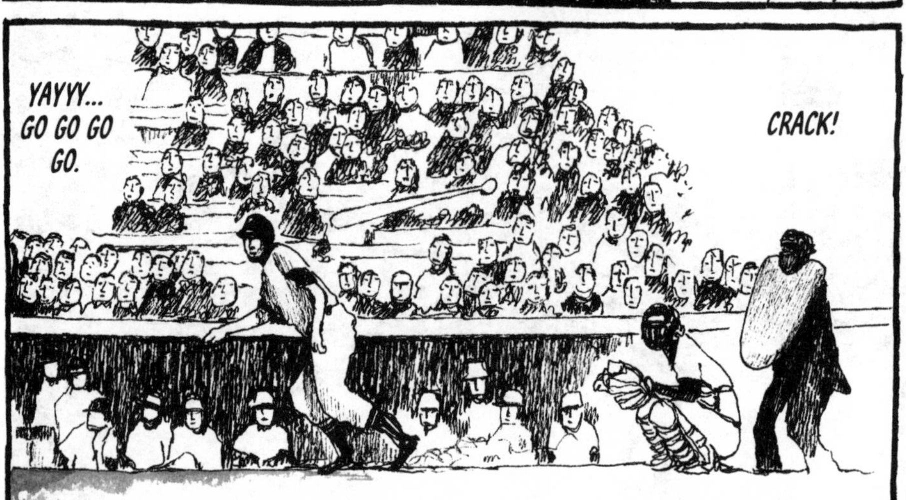
CRACK!
YAYYY... GO GO GO GO.

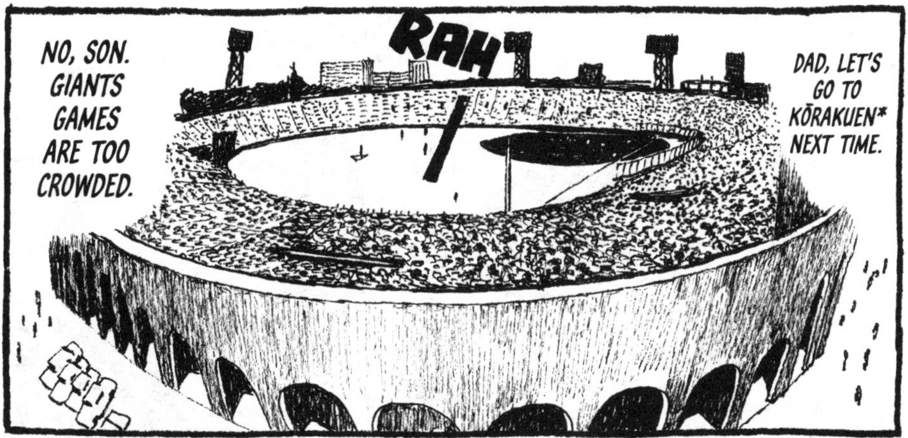
DAD, LET'S GO TO KŌRAKUEN* NEXT TIME.
RAH
NO, SON. GIANTS GAMES ARE TOO CROWDED.

*Kōrakuen = home of the Yomiuri Giants

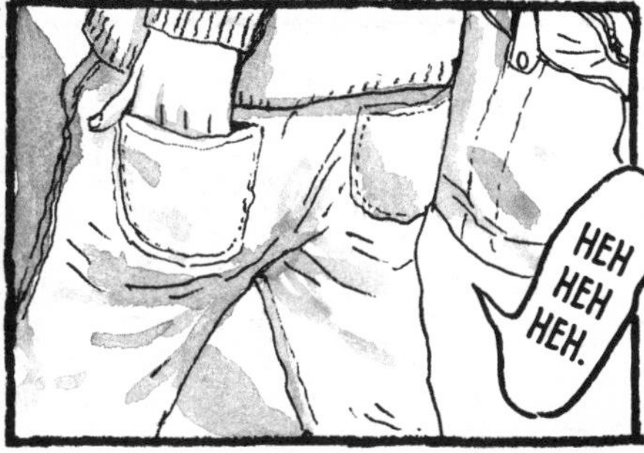
HEH HEH HEH.

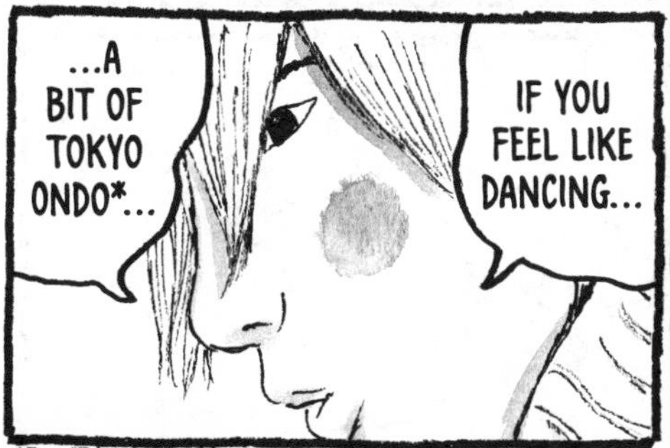
IF YOU FEEL LIKE DANCING...
...A BIT OF TOKYO ONDO*...

*From "Tokyo Ondo" ("Tokyo Spirits"), unofficial rally song for Yakult Swallows fans

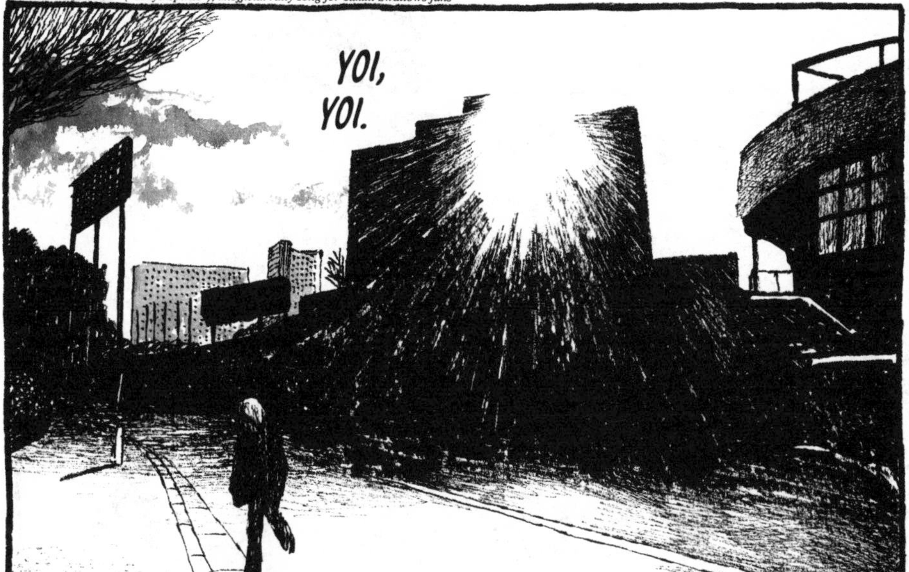
YOI, YOI.

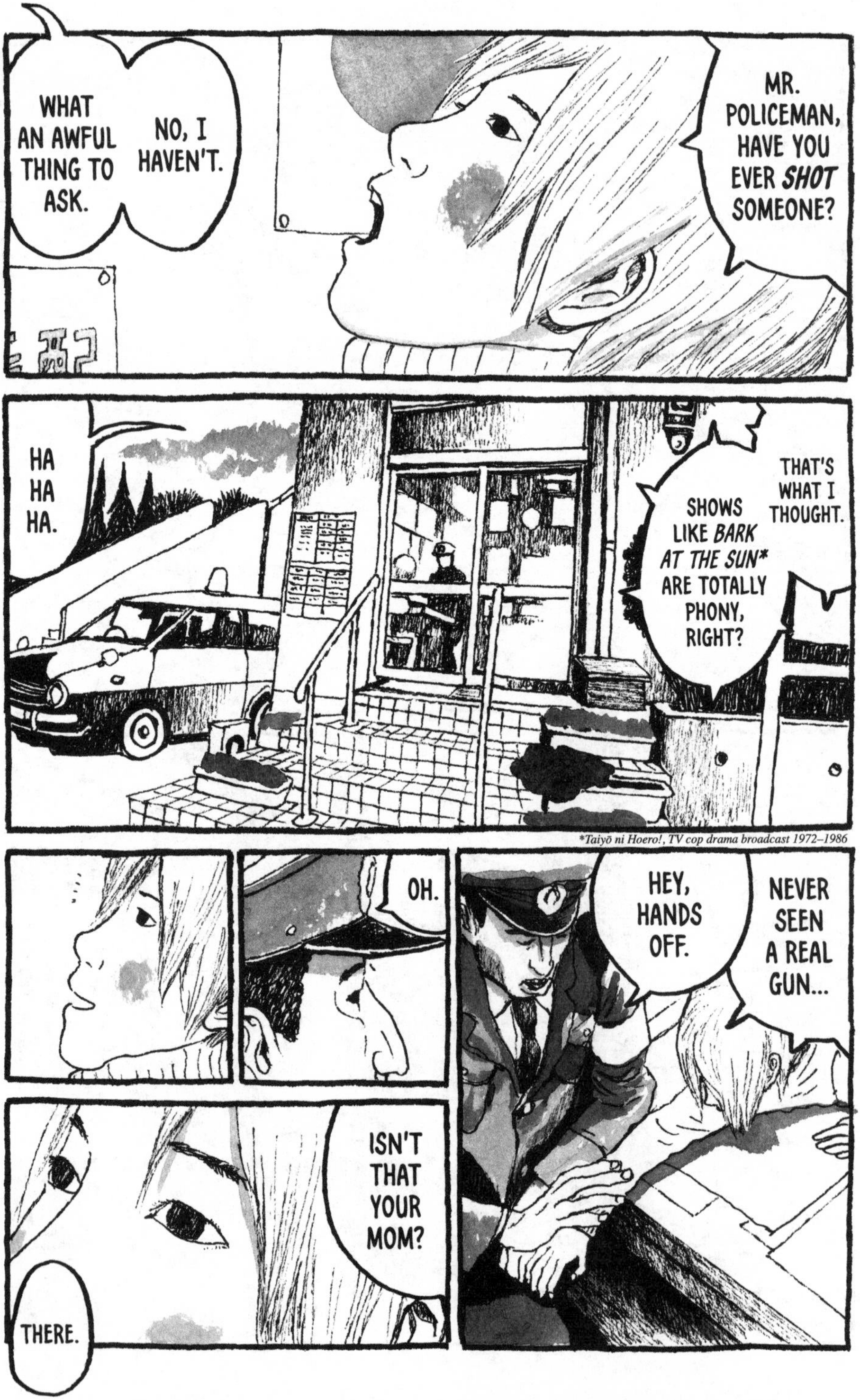
MR. POLICEMAN, HAVE YOU EVER SHOT SOMEONE?
NO, I HAVEN'T.
WHAT AN AWFUL THING TO ASK.
THAT'S WHAT I THOUGHT.
SHOWS LIKE BARK AT THE SUN* ARE TOTALLY PHONY, RIGHT?
HA HA HA.
NEVER SEEN A REAL GUN...
HEY, HANDS OFF.
OH.
ISN'T THAT YOUR MOM?
THERE.

*Taiyō ni Hoero!, TV cop drama broadcast 1972–1986

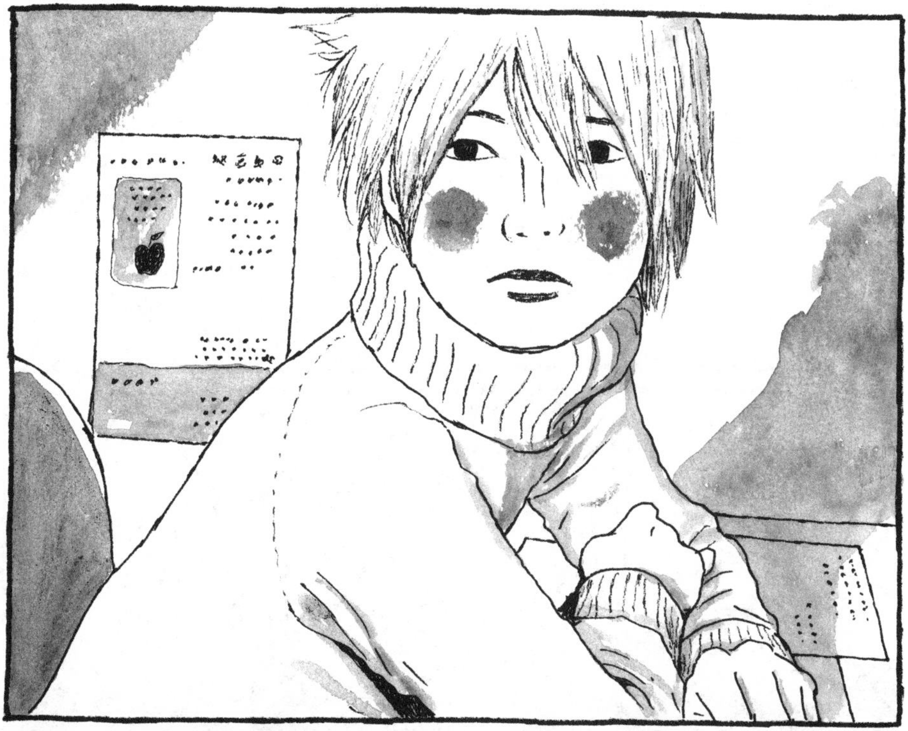

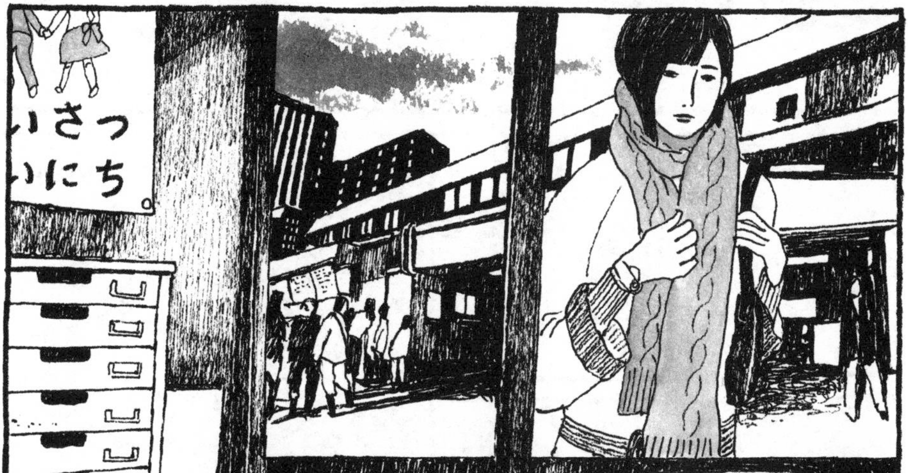
いさつ
いにち
手配

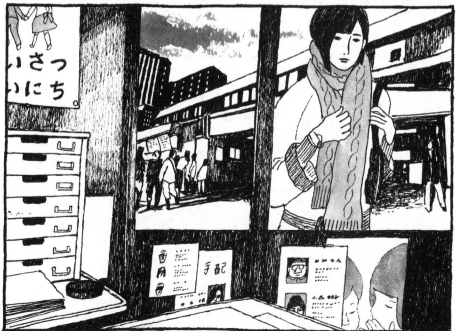

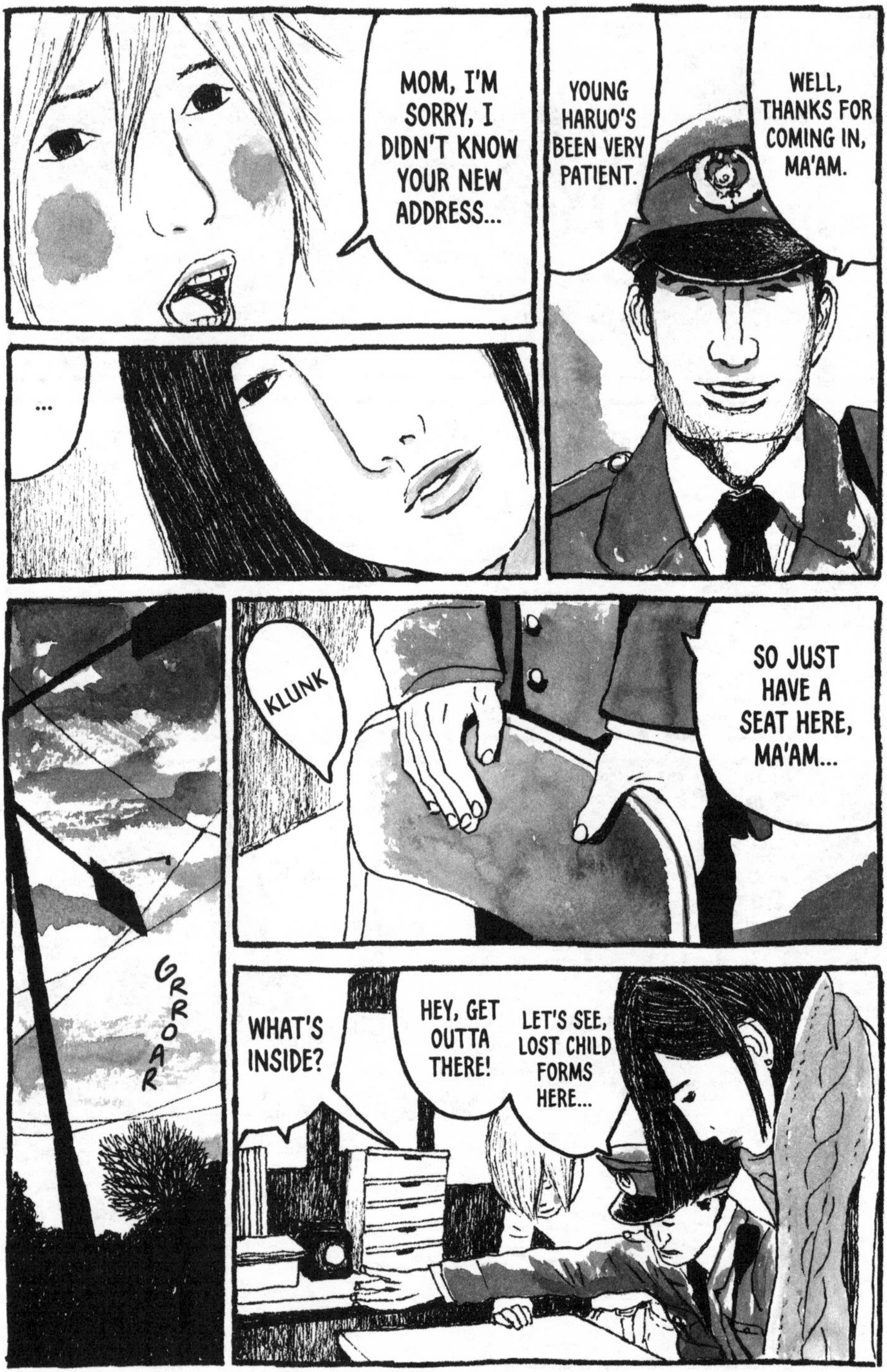
WELL, THANKS FOR COMING IN, MA'AM.
YOUNG HARUO'S BEEN VERY PATIENT.
MOM, I'M SORRY, I DIDN'T KNOW YOUR NEW ADDRESS...
...
SO JUST HAVE A SEAT HERE, MA'AM...
KLUNK
LET'S SEE, LOST CHILD FORMS HERE...
HEY, GET OUTTA THERE!
WHAT'S INSIDE?
GRROAR

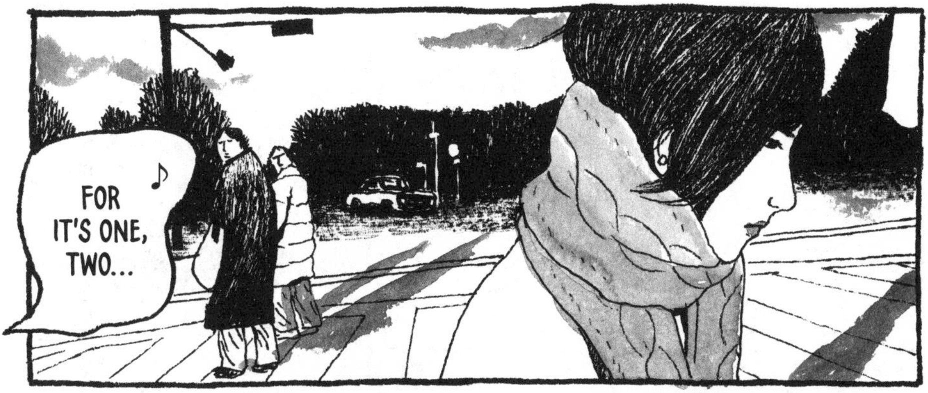
FOR IT'S ONE, TWO... ♪
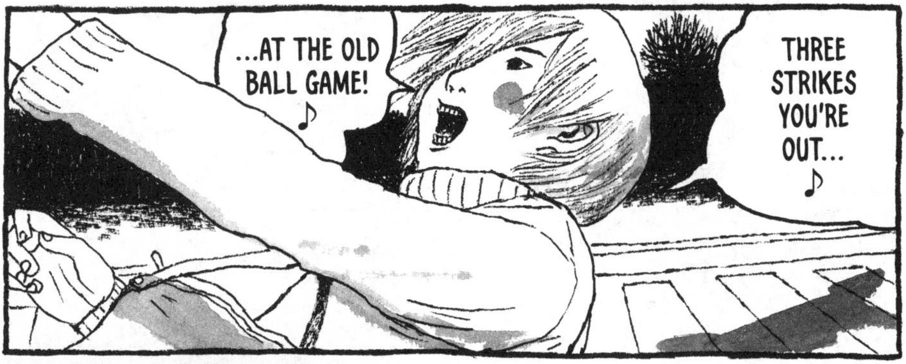
THREE STRIKES YOU'RE OUT... ♪
...AT THE OLD BALL GAME! ♪
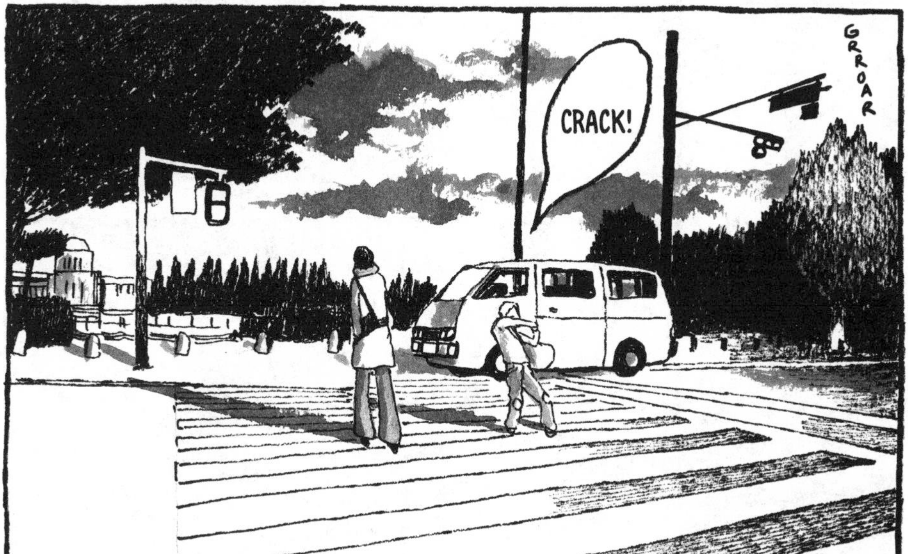
GRROAR
CRACK!

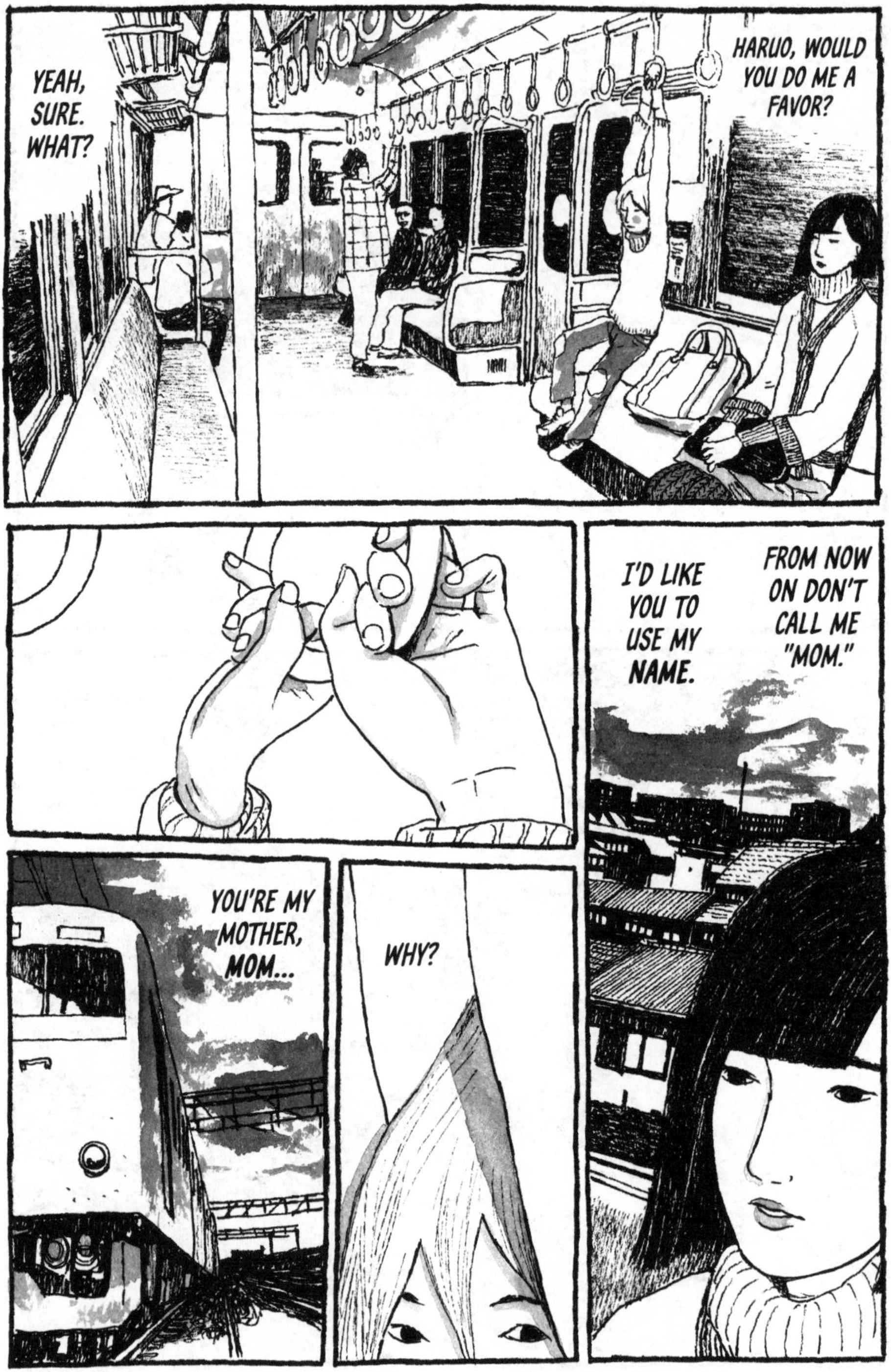
HARUO, WOULD YOU DO ME A FAVOR?
YEAH, SURE. WHAT?
FROM NOW ON DON'T CALL ME "MOM."
I'D LIKE YOU TO USE MY NAME.
WHY?
YOU'RE MY MOTHER, MOM...

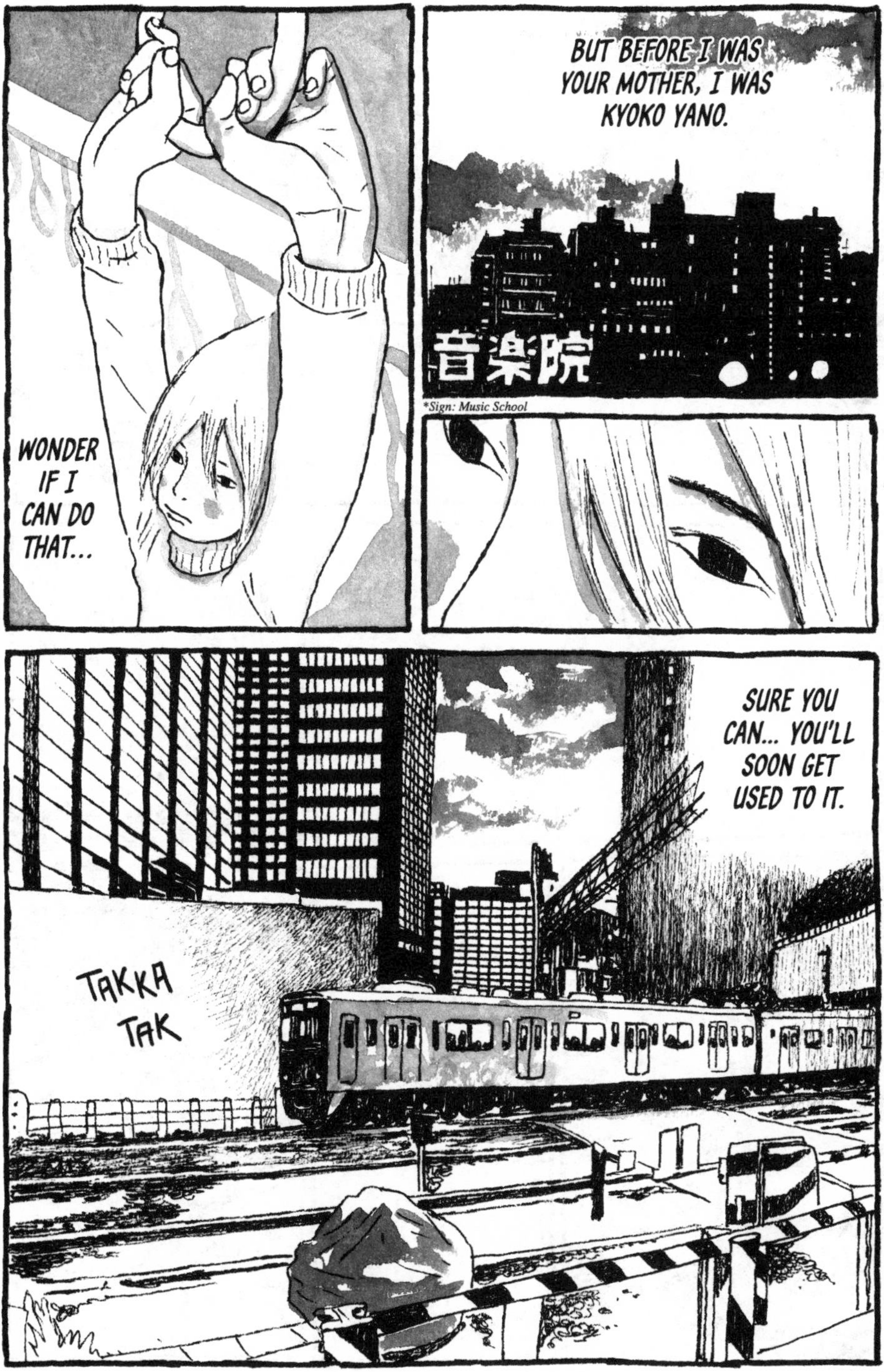
BUT BEFORE I WAS YOUR MOTHER, I WAS KYOKO YANO.
音楽院
*Sign: Music School
WONDER IF I CAN DO THAT...
SURE YOU CAN... YOU'LL SOON GET USED TO IT.
TAKKA TAK

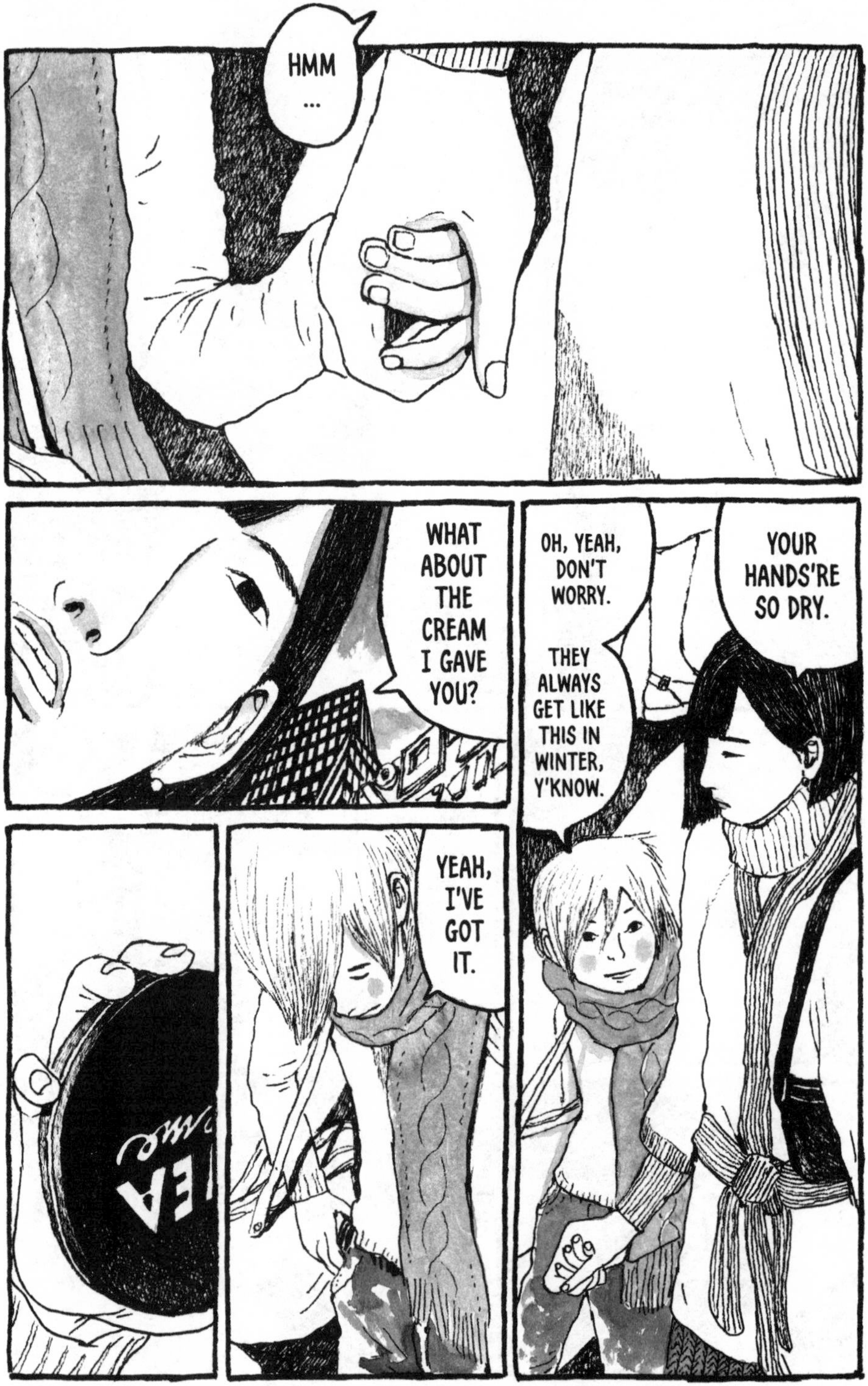
HMM ...
YOUR HANDS'RE SO DRY.
OH, YEAH, DON'T WORRY.
THEY ALWAYS GET LIKE THIS IN WINTER, Y'KNOW.
WHAT ABOUT THE CREAM I GAVE YOU?
YEAH, I'VE GOT IT.

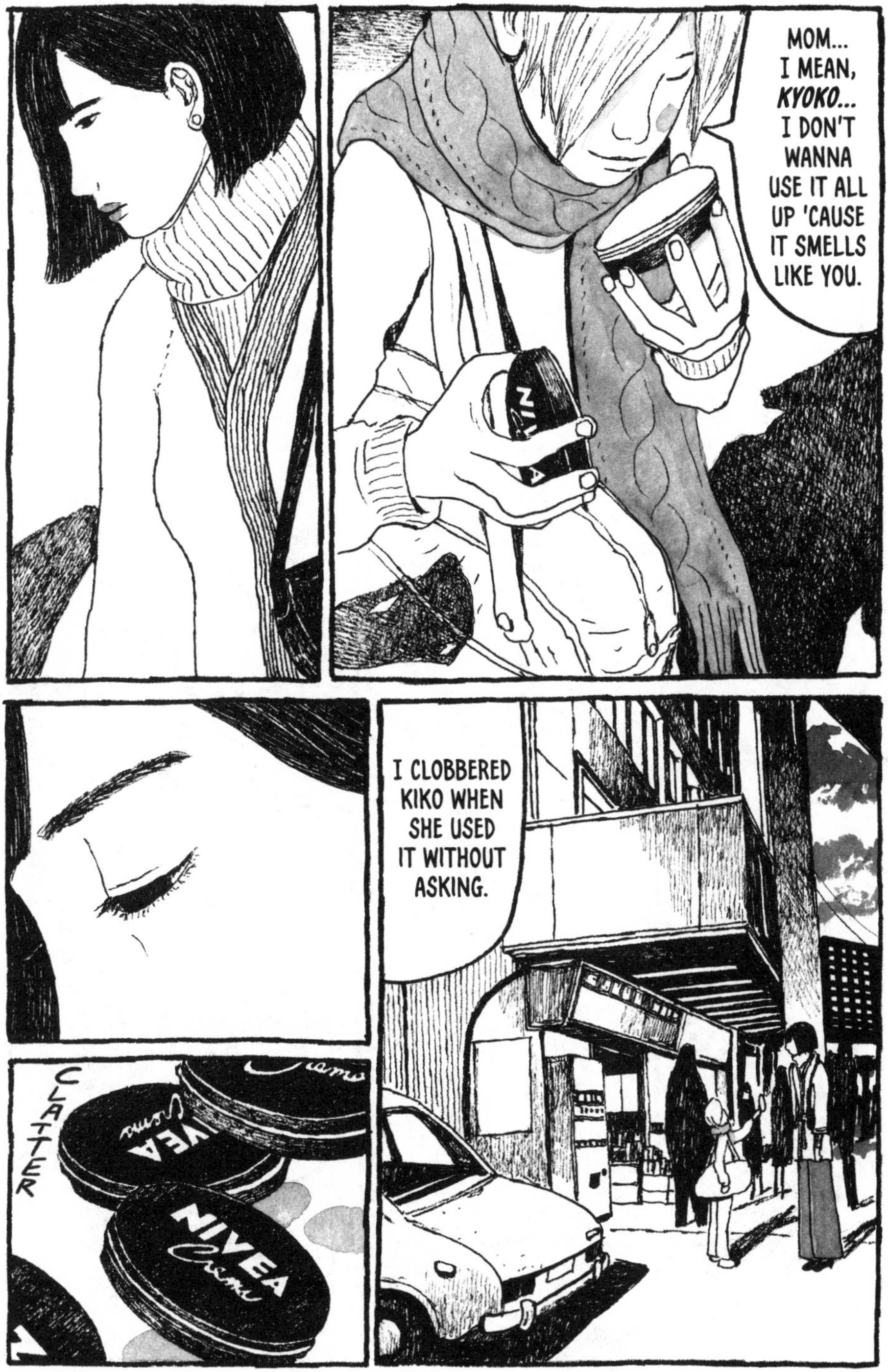
MOM... I MEAN, *KYOKO*... I DON'T WANNA USE IT ALL UP 'CAUSE IT SMELLS LIKE YOU.
NIVEA
I CLOBBERED KIKO WHEN SHE USED IT WITHOUT ASKING.
CLATTER
NIVEA
NIVEA

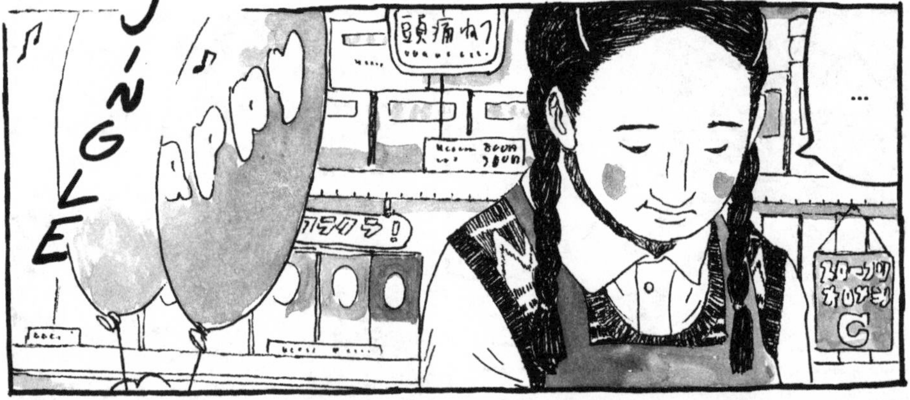
...
JINGLE

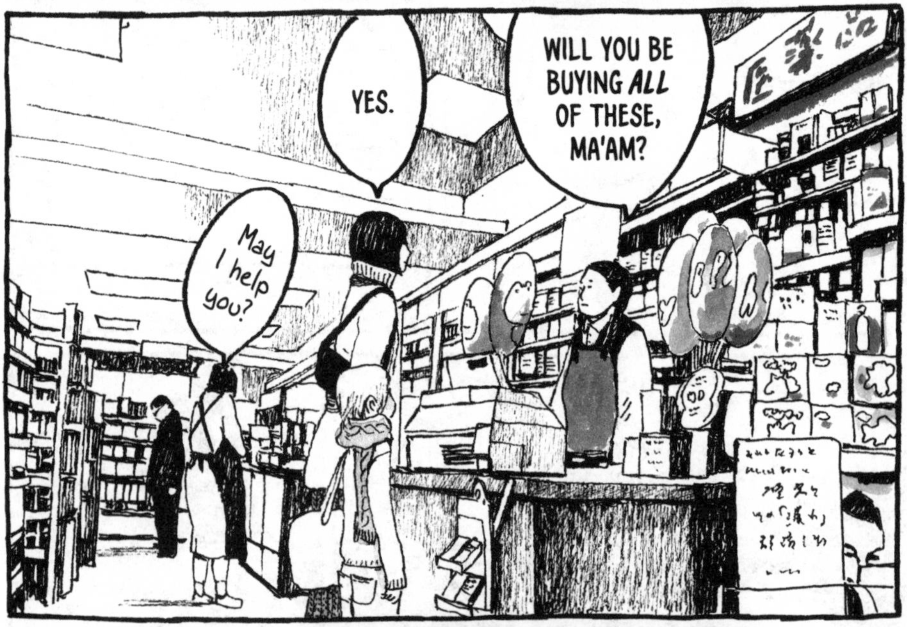
医薬品
WILL YOU BE BUYING *ALL* OF THESE, MA'AM?
YES.
May I help you?

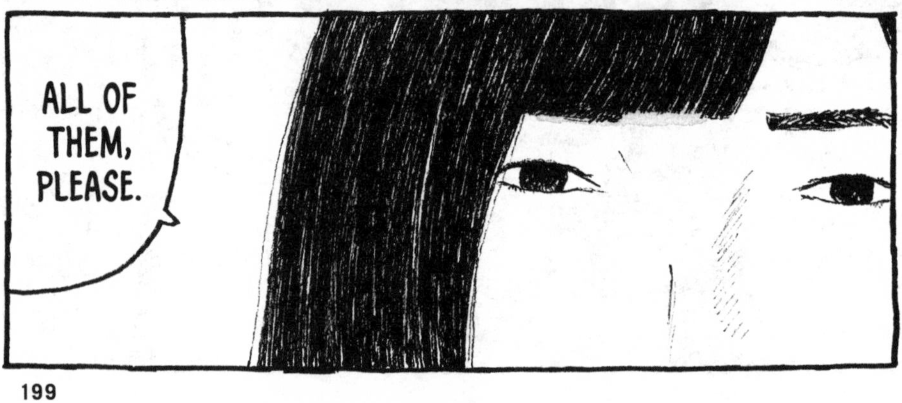
ALL OF THEM, PLEASE.

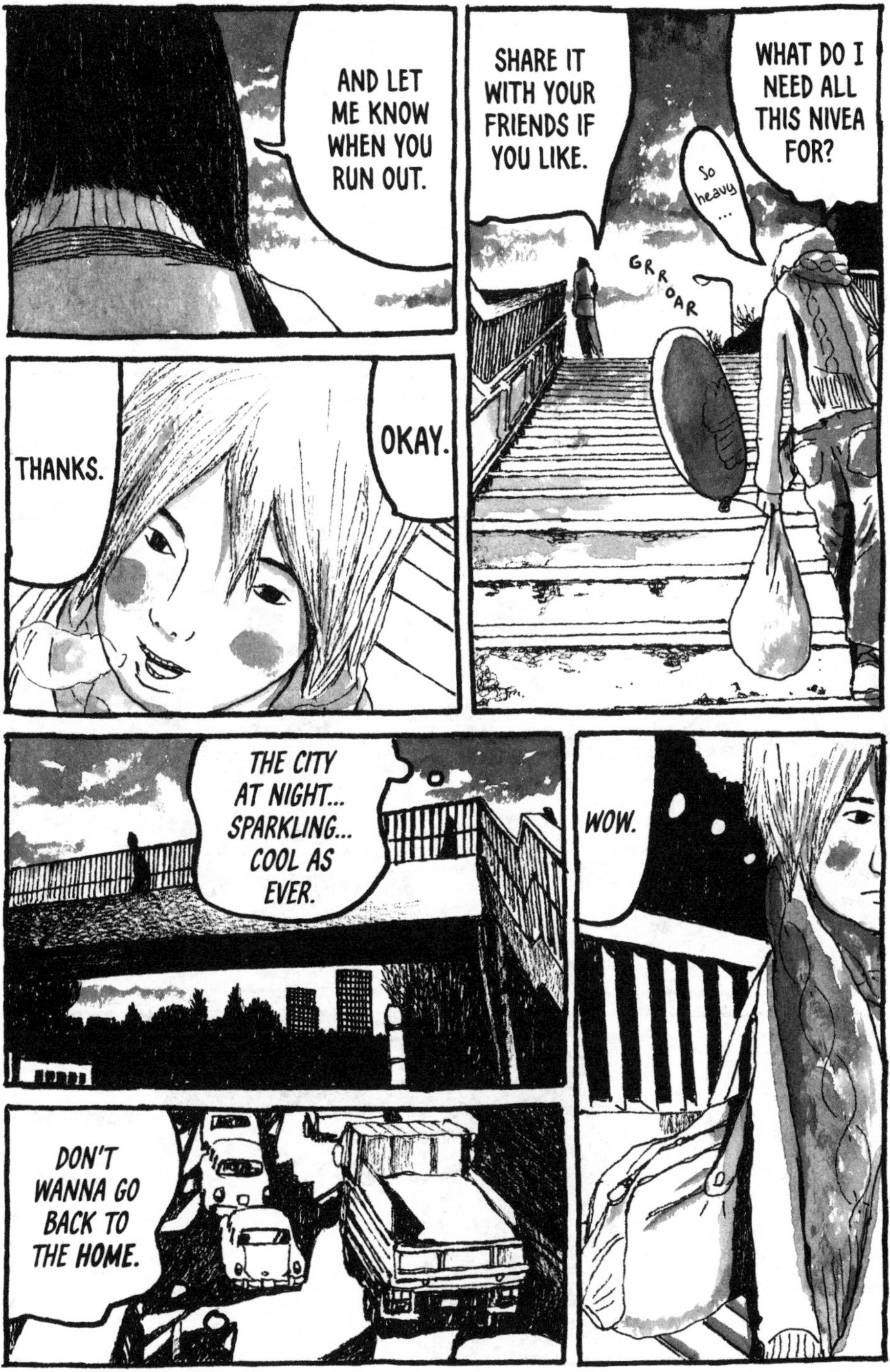
WHAT DO I NEED ALL THIS NIVEA FOR?
SHARE IT WITH YOUR FRIENDS IF YOU LIKE.
So heavy...
GRRROAR
AND LET ME KNOW WHEN YOU RUN OUT.
OKAY.
THANKS.
WOW.
THE CITY AT NIGHT... SPARKLING... COOL AS EVER.
DON'T WANNA GO BACK TO THE HOME.

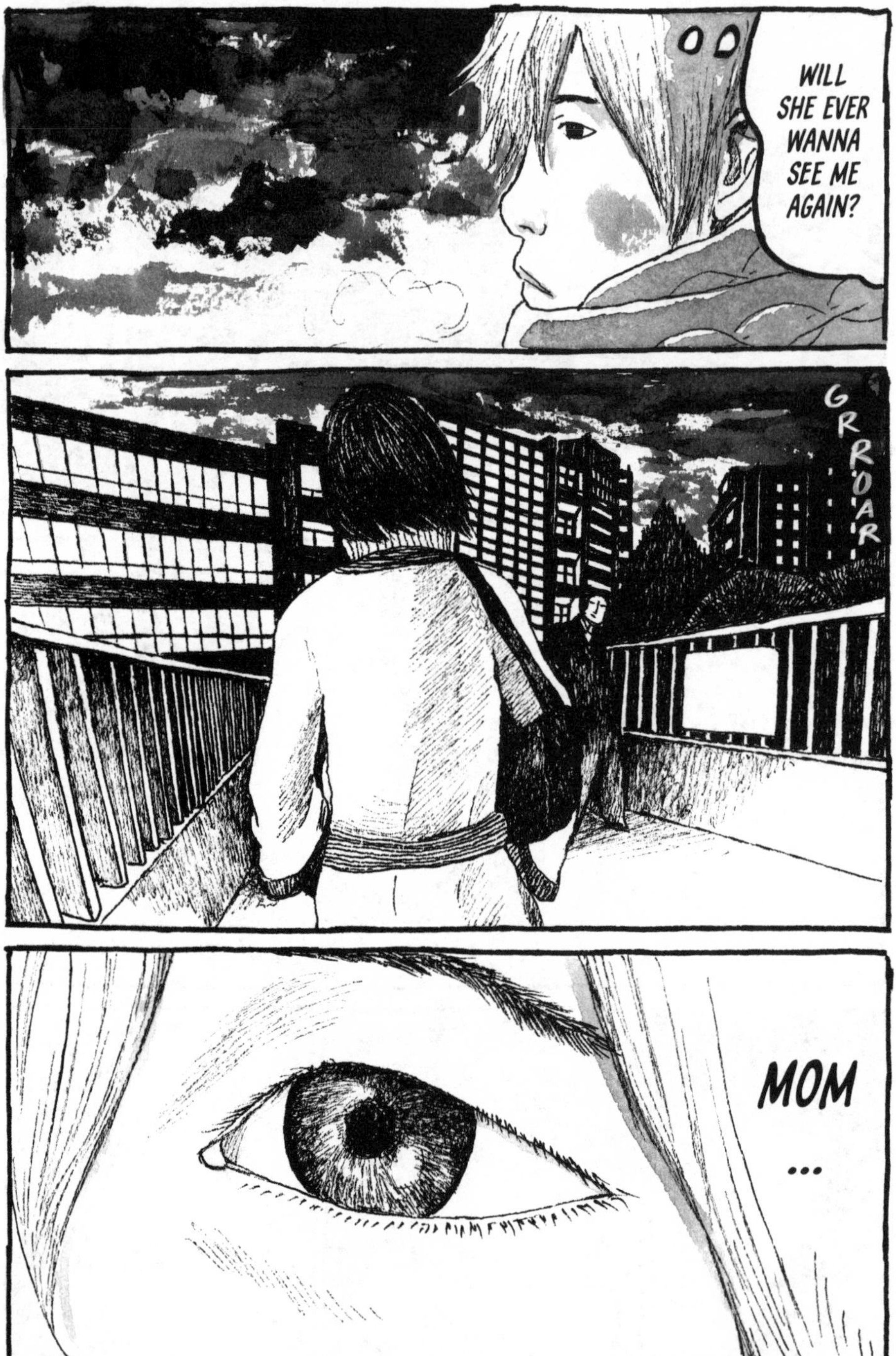
WILL SHE EVER WANNA SEE ME AGAIN?
GRROAR
MOM
...

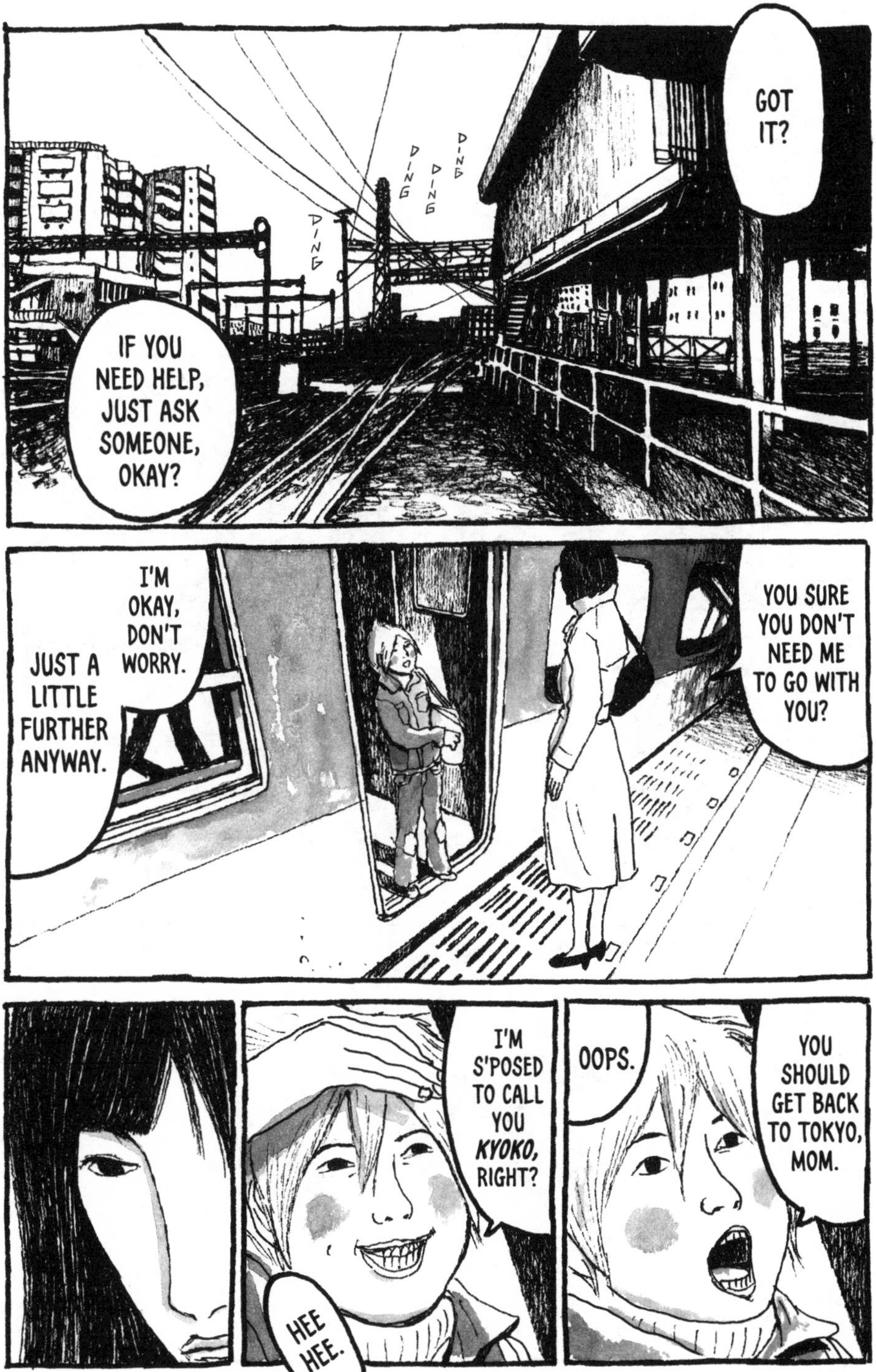
GOT IT?
DING
DING
DING
DING
IF YOU NEED HELP, JUST ASK SOMEONE, OKAY?
YOU SURE YOU DON'T NEED ME TO GO WITH YOU?
I'M OKAY, DON'T WORRY.
JUST A LITTLE FURTHER ANYWAY.
YOU SHOULD GET BACK TO TOKYO, MOM.
OOPS.
I'M S'POSED TO CALL YOU ***KYOKO,*** RIGHT?
HEE HEE.

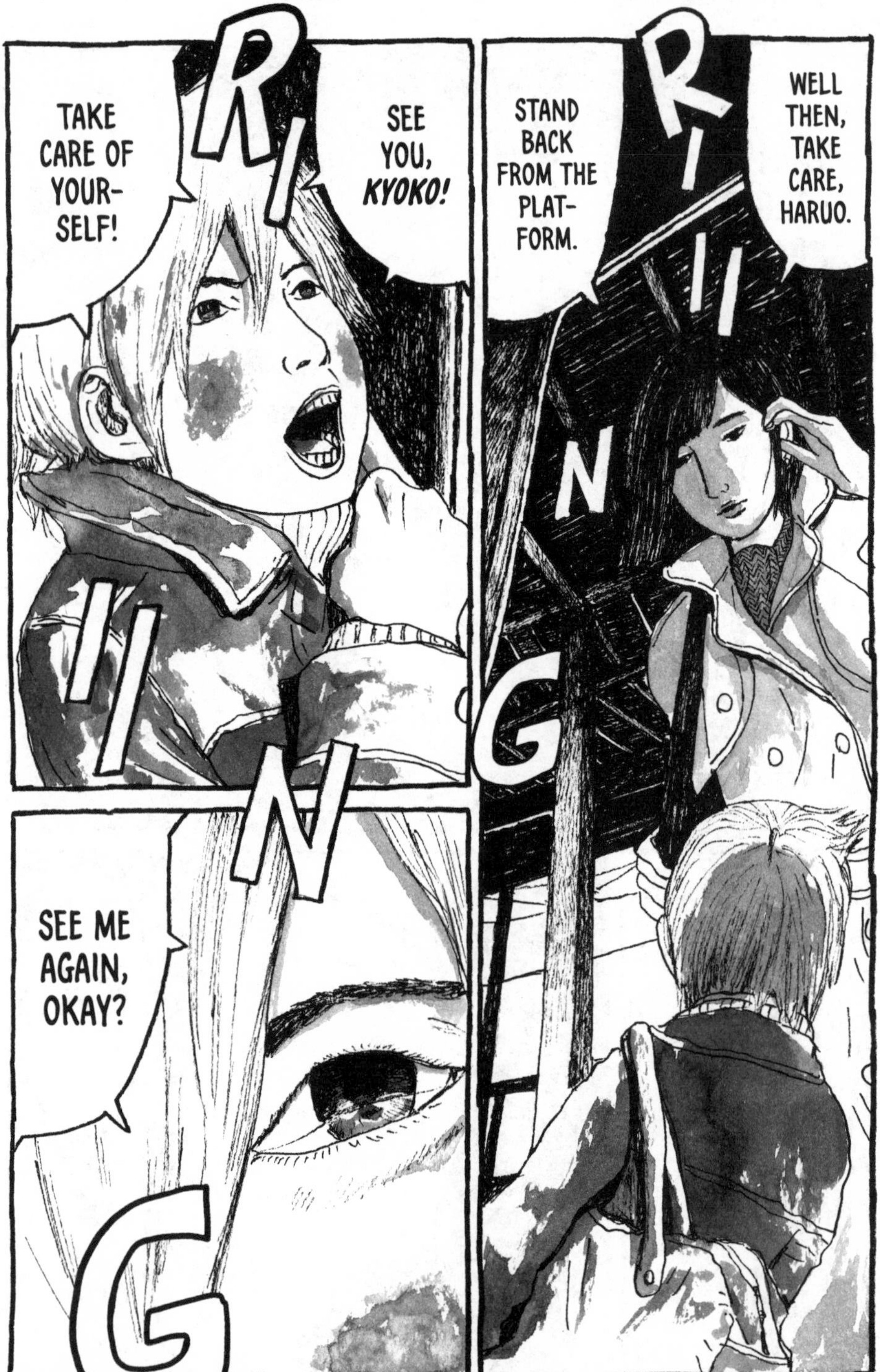
WELL THEN, TAKE CARE, HARUO.
STAND BACK FROM THE PLAT-FORM.
RIIING
SEE YOU, *KYOKO!*
TAKE CARE OF YOUR-SELF!
RIIING
SEE ME AGAIN, OKAY?

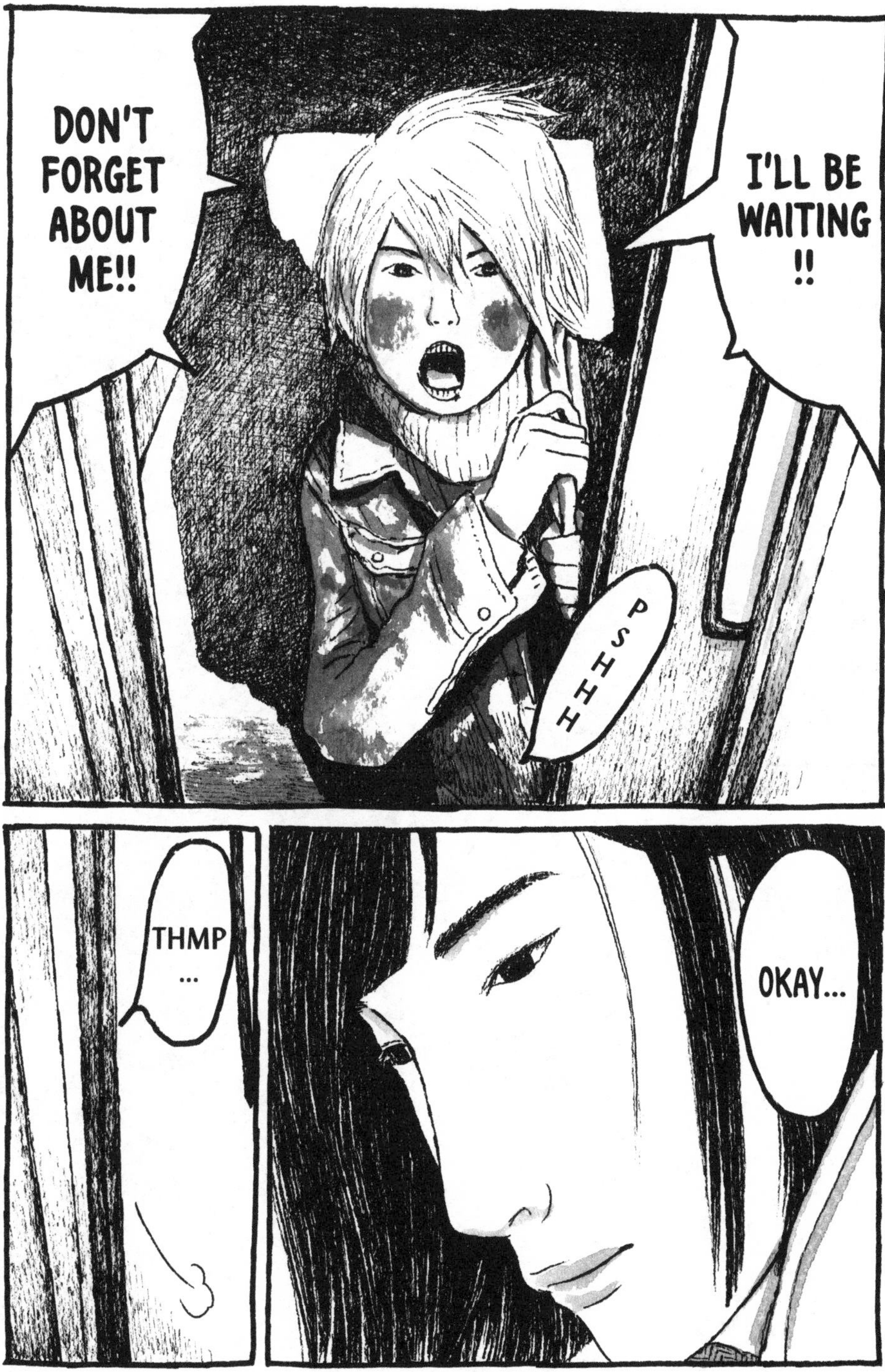

I'LL BE WAITING !!
DON'T FORGET ABOUT ME!!
PSHHH
OKAY...
THMP ...

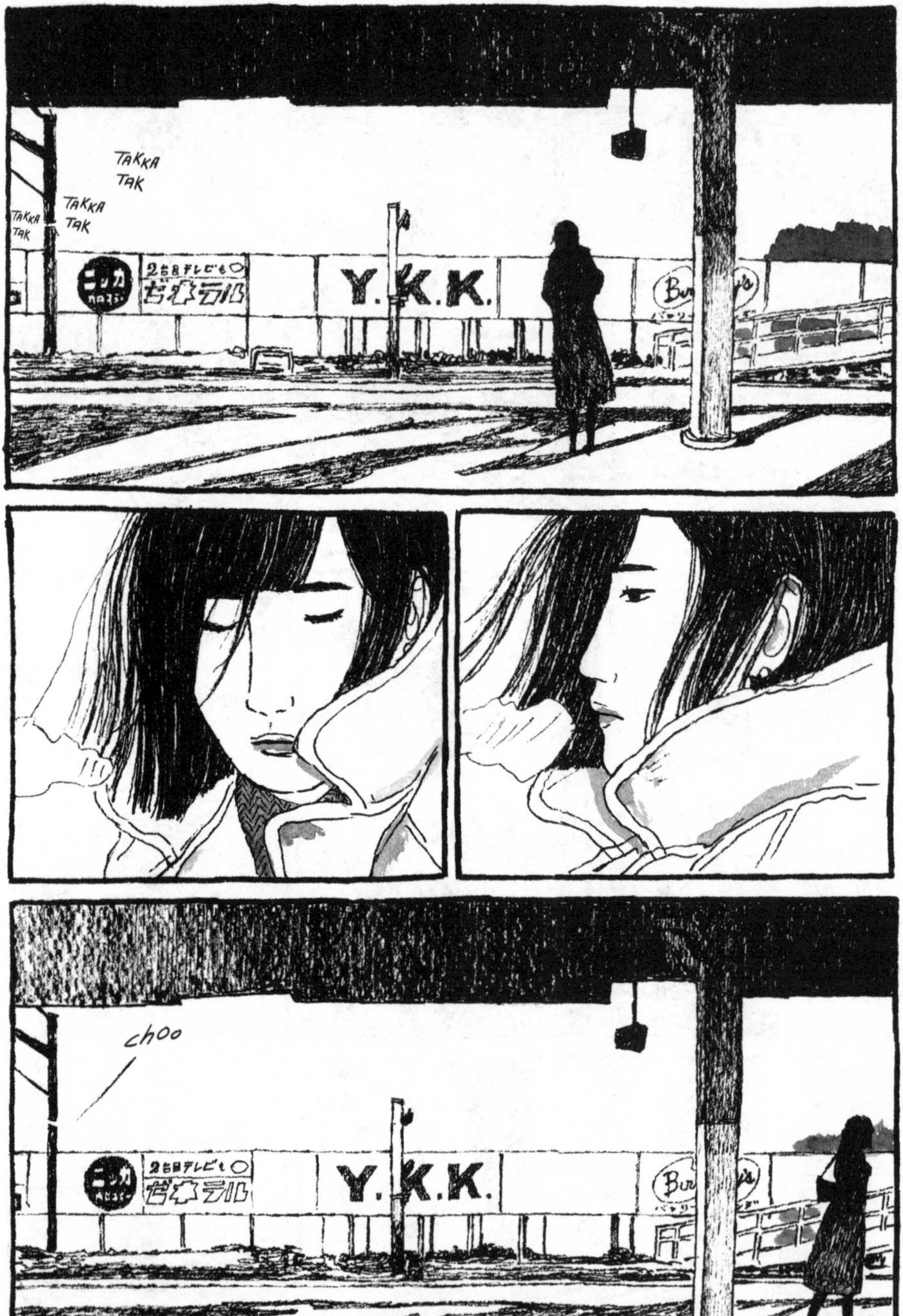
TAKKA
TAK
TAKKA
TAK
TAKKA
TAK
Y.K.K.
Y.K.K.
choo

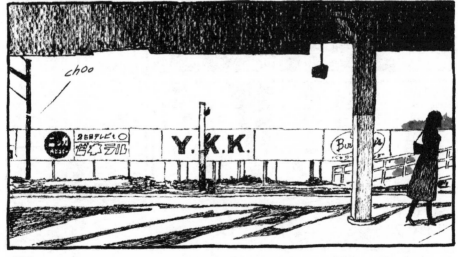

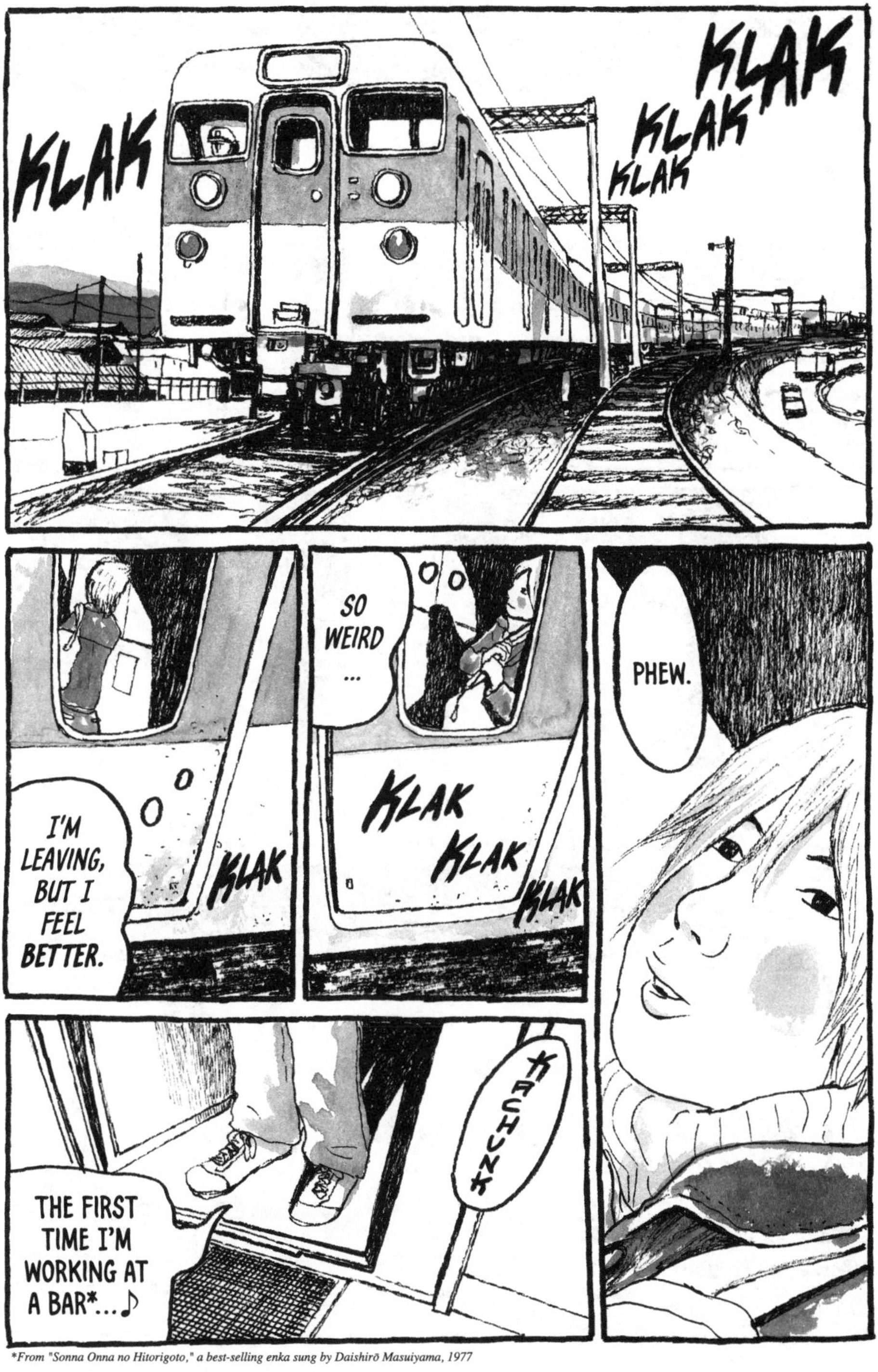
KLAK
KLAK
KLAK
KLAK
PHEW.
SO WEIRD ...
KLAK
KLAK
KLAK
I'M LEAVING, BUT I FEEL BETTER.
KLAK
KACHUNK
THE FIRST TIME I'M WORKING AT A BAR*...♪

*From "Sonna Onna no Hitorigoto," a best-selling enka sung by Daishirō Masuiyama, 1977

I SIT DOWN NEXT TO YOU. ♪
TAKKA
YOU SEEM LIKE A PLAYER. ♪
TAKKA
TAKKA
PHEW.
WHAT'S WITH THAT?
HAIR'S ALL WHITE.
TAKKA
S'CUSE ME, MISTER, CAN I SIT HERE?
TAKKA
WHY SURE Y'CAN.

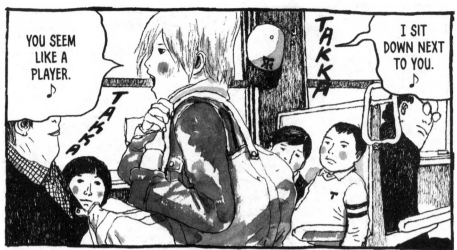

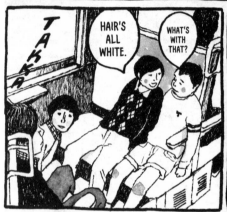

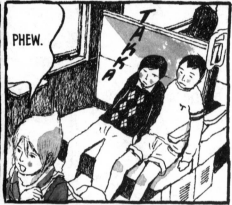

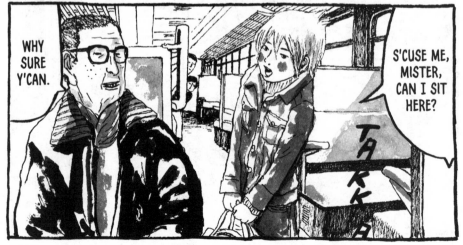

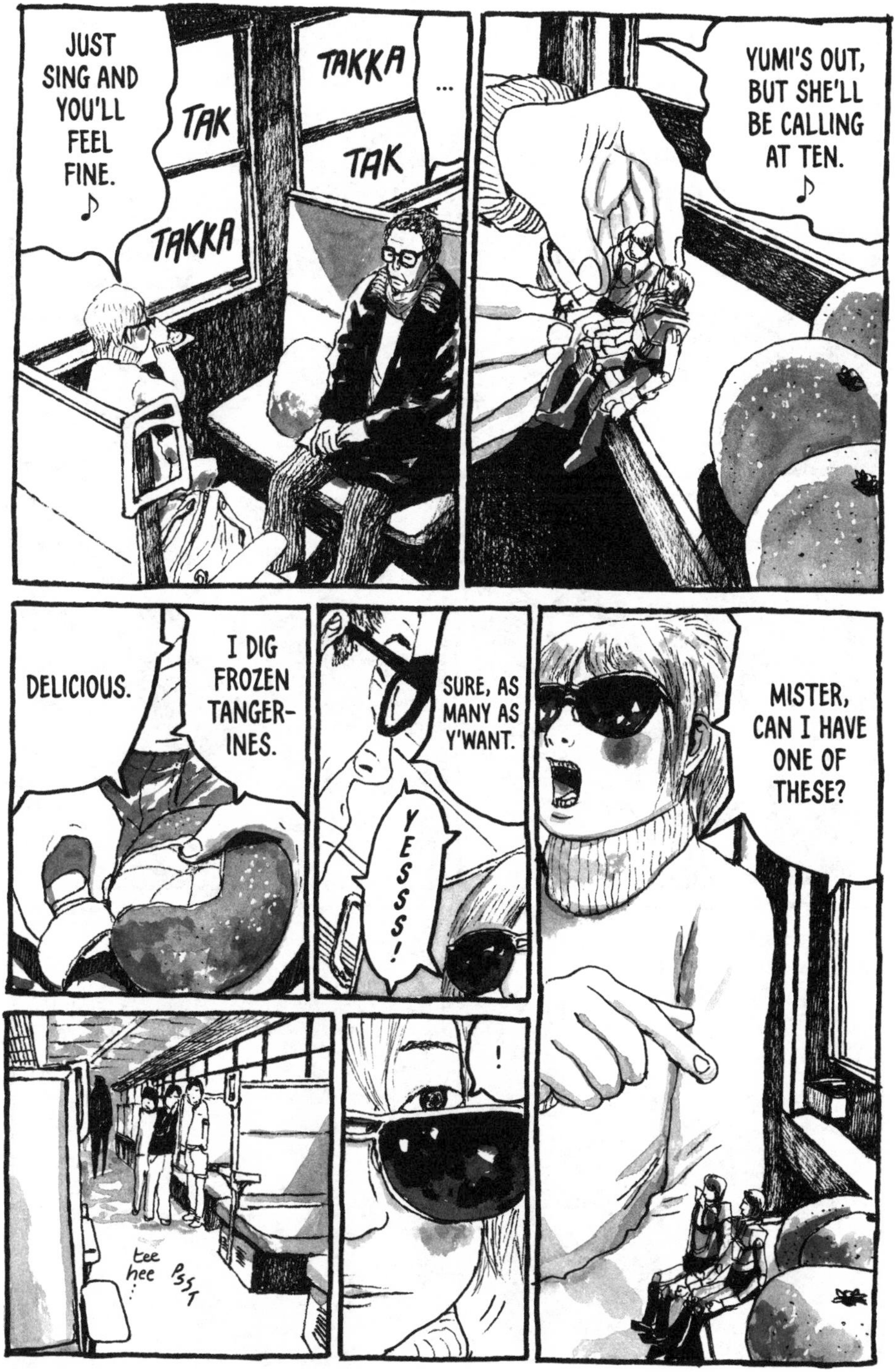
YUMI'S OUT, BUT SHE'LL BE CALLING AT TEN. ♪
...
TAKKA
TAK
TAK
TAKKA
JUST SING AND YOU'LL FEEL FINE. ♪
MISTER, CAN I HAVE ONE OF THESE?
SURE, AS MANY AS Y'WANT.
YESSS!
I DIG FROZEN TANGER-INES.
DELICIOUS.
!
tee hee
PSST

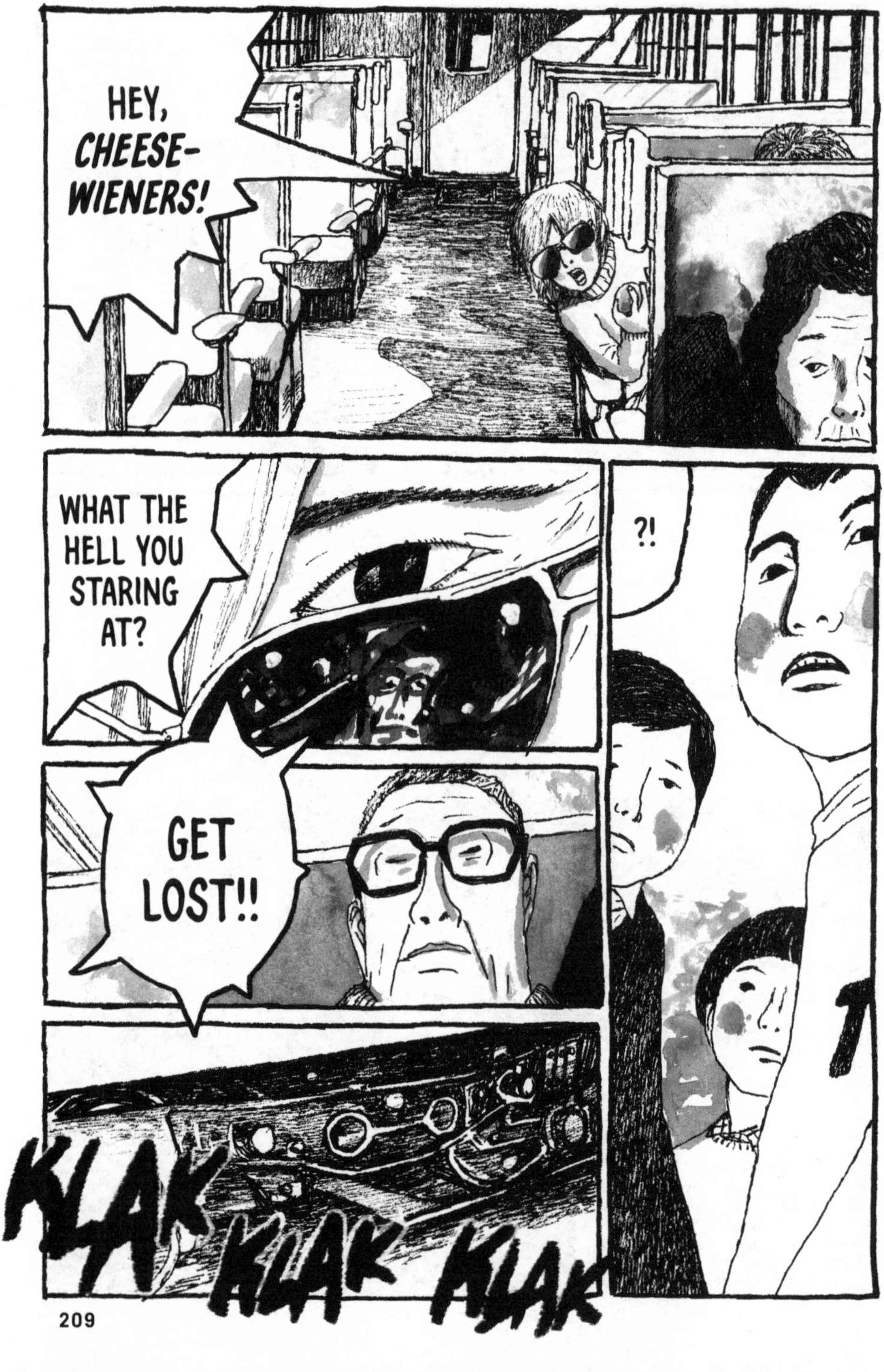
HEY, CHEESE-WIENERS!
?!
WHAT THE HELL YOU STARING AT?
GET LOST!!
KLAK KLAK KLAK

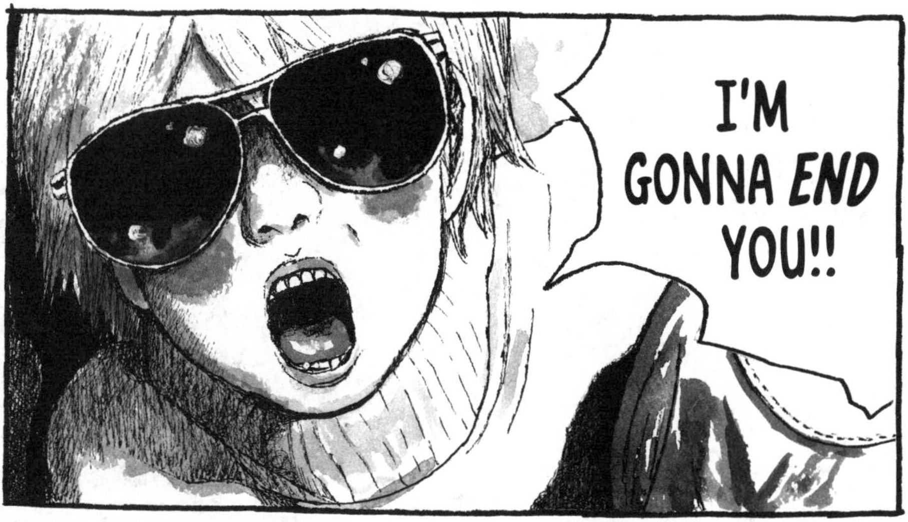
I'M GONNA *END* YOU!!

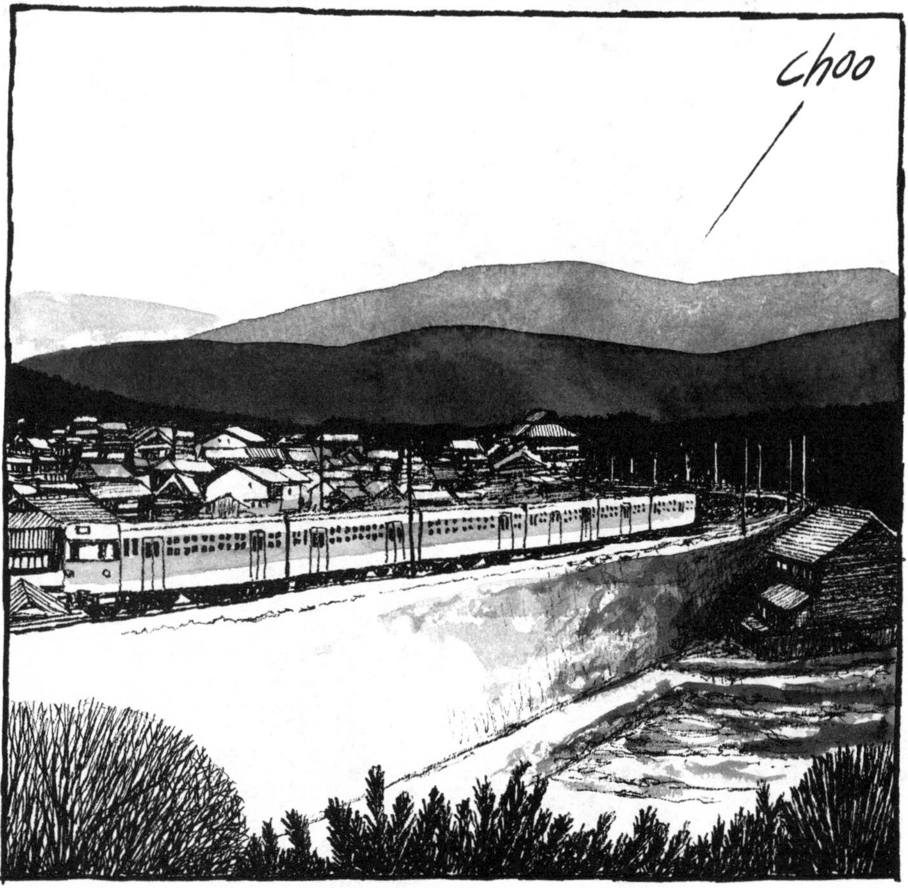
choo

Sunny

②

END

First serialized in Japanese in *IKKI*, October, November and December **2011**; January, February and March **2012**.

SUNNY
Volume 2
VIZ Signature Edition

Story and art by **Taiyo MATSUMOTO**

SUNNY Vol. 2
by Taiyo MATSUMOTO
© 2011 Taiyou MATSUMOTO
All rights reserved.
Original Japanese edition published by SHOGAKUKAN.
English translation rights in the United States of America and
Canada arranged with SHOGAKUKAN.

Original Japanese edition design by Sekine Shinichi Studio

With thanks to the Nissan Motor Co., Ltd.

Translation by **Michael Arias**
Lettering by **Deron Bennett**
Book design by **Fawn Lau**
Editing by **Hope Donovan**

The stories, characters and incidents mentioned
in this publication are entirely fictional.

Printed in the U. S. A.

Published by VIZ Media, LLC
PO Box 77010
San Francisco, CA 94107

10 9 8 7 6 5 4 3 2 1
First printing, November 2013

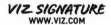
WWW.VIZ.COM

TAIYO MATSUMOTO

is best known to English-reading audiences as the
creator of *Tekkonkinkreet*, which in 2006 was made
into an animated feature film of the same name,
directed by Michael Arias. In 2007 Matsumoto was
awarded a **Japan Media Arts Festival Excellence
Award**, and in 2008 he won an **Eisner Award** for
the English publication of *Tekkonkinkreet*.

Also available in **ENGLISH** by **TAIYO MATSUMOTO**
● *Blue Spring* ● *Tekkonkinkreet* ● *GoGo Monster*

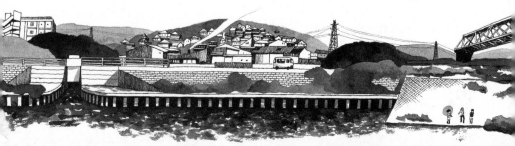